PLAGUES, PRIE

Drawing from anthropology, religious studies, history, and literary theory, *Plagues, Priests, and Demons* explores significant parallels in the rise of Christianity in the late Roman Empire and colonial Mexico. Evidence shows that new forms of infectious disease devastated the late Roman Empire and Indian America, respectively, contributing to pagan and Indian interest in Christianity. Christian clerics and monks in early medieval Europe, and later Jesuit missionaries in colonial Mexico, introduced new beliefs and practices as well as accommodated indigenous religions, especially through the cult of the saints. The book is simultaneously a comparative study of early Christian and later Spanish missionary texts. Similarities in the two literatures are attributed to similar cultural–historical forces that governed the "rise of Christianity" in Europe and the Americas.

Daniel T. Reff is an associate professor in the Department of Comparative Studies at Ohio State University. He is an anthropologist and ethnohistorian who has done research in northern Mexico, the American Southwest, Spain, and Portugal. He is the author of numerous articles on colonial Mexico in journals such as *American Anthropologist, American Antiquity,* and *Ethnohistory.* He is the author of *Disease, Depopulation, and Culture Change in Northwestern New Spain, 1518–1764* (1991), and editor and co-translator (with Maureen Ahern and Richard Danford) of the first critical, English-language edition of Andrés Pérez de Ribas's *History of the Triumphs of Our Holy Faith Amongst the Most Barbarous and Fierce Peoples of the New World* (1999 [1645]). He has been a resident scholar at the School of American Research and is the recipient of major research grants as well as a University Fellowship from the National Endowment for the Humanities.

"One thousand years apart, Christianity's rapid rise in Europe and in Mexico coincided with plague and social dislocation, but this was no coincidence. Crossing disciplines with apparent ease, Daniel Reff offers a fresh, erudite, and compelling explanation of how Jesuit missionaries in Mexico advanced their cause by echoing the rhetoric and strategies of early Christians."

> – David J. Weber, author of *The Spanish Frontier in North America* and the forthcoming *Spaniards and Their Savages in the Age of Enlightenment*

"Scholars have spent a generation abjectly recognizing that they cannot fully understand 'the other.' Now it is time to re-recognize that we are all members of the same species. In *Plagues, Priests, and Demons* we see that Europe in the first centuries AD and Mexico in the first post-Columbian centuries suffered similar pandemics and population crashes, and reacted similarly by accepting a new religion."

> – Alfred W. Crosby, Professor Emeritus in American Studies, History and Geography, University of Texas at Austin

"This work of original and innovative scholarship juxtaposes conversion to Christianity in late antique and medieval Europe and in early modern New Spain. Exploring the self-awareness of Jesuit missionaries in New Spain who viewed themselves as the successors of the church's earliest saints, Reff traces links of theological imagination and pastoral practice that span centuries and an entire ocean. Simultaneously, he explores the experience of conversion from the vantage point of the people who chose it, and describes their circumstances. Dread of cataclysmic change – whether the end of the Roman or of the Aztec empire – and of disease, death and demonic agency went hand in hand with the emergence of new bonds of piety, charity and community. An admirable, thought-provoking book awaits the reader."

> – Sabine MacCormack, University of Notre Dame

For Nancy and Zachariah

Contents

CONTENTS

List of Illustrations

Acknowledgments

This book was made possible by a University Fellowship from the National Endowment for the Humanities and grants from The Ohio State University College of the Humanities.

Joe Lynch, Thomas Kasulis, Jim Muldoon, Nicholas Howe, Clark Larsen, Daniel Gade, and Lindsay Jones generously read and commented on one or more chapters of the book. Special thanks are due Nancy Ettlinger, for reading and rereading the entire manuscript, all the while remaining supportive yet critical.

Ron McLean drafted the illustrations for the book.

ONE

———◆◇◆———

Introduction

During the century following the crucifixion of Christ, the apostles charged with spreading the "good news" of the Gospels enjoyed rather limited success. In an historical "blink of the eye" – during the late second and third century C.E. – people throughout a collapsing Roman Empire embraced Christianity. During the fourth century Christianity became the official religion of the Empire, and by the sixth century C.E., most Europeans – numbering in the millions – understood themselves as Christian.

Christianity experienced a similar history some 1,400 years later in Latin America. Here, too, the collapse of empires (e.g., Mexica, Inca) ushered in a period of several centuries during which millions of Indians came to understand themselves as Christian.

This book is a comparative study of early Christianity in the late Roman Empire (c. 150–800 C.E.) and in colonial Mexico (c. 1520–1720 C.E.). Following the early success of Mendicant missionaries in southern Mexico, the Jesuits, between 1591 and 1650, baptized over four hundred thousand Indians and established a vast network of Christian communities in northern Mexico. My central thesis is that the Mendicant and especially the Jesuit enterprise, although not on the same temporal or spatial scale as the rise of Christianity in Europe, nevertheless entailed similar processes. Perhaps most significant, the Christianization of pagan Europe and Indian Mexico was coincident with epidemics of acute and chronic infectious disease that undermined the structure and functioning of pagan and Indian societies, respectively.[1] Both pagans in Europe and Indians in Mexico were attracted to Christian beliefs and rituals because they provided a means of comprehending and dealing with epidemic disease and calamity. The organizational strategies based on charity and reciprocity that were implemented by early Christians and later by missionaries in Mexico also were particularly attractive in the context of profound sociocultural upheaval. Both medieval monks and Jesuit missionaries emphasized the cult of the saints and their relics, which, paradoxically, involved accommodation as much as suppression of indigenous belief systems. Significantly, the literature produced in Europe by early Christians, particularly sacred biography and history, was later used by Jesuit and, to a lesser extent, Mendicant missionary authors as literary models and sources of rhetoric to represent their New World experience. Pursuit of this "borrowing," which I attribute in significant part to demonstrable similarities in the two processes of Christianization, has resulted in a book that is a comparative study of Old and New World mission frontiers as well as early Christian literature and Spanish missionary texts.

The idea for this book began taking shape some twenty-five years ago, while doing archaeological research in Sonora, Mexico.[2] Living in northern Mexico made me aware that the people of Sonora carried on estimable traditions that were rooted in their Indian past. Our archaeological research indicated that this past encompassed lives that were at least as complex and presumably as fulfilling as the lives of contemporaries in early modern Europe. If so, then why did hundreds of thousands

---

[1] The term pagan at this point in time is fully loaded with unfortunate baggage. I use it as a referent for the mostly Celtic and German-speaking peoples of Western Europe who, in the context of a demographic collapse and migration, coalesced in late antiquity and the early Middle Ages, giving rise to better understood ethnic groups such as Franks, Saxons, and Irish. Sadly, when referring to the Indians of northern Mexico, I also gloss over what undoubtedly were innumerable differences among dozens of peoples; the differences and many of the cultures themselves have been lost to history.

[2] The Rio Sonora Project was funded by the National Science Foundation from 1975 to 1979 and was principally concerned with determining the broad outlines of Sonoran prehistory and the extent to which the region functioned prehistorically as a trade route linking Mesoamerica and the American Southwest. Richard A. Pailes and Daniel T. Reff, "Colonial Exchange Systems and the Decline of Paquime." In *The Archaeology of West and Northwest Mesoamerica*, eds. Michael S. Foster and Phil C. Weigand, pp. 353–363 (Boulder, CO: Westview Press, 1985).

of Indians embrace Jesuit missionaries and Christianity? About the time I started puzzling over this question I read William McNeill's *Plagues and Peoples* (1976) and Alfred Crosby's *The Columbian Exchange* (1972), which detail how epidemic disease changed the course of history in the Old World and the New. Their work compelled me to examine the accounts of Spanish explorers and Jesuit missionaries from northern Nueva España. To my suprise, I found considerable evidence that epidemics of smallpox, measles, typhus, and other maladies spread northward from central Mexico in advance of the generally northward-moving mission frontier, decimating Indian populations and contributing to Indian interest in baptism and missionization.[3]

My research on disease and its contribution to Jesuit success was made possible by a vast literature produced by the Jesuits. Ignatius Loyola and Jesuit superiors encouraged missionaries to write often. During the late sixteenth and seventeenth centuries, the Jesuits in Nueva España wrote thousands of letters and reports, including yearly summaries (*annuas*) for each province and its many subdivisions (e.g., *rectorados, colegios*). Some priests also took it upon themselves or were asked by superiors to write histories, synthesizing the observations and experiences of fellow missionaries.[4] The most detailed and informative narrative of the Jesuit experience in colonial Mexico was published in 1645, and was written by a former frontier missionary and Jesuit provincial, Andrés Pérez de Ribas. Titled in English *History of the Triumphs of Our Holy Faith Amongst the Most Barbarous and Fierce Peoples of the New World*,[5] the *Historia* is a wonderfully detailed commentary on Spanish and Indian relations in northern Nueva España.

Having satisfied, or so I thought, my interest in disease, I initiated in 1992 a National Endowment for the Humanities project to

---

[3] Daniel T. Reff, *Disease, Depopulation, and Culture Change in Northwestern New Spain, 1518–1764* (Salt Lake City: University of Utah Press, 1991).

[4] The fifth father general of the Jesuit order, Claudio Acquaviva (1581–1615), instructed each Jesuit province throughout the world to select a Jesuit to collect historical material and to compile a chronicle or history of the province. Magnus Morner, *The Political and Economic Activities of the Jesuits in the La Plata Region, The Hapsburg Era* (Stockholm: Library and Institute of Ibero-American Studies, 1953), 10.

[5] Andrés Pérez de Ribas, *History of the Triumphs of Our Holy Faith Amongst the Most Barbarous and Fierce Peoples of the New World*, trans. Daniel T. Reff, Maureen Ahern, and Richard Danford (Tucson: University of Arizona Press, 1999 [1645]).

prepare a critical, English-language edition of Pérez de Ribas's *Historia*. On previous occasions my reading of the text often entailed a mining operation of sorts; I read the book largely for ethnohistorical insights. Along the way I nevertheless became aware that the *Historia* was an often gripping, dramatic narrative, filled with demonic apparitions and miracles. Once I began the close reading implied by translation, I further discovered that Pérez de Ribas relied heavily on early Christian literature for literary models and rhetoric to represent the Jesuits' New World experience. Pérez de Ribas was not alone in this regard; other Jesuit as well as Franciscan authors used type scenes (e.g., "faith healing the blind"), metaphors, rhetoric, and explicit parallels from early Christian literature to describe the mission frontier in places such as New Mexico and Paraguay.[6] Jesuit narratives, for instance, tell of missionaries who were informed by God of their impending martyrdom through bleeding altar cloths, and of missionaries whose bodies, or body parts, remained incorruptible following death. The same or very similar incidents are recounted in the *Life of Saint Hilarion* and countless other sacred biographies. Similarly, the *Historia* recounts instances where Jesuits destroyed roadside cairns or trees that were "worshipped" by the Indians, replacing them with crosses. Almost identical pagan religious practices and "replacement strategies," used by medieval clerics and monks, are described in the fourth-century *Life of Saint Martin*.[7] Jesuit texts also abound in metaphors and epithets from early Christian literature, including references to the devil as "the enemy," "the infernal beast," or a "demonic kinsman." References to the devil's snares are as common in Jesuit missionary texts from Mexico as they are in Athanasius's *Life of Saint Antony*, which pertains to Mediterranean Europe during late antiquity. Perhaps most significant, Jesuit missionary texts abound in

---

[6] For instance, Fray A. Benavides, *The Memorial of Fray Alonso de Benavides*, trans. E. Ayers (Chicago: Privately Published, 1916 [1630]); Juan E. Nieremberg, S.J. (with Andrade Cassini), *Varones Illustres de la Compañia de Jesus.* 3 vols. (Bilbao, 1889 [1666]); Antonio Ruiz de Montoya, *Conquista Espiritual hecha por los religiosos de la Compañia de Jesus en las provincias del Paraguay, Parana, Uruguay y Tape* (Bilbao: Corazon de Jesus, 1892 [1639]).

[7] F. R. Hoare, trans. and ed., *The Western Fathers, Being the Lives of SS. Martin of Tours, Ambrose, Augustine of Hippo, Honoratus of Arles and Germanus of Auxerre* (New York: Sheed and Ward, 1954).

references to sickness and the miraculous cure; the latter is perhaps the most common "type scene" in early Christian sacred biography and history.[8]

Why would Iberian missionaries writing on the eve of the Enlightenment rely so heavily on literary models and rhetoric that were over one thousand years old to represent the missionary experience in the New World? The perhaps obvious answer, particularly in the wake of post-structuralism, is that Jesuit missionary authors were part of a "regime of power," the Counter-Reformation Church, with a particular discourse and rules for signification. Jesuits were formed as religious through their reading of the lives of the Church Fathers and saints and later, as authors, essentially were required by the Church and Spanish Crown to employ early Christian literature as a literary model and source of rhetoric.

In recent years I have employed the critique of ethnography and "constructivism" as an analytical framework, researching the contingent factors (e.g., theological, literary, political, institutional, historical) that encouraged Jesuit "borrowing" from early sacred biography and history.[9] As noted at the outset, perhaps the most significant finding of this research has been that the Jesuits employed early Christian literature not simply as a reflex of Counter-Reformation discourse but also because there were demonstrable parallels between their own experience and the experience of their missionary counterparts in late antique and early medieval Europe. The rise of Christianity in both the Old World and New was coincident with profound dislocations resulting from epidemics that undermined indigenous religions and society as a whole. The challenges that early Christian missionaries confronted and overcame, realizing sainthood in the process, were analogous to those that

---

[8] Clare Stancliffe, "From Town to Country: The Christianization of the Touraine, 370–600." In *The Church in Town and Countryside*, ed. Derek Baker, pp. 43–59 (Oxford: Basil Blackwell, 1979), 57.

[9] Some exemplifications of constructivism: Edward M. Bruner, "Abraham Lincoln as Authentic Reproduction: A Critique of Postmodernism." *American Anthropologist* 96 (1994): 397–415; Jean Comaroff, *Body of Power Spirit of Resistance, The Culture and History of a South African People* (University of Chicago Press, 1985); Marshall Sahlins, *Islands of History* (University of Chicago Press, 1985), 143–145; James Clifford and George Marcus, eds., *Writing Culture, The Poetics and Politics of Ethnography* (Berkeley: University of California Press, 1986); Clifford Geertz, *Works and Lives: The Anthropologist as Author* (Cambridge: Polity Press, 1988).

missionaries faced in the New World.[10] Medieval hagiography is replete with mention of roadside cairns, tree worship, ceremonial intoxication, flying witches, and other pagan practices that the Jesuits encountered in the New World one thousand years later. Both medieval missionaries and the Jesuits imagined themselves at war with Satan and his heathen familiars, the dreaded shamans. Both sets of missionaries directly challenged these religious leaders but accommodated indigenous beliefs and practices through the cult of the saints and other "Christian" rituals and devotions.[11]

I did not intend above that Jesuit missionary employment of early Christian literature was *not* affected by institutional/political contingencies. The Counter-Reformation Church certainly exercised a profound influence on contemporaries. However, "the Church," be it understood as theology, an institution, or as discourse, was not monolithic. Catholics disagreed – sometimes violently – over the sacraments, grace, illumination, perfection, and a host of other issues. Moreover, although authors in Iberia and America were encouraged by the Church as well as the Spanish Crown to embrace particular signifying practices (e.g., rhetoric and type scenes from early Christian literature), they did not necessarily affirm hegemonic positions. The much celebrated Mexican nun, Juana Ines de la Cruz, who challenged the authority of her male confessors by quoting scripture and Church authorities, was perhaps without peer. But *Sor* Juana was not the first or only colonial-period author to use authority to question authority.[12]

Jesuit authors in the New World used – and, one might say, *deployed* – early Christian literature in response to a variety of institutional/political contingencies but particularly to defend their mission enterprise and vocation. During the century following the foundation of the Society of Jesus, most members of the order came to prefer life as a teacher over

---

[10] McNeill, *Plagues and Peoples*, 181; John L. Phelan, *The Millennial Kingdom of the Franciscans in the New World*, 2nd ed. (Berkeley: University of California Press, 1970 [1956]), 92.

[11] Pamela Berger, *The Goddess Obscured* (Boston: Beacon Press, 1985); Valerie I. J. Flint, *The Rise of Magic in Early Medieval Europe* (Princeton, NJ: Princeton University Press, 1991), 76.

[12] Electra Arenal and Amanda Powell, trans. and eds., *Sor Juana Ines de la Cruz, The Answer/La Repuesta* (New York: Feminist Press, 1994).

the Ignatian ideal of itinerant missionary. By 1645, less than half of all Jesuits were missionaries.[13] This profound shift in vocations posed a threat to Jesuit missionaries in the New World, who depended on the Society of Jesus for money, men, and political support, particularly in dealings with the Spanish Crown, which funded and approved missionary enterprises in the New World. Jesuit missionary authors relied on sacred history and biography for narrative scenes and rhetoric to persuade their readers (i.e., Jesuit novices and superiors; royal and ecclesiastical officials) of the preeminent status of the missionary vocation. For instance, in recounting the heroic lives and martyrdom of fellow Jesuits, Julio Pascual and Manuel Martínez, Pérez de Ribas implicitly and explicitly invokes early Christian literature, particularly the *Roman Martyrology* and lives of the saints:

> They opened the portals and began shooting arrows inside so no one could escape. One arrow hit Father Julio Pascal in the stomach, at which point Father Manuel Martínez said: "Let us not die for Christ sadly and cowardly." Then he emerged from the house, at which point they furiously shot more arrows, pinning Father Martinez's arms to his torso. Father Julio Pascual followed, even though his stomach was pierced by an arrow. Full of devotion and with their rosaries in their hands (I myself have one of these, all covered with blood), they both fell to their knees and asked our Lord for His favor and grace. They began to be struck by thousands of arrows covered with a poisonous herb. These rained upon their bodies until they became two Saint Sebastians, and within a short time they fell to the ground.[14]

Jesuit "deployment" of type scenes and rhetoric from sacred biography and history was itself consistent with the experience of missionary authors in Europe during late antiquity and the early Middle Ages. In his late-fourth-century *Life of Saint Martin*, which became the most influential of all hagiographies in Western Europe, Sulpicius Severus confronted analogous "institutional" constraints Jesuit missionaries faced over one thousand years later. During the early Middle Ages, many monks and

---

[13] Joseph de Guibert, *The Jesuits, Their Spiritual Doctrine and Practice, A Historical Study* (Chicago: Loyola University Press, 1964), 288, f. 21.
[14] Pérez de Ribas, *History of the Triumphs*, 259.

ecclesiastics in Europe were convinced that a contemplative life rather than the active life of a missionary was the true path to religious perfection.[15] Moreover, many early medieval monks and clerics questioned, as did later Jesuit critics who disparaged the Indian, whether missions to "rustic" Celts and German "barbarians" were worthwhile.[16] In his *vita* of Saint Martin, Severus went out of his way to highlight Martin's missionary vocation, casting it as an *imitatio Christi*. Severus's recounting of Martin's miracles and his success converting pagans was "proof positive" that Martin was doing God's work. The *vita* is also peppered with subtle and not-so-subtle attacks on the complacent and withdrawn lives of contemporary clerics and monks:

> Indeed, I have come across some who were so envious of his [Martin's] spiritual powers and his life as actually to hate in him what they missed in themselves but had not the strength to imitate. And – oh, grievous and lamentable scandal! – nearly all his calumniators were bishops. There is no need to mention names, though several of them are barking now at me.[17]

There were, then, institutional/political as well as theological and cultural–historical parallels between the missionary experience in the Old World and New. As discussed later, although neither early Christian nor Jesuit literature mirror directly the reality of the mission frontier, both literatures nonetheless reflect the similar contingencies that governed the lives of missionaries and their pagan and Indian converts.

Previous Scholarship on the Rise of Christianity

To my knowledge, this is the first comparative study to pursue McNeill's provocative suggestion that epidemic disease may have played a dynamic

---

[15] Giles Constable, *Three Studies in Medieval Religious and Social Thought* (Cambridge, UK: Cambridge University Press, 1995).

[16] W. H. C. Frend, *Religion Popular and Unpopular in the Early Christian Centuries* (London: Variorum Reprints, 1976), 17; E. A. Thompson, *Romans and Barbarians: The Decline of the Western Empire* (Madison: University of Wisconsin Press, 1982), 231.

[17] Hoare, *The Western Fathers*, 43.

role in the rise of Christianity in both Europe and America.[18] Scholars have ignored or dismissed the possibility of New and Old World parallels.[19] Many it seems have assumed that the first, postapostolic Church was unique.[20] The study of the early Church in Europe has traditionally focused on Christian theology and theologians. Much has been written about men such as the Apostle Paul, Iraneus, Eusebius, Augustine, Cassian, and Gregory the Great. We know relatively little about the millions of "ordinary" people who embraced Christianity during the late Roman Empire.[21] Historiography, in general, has emphasized "great men." As Voltaire remarked, "For the last fourteen hundred years, the only Gauls, apparently, have been kings, ministers, and generals."[22]

Similarly, the study of Christianity in Latin America has emphasized "great men" and "great ideas." The great man theme is prominent in the earliest histories written by missionary authors,[23] who cast the friars

---

[18] Stark has pursued in persuasive fashion McNeill's argument as it pertains to the Old World. Rodney Stark, *The Rise of Christianity, A Sociologist Reconsiders History* (Princeton, NJ: Princeton University Press, 1996).

[19] For instance, Peter Brown, *The Cult of the Saints, Its Rise and Function in Latin Christianity* (Chicago: University of Chicago Press, 1981), 29.

[20] Jonathan Z. Smith, *Drudgery Divine, On the Comparison of Early Christianities and the Religions of Late Antiquity* (London: School of Oriental and African Studies, University of London, 1990), 143.

[21] T. Barnes, "Pagan Perceptions of Christianity." In *Early Christianity Origins and Evolution to A.D. 600*, ed. Ian Hazlett, pp. 231–244 (Nashville: Abingdon Press, 1991); Ramsay MacMullen, *Christianizing the Roman Empire (A.D. 100–400)* (New Haven, CT: Yale University Press, 1984), 8; "What Difference Did Christianity Make?" *Historia* 35(3) (1986): 322–343, 322–323; R. A. Markus, *The End of Ancient Christianity* (Cambridge University Press, 1990), 4; A. D. Wright, *Catholicism and Spanish Society Under the Reign of Philip II, 1555–1598, and Philip III, 1598–1621* (Lewiston, Australia: Edwin Mellen Press, 1991).

[22] Quoted in Marshall Sahlins, *Islands of History* (Chicago: University of Chicago Press, 1985), 32.

[23] Mendieta and López de Gómara were some of the earliest New World authors to advance the great man theory. See John L. Phelan, *The Millennial Kingdom of the Franciscans in the New World* (Berkeley: University of California Press, 1966), 37. With respect to the Jesuit authors, see Juan de Albieuri, "Historia de las missiones apostólicas, que los clerigos regulares de la Compañía de Jesús an echo en las Indias Occidentales del reyno de la Nueva Vizcaya," Mexican Manuscript #7, Hubert H. Bancroft Collection, Bancroft Library, University of California, Berkeley; Juan E. Nieremberg (with Andrade Cassini), *Varones Illustres de la Compañía de Jesus*, 3 vols. (Bilbao, 1896 [1666]); Andrés Pérez de Ribas, *Coronica y Historia Religiosa de la Provincia de la Compañía de Jesus de Mexico*, 2 vols. (Mexico: Sagrado Corazon, 1896 [1653]), *History of the Triumphs of*

and black robes as great civilizers, combating idolatry, drunkenness, warfare, laziness, and polygamy. During the Enlightenment, this discourse was accepted uncritically by the *philosophes*, who cited the Jesuit mission enterprises of the New World as proof of how the application of reason could create societies where once there was only chaos or uncertain relations.[24] This idea of the Jesuit missionary as the vanguard of civilization persisted well into the twentieth century and was taken up by Frederick Jackson Turner and his influential student, Herbert E. Bolton.[25] Throughout much of the twentieth century, anthropologists as well as historians cast the Jesuit missionary in a role analogous to a modern-day extension agent, the source of new crops, tools, cattle, and other innovations that purportedly attracted Indian converts and "revolutionized" aboriginal culture.[26]

In recent decades the pendulum has swung from a largely laudatory Church history to a poststructural, postcolonial history, which has been decidedly critical of the Church in both Europe and colonial Mexico. The Church of late antiquity and the early Middle Ages increasingly has been seen as a sexually repressive and exploitive institution that "talked" endlessly and glowingly of suffering and continence, convincing the masses to accept deprivation, all the while bishops lived comfortable,

---

Our Holy Faith; Ruiz de Montoya, *Conquista Espiritual*; José Cardiel, *Breve relacion del régimen de las misiones del Paraguay* (Madrid: Gráficas Nilo, 1989 [1767]), 51.

[24] Magunus Morner, *The Political and Economic Activities of the Jesuits in the La Plata Region: The Hapsburg Era* (Stockholm: Library and Institute of Ibero-American Studies, 1953), 195.

[25] Herbert E. Bolton, "The Mission as a Frontier Institution in the Spanish-American Colonies." *American Historical Review* 23 (1917): 42–61. For a discussion of Bolton's influence, see David J. Weber, "John Francis Bannon and the Historiography of the Spanish Borderlands." *Journal of the Southwest* 29 (1987): 331–336; David Sweet, "The Ibero-American Frontier Mission in Native American History." In *The New Latin American History*, eds. Erick Langer and Robert H. Jackson, pp. 1–48 (Lincoln: University of Nebraska Press, 1995).

[26] Clement J. McNaspy, S.J., *Conquistador without a Sword* (Chicago: Loyola University Press, 1984), 190; Alfred Métraux, "Jesuit Missions in South America, Part 2." In *Handbook of South American Indians, Volume 5*, ed. J. Steward, pp. 645–653 (Washington, DC: Smithsonian Institution Press, 1949), 646, 651; Silvio Palacios and Ena Zoffoli, *Gloria y Tragedia de las Misiones Guaraníes* (Bilbao: Mensajero, 1991), 191; Edward H. Spicer, *Cycles of Conquest: The Impact of Spain, Mexico, and the United States on the Indians of the Southwest, 1533–1960* (Tucson: University of Arizona Press, 1962), 285–298.

incontinent lives.[27] Similar arguments have surfaced in the last twenty years regarding the Jesuit and Franciscan enterprises in Nueva España. What were previously seen as "great men" on a mission of God and progress,[28] now are understood as sexually repressive agents of colonialism, exploitive, abusive and perversely hypocritical in their avowed concern for the Indian: "Missionaries had everything supplied to them, and they got Indians to work for them. They were never in want of anything: they had good horses, cattle, clothing, and sexual access to Indian women."[29]

[27] Peter Brown, *The Body and Society* (New York: Harper & Row, 1988); Michel Foucault, "Sexuality and Power." In *Religion and Culture*, ed. Jeremy R. Carrette, pp. 115–130 (New York: Routledge, 1999 [1978]; Ramsay MacMullen, "What Difference Did Christianity Make?," 322–343; Judith Perkins, *The Suffering Self: Pain and Narrative Representation in the Early Christian Era* (London: Routledge, 1995). Elsewhere, Brown went so far as to suggest that clerical affluence was such that bishops in the West "...had to invent new ways of spending money." Peter Brown, *The Cult of the Saints, Its Rise and Function in Latin Christianity* (Chicago: University of Chicago Press, 1981), 40.

[28] John F. Bannon, S.J., *The Mission Frontier in Sonora, 1620–1687* (New York: United States Catholic Historical Society, 1955); Peter Masten Dunne, S.J., *Pioneer Black Robes on the West Coast* (Berkeley: University of California Press, 1940); *Pioneer Jesuits in Northern Mexico* (Berkeley: University of California Press, 1944); Robert Ricard, *The Spiritual Conquest of Mexico* (Berkeley: University of California Press, 1966 [1933]). Note that, whereas Ricard gave voice to this great man theme (e.g., pp. 142–152, 194, 212, 267), he had many critics in 1932 because he did not go far enough casting the Mendicants as great civilizers (see p. 305).

[29] David L. Kozak and David I. Lopez, *Devil Sickness and Devil Songs, Tohono O'odham Poetics* (Washington, DC: Smithsonian Institution Press, 1999), 96. See also Ramón A. Gutiérrez, *When Jesus Came, the Corn Mothers Went Away: Marriage, Sexuality, and Power in New Mexico, 1500–1846* (Stanford University Press, 1991). It is significant that Gutiérrez's book was widely acclaimed, albeit not by his Pueblo subjects. Far less attention has been paid to analyses of the mission frontier that do not vilify the Franciscans and Jesuits. See, for instance, John Kessell, *Spain in the Southwest* (Norman: University of Oklahoma Press, 2002); Susan Deeds, "Rural Work in Nueva Vizcaya: Forms of Labor Coercion on the Periphery." *Hispanic American Historical Review* 69 (1989): 425–449, "Double Jeopardy: Indian Women in Jesuit Missions of Nueva Vizcaya." In *Indian Women of Early Mexico*, eds. S. Schroeder, S. Wood, and R. Haskett, pp. 255–272 (Norman: University of Oklahoma Press, 1997); Charlotte M. Gradie, *The Tepehuan Revolt of 1616* (Salt Lake City: University of Utah Press, 2000); Robert H. Jackson and Edwardo Castillo, *Indians, Franciscans, and Spanish Colonization* (Albuquerque: University of New Mexico Press, 1995); Cynthia Radding, *Wandering Peoples, Colonialism, Ethnic Spaces, and Ecological Frontiers in Northwestern Mexico, 1700–1850* (Durham, NC: Duke University Press, 1997); Thomas E. Sheridan, *Empire of Sand* (Tucson: University of Arizona Press, 1999).

The recent emphasis on viewing the early Church in Europe and Mexico as repressive institutions is part of a more tectonic upheaval regarding how we conceive of history and the historical record. Poststructural theorists have problematized the idea that texts mirror reality.[30] Scholars previously viewed sacred biography and history, be it Jesuit or early Christian, as windows on the past or as pious fictions, which convey symbolically (i.e., through miracles) theological "truths." Poststructuralist theorists have highlighted how all texts are constitutive of reality and invariably are caught up in the exercise of power, relying on the illusion of "the transcendental signified" to create and maintain subjects for exploitation.[31]

We are indebted to poststructuralist theorists for highlighting the complex ways in which texts reference and occlude various realities, and how our own interpretations entail yet another remaking of the past in the image of the present. The realization that historical narratives infrequently mirror reality directly is critical to imagining plausible alternatives to those inscribed by early Christian and later, Spanish missionary-authors. However, extreme poststructural interpretations can result in the Nihilist presupposition that the relationship between a text and the reality it purports to describe is so problematic that questions of pretextual reality are not worth pursuing.[32] It is not uncommon to find scholars of Spanish colonial literature and historiography ignoring or

---

[30] Roland Barthes, *S/Z*, trans. R. Miller (New York: Hill and Wang, 1977 [1970]); Jacque Derrida, *On Grammatology*, trans. G. Spivak (Baltimore, MD: Johns Hopkins Press, 1976 [1967]); Michel Foucault, *The Archaeology of Knowledge*, trans. A. Sheridan (New York: Vintage Books, 1969), *The Order of Things*, trans. A. Sheridan (New York: Vintage Books, 1970 [1966]). Poststructuralism and related intellectual challenges to the "Enlightenment project" owe their own origins in part to freedom movements of the post-1960s that ended colonial rule in Asia, Africa, and Latin America. Part of the success of these movements entailed challenging and discrediting celebratory colonial histories. Patricia Seed, "More Colonial and Postcolonial Discourse." *Latin American Research Review* 28 (1993): 146–152.

[31] Jacque Derrida, *Writing and Difference*, trans. A. Bass (London: Routledge and Kegan Paul, 1978 [1967]), 278–293.

[32] See Gesa Mackenthun, *Metaphors of Dispossession* (Norman: University of Oklahoma Press, 1997), 16–18; Daniel T Reff, "Text and Context: Cures, Miracles, and Fear in the Relación of Alvar Núñez Cabeza de Vaca." *Journal of the Southwest*: 38 (1996): 115–138.

even dismissing matters of truth and verification.[33] Frustrated by the inability to adequately know and thus speak for "the subaltern," some scholars of Latin America have made the difficulty of representing the subaltern the focus of study.[34] Similarly, prominent medievalists have implied or stated that it is "fruitless" trying to determine the real basis of miracle stories,[35] which are so characteristic of early Christian literature. Medievalists increasingly have focused on miracle stories as evidence of literary traditions or vehicles of social identity.[36]

Perhaps the most poignant example of this slighting of pretextual reality is an otherwise fascinating book by Judith Perkins, entitled *The Suffering Self*.[37] The central argument advanced by Perkins is that the extensive discourse on pain and suffering that characterized late antiquity in Mediterranean Europe was a social construction deployed by the Church and consumed by the masses: "Christianity was only able to create itself as an institution because cultural 'talking,' its own and others, had prepared a subject ready for its call – a subject that apprehended itself as a sufferer."[38]

One would never know from Perkins's book that there was any "real" suffering during late antiquity. The Antonine Plague, which lasted from 165 to 180 C.E, killed 10 million people, or 8 percent, of the population of the Roman Empire. As discussed in Chapter 2, the Antonine Plague was the first of a series of disease episodes that destroyed millions of

---

[33] Zamora has suggested what appears to be a more accommodating view: "one can read to understand the past or to understand how stories about the past are told." However, this view ignores the fact that understanding "how stories about the past are told" presupposes inferences about "the past." Margarita Zamora, *Reading Columbus* (Berkeley: University of California Press, 1993), 3.

[34] For instance, John Beverley, *Subalternity and Representation* (Durham, NC: Duke University Press, 1999).

[35] Richard Fletcher, *The Barbarian Conversion, From Paganism to Christianity* (Berkeley: University of California Press, 1997), 45.

[36] Joan M. Petersen, *The Dialogues of Gregory the Great in their late antique cultural background* (Toronto: Pontifical Institute of Medieval Studies, 1984), xxi; Raymond Van Dam, *Saints and Their Miracles in Late Antique Gaul* (Princeton, NJ: Princeton University Press, 1993), 84.

[37] Judith Perkins, *The Suffering Self: Pain and Narrative Representation in the Early Christian Era* (London: Routledge, 1995).

[38] Ibid., 9.

lives and had numerous unpleasant multipliers for the survivors, many of whose lives were made worse by invading armies, famine, still-born infants, anxiety, and so on. The notion of "the Dark Ages" is not entirely bankrupt. There was very real, perhaps unprecedented suffering underlying the discourse of pain and suffering that was embraced by Christians of all classes beginning in late antiquity. Often overlooked is that, alongside this discourse was another equally extensive and elaborate discourse on charity – a discourse that encouraged Christians to attend to the needs of fellow human beings.[39] Importantly, early Christians not only "talked" a lot about charity but made it central to their lives as lived (it wasn't that they simply imagined themselves as charitable).

The realization that reality infrequently is directly accessible through literature should not keep us from acknowledging that real things happen to real people.[40] No scholar of late antiquity has emphasized the power of ideas more than Peter Brown, yet Brown cautioned historians not to lose sight of the desperate choices that real men and women were forced to make in late antiquity.[41]

Acknowledging this desperation and its connection to epidemic disease does not preclude clerics of the post–Constantine Church having benefitted materially from a discourse of pain and suffering, nor does it negate many clerics having engaged a repressive discourse on sexuality. These are important "stories" but so, too, is the story of millions of pagans and Indians for whom Christianity – a Christianity that they helped define – provided a means of getting on with what were very difficult lives. Along these lines, "great men" like Augustine and Cassian, the "father" of Western monasticism, may have drawn up the blueprint for Christianity, but Christianity has never been a religion whose form and

---

[39] Neglect of this agency can be traced in part to the influential, early work of Foucault, which ignored human agency and emphasized how religion victimized populations. Ivan Strenski, "Religion, Power, and Final Foucault," *Journal of the American Academy of Religion* (1998), 345–367.

[40] Rolena Adorno, "Reconsidering Colonial Discourse For Sixteenth-And Seventeenth-Century Spanish America." *Latin American Research Review* 28 (1993): 135–145, 139; F. Jameson, *The Political Unconscious: Narrative as a Socially Symbolic Act* (Ithaca, NY: Cornell University Press, 1981); Sherry B. Ortner, "Resistance and the Problem of Ethnographic Refusal." *Comparative Studies In Society and History* 37(1995): 173–193, 188–191.

[41] *The Body and Society*, xviii.

content has been dictated solely from the top down. Actually, the "the top" always has been more like a plateau, because of jurisdictional wrangling, parochial jealousy, incompetence, and resistance from within the ranks of the privileged elite.[42] It also is the case that during late antiquity and the early Middle Ages ordinary people exercised a powerful voice through the cult of the saints, the election of bishops, and the simple decision to ignore some and not other aspects of Church teachings.[43] Similarly, in colonial Latin America, "the Church" was very much a contested institution, one that native peoples negotiated with as well as resisted creatively. Indians and mestizos did not simply acquiesce to the vision and demands of Mendicant and Jesuit missionaries. In thousands of small communities and urban *barrios* Christianity was reimagined, not simply accepted by Indians and mestizos. The cult of the Virgin of Guadalupe or the feast of Corpus Christi in Cusco are more than Old World transplants. Both bespeak not only resistance but also the mobilization of resources and identity by Indians and mestizos.[44]

[42] Robert Hefner, "Introduction: World Building and the Rationality of Conversion." In *Conversion to Christianity*, ed. R. Hefner, pp. 3–44 (Berkeley: University of California Press, 1993).

[43] Thomas Heffernan, *Sacred Biography, Saints and Their Biographies in the Middle Ages* (New York: Oxford University Press, 1988); Ramsay MacMullen, *Christianity and Paganism in the Fourth to Eight Centuries* (New Haven, CT: Yale University Press, 1997), 119.

[44] There have been numerous works of late that have pursued Indian agency: Thomas A. Abercrombie, *Pathways of Memory and Power* (Madison: University of Wisconsin Press, 1998); Elizabeth H. Boone and Walter D. Mignolo, eds., *Writing Without Words; Alternative Literacies in Mesoamerica and the Andes* (Durham, NC: Duke University Press, 1994); Louise M. Burkhart, *The Slippery Earth: Nahua-Christian Moral Dialogue in Sixteenth-Century Mexico* (Tucson: University of Arizona Press, 1989); Nancy Farris, *Maya Society Under Colonial Rule: The Collective Enterprise of Survival* (Princeton, NJ: Princeton University Press, 1984); J. Jorge Klor de Alva, "Spiritual Conflict and Accommodation in New Spain: Toward a Typology of Aztec Responses to Christianity." In *The Inca and Aztec State, 1400–1800: Anthropology and History*, eds. G. Collier, R. Renaldo, and J. Wirth, pp. 345–366 (New York: Academic Press, 1982); Kenneth Mills, *Idolatry and Its Enemies: Colonial Andean Religion and Extirpation, 1640–1750* (Princeton, NJ: Princeton University Press, 1997); Stafford Poole, C.M., *Our Lady of Guadalupe: The Origins and Sources of a Mexican National Symbol, 1531–1797* (Tucson: University of Arizona Press, 1995); Cynthia Radding, *Wandering Peoples, Colonialism, Ethnic Spaces, and Ecological Frontiers in Northwestern Mexico, 1700–1850* (Durham, NC: Duke University Press, 1997); William Rowe and Vivian Schilling, *Memory and Modernity: Popular Culture in Latin America* (London: Verso, 1991); Frank Salomon and George L. Urioste, trans. and eds., *The Huarochiri Manuscript: A Testament of Ancient and Colonial Andean Religion*

Early Christian and Jesuit Narratives of the Rise of Christianity

Although poststructuralism, in practice, often has tended to ahistoricism and a down-playing of human agency, theorists such as Foucault, Derrida, and Barthes have provided useful strategies for understanding the form and content of early Christian and Jesuit literatures, and how these literatures reflect, albeit indirectly, the pretextual reality of early Christianity in Europe and Mexico.[45] In the wake of the hermeneutics movement[46] as well as poststructuralism, it is now generally understood that between text and world there is a semi-autonomous author whose perception and representation of reality is governed by a host of contingencies, including prior texts and the author's own dynamic, cultural-historical context.[47]

Early Christian Literature

The most significant contingency for early Christian authors was their belief in God's design and continuing presence in the lives of human beings (following Christ's ascension to heaven). This preoccupation with the regular "in-breaking of the divine" is evident in the passions or stirring accounts of Christian martyrs who were steeled by the Holy Spirit during their persecution at the hands of the

---

(Austin: University of Texas Press, 1991); Steve J. Stern, *Peru's Indian Peoples and the Challenge of Spanish Conquest* (Madison: University of Wisconsin Press, 1982); William B. Taylor, *Magistrates of the Sacred: Priests and Parishioners in Eighteenth-Century Mexico* (Stanford, CA: Stanford University Press, 1996).

[45] Beside literary evidence, there has been considerable archaeological research during the last twenty years that sheds light on pagan and Indian cultures, early monasticism in Europe, and other aspects of the rise of Christianity in both the Old World and New.

[46] Hans-Georg Gadamer, *Truth and Method* (New York: Crossroad Press, 1975 [1960]).

[47] M. M. Bakhtin and V. N. Volosinov, *Marxism and the Philosophy of Language*, trans. L. Matejka and I. R. Titunik (Cambridge, MA: Harvard University Press, 1986); James Clifford, "Introduction, Partial Truths," In *Writing Culture, The Poetics and Politics of Ethnography*, eds. J. Clifford and G. Marcus, pp. 1–26 (Berkeley: University of California Press, 1986); Hayden White, *Tropics of Discourse: Essays on Cultural Criticism* (Baltimore, MD: Johns Hopkins University Press, 1978).

Romans.[48] With the Peace of Constantine in 313 C.E., the days of literal martyrdom largely came to an end for Christians. What was previously an underground movement persecuted by the state became the religion of the state, and in the process, an institution seriously compromised by bishops suddenly flush with privilege and power. The successors to the martyrs were the "desert saints" (e.g., Paul the Hermit, Saint Antony, Hilarion) who fled the cities and ecclesiastical privilege to live lives of asceticism, sustained as it were by God's grace.[49] The lives of these holy men and women, who gave birth to monasticism, differ from the passions in several important respects. Most notably the enemy is now Satan and not his surrogate, the Roman magistrate.[50] With the emphasis no longer on martyrdom but on the saint's ascetic and heroic life, the *vitae* tend to follow the structure of a quest tale, emphasizing a saint's various battles with the devil and his progression to sanctity. The narrative as such followed a set pattern: marvelous infancy and vocation; struggle and trials that proved the saint a true athlete of Christ; an account of the saints virtues, miracles, and prophecies, including his/her own approaching death, and the saint's death and postmortem miracles.

Between the fourth and sixth centuries various authors wrote lives of the desert saints and other "Church Fathers," which St. Jerome assembled along with the Fathers' "sayings" in a work known as the *Vitae Patrum.*

---

[48] Originally, in the second and third centuries, the passions were in the form of brief notes giving the time, place, and circumstances of various martyrs' deaths. In the Middle Ages, Bede and his students transformed the material into a collection of narrative martyrologies. Baronius published the first printed edition of the *Roman Martyrology* in 1586. Musurillo, *The Acts of the Christian Martyrs*; Duncan Robertson, *The Medieval Saints' Lives, Spiritual Renewal and Old French Literature* (Lexington: French Forum Publishers, 1995).

[49] Sacred biography is ambiguous about how one becomes a saint, one moment implying that would-be saint's cultivate sanctity by emulating Christ, and the next moment explicitly stating that God alone decides who will be a saint. Theologians such as Augustine and Eriugena "resolved" the apparent contradiction by suggesting concepts such as *theosis* – deification of the creature as a result of a dialectical, mystical conjunction of the ascending individual with the descending godhead. Stephen G. Nichols, Jr., *Romanesque Signs: Early Medieval Narrative and Iconography* (New Haven, CT: Yale University Press, 1983), 10–11.

[50] Alison Goddard Elliott, *Roads to Paradise: Reading the Lives of the Early Saints* (Hanover, NH: University Press of New England, 1987), 42.

Toward the end of the fourth century (c. 397 C.E.), Sulpicius Severus inaugurated an "episcopal" genre of sacred biography with his life of Bishop Martin of Tours, who is credited with converting the pagan population of northern Gaul.[51] Throughout the Middle Ages, hagiographers used *The Life of Saint Martin* as a literary model for thousands of saint's lives, which sprang from oral traditions about local clerics and monks who bridged heaven and earth.[52] It also was during the fourth century that Eusebius (d. 338/9) inaugurated the genre of ecclesiastical history, which was subsequently elaborated as a dramatic narrative by Gregory of Tours (539–595 C.E) and Bede (673–735 C.E.).[53]

Although there are significant differences between "passions," saints' lives, and sacred history, they all emphasize first and final causes (God and his often inscrutable intentions) rather than efficient or material causality.[54] Prosper, Sulpicius Severus, Jerome, and historians such as Bede and Gregory of Tours were principally concerned with showing how individual lives and historical events resembled events recounted in scripture, thus evidencing a divine plan.[55] This preoccupation with God's design and handiwork was championed by Augustine,[56] who both reflected and guided Christian thought during late antiquity and the early Middle Ages. History as well as nature itself was understood as evidencing the hand of God. Works on "the nature of things" (*De Natura Rerum*) were enormously popular during the early Middle Ages and presupposed a divine plan whose progress could be measured and judged

---

[51] Robertson, *The Medieval Saints' Lives*, 130; Stancliffe, *St. Martin and His Hagiographer*: Hoare, The Western Fathers.

[52] Heffernan notes that the *Bibliotecha Hagiographica Latina* alone lists more than eight thousand saints' lives. Heffernan, *Sacred Biography*, 13.

[53] Joaquín Martínez Pizarro, *A Rhetoric of the Scene: Dramatic Narrative in the Early Middle Ages* (Toronto: University of Toronto Press, 1989).

[54] Biraben and Le Goff, "The Plague in the Middle Ages," 49; Ernst Breisach, *Historiography, Ancient, Medieval & Modern* (Chicago: University of Chicago Press, 1983), 77–80; Johan Huizinga, *The Waning of the Middle Ages* (New York: St. Martin's Press, 1967 [1919]); Nichols, *Romanesque Signs*, 20–21; Stancliffe, *St. Martin and His Hagiographer*, 193, 210.

[55] Steven Muhlberger, *The Fifth-Century Chroniclers, Prosper, Hydatius, and the Gallic Chronicler of 452* (Leeds: Francis Cairns, 1990), 2; Nichols, *Romanesque Signs*, xi.

[56] Marcus Dods, trans. and ed., *The City of God by Saint Augustine*, 2 Vols. (New York: Hafner, 1948); G. Keyes, *Christian Faith and the Interpretation of History, A Study of St. Augustine's Philosophy of History* (Lincoln: University of Nebraska Press, 1966), 191.

by a spiritually informed reading of nature and natural phenomena (e.g., earthquakes, pestilence).[57]

Eusebius and other early Christian authors emphasized how the unfolding of God's plan, and more precisely, the spread of Christianity, presupposed a war against Satan and his legion of demons.[58] In the Old Testament (e.g., Book of Job) and the Gospels, Satan is an important yet largely undefined character. By the fourth century C.E., Christianity was a religion preoccupied with Satan. In narratives such as *The Life of Saint Antony*, Satan seemingly "is everywhere you want to be," obstructing the work of holy men.[59]

It is of course difficult to convey God and Satan working in and through mortal beings, nature, or historical events. To convey what essentially was ineffable (the immediate reality of an invisible world), sacred biographers and historians employed hyperbole, *superlatio* (e.g., "the tomb revealed a body as white as snow"), and other forms of "exaggerated speech."[60] Such language characteristically was embedded in dramatic narratives in which the author effaced himself as much as possible by allowing his characters to speak for themselves.[61] This oral quality was a rhetorical strategy that created the illusion that the reader witnessed events as they happened. Dramatized action (e.g., having a monk or cleric essentially reiterate Christ's Galilean ministry) also helped to

---

[57] Valerie I. J. Flint, "Thoughts About the Context of Some Early Medieval Treatises *De Natura Rerum*." In *Ideas in the Medieval West: Texts and their Contexts*, ed. Valerie I. J. Flint, pp. 1–31 (London: Variorum Reprints, 1988).

[58] de Nie, *Views From a Many-Windowed Tower*, 31; Glenn F. Chestnut, *The First Christian Histories: Eusebius, Socrates, Sozomen, Theodoret, and Evagrius* (Paris: Editions Beauchesne, 1986), 106. Eusebius's recounting of "the Martyrs of Lyon," for instance, blames the devil ("the adversary"; "the evil one") as much as Gallo-Romans for the persecution of the Christians of Lyon. Musurillo, *Acts of the Christian Martyrs*, 63.

[59] *The Life of Saint Antony* relates how Satan was always after Antony, and by extension, any and all Christians who "keep the faith." For instance, Satan tempts Antony by assuming human guises (e.g., an attractive woman); making noise at night outside Antony's cave; physically assaulting Antony at home; and tempting Antony by leaving gold coins along pathways in the desert.

[60] Heffernan, *Sacred Biography*, 11.

[61] Although the use of direct speech (e.g., Christ's many parables) was a preferred technique of biblical authors, early Christian authors systematically linked narrative events to create a dramatic narrative, which became the preferred literary style of early medieval sacred biographers and historians. R. Alter, *The Art of Biblical Narrative* (New York: Basic Books, 1981), 63ff; Pizarro, *A Rhetoric of the Scene*, 13.

convey a theological point, namely the paradigmatic status of Christ's life as revealed in the Gospels.[62] It is also the case that most sacred biographies originated as oral traditions and were committed to paper by monks and clerics who then read them aloud to their largely illiterate audiences on saint's feastdays.[63] In this regard, sacred biographies often were the outcome of "negotiations" between illiterate masses and privileged monks and clerics.

The rise of Christianity during the late Roman Empire is presented in early Christian literature as a story of martyrs, ascetics, monks, and clerics – all battling seen (e.g., Roman magistrates, Greek philosophers, pagan *magi* or shamans) and unseen enemies, notably Satan, aided as it were by the Holy Spirit. The hand of God turned hostile pagan mobs into doting listeners; on other occasions it caused a falling tree to suddenly alter its course, sparing the life of a missionary saint. Early Christian authors lived in awe of God's mysterious ways; rarely did it enter their minds to "forget about God" and focus systematically on material causality or what we today might term "real-world events." In his *Ecclesiastical History*, for instance, Eusebius mentioned epidemics,[64] but he invariably rendered them meaningful in terms of biblical precedents or as signs of God's power and transcendence.[65] Similarly, Eusebius's most prolific heir, Gregory of Tours, mentioned disease, but usually in a discussion of seemingly unconnected events or prodigies (e.g., comets, trees split by lightning). Gregory was not concerned with the role of disease in history but, rather, with how epidemics signaled God's anger and his impending wrath.[66] Likewise, Bede, when he chose to mention epidemics,[67] did so to make a point about God's enduring presence and power.[68]

---

[62] Heffernan, *Sacred Biography*, 5.   [63] Pizarro, *A Rhetoric of the Scene*.

[64] G. A. Williamson, trans., *Eusebius: The History of the Church from Christ to Constantine* (Harmondsworth, Middlesex, England: Dorset Press, 1965), 304–306, 365–368.

[65] Rebecca J. Lyman, *Christology and Cosmology* (Oxford: Clarendon Press, 1993), 92; see also Glenn F. Chestnut, *The First Christian Histories: Eusebius, Socrates, Sozomen, Theodoret, and Evagrius* (Paris: Editions Beauchesne, 1986), 100.

[66] de Nie, *Views From a Many-Windowed Tower*, 27–38.

[67] Colgrave and Mynors, *Bede's Ecclesiastical History*, 357–359, 377.

[68] Darrel W. Amundsen, "The Medieval Catholic Tradition." In *Caring and Curing, Health and Medicine in the Western Religious Tradition*, eds. R. Numbers and D. Amundsen, pp. 65–108 (London: Macmillan Publishing Company, 1986), 78–79.

Jesuit Narratives of the Early Church in Mexico

As noted, the Jesuits produced a voluminous literature, which is significantly more transparent with respect to material causality. That said, Jesuit authors had a great deal in common with their early Christian counterparts. Indeed, Jesuits were formed as religious through a reading of early Christian literature. The Jesuit "Father General" – the highest-ranking Jesuit superior – issued directives on which authors a Jesuit *should* read, *might* read (with caution), and *could not* read on pain of sin.[69] The *Ratio Studiorum* is particularly instructive in this regard. Implemented at the close of the late sixteenth century, the *Ratio* listed the authors and books that Jesuit novices were expected to read as part of their religious formation.[70] Included on the list is much of the early Christian literature cited above, including the *Roman Martyrology*.[71] It was a custom in Jesuit residences and colleges to read each day at supper a *passio* or stirring account of an early Christian martyr.[72] The lives and sayings of the desert saints and Church Fathers, the *Vitae Patrum*, likewise appears on the *Ratio Studiorum*. During the early seventeenth century (1615, 1628), a Jesuit, Herbert Rosweyd, compiled two editions of the *Vitae Patrum*,[73] which were read widely by religious, including Jesuit, novices.

Ignatius Loyola noted in his autobiography that his life was forever changed by his reading of the lives of the saints and Ludolph's *Life of Christ*.[74] Perhaps not surprisingly, recitation of the litany of the saints was a common practice in Jesuit schools and it was practically the only

---

[69] de Guibert, *The Jesuits*, 215–218; O'Malley, *The First Jesuits*, 313–315.

[70] See de Guibert, *The Jesuits*, 216.

[71] In 1643 the Jesuits at Antwerp under Jean Bolland began critically evaluating and establishing reliable texts of the acts or passions of the first Christian martyrs. Musurillo, *Acts of the Christian Martyrs*, xi.

[72] O'Malley, *The First Jesuits*, 340; Robertson, *The Medieval Saints' Lives*, 30.

[73] Henri-Jean Martin, *Print, Power, and People in 17th-Century France*, trans. David Gerard (Metuchen, NJ: The Scarecrow Press, 1993), 101–103; Robertson, *The Medieval Saints' Lives*, 77.

[74] George E. Ganss, Editor, *Ignatius Loyola: The Spiritual Exercises and Selected Works* (New York: Paulist Press, 1991), 70–71; O'Malley, *The First Jesuits*, 268–270. Note that Loyola's conversion was much like Augustine's; the latter was irrevocably changed by a reading of Athanasius's *Life of Saint Antony*.

occasion when Jesuits gathered regularly for prayer.[75] During the seventeenth century, it was the Jesuits led by Jean Bolland who took the lead in publishing sacred biographies, which were popular in Europe.[76] Not surprisingly, the lives of the saints, and Severus's *Life of Saint Martin*, in particular, appear on the *Ratio Studiorum*. The works of Eusebius, Bede, and two contemporaries of the late sixth century, Pope Gregory the Great (550–604 C.E.) and Bishop Gregory of Tours, also were required reading for Jesuits.

The relevance of early Christian literature was acknowledged by Jesuit missionary authors both in margin notes as well as explicit textual references. The *Historia*, for instance, contains innumerable references to not only the Bible but also the Fathers of the Church (e.g., Augustine, Cassiodorus) and sacred biography and history. The many explicit and implicit references to early Christian literature reflect the Jesuits' essentially Augustinian worldview, particularly the belief that God was intimately involved with his creation. Although separated in time by one thousand years, Gregory of Tours and Jesuits such as Pérez de Ribas saw God everywhere, and often in the very same places:

> The same is true indeed of the nature (natura) of trees, which, as I believe, is a sign (signat) of that same resurrection, when in the winter, denuded of leaves, they seem to be dead, and in the time of spring they are adorned with leaves and embellished by flowers, while in the summer full of apples. Which wonder, notwithstanding its being used in this way as a likeness (similitudo), exhibits a favour to the peoples [of the earth] here and now, so that man should know that he receives food from the One Who created him out of nothing (*creavit ex nihlo*). (Gregory of Tours, c. 590 C.E.).[77]

Let us turn to another natural wonder worthy of consideration, which is a tree often found in the valleys of Sinaloa and in other warm places. This tree, which has a very large crown, is called tucuchi in the language of this region. Its fruit is a small, sweet fig; some of its branches are very long and large, extending so far that they could no longer sustain themselves without forked branches to hold them up. The Lord

---

[75] O'Malley, *The First Jesuits*, 268.
[76] Martin, *Print, Power, and People*, 88, 101, 103.
[77] As quoted in de Nie, *Views From a Many-Windowed Tower*, 108.

aided them in a very unusual way: some trunks that are separate from the main trunk of the tree grow straight up out of the earth and under the tree branches.... We can therefore say that God wanted to leave in nature a sign of how the Holy Spirit flows from the Father and the Son, persons who are truly distinct, whom these works praise. (Pérez de Ribas, 1645)[78]

Early Christian and Jesuit missionaries truly believed that God was everywhere and his grace, ubiquitous. Grace sustained early Christian martyrs at the hour of death and empowered miracle workers such as Martin of Tours. Both types of holy people have their parallel among New World Jesuits. Most every Jesuit missionary who served on the northern frontier was threatened or wounded at some time or other by Indians who opposed or renounced baptism. Between 1591 and 1645, close to a dozen missionaries died as martyrs, killed by Indian apostates. Jesuits who were not "gifted" with martyrdom emulated Martin of Tours and "desert saints" such as Antony, wearing hair shirts and enduring all manner of personal sacrifice as well as trials and tribulations at the hand of Satan and his "familiars," Indian shamans.

Jesuits who served in the New World as missionaries were as convinced as Eusebius or Athanasius that the devil was real; Satan was no mere symbol or metaphor for evil, but a supernatural foe who, paradoxically, was powerless yet powerful. Along these lines, Jesuit missionary-authors shared Eusebius's conviction that "the rise of Christianity" presupposed a war with Satan. One reads in Pérez de Ribas's *Historia*, for instance:

But the more this primitive Church grew in Christian customs and the more gentile customs declined, the more the devil's rage grew. This principal enemy of mankind saw himself being stripped of the souls that he had dominated and possessed uncontested for so many years. On the occasion of the epidemics, many of the souls of baptized infants and newly-baptized adults no longer entered his infernal caverns as they used to, but instead went to heaven. He saw how the priests' talks revealed the web of lies with which his sorcerers and familiars (who are his tools) entangled and deceived so many people. The devil

---

[78] Pérez de Ribas, *History of the Triumphs*, 86.

understood that if he did not stem the course of the Gospel, he would soon be stripped of all the souls in Sinaloa.[79]

In significant ways the Jesuits had one foot in the Enlightenment and the other foot more firmly planted in the Middle Ages.[80] The Jesuits understood from experience and observation that many Indians were driven by desperation to Christianity. However, being largely "medieval" in their worldview,[81] they understood that the Indians' desperation was God's handiwork and that the "first and final cause" of Indian interest in baptism was the power of the Holy Spirit to attract people to God (as per Augustine). In Book II of the *Historia*, Pérez de Ribas recounted how in 1615 several hundred Nébome Indians beyond the mission frontier abandoned their pueblos and traveled for several days, seeking refuge in the Jesuit mission of Bamoa along the Río Sinaloa. Pérez de Ribas noted that a number of Indians died en route and another was covered from head to foot with what he referred to as leprosy. Still, he indicated: "The principal reasons why these people came [south] were to receive Holy Baptism, become Christians, and enjoy the catechism taught by the priests."[82] Nowhere did Pérez de Ribas acknowledge that the Indians came south hoping that the priests and their ritual cleansing might cure or protect them from typhus and other diseases that reached epidemic proportions at the time on the northern frontier.[83]

Other Story Lines

However much early Christian and Jesuit authors followed culturally defined rules and logic to produce convincing and meaningful stories,

---

[79] Ibid., 49.

[80] The Jesuits were "new rationalists," believing that revelation and metaphysics provided unique insights that became truths by subjecting them to natural reason. J. B. Russell, *Mephistopheles* (Ithaca, NY: Cornell University Press, 1986), 80–82.

[81] Huizinga conveyed this worldview in a sentence: "The Middle Ages never forgot that all things would be absurd, if their meanings were exhausted in their function and their place in the phenomenal world, if by their essence they did not reach into a world beyond this." Johan Huizinga, *The Waning of the Middle Ages* (New York: St. Martin's Press, 1967 [1919]), 183.

[82] Pérez de Ribas, *History of the Triumphs*, 185.

[83] Reff, *Disease, Depopulation and Culture Change*, 154–160.

their texts invariably evidence *punctum*, inconsistencies, gaps, and oc-
clusions that hint at other possibilities. As noted, Jesuit as well as early
Christian literature often take the form of a dramatic narrative,[84] replete with moments when early Christian and Jesuit authors switched to
direct discourse, seemingly relinquishing control of the text to converts,
shamans, and apostates. Although this relinquishment is orchestrated,[85]
direct discourse often reveals competing and conflicting voices and what
Barthes termed *punctum* – small details of a photograph or narrative that
convey realities such as epidemics that may have gone unnoticed by an
author or photographer, preoccupied with conveying "larger truths."[86]

The challenge with respect to early Christian and Jesuit literature is to
acknowledge as well as think past an author's own epistemologically informed construction, mindful of oppositions and rhetoric that evidence
"complex differences and differentiation" – other story lines besides the
author's own will to truth.[87] My own search for these story lines has
been guided by the assumption that cultural-historical analyses benefit
from cognizance of the day-to-day lives and struggles of ordinary people, even if those people did not have the privilege of writing their own
history.[88] Of course, just as poststructuralism taken too far can result in

---

[84] Alter, *Art of Biblical Narrative*; Pizarro, *A Rhetoric of the Scene.*
[85] James Clifford, "Introduction, Partial Truths." In *Writing Culture, The Poetics and Politics of Ethnography*, eds. J. Clifford and G. Marcus, pp. 1–26 (Berkeley: University of
California Press, 1986), 14–15; Peter Hulme, *Colonial Encounters: Europe and the Native
Caribbean, 1492–1797* (London: Methuen, 1986), 9.
[86] Mikhail Bakhtin, *The Dialogic Imagination: Four Essays*, trans. C. Emerson and M.
Holquist (Austin: University of Texas Press, 1981), 324. Barthes used the terms punctum
and studium to define how individuals relate to photographs, suggesting that studium
is the " . . . extension of a field, which I perceive quite familiarly as a consequence of my
knowledge, my culture," and that reveal the photographer's intentions. Punctum are
small details that break or punctuate the studium, " . . . rising of their own accord into
affective consciousness," overwhelming the entirety of the reading. Roland Barthes,
Camera Lucida, trans. Richard Howard (New York: Hill and Wang, 1981), 25–26,
49, 55.
[87] James Clifford, *The Predicament of Culture* (Cambridge, MA: Harvard University Press,
1988), 53; Stuart Hall, "Old and New Identities, Old and New Ethnicities." In *Culture,
Globalization and the World-System*, ed. A. King, pp. 41–68 (London: Macmillan, 1991);
Gyan Prakash, "Writing Post-Orientalist Histories of the Third World: Indian Historiography Is Good To Think." In *Colonialism and Culture*, eds. N. B. Dirks, pp. 353–388
(Ann Arbor: University of Michigan Press, 1992), 354.
[88] Karl Marx and Frederick Engels, *The German Ideology* (Moscow: Progress Publishers,
1964 [1845–1846]), 39–49.

Nihilism, so, too, a preoccupation with the material conditions of life can result in a reductionistic functionalism.[89] It is apparent that since the advent of state-level societies some seven thousand years ago, classes and institutions frequently have sustained themselves on fictions and social constructions that have seemingly dictated rather than responded to the material conditions of life. That said, it is a human conceit, exacerbated in the twentieth century through the uncritical acceptance of scientific progress, to conceive of history solely or largely in terms of power struggles realized through ideas or social constructions. "Men [people] make their own history, but they do not make it just as they please."[90] Throughout history, biological processes have asserted their power and influence over human beings,[91] despite social constructions that may imply otherwise. Hemorrhaging, ulcers, a helpless infant dying in a mother's arms – some things are hard to ignore or cast as something else.

Juxtaposition of what sometimes are several or more texts by contemporary authors facilitates supportable inferences regarding the pretextual reality of the mission frontier and the contingencies that governed the writing of early Christian and Jesuit texts.[92] Still, in the near total absence of pagan and Indian voices it is imperative to approach early Christian and Jesuit texts from an ethnographic perspective,[93] bringing the archaeological and anthropological literatures to bear on the question of pagan and Indian identities. Although anthropology has been complicit in colonialism and the "othering of others," cultural relativism offers the possibility of much thicker descriptions[94] of pagan and Indian

---

[89] Mircea Eliade, *Ordeal by Labrynth* (Chicago: University of Chicago Press, 1982), 137; Wayne A. Meeks, *The First Urban Christians, The Social World of the Apostle Paul* (New Haven, CT: Yale University Press, 1983), 20–21.

[90] Karl Marx, *The Eighteenth Brumaire of Louis Bonaparte* (New York: International Publishers, 1963 [1852]), 15.

[91] The inseparability of the history of nature and the history of man was explicitly noted by Marx and Engels in a passage crossed out of the original manuscript of the thesis on Feuerbach (Marx and Engels, *The German Ideology*, 28).

[92] Caroline W. Bynum, *Fragmentation and Redemption, Essays on Gender and the Human Body in Medieval Religion* (New York: Zone Books, 1991), 23.

[93] Sherry B. Ortner, "Resistance and the Problem of Ethnographic Refusal." *Comparative Studies In Society and History* 37 (1995): 173–193.

[94] Clifford Geertz, *The Interpretation of Cultures* (New York: Basic Books, 1973).

cultures and the dynamics of conversion than would otherwise be the case.

As noted earlier, the explicit "story"[95] told by early Christian and Jesuit authors is almost always about how God and, more precisely, the Holy Spirit, working with and through Christian missionaries, successfully defeated Satan and his pagan and Indian "familiars," the dreaded *magi* and shamans. In narrating this triumph of the Holy Spirit, early Christian and Jesuit authors inscribed or alluded to another story line that pagans and Indians might recognize, and perhaps have voiced. This other story is not predicated on the assumption that pagans and Indians were backward and prisoners of Satan, nor does it understand the spread of Christianity in terms of a wholesale change wrought by the Holy Spirit. Rather, unprecedented calamity is suggested as having paved the way for Christianity. Moreover, rather than vanquishing heathenism and the devil, Christianity accommodated both! This is the "unthinkable" implied but never made explicit in early Christian and Jesuit narratives.[96]

But who is to say that this is indeed the story lurking beneath the surface of Bede's *Ecclesiastical History* or Perez de Ribas's *History of the Triumphs of Our Holy Faith*? And who is to say that this is the story pagans and Indians would tell, or would have told? Spivak is correct in her assertion that academic knowledge is inadequate to the task of representing subalterns. However, it is not as if we have a choice about whether a story, and preferably, stories, will be told; they are told every day in textbooks, the media, and so on, with profound consequences for everyone and particularly for subalterns. I proffer the foregoing story because it assumes that pagans and Indians were agents – not simply victims. Too often the laudable pursuit of oppressive institutions and discourses has

---

[95] Here I follow Ricouer who suggests that it is through narrative that historical understanding is conveyed. Paul Ricouer, *Time and Narrative*, Vol. 1., trans. Kathleen McLaughlin and David Pellauer (Chicago: University of Chicago Press, 1984).

[96] For the "unthinkable" see Barthes, *S/Z*; Derrida, *On Grammatology, Writing and Difference*, trans. A. Bass (London: Routledge and Kegan Paul, 1978 [1967]; F. Jameson, *The Political Unconscious: Narrative as a Socially Symbolic Act* (Ithaca, NY: Cornell University Press, 1981), 35, 82–83; Pierre Macherey, *A Theory of Literary Production* (London: Routledge, 1978), 80.

had the unfortunate consequence of "othering others." Although I am in fundamental agreement with the many scholars who have highlighted the oppression and repression carried out in the name of Christianity,[97] I doubt that medieval pagans and Indians were duped into abandoning "cheerful other worlds" for a preoccupation with purgatory and hell (as per Le Goff) and "exhaustive and permanent confession" (as per Foucault). Indians and mestizos in colonial Mexico certainly were not "duped." Despite confession and the coercive influence of ecclesiastical rules and courts, the people as a whole were rather tolerant of consensual unions, illegitimate children, and ethnic mixing.[98]

Recent, yet now orthodox formulations of "the Church" and "state" strike me as unduly reductionistic, not only in their imagining of regimes of power that are monolithic but also because they essentially imply and embrace Greco-Roman stereotypes of pagans as rustics and barbarians, and Native Americans who are likewise less-than-rational or backward.[99] And how are we to understand the millions of Europeans as well as Indians and mestizos who today bloody their knees and spend their hard-earned wages on candles consumed before plaster images of the Virgin and innumerable other saints?[100] Are we to understand these people as puppets – prisoners of an imposed "habitus?"[101]

Although the rise of Christianity is very much a story of sexual repression, abusive clerics, unholy wars, and so on, it is also a story of

---

[97] For instance, Foucault, "Politics and Reason," 63; David E. Stannard, *American Holocaust* (New York: Oxford University Press, 1992).

[98] Asunción Lavrin, *Sexuality and Marriage in Colonial Latin America* (Lincoln: University of Nebraska Press, 1989), 78–80.

[99] Foucault's *Discipline and Punish* has had a significant impact on recent scholars, many of whom seemingly may have lost sight of the fact that the all-encompassing "terrific" exercise of power that Foucault described for Europe in circa 1800 may not be generalizable. Joanne P. Sharp et al., "Entanglements of Power, Geographies of Domination/Resistance." In *Entanglements of Power: Geographies of Domination/Resistance*, eds. J. P. Sharp et al., pp. 1–42 (London: Routledge, 2000), 14–16.

[100] The paradoxical nature of the cult of the saints (undercutting yet empowering individual agency) is powerfully conveyed in Robert Orsi's, *Thank You, St. Jude: Women's Devotion to the Patron Saint of Hopeless Causes* (New Haven, CT: Yale University Press, 1999).

[101] Pierre Bourdieu, "Legitimation and Structured Interest in Weber's Sociology of Religion." In *Max Weber: Rationality, and Modernity*, eds. Samuel Whimster and Scott Lash, pp. 119–136 (London: Allen and Urwin, 1987), 126.

human beings responding in novel ways to unprecedented adversity.[102] Rigoberta Menchú is perhaps the most celebrated, recent example of such agency. Is she truly exceptional or is she one of countless people who have made a difference in not only the lives of others but also in various institutions and regimes of power, including "the Church"?

Note that in arguing for the agency of pagans and Indians I am not assuming some consciousness of subjectivity – that pagans and Indians necessarily understood themselves as in opposition to established authorities within the Church (e.g., bishops or Jesuit missionaries), battling as it were to define Christianity. As Asad has reminded us, those who make history rarely are altogether conscious of what they are doing; their acts are more (and less) than their consciousness of those acts.[103] Perhaps as significant as pagan or Indian consciousness of subjectivity was the cultural–historical context of late antiquity and colonial America, respectively. Epidemics, population collapse, and internal migration rendered economic, political, and social structures unstable and fluid, requiring new forms of economic, social, and religious life that nevertheless were bound to the past. During epidemics, "ideology" as a coercive system of meanings inscribed on bodies and reality writ large,[104] necessarily faltered along with the purveyors of socially constructed "truths."

During the nineteenth and early twentieth century, it was assumed that pagans and Indians were attracted to Christianity because of Christianity's greater intellectual coherence and moral rigor, as evident in the works of its great theologians, notably Augustine and Thomas Aquinas. After World War II, this view was supplanted by the Weberian notion that Christianity offered a cultural logic that was adapted to the

---

[102] Gabrielle Spiegel, "History, Historicism and the Social Logic of the Text in the Middle Ages." In *The Postmodern History Reader*, ed. Keith Jenkins, pp. 180–203 (London: Routledge, 1997), 195; Ivan Strenski, "Religion, Power, and Final Foucault." *Journal of the American Academy of Religion* (1998): 345–367, 354.

[103] Talal Asad, *Genealogies of Religion, Discipline and Reasons of Power in Christianity and Islam* (Baltimore, MD: Johns Hopkins University Press, 1993), 15.

[104] Louise Althusser, "Ideology and Ideological State Apparatuses." In *Reading Popular Narrative: A Source Book*, ed. Bob Ashley (London: Leicester University Press, 1997 [1971]); Bourdieu, *Outline of A Theory of Practice*; Michel Foucault, "Nietzsche, Genealogy, History." In *The Foucault Reader*, ed. Paul Rabinow, pp. 76–100 (New York: Pantheon Books, 1984).

"civilized macrocosm."[105] Once a pagan or Indian became a citizen of the Roman or Spanish empires, respectively, his or her thoughts and concerns were no longer local, and thus required religious beliefs and practices that were less instrumental and more universal in scope.[106] Archaeological and ethnohistorical research have made abundantly clear that Neolithic Celts and pre-Columbian Indians were quite familiar with what was their own civilized macrocosm.[107] Long before Caesar invaded Gaul, or Cortés set foot in Mexico, pagans and Indians had known town life, surplus production, philosophy, far-reaching trade, exploitive elites, and other hallmarks of civilization. Ethnographically informed research has likewise revealed that Christianity always has been instrumental, even if its doctrines and rhetoric have suggested otherwise.[108] Indeed, a major argument of this book is that Christianity's success in both the Old World and the New was due in part to the instrumentality of Christian rituals and practice, particularly in the context of a disease environment. Similarly, whereas Christian theology may be universal

---

[105] Hefner, "Introduction: World Building and the Rationality of Conversion," 6–10.

[106] This logic has been embraced by a number of prominent theorists: Robert Bellah, "Religious Evolution." In *Sociology of Religion*, ed. R. Robertson, pp. 262–292 (Baltimore, MD: Penguin Books, 1969), 276–277; Arnold Toynbee, *An Historian's Approach to Religion*, 2nd ed. (Oxford, UK: Oxford University Press, 1979), 76–77; Max Weber, *The Sociology of Religion*, trans. Ephraim Fischoff (Boston: Beacon Press, 1956). No less a scholar than Stancliffe embraced this logic when she suggested that the "seedbed" for a great number of conversions to Christianity in Gaul was "a world that had grown frighteningly large." Clare Stancliffe, "From Town to Country: The Christianization of the Touraine, 370–600." In *The Church in Town and Countryside*, ed. Derek Baker, pp. 43–59 (Oxford: Basil Blackwell, 1979), 46. More recently, Russell has embraced a similar Weberian notion, arguing that Christianity was essentially "world-rejecting," explaining in part the reluctant embrace of Germanic peoples. James C. Russell, *The Germanization of Early Medieval Christianity* (Oxford, UK: Oxford University Press, 1994).

[107] Robert M. Carmack, "Chapter 3, Mesoamerica at Spanish Contact." In *The Legacy of Mesoamerica*, eds. R.M. Carmack, Janine Gasco, and Gary H. Gossen, pp. 80–121 (Upper Saddle River, NJ: Prentice Hall, 1996); Peter S. Wells, *The Barbarians Speak: How The Conquered Peoples Shaped Roman Europe* (Princeton, NJ: Princeton University Press, 1999).

[108] William Christian's study of local religion in sixteenth-century Spain is one of numerous studies that convincingly point to the instrumental nature of Catholicism as it was and is practiced in Europe. William Christian, *Local Religion in Sixteenth-Century Spain* (Princeton, NJ: Princeton University Press, 1981). See also Jane Schneider, "Spirits and the Spirit of Capitalism." In *Religious Orthodoxy and Popular Faith in European Society*, ed. E. Badone, pp. 24–53 (Princeton, NJ: Princeton University Press, 1990).

in scope, and in part world-rejecting, the history of Christianity has been characterized by the adaptation of this theology to local settings; Christian beliefs and rituals are not everywhere the same, however much the Vatican and Church hierarchy may endeavor to legislate norms.[109]

In his study of colonial Peru, Salomon noted that the absolute demand of conversion makes it nightmarish; if conversion were ever complete, the subject would not exist any more.[110] "Jews for Jesus" are precisely that. Conversion rarely is such; usually it amounts to a reworking of identity and an acceptance of rituals and beliefs that are deemed useful or true.[111] As Valerie Flint demonstrated in her aptly titled book, *The Rise of Magic in Early Medieval Europe*, Christianity did not so much supplant paganism as find common ground with centuries-old Celtic, Teutonic, and Mediterranean religious traditions. This process of accommodation – "the rise of Christianity" – occurred mostly in Europe's interior, far from the towns and cities of the eastern Mediterranean where Christianity had its origins. Lost to history are the countless monks, clerics, and ascetics who interpreted the Gospels and Augustine for their fellow countrymen.[112] That many did so in an expansive fashion, accommodating as much rejecting pagan traditions, is apparent from the innumerable complaints of bishops during the early Middle Ages.[113] Relatedly, the acts of provincial synods from the early Middle Ages are replete with legislation that sought to do away with "vagrant" monks

[109] Ellen Badone, ed., *Religious Orthodoxy and Popular Faith in European Society* (Princeton, NJ: Princeton University Press, 1990); K. S. Latourette, *A History of the Expansion of Christianity, Seven Vols.* (London: Eyre & Spottiswood, 1937–1945); Jane Schneider and Shirley Lindenbaum, eds., "Frontiers of Christian Evangelism." *American Ethnologist* (Special Issue) (1987): 14.

[110] Frank Salomon, "Nightmare Victory, The Meaning of Conversion among Peruvian Indians (Huarachorí, 1608)." Discovering the Americas 1992 Lecture Series, Working Papers No. 7 (College Park: Department of Spanish and Portuguese, University of Maryland, 1990), 18.

[111] Hefner, "Introduction: World Building and the Rationality of Conversion," 17.

[112] Ian Wood, "The Missionary Life." In *The Cult of the Saints in Late Antiquity and the Middle Ages*, eds. James Howard-Johnston and Paul Antony Hayward, pp. 167–183 (Oxford, UK: Oxford University Press, 1999), 180–181; *The Missionary Life: Saints and the Evangelisation of Europe, 400–1050* (London: Longman, 2001), 7–17, 247–250.

[113] This fear is evident in the fourth-century *Life of Saint Antony* – a narrative by a bishop (Athanasius) who sought to reign in would-be ascetics and their anti-institutional reading of the Gospels. Michael A. Williams, "The Life of Antony and the Domestication of Charismatic Wisdom." *JARR Thematic Studies* 48 (1982): 23–45.

and ascetics who were not under the authority of bishops or abbots.[114]
In a sermon "On Seeking Health of Soul Rather Than of Body, And on
Avoiding Soothsayers," Bishop Caesarius of Arles (470–543 C.E.) implied
that there were many Christian deacons and priests who had accommodated paganism:[115]

> What is deplorable it that there are some who seek soothsayers in
> every kind of infirmity. They consult seers and diviners, summon en-
> chanters, and hang diabolical phylacteries and magic letters on them-
> selves. Often enough they receive charms even from priests and reli-
> gious, who, however, are not really religious or clerics but the Devil's
> helpers. See, brethren, how I plead with you not to consent to accept
> these wicked objects, even if they are offered by clerics.[116]

Caesarius was perhaps the most influential of all early Gallic bishops, yet
two hundred years after his death the Church in Gaul still was struggling
with pagan practices.[117]

The mission frontier in America where the Jesuits labored one thousand years later was in significant ways like early medieval Europe. The
Jesuits were members of a religious order, embedded in a larger institution, "the Church," which regularized clerical roles, standardized ritual,
formalized doctrine, and otherwise worked to create an authoritative
culture and cohesive religious structure. It nevertheless was difficult to
extend and maintain this religious culture on the frontier. Accordingly,
as early as 1610, Jesuit superiors drew up rules and regulations governing the activities of missionaries on the frontier.[118] Because of a shortage

---

[114] Roger Collins, *Early Medieval Europe 300–1000* (New York: St. Martin's Press, 1999), 249.

[115] What was true of Gaul was true elsewhere; sorcery was rife, for instance, among the Syrian clergy of the fifth century. Peter Brown, *Religion and Society in the Age of Saint Augustine* (New York: Harper & Row, 1972), 129.

[116] Sister Mary Magdeleine Mueller, O.S.F., trans. and ed., *Saint Caesarius of Arles, Sermons*, Vol. I (1–80) (New York: Fathers of the Church, 1956), 254.

[117] R. A. Markus, *The End of Ancient Christianity* (Cambridge, UK: Cambridge University Press, 1990).

[118] Rodrigo de Cabredo, "Ordenaciones del Padre Rodrigo de Cabredo para las Mis-siones, January 1, 1611, Durango." Latin American Manuscripts, Mexico II, Lily Li-brary, Indiana State University; Charles W. Polzer, S.J., *Rules and Precepts of the Jesuit*

of priests, most Jesuit missionaries worked by themselves and only occasionally saw another priest, never mind a Jesuit superior. Physical separation as well as slow and imperfect communication meant that priests
on the frontier often made decisions on their own. Obedience to superiors, which was celebrated in Jesuit discourse, correlated poorly with
reality.[119]

Jesuit missionaries infrequently escaped their Spanish-Catholic culture and particularly Jesuit worldview. That said, Jesuits who disem-
barked in Veracruz did experience a New World – a world in which
sights, sounds, and other human beings did not conform to preexisting
concepts, words, or narratives. The very "newness" of Mexico became
inescapable as a consequence of the Jesuit imperative that all missionaries master the language of their Indian neophytes. This imperative,
discussed in Chapter 3, forced missionaries to contemplate and at times
acknowledge the worth and complexity of Indian culture and experience.
Thus, Jesuits such as Pérez de Ribas employed native terms, or native
terms alongside Spanish lexical items, and empowered Indians to express views on topics such as infanticide that a Spaniard could or would
not express. More important, Jesuit missionaries allowed for Indian in-
put and refashioning of Christianity in ways that resonated with Indian
traditions. Paradoxically, the Jesuits were at the same time immovable
in their possession of the truth, and often they evoked Indian resistance,
which was ambiguous as well as outrightly hostile and subversive.[120]

The Christianity that "arose" in Latin America as well as medieval
Europe encapsulated many stories, not one:

> Catholicism in medieval times was enormously diverse – there were not
> only French, German, Spanish, Irish "churches," but within each there
> were hundreds of divisions subdivided again into thousands of smaller
> units, ending at last with a semi-literate cleric in some rude chapel in

---

Missions of Northwestern New Spain, 1600–1767 (Tucson: University of Arizona Press,
1976).

[119] The Jesuit Constitution mandated that Jesuit superiors "interview" Jesuit inferiors on
a regular basis, to ensure that each Jesuit did not violate rules and precepts of the
order. See John W. O'Malley, *The First Jesuits* (Cambridge, MA: Harvard University
Press, 1993), 354–355.

[120] Ortner, "Resistance and the Problem of Ethnographic Refusal," 175.

the midst of inhospitable forests or fields, surrounded by peasants who muttered charms over their ploughs and whispered magic words at crossroads.[121]

Finucane overstated the simplicity of medieval peasants and their religious practices, but he was correct in emphasizing the local character of Christianity during the early medieval period. In both the Old World and the New it was Catholicism's "reflexivity" – the manner in which it adapted to local conditions – that helps explain its successful spread. In this regard, "world religions" are successful not because they are more rational or because they emancipate the individual from tradition,[122] but because they preserve tradition and are instrumental in daily life, all the while they hold out the promise of a world beyond the known.

[121] Ronald C. Finucane, *Miracles and Pilgrims, Popular Beliefs in Medieval England* (Totowa, NJ: Rowman and Littlefield, 1977), 10.
[122] Bellah, "Religious Evolution," 177.

————◀◉▶————

TWO

Disease and the Rise of Christianity
in Europe, 150–800 C.E.

Through him [Saint Antony], the Lord healed many of those present who were suffering in body and freed others from evil spirits.

> (Anthanasius's *Life of St. Antony*, c. 360 C.E.)[1]

A letter from Martin happened to be brought to him and he placed it in her bosom at the very moment when her temperature was rising and at once the fever left her.

> (Sulpicius Severus's *Life of Saint Martin*, c. 396 C.E.)[2]

The glorious tomb of the blessed martyr Baudilius is in Nimes...The inhabitants of the region realized that this tomb often possessed a heavenly remedy for many illnesses.

> (Gregory of Tours's *Glory of the Martyrs*, c. 590 C.E.)[3]

Early Christian literature abounds in references to sickness and the miraculous cure. Indeed, the miraculous cure is perhaps the most common type scene in sacred biography and history.[4] Why are stories of sick

---

[1] Sister Mary Emily Keenan, S.C.N., trans., "Life of St. Antony by St. Athanasius." In *The Fathers of the Church, Volume 15, Early Christian Biographies*, ed. Roy J. Deferrari, pp. 127–216 (New York: Fathers of the Church, Inc., 1952), 148.

[2] F. R. Hoare, trans. and ed., *The Western Fathers, Being the Lives of SS. Martin of Tours, Ambrose, Augustine of Hippo, Honoratus of Arles and Germanus of Auxerre* (New York: Sheed and Ward, 1956), 32.

[3] Raymond Van Dam, trans., *Gregory of Tours: Glory of the Martyrs* (Liverpool, UK: Liverpool University Press, 1988), 100.

[4] Clare Stancliffe, "From Town to Country: The Christianization of the Touraine, 370–600." In *The Church in Town and Countryside*, ed. Derek Baker, pp. 43–59 (Oxford: Basil Blackwell, 1979), 57.

people who are cured by monks and bishops so common, particularly relative to accounts of other "miracles" such as villages saved from marauding enemies or of crops saved from locusts or drought? To date, scholars of late antiquity and the early Middle Ages have shied away from this question. To quote one distinguished historian, "It is usually fruitless to indulge in speculation about what might have been the 'real' basis of miracle stories."[5] Since the Enlightenment, miracles largely have been seen as beyond the bounds of historical analysis.[6] Correspondingly, sacred biography and history, because they are replete with miracles, have been ignored or cast as overly fictitious. More recently, poststructural theorists have not only eschewed metaphysical inquiry but also have questioned the ontological status of language itself; for many, narrative cannot reflect any reality other than its own.[7] The very notion of historical processes that reflect cause and effect has been cast as symptomatic of an Enlightenment project that occludes ". . . the accidents, the minute deviations – or conversely, the complete reversals – the errors, the false appraisals, and the faulty calculations."[8]

Rather than pursue the question of a pretextual reality underlying the miraculous cure, scholars have turned to literary–critical analysis of what is understood as a biblical type scene.[9] It is generally assumed

[5] Richard Fletcher, *The Barbarian Conversion: From Paganism to Christianity* (Berkeley: University of California Press, 1997), 45.

[6] Raymond Van Dam, *Saints and Their Miracles in Late Antique Gaul* (Princeton, NJ: Princeton University Press, 1993), 84.

[7] Thomas J. Heffernan, *Sacred Biography: Saints and Their Biographies in the Middle Ages* (New York: Oxford University Press, 1988), 17.

[8] Michel Foucault, "Nietzsche, Genealogy, History." In *The Foucault Reader*, edited by Paul Rabinow, pp. 76–100 (New York: Random House, 1984), 81.

[9] In her study of the Dialogues of Gregory the Great, Petersen comments: "It is not my intention to search for some kind of scientific basis for miracle stories. . . . My efforts . . . will be directed chiefly towards showing that there was in the Mediterranean area a common fund of stories and teaching, upon which Eastern and Western Christian writers alike could draw." Joan M. Petersen, *The Dialogues of Gregory the Great in Their Late Antique Cultural Background* (Toronto: Pontifical Institute of Medieval Studies, 1984), xxi. A number of scholars have remarked on this trend of literary–critical analysis: Caroline W. Bynum, *Fragmentation and Redemption: Essays on Gender and the Human Body in Medieval Religion* (New York: Zone Books, 1991), 44; Averil Cameron, "On Defining the Holy Man." In *The Cult of the Saints in Late Antiquity and the Middle Ages*, eds. James Howard-Johnston and Paul Antony Hayward, pp. 27–45 (Oxford: Oxford University Press, 1999), 36–37; Karen Winstead, *Virgin Martyrs, Legends of Sainthood in Late Medieval England* (Ithaca, NY: Cornell University Press, 1997), 16.

that early Christian authors – most of whom were clerics or monks – borrowed the miraculous cure from the Gospels to impart authority to their own works and to restate what is perhaps the most fundamental of Christian beliefs: that God became man. Like the *Song of Songs*, which speaks of human love yet purportedly is about loving God,[10] miracle stories purportedly are not about sickness but Christ's enduring promise.

More recently, Van Dam has suggested that the miraculous cure and early medieval notions of illness and healing provided a powerful idiom with which people could think about and describe not only God but also their own identities.[11] Following Foucault, Perkins has argued that this identity – "the suffering self" – was more imagined than real and essentially was imposed on the masses by bishops seeking to maintain and extend their own privileges as elites.[12]

Early Christian literature reflects a variety of contingencies (e.g., theological, political/institutional, literary, historical), and thus it is true that references to diseased bodies at times had little or nothing to do with sickness or epidemics. That said, the question remains as to why sacred biography and history focus so much on physical illness, suffering, and bodily resurrection, and why this discourse proliferated when it did, in late antiquity. Is it just fortuitous that "sickness" became such a popular signifier at this time?

The central argument of this chapter is that the miraculous cure and other referents to illness and healing were not just another powerful idiom, but a *particularly* powerful idiom by virtue of the appearance of new and more virulent strains of infectious disease. If people understood their lives as short and prone to sickness, it was not simply because sickness was a powerful metaphor or that a regime of power convinced the masses to value their own suffering. People were sicker and died prematurely in greater numbers during late antiquity and the early Middle

---

[10] For a more literal interpretation of *Songs*, see Marcia Falk, *Love Lyrics from the Bible* (Sheffield: Almond Press, 1982).

[11] Van Dam, *Saints and Their Miracles in Late Antique Gaul*, 84, 91.

[12] Judith Perkins, *The Suffering Self, Pain and Narrative Representation in the Early Christian Era* (London: Routledge, 1995). Although Foucault was less than explicit naming the agents of what he refers to as "pastoral technology," it is apparent that he had bishops, abbots, monks, and deacons in mind. See Michel Foucault, "Politics and Reason." In *Michel Foucault, Politics, Philosophy, Culture*, ed. L. D. Kritzman, trans. A. Sheridan et al. (New York: Routlege, 1988), 63.

Ages, as compared with the earlier reign of Augustus. As detailed later, smallpox, measles, plague, and malaria devastated Europe during the early Christian era and the subsequent early Middle Ages. Christianity provided a belief system as well as rituals to deal with disease and its profound consequences. Beginning with the earliest *ekklésiae*, and continuing with the rise of monasticism during the fourth century, the Church made charity, particularly care of the sick and orphans, central ministries of priests and monks. In what essentially was a disease environment, *ekklésiae* and monasteries functioned as centers for organizing and reorganizing lives that were shattered by epidemic disease as well as migration, warfare, and social unrest.

In pursuing the above argument, I focus on the western Roman Empire and especially Gaul (modern France, Belgium, and westernmost Germany) during the period 150–800 C.E. (Figure 1). My restricted temporal and spatial analysis of formative Christianity has been dictated by both the enormity of the subject and the fact that it is the Christian literature of the western Empire, and again, especially Gaul, that informed Jesuit missionary texts in the seventeenth century. Jesuit favorites such as Sulpicius Severus, Caesarius of Arles, Gregory the Great, and Gregory of Tours all focused on Gaul. I have not explored in earnest the early Byzantine world, except where it seems directly relevant, as in the diffusion of Eastern ascetic practices and monasticism to the West. It should be noted, however, that the argument advanced for the western Empire appears applicable to the eastern Roman Empire. Here, too, epidemic disease undermined the structure and functioning of communities and Christianity provided "social welfare programs" as well as beliefs and rituals that benefitted the sick and needy.[13] Correspondingly, the literature produced by Eastern authors abounds in miraculous cures. Written accounts of cures performed by patron saints ("miracle collections") survive in hundreds of versions and manuscripts dating to the fifth through seventh centuries.[14]

---

[13] See H. J. Magoulias, "The Lives of the Saints as Source of Data for the History of Byzantine Medicine in the Sixth and Seventh Centuries." In *Byzantinische Zeitscrhrift, Bergrundet Von Karl Krumbacher*, eds. Hans-Georg Beck, F. W. Deichmann, and H. Hunger, pp. 127–150 (Munich: C.H. Beck'sche, 1964).

[14] D. Abrahamse, "Hagiographic Sources for Byzantine Cities, 500–900 AD" (Ann Arbor: University Microfilms, 1967).

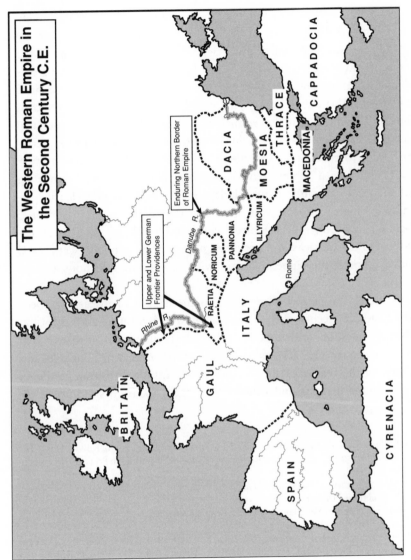

Figure 1. The Western Roman Empire in 200 C.E.

With few exceptions, notably McNeill and Stark, scholars largely have ignored the evidence of disease from late antiquity and the early Middle Ages.[15] The writing and rewriting of history always entails the present intruding on the past. Our "present" largely is free of epidemic disease; it has been that way for Americans and Europeans since the great flu pandemic of 1917. Arguably, our relative success controlling and eradicating maladies such as smallpox has made it difficult to imagine epidemic disease having changed the course of history, contributing to the rise of something so otherworldly as Christianity.[16] In keeping with recent trends in theory, particularly the eschewing of material causality, many scholars in the humanities[17] clearly perceive biological processes as somehow too mundane or irrelevant.[18] Scholars who have been entirely comfortable talking about the east-to-west flow of ideas and practices such as the Egyptian ascetic ideal have ignored the same dynamic with respect to infectious disease agents.[19]

Perhaps the biggest contributor to the neglect of disease has been the historical record itself. Late Roman and Byzantine chronicles frequently mention epidemics but infrequently elaborate on their extent and consequences.[20] Typical is Jerome's *Chronicon*, which includes this entry for the year 332 C.E.: "A countless multitude died from pestilence and famine in Syria and Cilicia."[21] Gregory of Tours's *History of the*

---

[15] William McNeill, *Plagues and Peoples* (New York: Doubleday, 1976); Rodney Stark, *The Rise of Christianity: A Sociologist Reconsiders History* (Princeton, NJ: Princeton University Press, 1996).

[16] William Johnston, *The Modern Epidemic: A History of Tuberculosis in Japan* (Cambridge, MA: Harvard University Press, 1995), 9.

[17] See, for instance, Van Dam, *Saints and Their Miracles*, 84.

[18] Stark, *The Rise of Christianity*, 74.

[19] For instance: Averil Cameron, *The Later Roman Empire* (Cambridge, MA: Harvard University Press, 1993), 10; Adolf Harnack, *Militia Christi: The Christian Religion and the Military in the First Three Centuries*, trans. D. M. Grace (Philadelphia: Fortress Press, [1905] 1981), 171–173; Van Dam, *Saints and Their Miracles in Late Antique Gaul* (Princeton, NJ: Princeton University Press, 1993), 82.

[20] Michael Whitby and Mary Whitby, trans., *Chronicon Paschale 284–628 AD* (Liverpool, UK: Liverpool University Press, 1989), 196.

[21] Malcolm D. Donalson, trans., *A Translation of Jerome's Chronicon with Historical Commentary* (Lewiston, Australia: Mellen University Press, 1996), 41.

Franks is likewise replete with passing comments about sickness and epidemics: "The plague ravaged the cities of Viviers and Avignon."[22] This frequent yet brief mention of disease has led scholars in different directions. Some have concluded that disease was indeed a fact of life in antiquity; so common, however, that it seems hardly worth considering as a dynamic force, contributing, for instance, to the development of Christian rhetoric or Christianity in general.[23] At the other extreme are scholars who have dismissed disease as important because particular authors or extant sources make no mention of epidemics.[24]

As Biraben and Le Goff pointed out many years ago, contemporaries of the plague often completely ignored its devastating consequences, even though they were aware that it killed tens of thousands of people.[25] Eusebius, Theodoret, Jerome, Isidore, and Gregory the Great and Gregory of Tours all were preoccupied with "invisible" truths and first and final causes (God and God's often inscrutable intention). We forget that the Renaissance and Enlightenment relegated God to the status of a distant observer; humankind has since held center stage as both the maker and interpreter of history.

Fifteen hundred years ago, historians thought it foolish and presumptuous to construe history in terms of efficient or material causality; history was more a matter of showing how events were a fulfillment of prophecy or reiteration of a truth revealed in scripture.[26] Given this preoccupation with God's unfolding plan for humankind, it is understandable that late antique and early medieval authors ignored the consequences of disease. Only occasionally did writers deem it useful to detail how smallpox or the plague impacted populations. For instance,

---

22 O. M. Dalton, trans., *The History of the Franks, by Gregory of Tours*, 2 Vols. (Oxford: Clarendon Press, 1927), II, 459.

23 Cameron, *The Later Roman Empire*, 10.

24 Malcolm Todd, "*Famosa Pestis* and Britain in the Fifth Century." *Britania* 8 (1977): 319–325, 322.

25 J. N. Biraben and Jacques Le Goff, "The Plague in the Early Middle Ages." In *Biology of Man in History*, eds. E. Forster and O. Ranum, trans. E. Forster and P. Ranum, pp. 48–80 (Baltimore, MD: Johns Hopkins University Press, 1975), 49.

26 Stephen G. Nichols, Jr., *Romanesque Signs: Early Medieval Narrative and Iconography* (New Haven, CT: Yale University Press, 1983), 20–21; Clare Stancliffe, *St. Martin and His Hagiographer* (Oxford: Clarendon Press, 1983), 193, 210.

Gregory of Tours, who often mentioned "great plagues" in passing, offered the following detailed comments on an epidemic in 589 C.E.:

> The city of Marseilles being afflicted, as I have just said, by a most grievous pestilence, I deem it well to unfold from the beginning how much it endured. At that time Bishop Theodore had journeyed to the king to make complaint against the patrician Nicetius. King Childebert would scarce give ear to the matter, so he prepared to return home. In the meantime a ship had put into the port with usual merchandise from Spain, unhappily bringing the tinder which kindled the disease. Many citizens purchased various objects from the cargo, and soon a house inhabited by eight people was left empty, every one of them being carried off by the contagion. The fire of this plague did not spread immediately through all the houses in the place; but there was a certain interval, and then the whole city was blazed with the pest, like a cornfield set aflame.... After two months the affliction ceased, and the people returned, thinking the danger overpast. But the plague began once more, and all who had returned perished. On several other occasions Marseilles was afflicted by this death.[27]

The above quote is unusual in its epidemiological insight.[28] Note, however, that even detailed descriptions of an epidemic such as Gregory of Tours's comments above are likely to be insufficient in terms of determining the extent and consequences of a disease episode. Because disease is dynamic and changeable, and often several rather than one disease agent are responsible for epidemics, it is difficult to say with any certainty whether measles, smallpox, typhus, plague, and so on, were responsible for a contagion mentioned by early chroniclers, historians, or hagiographers.[29] This uncertainty makes it hard to fully

---

[27] Dalton, *History of the Franks*, II, 395–396.

[28] Giselle de Nie, *Views From a Many-Windowed Tower: Studies of Imagination in the Works of Gregory of Tours* (Amsterdam: Rodopi, 1987), 56.

[29] P. M. Ashburn, *The Ranks of Death* (New York: Coward-McCann, 1947), 92; J. R. Busvine, *Insects, Hygiene and History* (London: Athlone Press, 1976), 53; A. Lynn Martin, *Plague? Jesuit Accounts of Epidemic Disease in the 16th Century* (Kirksville, MO: Sixteenth Century Journal Publishers, 1996); Jean-Pierre Peter, "Disease and the Sick at the End of the Eighteenth Century." In *Biology of Man in History*, eds. E. Forster and O. Ranum, trans. E. Forster and P. Ranum, pp. 81–94 (Baltimore, MD: Johns Hopkins University Press, 1975).

model and assess the spread of disease and its demographic and cultural consequences.

Disease and Its Consequences in Late Antiquity and the Early Middle Ages, 150–800 C.E.

When early Christian literature is systematically scrutinized from an epidemiological perspective,[30] linking disparate and sometimes disguised mentions of disease (disguised in the sense that an epidemic may be represented in one or more texts by accounts of miraculous cures or brief suggestive comments such as "fevers laid waste the province"), it becomes apparent that infectious diseases played a dynamic role in the synchronous fall of the Roman Empire and rise of Christianity.

During the second century C.E., the Roman Empire was at its height, including the size of its population, which peaked at near fifty million. By 150 C.E., the Romans had introduced or encouraged urban life throughout Europe; the city of Rome in the second century C.E. had a population of close to one million.[31] Cities and towns with populations numbering in the thousands were spread throughout the Middle East, southwestern Asia, northern Africa, and Europe, and were everywhere linked by regular trade and communication, particularly along the Mediterranean, the heart of the Roman world (Figure 2).[32] Ships carrying wine, grain, slaves, or other commodities sailed in three weeks' time from one end of the Mediterranean to the other.[33] Road and water transport systems that were developed under Augustus during the first century B.C.E. extended

---

[30] Here I am thinking of Biraben and Le Goff, "Plague in the Early Middle Ages"; McNeill, *Plagues and Peoples*.

[31] George La Piana, "Foreign Groups in Rome During the First Centuries of the Empire." *The Harvard Theological Review* XX (1927): 183–403, 188–195.

[32] Tonnes Bekker-Nielsen, *The Geography of Power, Studies in the Urbanization of Roman North-West Europe* (Oxford: BAR International Series, 1989), 477; J. F. Drinkwater, *Roman Gaul: The Three Provinces, 58 BC–AD 260* (London: Croom Helm, 1983), 127, 239; Ray Laurence, "Afterword: Travel and Empire." In *Travel and Geography in the Roman Empire*, eds. Colin Adams and Ray Laurence, pp. 167–176 (London; Routledge, 2001); Wayne A. Meeks, *The First Urban Christians: The Social World of the Apostle Paul* (New Haven, CT: Yale University Press, 1983), 17–18; N. J. Pounds, *An Historical Geography of Europe* (Cambridge, UK: Cambridge University Press, 1990), 52–53; Benet Salway, "Travel, Itineria and Tabellaria." In *Travel and Geography in the Roman Empire*, eds. Colin Adams and Ray Laurence, pp. 22–66 (London; Routledge, 2001).

[33] Peter Brown, *The World of Late Antiquity* (London: Thames and Hudson, 1971), 11.

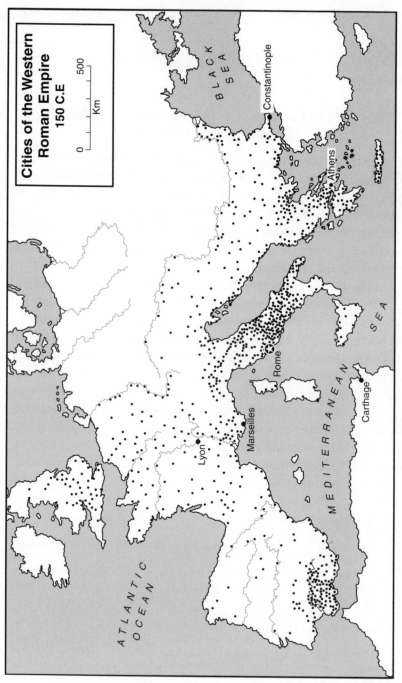

Figure 2. Distribution of Cities in the Western Roman Empire (After Pounds, *An Historical Geography of Europe*, 56).

Rome's reach far to the north and west, as evidenced by the ruins of innumerable Roman villas in present-day France and Iberia, and large numbers of trade goods recovered from archaeological sites in Germany, Britain, Denmark, and the Baltic region.[34]

No civilization that unites tens of millions of people for the first time can escape the appearance of new forms of infectious disease. The question is not whether new diseases will arise, but whether for reasons of disease ecology and chance they will become both easily spread and lethal to their human hosts. Those who have escaped the ravages of AIDS, an apparent byproduct of our own global economy,[35] are fortunate that the disease has not evolved along the lines of measles or smallpox, which literally are spread by a mere cough. (As I write, the world is holding its breath, literally and figuratively, fearing SARS, which apparently is spread by a mere cough.)

The citizens of Rome also were fortunate, at least for a while. Besides luck, the Romans' impressive feats of engineering in public sanitation and water control helped keep infectious diseases in check.[36] In time, however, the Greco-Roman proclivity for urban life, rapid transportation, and, paradoxically, improvements in sanitation,[37] increased the populations' vulnerability to new forms of acute and chronic infectious disease. By the late second century, cities such as Rome had become very unhealthy places to live; the same was true of distant towns in Roman Gaul.[38]

---

[34] Michael McCormick, *Origins Of The European Economy: Communications and Commerce, A.D. 300–900* (Cambridge, UK: Cambridge University Press, 2001), 53–63; E.A. Thompson, *The Huns* (Oxford: Blackwell Publishers, 1996), 191.

[35] Carl Zimmer, *Evolution: The Triumph of an Idea* (New York: HarperCollins, 2001), 216–222.

[36] Angelo Celli, *The History of Malaria in the Roman Campagna from Ancient Times*, ed. and enlarged by Anna Celli-Fraentzel (London: J. Bale, Sons & Danielsson, 1933); J. L. Cloudsley-Thompson, *Insects and History* (New York: St. Martin's Press, 1976), 91.

[37] Exposure generally promotes resistance to what otherwise become more virulent forms of disease. See Arno G. Motulsky, "Metabolic Polymorphisms and the Role of Infectious Diseases in Human Evolution." In *Human Populations, Genetic Variation, and Evolution*, ed. Laura N. Morris, pp. 222–252 (San Francisco: Chandler Publishing Company, 1971).

[38] Drinkwater, *Roman Gaul*, 157; Stark, *The Rise of Christianity*, 154–156. Note that the towns and cities of medieval Europe remained very unhealthy places well into the

The appearance and rapid diffusion of new forms of infectious disease were made possible by Rome's legions, caravans, and sailing ships,
which apparently brought new and often more virulent strains of disease
back from southwest Asia and beyond. Incursions of Huns and Goths
from eastern Europe, beginning in the third century, contributed further to what McNeill termed a "confluence of disease pools."[39] Indeed,
McNeill has suggested that by the early Christian era the Roman Empire was in an epidemiological position analogous to America in 1492.
Although authors such as Livy, Suetonius, and Orosius recorded serious
epidemics during the pre-Christian era, few seem to compare with the
series of disease episodes that began in the mid-second century C.E.[40] At
this time and on numerous occasions during the centuries that followed,
variants of the same diseases that later devastated Amerindian populations (smallpox, measles, malaria, plague) regularly wrecked havoc on
the Roman Empire.

The first such disease episode was a true pandemic of what appears to have been at least in part smallpox.[41] Known as the "Antonine Plague," the disease episode affected the Roman world for close
to two decades, beginning in about 165 C.E. Roman soldiers fighting at
the time in Mesopotamia were stricken with smallpox and subsequently

---

modern period. See Chris Wilson, "Understanding the Nature and Importance of Low-
growth Demographic Regimes." In *Asian Population History*, ed. Ts'ui-jung Liu et al.,
pp. 24–44 (Oxford, UK: Oxford University Press, 2001), 32.

[39] It has been argued that the initial westward migration of the Huns from Asia, which
began in 80 C.E., actually was coincident with an epidemic that killed horses and cattle
as well as large numbers of Huns. Zinsser, *Rats, Lice and History*, 135.

[40] Hopkins, *Princes and Peasants*, 22; McNeill, *Plagues and Peoples*, 115–116. Note that
whereas Orosius's *The Seven Books of History Against the Pagans*, which was written
around 414 C.E., casts the centuries prior to the Christian era as a time of numerous
"unspeakable disasters and intolerable plagues," Orosius was a Christian apologist
rather than a historian; he wrote to defend Christianity from the attacks of Romans
who noted a correlation between the rise of Christianity and the demise of the Roman
Empire from disease and other calamities. See Roy J. Deferrari, trans., *Paul Orosius:
The Seven Books Of History Against The Pagans* (Washington, DC: Catholic University
of America Press, 1964), xx.

[41] Smallpox is suggested by clinical characterizations of the disease, such as Galen's references to a rash and skin ulcers, which is consistent with modern descriptions of *variola
major*. C. W. Dixon, *Smallpox* (London: J. and A. Churchill Ltd, 1962); Hopkins, *Princes
and Peasants*, 22–23; Zinsser, *Rats, Lice, and History*, 101.

introduced *variola* to Syria and then Italy.[42] At the outset of the epidemic, two thousand people a day died in Rome. Smallpox raged on and off in the city and its environs for fifteen years,[43] eventually killing the emperor, Marcus Aurelius.[44] Roman doctors, annalists, and historians such as Galen, Cassius Dio, and Ammianus Marcellinus reported that the epidemic spread throughout Europe ("from the frontiers of the Persians to the Rhine and Gaul"), contributing to widespread famine.[45]

It has been conservatively estimated that during the first three years of the pandemic, between 3.5 million and 5 million people died;[46] ten million people, about 8 percent of the population of Europe, died before smallpox at last subsided in 190 C.E.[47]

The Antonine Plague was perhaps the most devastating disease episode in late antiquity. It was not, however, the last time that the Roman world experienced smallpox. The historical record mentions or alludes to what appear to have been frequent outbreaks of *variola* during late antiquity and the early Middle Ages.[48] Eusebius, for instance, mentions an epidemic in 312–313 C.E. whose clinical symptoms (e.g., malignant pustules; blindness) are highly suggestive of smallpox;

---

[42] J. F. Gilliam, "The Plague under Marcus Aurelius." *American Journal of Philology* 82 (1961): 225–251.

[43] The epidemic apparently began in Smyrna in 165 C.E. and reached Rome the following year; after subsiding in 180 C.E., it reappeared in Rome in 189 C.E. Richard Duncan-Jones, *Structure and Scale in the Roman Economy* (Cambridge, UK: Cambridge University Press, 1990), 72; Zinsser, *Rats, Lice, and History*, 136.

[44] Donald R. Hopkins, *Princes and Peasants: Smallpox in History* (Chicago: University of Chicago Press, 1983), 22–23.

[45] Roger S. Bagnall and Bruce W. Frier, *The Demography of Roman Egypt* (Cambridge, UK: Cambridge University Press, 1994), 174; A. E. Boak, *Manpower Shortage and the Fall of the Roman Empire in the West* (Ann Arbor: University of Michigan Press, 1955), 109–110; Malcolm Todd, "*Famosa Pestis*," 323.

[46] More liberal estimates are that 10 percent of the empire's population was destroyed; large cities and military camps were particularly hard-hit and may have lost 20 percent of their population. Bagnall and Frier, *The Demography of Roman Egypt*, 174.

[47] R. J. Littman and M. L. Littman, "Galen and the Antonine Plague." *American Journal of Philology* 94 (1973): 243–255, 254–255.

[48] Adolf Harnack, *Militia Christi: The Christian Religion and the Military in the First Three Centuries*, trans. by D. M. Grace (Philadelphia: Fortress Press, 1981[1905]), 171–173; Hopkins, *Princes and Peasants*, 23–24, 230.

the epidemic devastated the Middle East and the southern part of Asia Minor:

> It was the winter season, and usual rains and showers were withholding their normal downpour, when without warning famine struck, followed by pestilence and an outbreak of a different disease – a malignant pustule, which because of its fiery appearance was known as a carbuncle. This spread over the entire body, causing great danger to the sufferers; but the eyes were the chief target for attack, and hundreds of men, women, and children lost their sight through it....In the Armenian war the emperor [Maximinus Daia] was worn out as completely as his legions: the rest of the people in the cities under his rule were so horribly wasted by famine and pestilence that a single measure of wheat fetched 2,500 Attic drachmas. Hundreds were dying in the cities, still more in the country villages, so that the rural registers which once contained so many names now suffered almost complete obliteration; for at one stroke food shortage and epidemic disease destroyed nearly all the inhabitants.[49]

The destruction wrought by smallpox appears to have been equaled by epidemics of measles, including a pandemic in 251 C.E., which once again was said to have devastated parts of the Roman Empire. At the height of the pandemic, five thousand people a day died in Rome.[50] How many died elsewhere is unknown. As Drinkwater[51] has pointed out, the history of the Roman world during the third century C.E. is extremely difficult to reconstruct, owing to a paucity of literary texts. Still, historians such as Zosimus wrote of several devastating plagues, including one in 251 C.E. that was unprecedented: "With war thus pressing heavily on the empire from all sides, a plague afflicted cities and villages and destroyed whatever was left of mankind; no plague in previous times wrought such destruction of human life."[52]

---

[49] G. A. Williamson, trans. *Eusebius: The History of the Church from Christ to Constantine* (Harmondsworth, Middlesex, England: Dorset Press, 1984), 365–366.

[50] Boak, *Manpower Shortage*, 26, 111.

[51] *The Gallic Empire* (Stuttgart: Franz Steiner Verlag Wiesbaden GMBH, 1987) 45.

[52] Ronald T. Ridley, trans. and ed., *Zosimus, New History* (Sydney: Australian Association for Byzantine Studies, 1982), 8, 12, 14.

The pandemic of 251 C.E. is known as the "plague of Cyprian," owing to the saint's detailed account of the disease episode in his *De Mortalitate*.[53] As McNeill suggests, the Cyprian and earlier Antonine Plague were co-conspirators in the devolution of the Roman Empire:

> What seems to have occurred in the Mediterranean lands was that a tolerable macroparasitic system – the imperial armies and bureaucracy of the first century A.D. superimposed upon a diverse muster of local landlords who generally aspired to an urban, Greco-Roman style of life – became unbearably top-heavy after the first disastrous ravages of epidemic disease hit home in the second and third centuries. Thereafter the macroparasitic elements in Roman society became agents of further destruction to population and production, and the resultant disorders, famines, migrations, concentrations of human flotsam and jetsam, in turn, created fresh opportunities for epidemic diseases to diminish population still more.[54]

The Roman Empire's failure to rebound from successive epidemics of smallpox and measles as well as other calamities (e.g., wars, invasions) is partially explained by chronic infectious diseases, particularly malaria (*Plasmodium vivax*). Human populations can relatively quickly replace numerical losses from war or epidemics, even when acute infectious diseases claim a third or more of a population. However, it is very difficult to recoup population losses when they occur in the context of endemic, chronic infectious diseases such as malaria. Malaria, once it becomes endemic, kills large numbers of infants and leaves those who survive with anemia and poor general health.[55]

During the pre-Christian era, the Romans worshipped a goddess of fevers (*Dea Febris*) who seemingly kept malaria at bay in southern Italy.[56]

---

53 Daniel D. Sullivan, *The Life of the North Africans as Revealed in the Works of Saint Cyprian* (Washington, DC: Catholic University of America, 1933); Zinsser, *Rats, Lice and History*, 138–141.

54 McNeill, *Plagues and Peoples*, 120.

55 Mark F. Boyd, "Epidemiology of Malaria: Factors Related to the Intermediate Host." In *Malariology, Vol. I*, ed. Mark F. Boyd, pp. 551–607 (Philadelphia: W.B. Saunders, 1949), 566; Cloudsley-Thompson, *Insects and History*, 76; Daniel Gade, *Nature and Culture in the Andes* (Madison: University of Wisconsin Press, 1999), 75–101; Robert Sallares, *The Ecology of the Ancient Greek World* (London: Duckworth, 1991), 273.

56 Cloudsley-Thompson, *Insects and History*, 90.

However, by the Christian era, Rome had become highly malarious.[57] Writers such as Celsus make clear that malaria became an even greater problem during the latter part of the second century.[58] The third and fourth centuries were no better; Constantine the Great (337 C.E.) and his son Constantius (363 C.E.) are two of many who apparently succumbed to malaria.[59] Alaric (c. 370–419 C.E.) – the first of the "barbarians" to sack Rome – apparently died from malaria, as did many subsequent Vandals and Goths.[60]

As the fourth century unfolded and Roman infrastructure and water control devices deteriorated, the incidence of malaria increased dramatically.[61] Writing in circa 359 C.E., the historian Ammianus Marcellinus outlined what became a centuries-old pattern of malaria in Rome and southern Italy:

> Now the first kind of plague is called endemic, and causes those who live in places that are too dry to be cut off by frequent fevers. The second is epidemic, which breaks out at certain seasons of the year, dimming the sight of the eyes and causing a dangerous flow of moisture. The third is *loemodes* [pestilential], which is also periodic, but deadly from its winged speed.[62]

Consistent with Marcellinus's observation, the exceptionally dry hills to the south of Rome and the islands of Sardinia and Sicily historically had the highest incidence of malaria.[63] (It is a misconception that malaria occurred only in lowlands or in southern Europe.)

---

[57] George W. Bryun, *An Illustrated History of Malaria* (New York: Parthenon Publishing Group, 1999), 7.

[58] Sallares, *Ecology of the Ancient Greek World*, 278.

[59] Ammianus Marcellinus's account of Constantius's demise is highly suggestive of malaria, inasmuch as Constantius came down with a slight fever that grew increasingly worse: "Gradually the extreme heat of the fever so inflamed his veins that his body could not even be touched, since it burned like a furnace; . . . Then the death-rattle began and he was silent, and after a long struggle gave up the ghost." Rolfe, *Ammianus Marcellinus*, II, 171; see also Bryun, *Illustrated History of Malaria*, 7.

[60] Cloudsley-Thompson, *Insects and History*, 91–92, 94.

[61] Celli, *History of Malaria*; Cloudsley-Thompson, *Insects and History*, 84; McCormick, *Origins of the European Economy*, 38–41; L.W. Hackett, *Malaria in Europe* (London: Oxford University Press, 1937), 7.

[62] Rolfe, *Ammianus Marcellinus*, I, 489.   [63] Hackett, *Malaria in Europe*, 11.

In the fourth century, if not sooner, malaria escaped from the narrow bounds within which it had been confined by drainage, sanitation, and agriculture.[64] Malaria became widespread in Europe, apparently in part because of the abandonment of villas and towns.[65] The corresponding devolution of agriculture and animal husbandry encouraged mosquitoes, in general, and certain subspecies of anopheline mosquitoes,[66] which fueled epidemics of malaria among humans.[67] During the fifth and sixth centuries, when many previously abandoned farms or secondary forests were resettled by monks and internal migrants,[68] malaria was further encouraged.[69] Thus, medieval texts such as the *Life of the Fathers*, written by Gregory of Tours (592 C.E.), and *The Life of Saint Columban* (642 C.E.) often speak of individuals incapacitated by fever:

Today many people who are sunk in melancholy obtain at his tomb [Bishop Quintianus] relief from their quartan fever and from their illness. (*Life of the Fathers*)[70]

...he began to ask earnestly that the holy man should pray to God on behalf of his wife, who for a whole year had been burning with so violent a fever that it now seemed impossible that she could be restored to health. (*Life of St. Columban*)[71]

Fevers of one kind or another – reflecting malaria as well as other infectious diseases – abound in literature from late antiquity and the

---

[64] Cloudsley-Thompson, *Insects and History*, 91.

[65] Boak, *Manpower Shortage*, 127; J. C. Russell, "Late Ancient and Medieval Population." *Transactions of the American Philosophical Society*, New Series, Volume 48, Part 3 (Philadelphia: American Philosophical Society, 1958), 39–40.

[66] Europe historically has been home to a number of species of anopheline mosquito that evolved to survive the coldest winters (mostly by moving indoors); the mosquitoes also have remarkable flight ranges (three to ten miles). See Hackett, *Malaria in Europe*, 206–207.

[67] Bryun, *Illustrated History of Malaria*, 21–22; W. H. S. Jones, *Malaria: A Neglected Factor in the History of Greece and Rome* (Cambridge, UK: Bowes & Bowes, 1907), 75.

[68] J. N. Hillgarth, *Christianity and Paganism, 350–750* (Philadelphia: University of Pennsylvania Press, 1986), 21–22.

[69] Hackett, *Malaria in Europe*, 90, 225.

[70] Edward James, trans., *Gregory of Tours: Life of the Fathers* (Liverpool, UK: Liverpool University Press, 1991), 27.

[71] Dana C. Munro, trans., *Life of St. Columban by the Monk Jonas* (Felinfach: Llanerch Publishers, 1993), 24.

early Middle Ages. During the sixth century C.E., there appeared a new contributor to these fevers: plague. What came to be known as the Justinian plague raged in Mediterranean Europe in 542–543 C.E. Procopius reported that the epidemic persisted for four months in Constantinople and that at the height of the epidemic ten thousand people died per day.[72] For the next two hundred years,[73] the plague reached epidemic proportions every nine to twelve years, affecting primarily Mediterranean Europe, Spain, Gaul, and Italy. On the basis of miracles recorded in hagiographic texts, Biraben and Le Goff[74] believe the plague spread as far north as the Loire, Marne, and Rhine rivers, and the Alps. One should not assume from this statement that northern Europe escaped the plague entirely or did not suffer from epidemic disease. Anglo-Saxon records mention at least forty-nine disease episodes or epidemics between 526 and 1087 C.E.[75]

The consequences of plague were everywhere severe, particularly when the disease occurred with other maladies. In 570 C.E., the plague as well as smallpox affected much of continental Europe.[76] Gregory of Tours has a telling description of its impact:

> At the coming of the disaster itself, there was made much slaughter of the people through all the region, that the legions of men who fell there might not even be numbered. When coffins and planks failed, ten dead or more were buried in a common pit. In the single church of Saint Peter there were counted on a certain Sunday three hundred corpses.[77]

The Demographic Consequences of Disease

What were the consequences of the Antonine, Cyprian, and Justinian plagues and endemic or near-endemic chronic diseases such as malaria?

---

[72] McNeill, *Plagues and Peoples*, 127.
[73] For reasons that are not known, the plague appears to have disappeared around 750 C.E., not appearing again until the fourteenth century. Biraben and Le Goff, "The Plague in the Early Middle Ages," 63.
[74] Ibid., 62.
[75] Bertram Colgrave and R. A. B. Mynors, eds., *Bede's Ecclesiastical History of the English People* (Oxford: Clarendon Press, 1969), 288n; McNeill, *Plagues and Peoples*, 128–129.
[76] Biraben and Le Goff, "The Plague in the Early Middle Ages," 60.
[77] Dalton, *The History of the Franks, by Gregory of Tours*, II, 143.

The question is not easily answered, given the fragmentary nature of the historical record and the fact that civil disorders, famine, and migration were coincident with many disease episodes. Although scholars may disagree over the numbers and the relative importance of disease, there is a consensus that the population of Europe experienced a significant decline or collapse in late antiquity; this collapse continued well into the Middle Ages.[78] Russell[79] estimated that the population of the Roman Empire declined by half during the first five centuries of the Christian era (by 543 C.E.). Biraben and Le Goff suggest that the great plagues of the sixth century, combined with smallpox, caused further catastrophic losses.[80] Between 300 C.E. and 530 C.E., the population of the city of Rome declined by over 90 percent, from eight hundred thousand to sixty thousand.[81]

Egyptian census records, which provide some of the most credible demographic evidence from the Greco-Roman world, indicate that the chances of surviving to adulthood in the Roman Empire declined appreciably during the second and third centuries. Life expectancy at birth during this time was twenty-two to twenty-five years of age[82] – about what it was during the late Neolithic.[83] Detailed research on life expectations in the Danube provinces indicate that only one out of five people lived to age sixty-two.[84]

Epidemic disease was not the ultimate cause of Europe's population decline, inasmuch as natural selection operates on fertility not mortality.[85] Repeated epidemics contributed to failed harvests and the abandonment of villas and farms, which resulted in famines and chronic

---

[78] Boak, *Manpower Shortage*, 111; McCormick, *Origins of the European Economy*, 38–41; McNeill, *Plagues and Peoples*, 116; Pounds, *Historical Geography of Europe*, 77; Wilson, "Understanding the Nature and Importance of Low-growth Demographic Regimes," 28.

[79] Russell, "Late Ancient and Medieval Population."

[80] Biraben and Le Goff, "Plague in the Early Middle Ages," 62.

[81] McCormick, *Origins of the European Economy*, 66.

[82] Disaggregation of the data suggests that life expectancy at birth was thirty-two for upper-class Romans and less than twenty for slaves and freedmen. Duncan-Jones, *Structure and Scale in the Roman Economy*, 103.

[83] Bagnall and Frier, *The Demography of Roman Egypt*, 109–110.

[84] A. R. Burn, "*Hic Breve Vivitur*: a Study of the Expectation of Life in the Roman Empire." *Past and Present* 4(1953): 2–31, 23.

[85] Sallares, *The Ecology of the Ancient Greek World*, 222–224.

malnourishment, and in turn, declining fertility.[86] There is evidence that men outnumbered women during the early Middle Ages,[87] implying that young, married women often died during pregnancy and childbirth, presumably from concurrent infections. As early as the reign of Diocletian (285–305 C.E.), Roman emperors sought to address the twin problems of famine and population decline by passing laws that prohibited farm laborers from leaving their land or even entering the army.[88] Archaeological evidence also attests to widespread abandonment of villas and other profound settlement system changes in Gaul beginning around the time of the Antonine Plague.[89] Where town or urban life continued it was much attenuated.[90] During the late third century, following the measles pandemic of 251–270 C.E., Roman defenses against barbarian incursions became tenuous and many towns drastically reduced the area contained within newly fortified walls.[91] It is perhaps a testament to the consequences of "crowd infections" that many of these newly fortified towns, after a brief revival, subsequently became impoverished and perished.[92] Boak noted that by the early fifth century the area of untilled

---

[86] Pierre Riché, *Daily Life In The World Of Charlemagne*, trans. Jo Ann McNamara (Philadelphia: University of Pennsylvania Press, 1978[1973]), 47–49. One can imagine any number of scenarios whereby fertility was undermined. Chronic malnourishment, for instance, would have meant women lacked sufficient body fat for ovulation and lactation.

[87] Joseph Lynch, *The Medieval Church* (New York: Longman, 1992), 213.

[88] Dom John Chapman, *Saint Benedict and the Sixth Century* (New York: Longmans, Green and Co., 1929), 155; McNeill, *Plagues and Peoples*, 118; Pounds, *Historical Geography of Europe*, 77.

[89] William E. Klingshirn, *Caesarius of Arles: The Making of a Christian Community in Late Antique Gaul* (Cambridge, UK: Cambridge University Press, 1994), 203–206; C. R. Whittaker, *Frontiers of the Roman Empire: A Social and Economic Study* (Baltimore, MD: Johns Hopkins University Press, 1994), 232.

[90] Pounds, *Historical Geography of Europe*, 70.

[91] Christopher Pickles, *Texts and Monuments: A Study of Ten Anglo-Saxon Churches of the Pre-Viking Period* (Oxford, UK: Archaeopress, 1999), 102; Whittaker, *Frontiers of the Roman Empire*, 207–208. Note that archaeological research in northern France, Belgium, and the left bank of the German Rhineland indicate that at least some settlements were being abandoned even before the destructive invasions of the late third century. Although Whittaker has speculated that this abandonment may have been for economic reasons, epidemic disease also may have played a part. Whittaker, *Frontiers of the Roman Empire*, 211.

[92] Drinkwater, *Roman Gaul*, 157–158; Guy Halsall, "Social Identities and Social Relationships in Early Merovingian Gaul." In *Franks and Alamanni in the Merovingian Period: An Ethnographic Perspective*, ed. Ian Wood, pp. 141–165 (Rochester, NY: Boydell

land had reached astonishing proportions, and many of the cities of the Roman Empire had become ghost towns.[93] As noted, by the turn of the sixth century, the population of the city of Rome had plummeted to around sixty thousand (down from over a million in the late second century and perhaps eight hundred thousand at the outset of the fourth century C.E.).

What is especially striking about the population collapse in Western Europe during late antiquity and the early Middle Ages is that it seems not to have been slowed by the steady and sometimes rapid in-migration of large numbers of peoples from eastern and central Europe (Figure 3). The Visigoths and Ostrogoths, who were driven across the Danube by the Huns in 376 C.E., are thought to have numbered at least one hundred thousand.[94] In 406–407 C.E., tens of thousands of Vandals, Alans, and Sueves crossed the Rhine. In 454 C.E., the collapse of Attila's empire sent thousands more "barbarians" streaming across the Danubian frontier.[95] Numerically speaking, these three major incursions represent the tip of the iceberg, as most scholars today acknowledge that the majority of Goths and other "barbarians" crossed the frontier into the Roman Empire in small bands.[96] In this regard, terms like Goths, Franks, and Alamanni are generic terms that elide the multiple and often separate identities of barbarian invaders. The Gothic migration in 376 C.E., for instance, was led by at least seven or eight different chieftains who often fought with each other.[97]

Press, 1998), 146; Colin Haselgrove, "Roman Impact on Rural Settlement and Society in Southern Picardy." In *From the Sword to the Plough: Three Studies on the Earliest Romanisation of Northern Gaul*, ed. N. Roymans, pp. 127–189 (Amsterdam: Amsterdam University Press, 1996), 166–168; Whittaker, *Frontiers of the Roman Empire*, 211.

[93] *Manpower Shortage*, 127.

[94] P. J. Heather, *Goths and Romans* (Oxford: Clarendon Press, 1991), 327.

[95] E. A. Thompson, *Romans and Barbarians: The Decline of the Western Empire* (Madison: University of Wisconsin Press, 1982), 15–19.

[96] Patrick Geary, "Barbarians and Ethnicity." In *Late Antiquity: A Guide to the Postclassical World*, ed. G. W. Bowerstock, P. Brown, and O. Grabar, pp. 107–130 (Cambridge: Belknap Press, 1999); Brent Shaw, "War and Violence." In *Late Antiquity, A Guide to the Postclassical World*, pp. 130–170; Whittaker, *Frontiers of the Roman Empire*, 209.

[97] Hans J. Hummer, "Franks and Alamanni: A Discontinuous Ethnogenesis." In *Franks and Alamanni in the Merovingian Period An Ethnographic Perspective*, ed. Ian Wood, pp. 9–21 (Rochester, NY: The Boydell Press, 1998); Whittaker, *Frontiers of the Roman Empire*, 212–213.

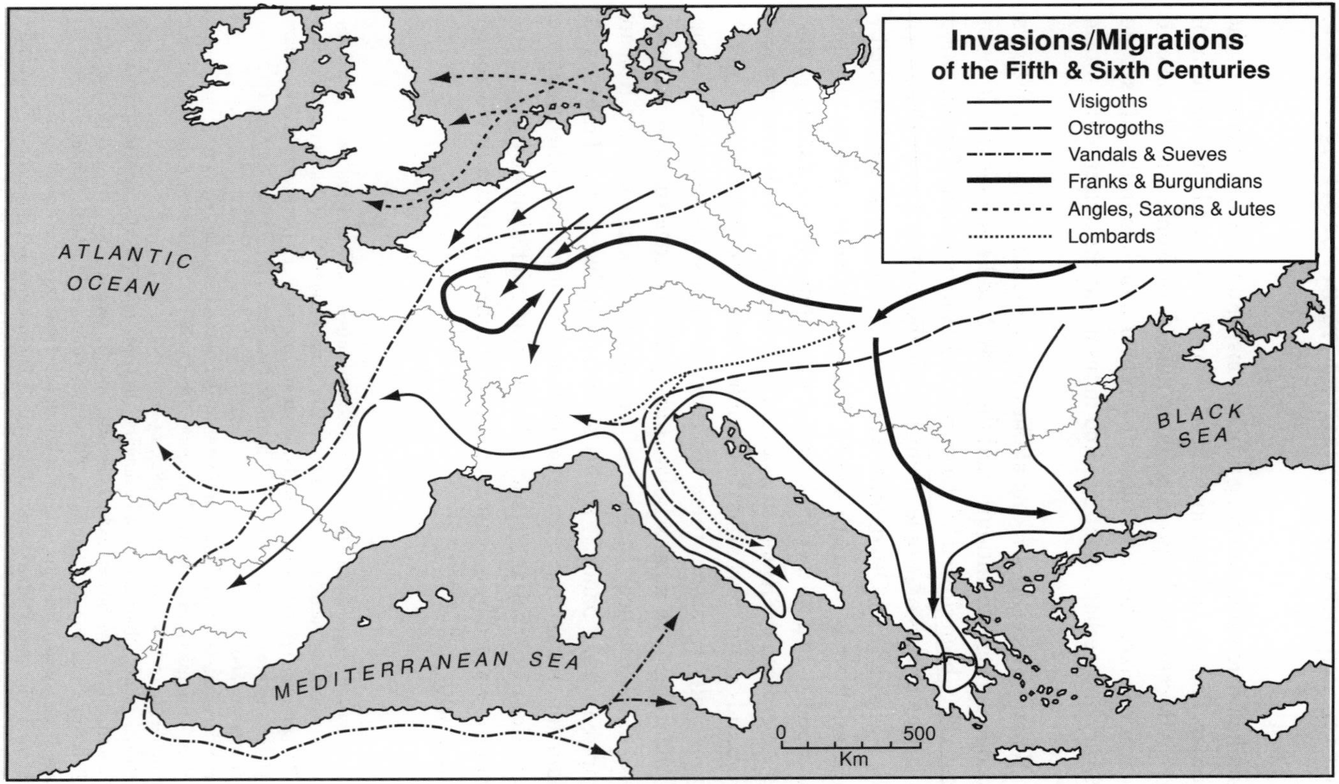
Invasions/Migrations
of the Fifth & Sixth Centuries
Visigoths
Ostrogoths
Vandals & Sueves
Franks & Burgundians
Angles, Saxons & Jutes
Lombards
ATLANTIC
OCEAN
BLACK
SEA
MEDITERRANEAN SEA
0
500
Km

Figure 3. Invasions and Migrations of the Fifth and Sixth Centuries (After Pounds, *An Historical Geography of Europe*, 79).

It has been suggested that well over a million foreigners crossed the Rhine and Danube frontiers during just one century, from circa 250 to 350 C.E.[98] One would think that such significant migration would have offset Europe's pronounced population decline in late antiquity. But the "barbarians" themselves were ravaged by epidemics.[99] Moreover, those barbarians who survived and then settled within the empire – becoming more sedentary in the process – suffered further from disease.

Goths, Franks, Burgundians, and so on often supplemented rather than displaced what was a disappearing Gallic population. This perhaps explains why Gallic nobles were willing to part with gold rather than agricultural laborers, and why native Gauls offered little or no resistance to invaders.[100] Although the Gallic Chronicle of 452 suggests that the settlement of barbarians was encouraged by the Roman government, there clearly were significant tracts of land available for settlement, pre-sumably owing to disease-induced reductions in the native Gaulish pop-ulation. Thus, the Chronicle tells of Alans who were allotted "deserted lands" around the city of Valence and still other invaders who divided the land with the Gauls.[101] In the region about Tours, there is likewise archaeological evidence of dramatic settlement shifts in circa 270 C.E. that may reflect reoccupation of Roman villas by Germanic invaders and the withdrawal of remnant groups of Gallic speakers to hamlets in the more remote parts of the Touraine.[102] In northern Gaul and in the lower German province, there is clear evidence that the Franks, who were an amalgamation of small tribes who came together in the first and second centuries between the Weser and Rhine rivers, expanded for the most part peacefully across the Rhine and into Belgium, settling in

---

[98] Whittaker, *Frontiers of the Roman Empire*, 231.

[99] Boak, *Manpower Shortage*, 112, 128–129; Hopkins, *Princes and Peasants*, 23; E. A. Thompson, *Romans and Barbarians: The Decline of the Western Empire* (Madison: University of Wisconsin Press, 1982), 236; Zinsser, *Rats, Lice and History*, 136; Whittaker, *Frontiers of the Roman Empire*, 220–222.

[100] Thompson, *Romans and Barbarians*, 16, 37, 239.

[101] The chronicle does include one instance where Alans were opposed by local inhabitants. See Steven Muhlberger, *The Fifth-Century Chroniclers: Prosper, Hydatius, and the Gallic Chronicler of 452* (Leeds: Francis Cairns, 1990), 176–177.

[102] Clare Stancliffe, "From Town to Country: The Christianization of the Touraine, 370–600." In *The Church in Town and Countryside*, ed. Derek Baker, pp. 43–59 (Oxford: Basil Blackwell, 1979), 45–48.

areas abandoned by Gallo-Roman landlords, and coexisting with what remained of the local Gallic-speaking population.[103] What happened in Gaul happened in Spain. According to Isidore of Seville (570–636 C.E.), epidemics devastated the indigenous population of Spain, paving the way for the "barbarians:"

> In the era 449 (411), after the terrible destruction of the plagues by which Spain was destroyed, finally through God's mercy the barbarians were moved to make peace and divided Spain's provinces by lot for their occupation. The Vandals and Suevi took Galicia. The Alani obtained the provinces of Lusitania and Cartagena, and the Vandals called Silingians received Baetica. But the Spaniards in the remaining cities and strongholds, having been struck down by the plagues, placed themselves in subjection to the ruling barbarians.[104]

The Sociocultural Consequences of Epidemic Disease: The Case of Gaul

In Spain, Gaul, Britain, and elsewhere, ethnogenesis, or the reforging of cultural identities and sociocultural systems, largely was a consequence of disease, famine, and warfare during the period 150–600 C.E. In Gaul, legal protection afforded Roman subjects by barbarian kings encouraged the "mixing" of Germanic peoples with what was once a large, native population of Gallic-speakers.[105] At the height of the Roman Empire, during the mid-second century C.E., the three Gallic-speaking provinces of Gaul had a thriving population of twelve million.[106] Indeed, Gallic flourished to the point that the emperor Severus in circa 200 C.E. permitted the use of Gallic in courts of law; also at this time native leagues officially replaced Roman miles on road signs in Gaul.[107] If the demise

---

[103] Whittaker, *Frontiers of the Roman Empire*, 237, 240.
[104] Guido Donini and Gordon B. Ford, Jr., trans., *Isidore of Seville's History of the Kings of the Goths, Vandals, and Suevi* (Leiden: E.J. Brill, 1966), 35.
[105] Ralph Mathisen, *Roman Aristocrats in Barbarian Gaul* (Austin: University of Texas Press, 1993), 133.
[106] Drinkwater, *Roman Gaul*, 170; Russell, *Late Ancient and Medieval Population*, 83–85.
[107] Drinkwater, *Roman Gaul*, 83.

of a language is any indication of cultural processes as a whole, it is telling that by 500 C.E. the Gallic language had all but vanished.[108]

If the language vanished, what happened to the Gallic and Gallo-Roman cultures of Gaul, including the religious beliefs and "holy men" who played a vital part in maintaining the identity and well-being of Gallic society? Relatively little is known about Gallic or Celtic religion, excepting the formal priesthood of the Druids. In his *Gallic War*, Caesar noted that the Druids:

> ...are concerned with divine worship, the due performance of sacrifices, public and private, and the interpretation of ritual questions: a great number of young men gather about them for the sake of instruction and hold them in great honour. In fact it is they who decide in almost all disputes, public and private; and if any crime has been committed, or murder done, or if there is any dispute about succession or boundaries, they also decide it, determining rewards and penalties.[109]

The Gauls and other "Celts"[110] are thought to have had various orders of holy men, including priests, diviners, and what some Roman observers referred to as "natural philosophers."[111] Together they fulfilled various functions, principally maintaining the calendar and fixing dates for festivals, sowing, and so on, and acting as go-betweens with Celtic gods, the dead, and various spirits of rivers, springs, forests, and other natural "sites."[112] Long before they had been incorporated into the Roman

---

[108] Simon James, *Exploring the World of the Celts* (London: Thames and Hudson, 1993), 151; Alex Woolf, "Romancing the Celts, A Segmentary Approach to Acculturation." In *Cultural Identity in the Roman Empire*, eds. Ray Laurence and Joanne Berry, pp. 111–124 (London: Routledge, 1998).

[109] H. J. Edwards, trans., *Caesar: The Gallic War* (London: William Heinemann, 1916), 337.

[110] My use of "the Celts" or "Celtic society" represents a lumping together of what apparently were diverse peoples in Western Europe. Unfortunately, neither the archaeological or historical records have shed sufficient light on this diversity to provide alternative designations. See Stephen D. Jones, *Deconstructing the Celts: A Skeptic's Guide to the Archaeology of the Auvergne* (Oxford: Archaeopress/British Archaeological Reports, 2001), 4–5.

[111] James, *Exploring the World of the Celts*, 90; Bruce Lincoln, *Myth, Cosmos, and Society: Indo-European Themes of Creation and Destruction* (Cambridge, MA: Harvard University Press, 1986), 164–165.

[112] James, *Exploring the World of the Celts*, 52–53.

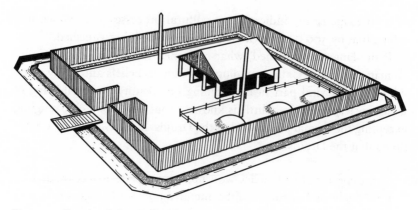

Figure 4. Sketch of the Gallic Shrine at Gournay (After James, *Exploring the World of the Celts*, 93).

Empire, the Gauls as well as Germanic groups (east of the Rhine) erected shrines or temples in what were perceived as sacred places (e.g., springs, caves) (Figure 4).[113] The Gauls offered sacrifices (material and human) and left votive offerings to what appear to have been rather abstractly conceived supernaturals, such as shape-shifters.[114] As a result of Roman influence, which encouraged the personification of deities, the Gauls by the second century C.E. had turned some of their shrines or sanctuaries into "homes" for mostly local but also some Roman deities (e.g., Mercury), to whom private and communal offerings were left to ensure

---

[113] Celtic sanctuaries or centers of pilgrimage consisted of a sacred enclosure (*nemeton*) with a Celtic temple (*cella* and ambulatory), which, by the second century, were richly built and decorated in the Roman fashion; the enclosure might also have a nearby complex of buildings including a residence for a temple priest, baths, theater, and buildings and open spaces to accommodate visitors. See Drinkwater, *Roman Gaul*, 179.

[114] Ton Derks, *Gods, Temples and Ritual Practices: The Transformation of Religious Ideas and Values in Roman Gaul* (Amsterdam: Amsterdam University Press, 1998), 78–79; James, *Exploring the World of the Celts*; Thomas Taylor, trans., *The Arguments of the Emperor Julian Against the Christians* (Chicago: Ares Publishing, 1980), 35; Robert L. Wilken, "Pagan Criticism of Christianity: Greek Religion and Christian Faith." In *Early Christian Literature and the Classical Intellectual Tradition*, eds. W. R. Schodel and R. L. Wilken, pp. 117–134 (Paris: Editions Beauchesne, 1979); *The Christians as the Romans Saw Them* (New Haven, CT: Yale University Press, 1984), 148–149.

inspiration, healing, and knowledge.[115] In more urban areas, where Roman power and influence were largely felt, tax-supported temples with priests and magistrates enacted rituals and received sacrifices on behalf of Roman state religion. Although these cultic centers were decidedly Roman, votive inscriptions indicate that over time Roman deities became a syncretic blend, as reflected in names that were at once Roman and Celtic (e.g., Mars Camulus).[116]

By the second century C.E., Gaul was the "strategic linchpin of the Roman West," providing communications between Spain, Britain, Italy, and the Danube.[117] It is hard to believe that Gaul escaped the devastation wrought by disease elsewhere in the Roman Empire.[118] There apparently are no eyewitness accounts of how the Antonine Plague or subsequent epidemics affected Gallic religion and the power and influence of Gallic shamans and priests. The first two centuries of the Christian era in areas such as Gaul have been described as "an age without history."[119] Ecclesiastical and secular texts from the early Middle Ages nevertheless suggest that by the fifth century most Gallic temples had disappeared, along with whatever formal priesthood once existed among the Gauls.[120] In their stead were simple shrines or open-air sites where a seemingly disparate group of *harioli, haruspices, sortilegi, incantores,* and other claimants to the supernatural drew from Celtic, Roman, and Germanic traditions.[121]

Of course, farming communities do not fare well during epidemics that kill one in five people and leave another 20 percent or 30 percent of the population incapacitated for days or weeks on end.[122] Although kinship, particularly lineage and clan systems, may have mattered less in Gallic *civitates* (more urban areas that were administrative units of the Roman Empire), they undoubtedly defined economic and

---

[115] H. R. Ellis Davidson, *Gods and Myths of Northern Europe* (Baltimore, MD: Penguin, 1964), 34–55; Derks, *Gods, Temples and Ritual Practices,* 244.

[116] Derks, *Gods, Temples and Ritual Practices,* 242–244.

[117] James, *Exploring the World of the Celts,* 141.

[118] Drinkwater, *Roman Gaul,* 76.   [119] Ibid., 72.

[120] Halsall, "Social Identities," 157; Yitzhak Hen, *Culture and Religion in Merovingian Gaul A.D. 481–751* (New York: Brill, 1995), 10, 160.

[121] Flint, *The Rise of Magic,* 61.

[122] Klingshirn, *Caesarius of Arles,* 207–209, 221–223.

social life on the large farms or estates (*villas*), and small farms (*aedifica*) and hamlets where 90 percent of Gauls lived.[123] Among other things, kinship determined where one looked for a marriage partner or to whom one turned for help when harvesting a crop or caring for a sick child. When 20 percent or more of a village's population suddenly dies, seemingly at random, the very structure and functioning of the community is called into question. Of course, when the dead include trusted elders, bards, and religious specialists – the "bearers" of what was largely an oral culture – the future as well as the present are in jeopardy. Doubts about the future are perhaps reflected in the patterning of coin offerings at water shrines, which were very popular among Gallo-Roman and Germanic peoples. Rouselle's analysis of coins from over ninety shrines and sanctuaries in Gaul[124] indicates that in the late third century, and even more so during the fourth century, when abandonment of villas was widespread throughout Gaul,[125] water shrines were no longer the site of offerings and presumably pagan devotions.[126] At roughly this same time (mid-third century), there was a distinct wave of hoarding (burial of coins and objects of value) in northern Gaul and Britain. Drinkwater[127] has noted that this hoarding can not be entirely explained in terms of barbarian invasions or civil strife; something else had rendered life both difficult and unpredictable.

The demise of the Celtic-speaking population of Gaul (the apparent disappearance of millions of people) was not unusual. Between 200 and 359 C.E., the peoples of western Germany previously described by Tacitus seem to disappear from history and are replaced by Alamanni, Franks, Burgundians, and Saxons.[128] Similarly, in Britain, the successful Saxon invasion in the fifth century followed or was coincident with the still unexplained end of town life and the disappearance of countless native

---

[123] See M. Millett, *The Romanization of Britain* (UK: Cambridge University Press, 1990); Woolf, "Romancing the Celts."

[124] *Croire et Guérir: La Foi en Gaule dans l'Antiquité Tardive.* (Paris: Fayard, 1990), pp. 109–132.

[125] Klingshirn, *Caesarius of Arles*, 205.

[126] See also Clare Stancliffe, *St. Martin and His Hagiographer* (Oxford: Clarendon Press, 1983), 333–335.

[127] J. F. Drinkwater, *The Gallic Empire* (Stuttgart: Franz Steiner Verlag Wiesbaden GMBH, 1987), 198–199.

[128] E. A. Thompson, *The Early Germans* (Oxford: Clarendon Press, 1965), 150.

Britons.[129] Not insignificantly, Gildas, who wrote the only surviving narrative history of fifth-century Britain, noted that the coming of the Saxons followed a deadly plague that "laid low so many people, . . . that the living could not bury all the dead."[130]

The Rise of Christianity to 313 C.E.

Whether as fertility cult, or as calendar and astrological calculation, or as covenant, the impulse in all thanatologies is to secure human life by an alliance with divinities who will control nature by making it predictable.[131]

What role did infectious diseases and their consequences play in the spread of Christianity in late antiquity and the early Middle Ages? With the notable exception of Stark,[132] the question has not been pursued vigorously by scholars, most of whom readily acknowledge that we know relatively little about the growth of the early Church following the apostolic age. Our principal sources for the period reflect largely the concerns and views of a relatively small Greek and Latin-speaking minority.[133] Sadly, some of the more insightful Latin authors are known only from fragmentary works. For instance, Ammianus Marcellinus authored a detailed history of the Roman Empire, but only a portion of the

---

[129] E. A. Thompson, "Britain, A.D. 406–410." *Britannia* 8 (1977): 303–318, 314; E. A. Thompson, *Saint Germanus of Auxerre and the End of Roman Britain* (Woodbridge, Suffolk, England: Boydell Press, 1984); John Wacher, *The Towns of Roman Britain* (London: B.T. Batsford, 1975), 444.

[130] Michael Winterbottom, trans. and ed., *Gildas, The Ruin of Britain and other works* (London: Phillimore, 1978[540 C.E.]), 25. Note that Bede ([731 C.E.], who apparently drew from Gildas, also reported that the Britons were devastated by a plague that prompted them to call the Saxons to their aid from across the sea. Colgrave and Mynors, *Bede's Ecclesiastical History*, 49.

[131] Jon Davies, *Death, Burial and Rebirth in the Religions of Antiquity* (London: Routledge, 1999), 210.

[132] *The Rise of Christianity.*

[133] Averil Cameron, *Christianity and the Rhetoric of Empire: The Development of Christian Discourse* (Berkeley: University of California Press, 1991), 5; W. H. C. Frend, *Religion Popular and Unpopular in the Early Christian Centuries* (London: Variorum Reprints, 1976), 3, 488.

history is extant; missing are the first thirteen books, which deal with the all-important period prior to 354 C.E.

Neither Church apologists and theologians nor critics of Christianity (e.g., Celsus, Porphyry) were especially concerned with the lives of the many thousands who embraced Christianity during late antiquity.[134] Scholars have followed the theologians, focusing on doctrinal debates and controversies (e.g., Arianism, Pelageism). The concerns and motivations of the vast majority of illiterate Christians have not been afforded the same research priority.[135] As Brown[136] has suggested, there is a long scholarly tradition of ignoring, and even embarrassment with "popular religion."

During the first and much of the second century, Christianity was a small movement struggling to resolve a host of issues surrounding its founder, his message, and, in general, what it meant to be a Christian.[137] Note that it was not until the end of the second century that a general consensus emerged with respect to the scriptural canon of the New Testament and a ministry based on the episcopate. Paul's epistles testify to the theological and behavioral issues that threatened the growth, and in some cases, the survival of the various churches clustered in the eastern Mediterranean. Paul's missionary strategy, as detailed in his letters and *The Acts of the Apostles*, was to preach in select cities in different provinces and in the process to establish Christian communities,

---

[134] T. Barnes, "Pagan Perceptions of Christianity." In *Early Christianity Origins and Evolution to AD 600*, ed. Ian Hazlett, pp. 231–244 (Nashville: Abingdon Press, 1991); Ramsay MacMullen, "What Difference Did Christianity Make?" *Historia* 35 (1986): 322–343, 322–323; A.D. Wright, *Catholicism and Spanish Society Under the Reign of Philip II, 1505–1598, and Philip III, 1598–1621* (Lewiston, Australia: Edwin Mellen Press, 1991).

[135] R. A. Markus, *The End of Ancient Christianity* (UK: Cambridge University Press, 1990), 4; Ramsay MacMullen, *Christianizing the Roman Empire (A.D. 100–400)* (New Haven, CT: Yale University Press, 1984), 8.

[136] Peter Brown, *The Cult of the Saints* (Chicago: University of Chicago Press, 1981), 12–22.

[137] Ramsay MacMullen, *Christianity and Paganism in the Fourth to Eight Centuries* (New Haven, CT: Yale University Press, 1997); Denis Minns, O.P., *Irenaeus* (Washington, DC: Georgetown University Press, 1994); Jonathan Z. Smith, *Drudgery Divine: On the Comparison of Early Christianities and the Religions of Late Antiquity* (London: School of Oriental and African Studies, University of London, 1990), 129–130; Joseph B. Tyson, *A Study of Early Christianity* (New York: Macmillan, 1973).

whence knowledge of Christ's teachings were spread by elders to outlying settlements.[138]

At the turn of the second century, there were perhaps forty or fifty cities within the Roman Empire with one or more Christian sects. These almost exclusively urban groups (*ekklésiae*), being offshoots of Judaism, often modeled themselves on the diaspora synagogue, consisting of an extended family or slightly larger gathering of people who lived and ate together and who regularly met to study scripture and recite hymns and prayers.[139] Most *ekklésiae* were small and had perhaps several dozen people; Christian communities of several hundred were unusual in circa 100 C.E. The total number of Christians at this time was probably less than fifty thousand (in a society or empire of sixty million).[140]

It was following the Antonine Plague and during the first half of the third century that Christianity began to win significant numbers of converts.[141] Many of these conversions were among the underprivileged of the urban, Greco-Roman world.[142] Celsus (160 C.E.), an early critic of Christianity, sarcastically described the leaders of the Church as "wool workers, cobblers, laundry-workers, and bucolic yokels." Worse yet, from Celsus's perspective, were the rank and file of the Church: women, children, and slaves.[143] Whereas poor immigrants and rootless peasants swelled the ranks of Christianity, it is clear that men and especially women of the middle and upper classes also played a prominent role in the early Church.[144] Thus, Pliny the Younger (110 C.E.) wrote to the

---

[138] Glenn E. Hinson, *The Evangelization of the Roman Empire* (Macon, GA: Mercer University Press, 1981), 33–38.

[139] Howard Clark Kee, "From the Jesus Movement toward Institutional Church." In *Conversion to Christianity*, ed. R. Hefner, pp. 47–63 (Berkeley: University of California Press, 1993); Wayne A. Meeks, *The First Urban Christians, The Social World of the Apostle Paul* (New Haven, CT: Yale University Press, 1983), 82–83.

[140] Wilken, *The Christians as the Romans Saw Them*, 31.

[141] Terrance L. Tiessen, *Irenaeus on the Salvation of the Unevangelized* (Metuchen, NJ: Scarecrow Press, 1993), 67–81.

[142] Cameron, *Christianity and the Rhetoric of Empire*, 44; Frend, *Religion Popular and Unpopular*, 9; Knut Schaferdick, "Christian Mission and Expansion." In *Early Christianity Origins and Evolution to AD 600*, ed. Ian Hazlett, pp. 65–78 (Nashville: Abingdon Press, 1991).

[143] Barnes, "Pagan Perceptions of Christianity," 238.

[144] Peter Brown, *Religion and Society in the Age of Saint Augustine* (New York: Harper & Row, 1972), 134; Meeks, *The First Urban Christians*; Jo Ann McNamara, *A New Song: Celibate Women in the First Three Christian Centuries* (New York: The Institute for

---

emperor Trajan that he anticipated persecuting Christians "... of all ages and ranks, and of both sexes."[145]

During the mid-third century, the emperors Decius (249–251 C.E.) and Valerian (253–260 C.E.) both tried unsuccessfully to halt the spread of Christianity. This first systematic persecution continued, indeed worsened, under Diocletian and Galerius. Intellectuals of the time such as Porphyry (c. 270 C.E.) blamed Christianity for the decline of the cult of Asklepios and frequent epidemics.[146] Despite such charges and persecution, the Church continued to grow in numbers, while pagan cults continued to decline.[147] In Roman North Africa, for instance, Numidian villagers adopted Christianity in large numbers, abandoning the cult of Saturn. Frend,[148] after noting that there is no satisfactory explanation for the Numidian embrace of Christianity, points out that it was correlated with a decline in urban life and institutions. The North African saint, Cyprian, in his *De Mortalitate*,[149] was quite explicit that plague as well as chronic infectious diseases had ravaged North Africa. The biography of Gregory of Nyssa, whose thirty-year mission (243–272 C.E.) to Pontus and Cappadocia coincided with the great measles epidemic, recounts how Gregory broke the hold of traditional priestly families by directly challenging their oracles and cures and replacing their festivals for pagan idols with celebrations for Christian martyrs.[150]

With the conversion of the emperor Constantine in 313 C.E., the Church emerged victorious from the shadows of a failing empire. Christian communities could be found at the time in Spain, Italy, North Africa, and Britain. Christianity also had spread up the Rhine to Cologne,

---

Research and in History, 1983), 56–67; Schaferdick, "Christian Mission and Expansion," 67; see also Cameron, *Christianity and the Rhetoric of Empire*, 36–37; Elizabeth A. Petroff, "Women in the Early Church, St. Perpetua and St. Macrina." In *Medieval Women's Visionary Literature*, ed. E. A. Petroff, pp. 60–69 (New York: Oxford, 1986).

[145] Thomas M. Lucas, S. J., *Landmarking, City, Church and Jesuit Urban Strategy* (Chicago: Loyola Press, 1997), 42.

[146] E. R. Dods, *Pagan and Christian in an Age of Anxiety* (UK: Cambridge University Press, 1968), 114–115.

[147] Ibid., 105–115.

[148] *Religion Popular and Unpopular*, 487–497.

[149] Daniel D. Sullivan, *The Life of the North Africans as Revealed in the Works of Saint Cyprian* (Washington, DC: Catholic University of America, 1933), 13–15.

[150] Frend, *Religion Popular and Unpopular*, 8.

throughout the Rhone Valley, in eastern Gaul, most of Auvergne, south Aquitaine, and along the Seine River.[151]

Christianity as Protector from Evil and Sickness

What attracted tens of thousands of people throughout the Roman world to Christianity during late antiquity? Porphyry is said to have remarked that only sick souls needed Christianity, to which Dods[152] countered, "But sick souls were numerous in our period."

During the early Christian era there was a proliferation of medical texts and shrines to the Roman god of health, Asclepius.[153] However, neither Greco-Roman medicine nor Asclepius and other Roman deities (e.g., *Dea Febris*) apparently were much help dealing with new forms of infectious disease. Christianity asserted itself in this vacuum, providing a new and alternative understanding of sickness. Christian theologians and preachers took the previously ambivalent and often faceless *daemons* of pagan belief and gave them a new valence: Satan and his cohort were identified and exposed as the efficient cause of both psychological and physical disorder.[154] By exorcising demons and disease, and by bestowing this power on his apostles and later clerics, Jesus provided a means by which late antique peoples could wage war upon Satan.[155] Exorcism both reestablished the tranquil integrity of the individual body and provided a public ritual by which individuals could be reincorporated into the small, face-to-face world that was basis of socioreligious life in late antiquity.[156] As we have seen, this world was seriously fragmented

[151] Hen, *Culture and Religion in Merovingian Gaul*, 8.

[152] Dods, *Pagan and Christian in an Age of Anxiety*, 135.

[153] Perkins, *The Suffering Self*, 2.

[154] Brown, *Religion and Society*, 132; Norman Cohn, *Europe's Inner Demons: An Enquiry Inspired by the Great Witch-Hunt* (New York: Basic Books, 1975), 66; Flint, *The Rise of Magic*; Harnack, *Militia Christi*: I, 129; Meeks, *The First Urban Christians*, 189.

[155] J. B. Russell, *The Devil: Perceptions of Evil from Antiquity to Primitive Christianity* (Ithaca, NY: Cornell University Press, 1977), 237–240; Stancliffe, *St. Martin and His Hagiographer*, 210; Peter Stanford, *The Devil: A Biography* (New York: Henry Holt and Company, 1996), 62.

[156] Peter Brown, *Society and the Holy in Late Antiquity* (Berkeley: University of California Press, 1982), 18–19; Fritz Graf, *Magic in the Ancient World* (Cambridge, MA: Harvard University Press, 1997), 167.

beginning in the late second century, when face-to-face contacts literally implied death and disease.

Augustine's "On the Divination of Demons" became the foremost general treatise promoting the idea of demons, including the notion that they often induced diseases by rendering the air unwholesome.[157] Augustine and other theologians such as Caesarius of Arles were quite explicit that demons did nothing without divine permission. As Flint has pointed out, this theological position on demons both explained events beyond human understanding and saved humankind from having to take full responsibility for calamity:

> Demons do not here play that role for which they are later to become so famous in witchcraft trials; the role, that is, of active agents in a drama of fear and repression. Rather they play an almost exactly opposite one. They are used to take the panic, much of the blame, and the extreme penalties from the accused maleficus upon themselves. This humane use of a belief in the magical powers of demons by the early medieval church is one deserving of some emphasis, for, in light especially of later abuses, sight of it can easily be lost.[158]

The Christian redefinition of misfortune lifted the burden of guilt from the shoulders of people, and at the same time, through exorcism and baptism, empowered the individual against Satan, who became the cause of disease and death.

Did pagans perceive baptism as an alternative form of "magic" – one that protected them from the demon/devil and the diseases he spread through the Roman world? The Emperor Julian (331–363 C.E.) – a hostile critic of Christianity – certainly suggested as much:

> And baptism, indeed, does not take away the spots of leprosy, nor ringworms, nor warts, nor the gout, nor the dysentery, nor the dropsy, nor the reduvia.[159]

---

[157] Flint, *The Rise of Magic*, 148.
[158] Ibid., 153–154. See also Cohn, *Europe's Inner Demons*, 67–68.
[159] Taylor, *The Arguments of the Emperor Julian*, 74–75.

Christian rhetoric, which beginning with Christ's own parables was highly figural and metaphorical,[160] held out the promise that baptism was indeed more than a spiritual cleansing of the soul. Early Christian texts such as the apocryphal *Acts of Thomas* clearly indicate that pagans viewed baptism and chrismation as magical charms with immense healing powers.[161] The oldest liturgical texts, the *Apostolic Tradition of Hippolytus* (c. 200 C.E.) and the late-fourth-century *Apostolic Constitutions*, indicate that the ingestion or application of holy oil and water were understood exclusively as a means to physical health.[162] Lynch[163] notes that the "folk interpretation" of baptism was that it drove out the demons who caused sickness, preserving or providing good health.

The sacraments of Confession and the Eucharist also were perceived as a kind of magical talisman against evil spirits, sickness, and death.[164] This interpretation certainly was consistent with the use of medical or disease metaphors in early Christian literature. In Origen's *Contra Celsum* (c. 248 C.E.), Christ is represented as the "universal doctor" of mankind. Ignatius of Antioch referred to the "Bread of Life" in John's Gospel as the "medicine of immortality."[165] Amulet collections and ritual manuals from various parts of the late antique world lend further support to the idea that many Christians understood their newfound religion as particularly potent dealing with sickness.[166]

---

[160] Cameron, *Christianity and the Rhetoric of Empire*.

[161] Montague Rhodes James, *The Apocryphal New Testament* (Oxford: Clarendon Press, 1963); Hinson, *The Evangelization of the Roman Empire*, 221.

[162] Frederick Paxton, *Christianizing Death: The Creation of a Ritual Process in Early Medieval Europe* (Ithaca, NY: Cornell University Press, 1990), 29–30, 32.

[163] Lynch, *Christianizing Kinship*, 129. See also Ramsay MacMullen, *Christianity and Paganism in the Fourth to Eight Centuries* (New Haven, CT: Yale University Press, 1997), 140.

[164] Darrel W. Amundsen, "The Medieval Catholic Tradition." In *Caring and Curing, Health and Medicine in the Western Religious Tradition*, eds. R. Numbers and D. Amundsen, pp. 65–108 (London: Macmillan Publishing, 1986), 97; Hinson, *The Evangelization of the Roman Empire*, 231.

[165] G. Hall, "Ministry, Worship and Christian Life." In *Early Christianity Origins and Evolution to AD 600*, ed. Ian Hazlett, pp. 101–112 (Nashville: Abingdon Press, 1991), 105.

[166] David Frankfurter, "Amuletic Invocations of Christ for Health and Fortune." In *Religions of Late Antiquity in Practice*, ed. R. Valantasis, pp. 340–343 (Princeton, NJ: Princeton University Press, 2000).

Of course, there were many for whom baptism and other sacraments did not provide a cure or protection from disease. Modern medical research nevertheless suggests that the mortality rate among Christians or would-be Christians probably was significantly lower than among contemporaries who rejected Christian rhetoric and promises. Faith can have a very significant impact on whether someone contracts or recovers from all manner of sickness.[167] Perhaps just as important, Christianity held out the promise that those who did suffer and die would nevertheless be healed and made whole again. Prior to the late second century (and the Antonine Plague), most Christians were unsure what to make of Paul's confident assertion that "God having raised Jesus, will also raise us."[168] Christ's bodily resurrection was not a certainty (even if he ascended in spirit to the Father), and most Christians harbored doubts about their own corporal resuscitation. Christians as well as many non-Christians believed that the dead traveled to another realm, separate from the living, although there was contact and continuity of relationships (thus Christians ate with the dead in an extended kinship meal).[169]

Sometime during the mid- or late second century, Christianity and other mystery cults switched gears, holding out the promise that human tragedy, which weighed so heavily on the minds of people,[170] was negated by bodily resurrection. Why, Bynum[171] has asked, did resurrection become a major theme of Christian discussion and apologetics? Although we may agree with her answer that the promise of resurrection (body restored to soul) made it possible for people, and those they

---

[167] Ann McElroy and Patricia A. Townsend, *Medical Anthropology in Ecological Perspective* (North Scituate, MA: Duxbury Press, 1979); Jean-Pierre Peter, "Disease and the Sick at the End of the Eighteenth Century." In *Biology of Man in History*, eds. R. Forster and O. Ranum, pp. 81–94 (Baltimore, MD: Johns Hopkins University Press, 1975), 123.

[168] Meeks, *The First Urban Christians*, 182.

[169] Jonathan Z. Smith, *Drudgery Divine: On the Comparison of Early Christianities and the Religions of Late Antiquity* (London: School of Oriental and African Studies, University of London, 1990), 193.

[170] Karl Baus et al., *The Imperial Church from Constantine to the early Middle Ages*, trans. Anselm Biggs (New York: Seabury Press, 1982), 92–93.

[171] Caroline W. Bynum, "Images of the Resurrection Body in the Theology of Late Antiquity." *The Catholic Historical Review* LXXX (1994): 179–237.

loved, to face death,[172] the question remains as to why this seemingly universal need apparently became an imperative during the late second century. The period 150–300 C.E. has been aptly described as an age of anxiety – a time when philosophers increasingly asked the question "what are we here for?" People who are content with their lives do not ask such questions – at least not repeatedly.[173]

The optimistic Christian discourse of resurrection followed or was coincident with the unprecedented and inexplicable suffering and death caused by the Antonine Plague (166–190 C.E.).[174] Arguably at this time, and with succeeding epidemics and disasters, it became particularly comforting to the living to know that they and the deceased would be reunited and that interrupted lives would be continued.[175] Christians presumably took comfort in the idea that an inscrutable but just God had taken their loved ones who were enjoying, or would enjoy, a blissful life in heaven. This promise of life after death is powerfully conveyed in the early-third-century Passion of St. Perpetua (203 C.E.). During her trials and tribulations and prior to her martyrdom, Perpetua had a vision in which she saw a heavenly paradise that martyrs enjoyed immediately upon their self-sacrificing death. Perpetua had two subsequent visions, the first revealed her long-dead brother, still suffering in what amounted to purgatory; in the second vision, which followed Perpetua's prayers for her brother, he is "released from punishment."[176]

---

[172] In a subsequent, book-length study of resurrection, Bynum attributed "a good deal" of the late-second-century Christian embrace of bodily resurrection to a context of persecution, which led to the scattering and dishonoring of martyrs' remains. There may be some truth to this argument, but I find the evidence for epidemic disease and its devastating consequences more compelling than persecution as a contextual explanation. Caroline W, Bynum, *The Resurrection of the Body in Western Christianity, 200–1336* (New York: Columbia University Press, 1995), 58.

[173] Dods, *Pagan and Christian in an Age of Anxiety,* 21–22.

[174] On the optimistic quality of Christian discourse, see Davies, *Death, Burial and Rebirth,* 196–200; Megan McLaughlin, *Consorting with Saints: Prayer for the Dead in Early Medieval France* (Ithaca, NY: Cornell University Press, 1994), 185.

[175] Eamon Duffy, *The Stripping of the Altars* (New Haven, CT: Yale University Press, 1992), 303.

[176] Herbert Musurillo, trans. and ed., *The Acts of the Christian Martyrs* (Oxford: Clarendon Press, 1972).

With the advent of the cult of the saints in late antiquity, Christians could take comfort not only in the promise of resurrection, but also the belief that saints such as Martin of Tours would see to it that all but the utterly damned would realize heaven:

> And when, at the Last Judgement, I am to be placed on the left hand, [Saint] Martin will deign to pick me out from the middle of the goats with his sacred right hand. He will shelter me behind his back. And when, in accordance with the Judge's sentence, I am to be condemned to the infernal flames, he will throw over me that sacred cloak, by which he once covered the King of Glory [in the form of a beggar with whom martin once shared his officer's cloak] and will gain a reprieve for me, as angels tell the King.... This is the man for whom Saint Martin pleads.[177]

It is worth emphasizing that Stoic and other pagan philosophers, with their emphasis on self-sufficiency, impersonal processes, and natural law, could neither explain the random deaths of young and old, rich and poor, nor alleviate grief through altruism and promises of a compensatory afterlife.[178]

Early Christian theologians such as Irenaeus were horrified at Gnosticism, Docetism, and other "heresies" that spoke of the body as some unfortunate epiphenomenon of creation.[179] Around the turn of the third century – again, not long after the Antonine Plague – Christian theologians increasingly began talking about the "enigmatic," rather than hallowed, joining of body and soul.[180] Within a century, theologians as well as the laity were viewing the body as sinful and an impediment to salvation.[181] At this same time, Christian literature and discourse championed human suffering or the "suffering self."[182] Simultaneously there

---

[177] Gregory of Tours, quoted in Peter Brown, "The Decline of the Empire of God." In *Last Things: Death and the Apocalypses in the Middle Ages*, eds. C. W. Bynum and P. Freedman, pp. 41–59 (Philadelphia: University of Pennsylvania Press, 2000), 50.

[178] Hinson, *The Evangelization of the Roman Empire*, 27–28; McNeill, *Plagues and Peoples*, 122–123.

[179] Minns, *Irenaeus*.

[180] Peter Brown, *The Body and Society* (New York: Harper & Row, 1988), 235–236.

[181] Brown, *The Body and Society*; Jacques Le Goff, *The Medieval Imagination*, trans. Arthur Goldhammer (Chicago: University of Chicago Press, 1985), 14, 96.

[182] Perkins, *The Suffering Self*.

emerged "a strange technology of power treating the vast majority of men as flock with a few as shepherds."[183]

Why fear or hate the body and seemingly value human suffering? Why all the talk of shepherds and their flocks? Certainly the shepherd theme and the idea of the body as an impediment to spiritual perfection or requiring discipline was not new to the third century.[184] One can agree as well with Perkins and Foucault that many bishops found a discourse of the suffering self a source of empowerment, inasmuch as the exercise of power could be justified on the basis of attending to the poor and needy. The poor and suffering presumably were placated by sermons that championed impoverishment or that implied that individual sheep should be ruled in a continuous and permanent way by their pastors.[185]

It is quite another thing, however, to suggest that sickness (consciousness of being sick) was largely a social construction,[186] and bore no relation to the Antonine and Cyprian Plagues, or near-endemic malaria, which literally killed many millions of people in the late second and third centuries. Arguably, if people were conscious of sickness, it was because they had ample experience with smallpox, measles, plague, and so on. Once the body's diseased state became a "fact of life" during the late second century, it made sense for Christians to embrace a discourse that effectively separated the body and soul (a discourse previously articulated through Neo-Platonism and Gnosticism). Moreover, while some and perhaps many bishops and clerics may have found the discourse of suffering useful in their accumulation and exercise of power, the Church, be it conceived as a discourse or an institution, spent as much time "talking" about charity as it did suffering. Even more important, this

---

[183] Michel Foucault, "Politics and Reason." In *Michel Foucault, Politics, Philosophy, Culture*, ed. L. D. Kritzman, trans. A. Sheridan and others (New York: Routlege, 1988), 63.

[184] Brown, *The Body and Society*; Foucault, "Politics and Reason"; Le Goff, *Medieval Civilization: 400–1500*, trans. Julia Barrow (Oxford: Basil Blackwell, 1988), 96–100; Markus, *The End of Ancient Christianity*, 59; Margaret Miles, *Plotinus on Body and Beauty* (Oxford: Blackwell Publishers, 1999).

[185] Foucault, "Politics and Reason," 60.

[186] Perkins, *The Suffering Self*, 11. Foucault did not deny that late antiquity was a time of great sickness; arguably he was not interested in material causality: "I will pass over the manner in which these things concretely happened." Michel Foucault, *The History of Sexuality I: An Introduction*, trans. R. Hurley (New York: Random House 1978), 123.

extensive discourse on charity was matched by heroic deeds of compassion. For every "suffering self" there was a "giving self."

Christianity as Social Welfare

Most of our brother-Christians showed unbounded love and loyalty, never sparing themselves and thinking only of one another. Heedless of the danger, they took charge of the sick, attending to their every need and ministering to them in Christ, and with them departed this life serenely happy; for they were infected by others with the disease, drawing on themselves the sickness of their neighbours and cheerfully accepting their pains. Many, in nursing and curing others, transferred their death to themselves and died in their stead, turning the common formula that is normally an empty courtesy into a reality: "Your humble servants bid you goodbye."...The heathen behaved in the very opposite way. At first onset of the disease, they pushed the sufferers away and fled from their dearest, throwing them into the roads before they were dead and treating unburied corpses as dirt, hoping thereby to avert the spread and contagion of the fatal disease; but do what they might, they found it difficult to escape.[187]

The above quote is from a letter written by Bishop Dionysius, describing the very different reaction of Christians and non-Christians to the epidemic that raged in Alexandria in circa 259 C.E. Christian communities of Roman antiquity responded to epidemics with not only prayer and healing rituals but also awe-inspiring charity.[188] Although love of one's neighbor was not exclusively a Christian virtue, Christians apparently practiced it much more effectively than did other groups in late antiquity.[189] Whereas Roman munificence traditionally entailed wealthy citizens raising votive stones, temples, colonnades, baths, and so on, Christian charity was focused on basic needs of food and shelter.[190]

---

[187] G. A. Williamson, trans., *Eusebius: The History of the Church from Christ to Constantine* (Harmondsworth, Middlesex, England: Dorset Press, 1965), 305–306.

[188] Stark, *The Rise of Christianity*, 83–88.

[189] Peter Brown, *The World of Late Antiquity* (London: Thames and Hudson, 1971), 68; Dods, *Pagan and Christian in an Age of Anxiety*, 137.

[190] J. H. W. G. Liebeschuetz, *Barbarians and Bishops: Army, Church, and State in the Age of Arcadius and Chrysostom* (Oxford: Clarendon Press, 1990), 187.

Along these lines, the agape or "love feast," which was caricatured as a *bacchanalia* by critics of Christianity, was a religious rite that welcomed the poor, who were at first fed and then invited to participate in prayers and psalms.[191]

As McNeill has pointed out, something as basic as providing the ill with food and water can have an enormous positive impact, particularly when, as is the case with epidemics of measles or smallpox, secondary infections (pneumonia, streptococci) often contribute substantially to disease mortality.[192] The Christian concern with, and indeed, ritual duty, to care for the sick undoubtedly served to increase Christian conversions during late antiquity, when the imperial government was collapsing.[193] In a fragment of a letter written to a priest of the Roman state religion, the emperor Julian, who also was supreme pontiff, admonished the priest to, in effect, be more like the Christians, attending to the needs of the poor and those in prison. Toward the end of his letter Julian noted that the Christians (Galatians) had won many converts because of their philanthropy:

> For when it came about the poor were neglected and overlooked by the priests [of the Roman state religion], then I think the impious Galatians observed this fact and devoted themselves to philanthropy. And they have gained ascendancy in the worst of their deeds through the credit they win for such practices.[194]

It has been suggested that nothing was more important to the spread of Christianity than the charities that were offered to so many without regard for class, condition, or status.[195] Compassion for others is a prominent theme of the Gospels as well as early Church records

---

[191] Cohn, *Europe's Inner Demons*, 10.
[192] James V. Neel et al. "Notes on the Effects of Measles and Measles Vaccine in a Virgin Soil Population of South American Indians." *American Journal of Epidemiology* 91 (1970): 418–429.
[193] Harnack, *Militia Christi*, 171.
[194] Wilmer C. Wright, trans., *The Works of the Emperor Julian*, Vol. 2 (London: William Heinemann, 1913), 337.
[195] Robin L. Fox, *Pagans and Christians* (New York: Knopf, 1987), 335; Hinson, *The Evangelization of the Roman Empire*, 51; Schaferdick, "Christian Mission and Expansion," 68.

and liturgy, which repeatedly emphasize the importance of supporting widows and orphans and caring for the sick.[196] Influential theologians such as Origen (c. 185–253), who is credited with the most successful synthesis of pagan Hellenism and Christianity, saw works of charity as the vehicle to perfection.[197] That Origen's views were shared by many others is suggested by the fact that the purpose of the catechumenate (the time leading up to baptism) was to judge whether a would-be Christian knew how to behave – "...whether they honored the widows, whether they visited the sick, whether they did every sort of good thing" – rather than simply a period in which to master the rudiments of Christian theology or rid one's soul of evil spirits.[198]

Christians did indeed put their trust in a pastorate (a priesthood) whose principal function was to ensure "the provision of subsistence for the flock."[199] And why not? In the mid-third century, the Christian community in Rome supported over fifteen hundred widows and poor persons.[200] Many Christian communities established a "community chest" from which funds were drawn to support the clergy, the needy, and those who gave up a profession (e.g., prostitutes, idol makers) because of conversion.[201] In his *Apologeticus*, Tertullian clarified how these community chests functioned:

> Even if there is a chest of a sort, it is not made up of money paid in entrance-fees, as if religion were a matter of a contract. Every man once a month brings some modest coin – or whenever he wishes, and

---

[196] Harnack, *Militia Christi*, I, 159.

[197] Thomas M. Gannon, S.J., and George W. Traub, S.J., *The Desert and the City, an Interpretation of the History of Christian Spirituality* (London: Macmillan Company, 1969), 40.

[198] This would change in the fourth century when a flood of people seeking conversion made baptism more of a ritual than the culmination of moral testing. Also, during the fourth and fifth century, many delayed baptism until old age or impending death to limit their sins at death. See Lynch, *Godparents and Kinship*, 94. Such changes do not necessarily imply, however, that charity was no longer valued by Christians.

[199] Foucault, *The History of Sexuality*, 123.

[200] Dods, *Pagan and Christian in an Age of Anxiety*, 27.

[201] Ibid., 137; Hall, "Ministry, Worship and Christian Life," 105; Harnack, *Militia Christi*, I, 147–198.

only if he does wish, and if he can; for nobody is compelled; it is a voluntary offering. You might call them the trust funds of piety. For they are not spent upon banquets nor drinking-parties nor thankless eating-houses; but to feed the poor and to bury them, for boys and girls who lack property and parents, and then for slaves grown old and ship-wrecked mariners; and any who may be in mines, islands or prisons, provided that it is for the sake of God's school, become the pensioners of their confession.[202]

Christianity was very much an alternative society in the sense of in-dependent, self-sufficient, and self-reproducing communities.[203] In this regard, Christianity had a decided advantage over competing "mystery cults," which lacked the formal organization of *ekklésia*, which was so effectively mobilized to alleviate real-life suffering. The fact that Christianity accepted all comers also distinguished itself from competing mysteries. The emperor Julian offered this sarcasm:

And if it be requisite to speak the truth, you have ambitiously endeav-ored to extend your confusion. This, however, I think happens very properly, that you have conceived your doctrines ought to be adapted to all nations and lives of other men, such as inn-keepers, publicans, dancers, and others of the like kind![204]

Early Christian communities emulated and often supplanted the so-ciobiological relationships of the family unit and the larger ethnic com-munity.[205] Although the eschatological orientation of early Christianity

---

[202] T. R. Glover and Gerald H. Rendall, trans., *Tertullian [Apologeticus and De Spectaculis] Minucius Felix [Octavius]* (Cambridge, MA: Loeb Classical Library, Harvard University Press, 1931), 175–176.

[203] Walter Burkert, *Homo Necans: The Anthropology of Ancient Greek Sacrificial Ritual and Myth*, trans. Peter Bing (Berkeley: University of California Press, 1983), 51.

[204] Taylor, *The Arguments of the Emperor Julian*, 72–73.

[205] Peter Brown, *The Cult of the Saints* (Chicago: University of Chicago Press, 1981), 31; James C. Russell, *The Germanization of Early Medieval Christianity* (New York: Oxford University Press, 1994), 81. Brown perceptively suggested that these com-munities may have resembled Shaker "families" from nineteenth-century America. Curiously, Brown further suggested they sprang from "...a tendency built into the Near Eastern landscape itself." Brown, *The Body and Society*, 101. For a discussion of

(e.g., Paul's exhortation to celibacy) undoubtedly moved many individuals to abandon their biological families,[206] there obviously were large numbers of people during the second and third centuries whose families were taken from them during epidemics. This inference is suggested by not only early Christian literature, but also texts like Porphyr's *On the Life of Plotinus and the Order of His Works*. In his biographical introduction, Porphyr noted that Plotinus, who lived from 205 to 269 C.E., turned his house into an orphanage of sorts.[207] The fragmentation and destruction of families clearly was an issue of concern for the author of the *Apostolic Constitutions*, which enjoined Christians (including bishops) to adopt and care for orphans.[208]

In late antiquity no less than today, gender was a social construction defined through performative acts prescribed by society.[209] In Roman society the gender "performed" by women entailed far fewer rights and opportunities, relative to men; legally, women were dependent on fathers and husbands. As Weber suggested, religious movements often are sustained by "out-groups" seeking social status, or by in-groups aiming to retain their social dominance. Interestingly, many Christian converts were independent women with moderate wealth who were effectively "in and out," to quote Weber.[210] Christian assemblies mentioned in *Acts* and the *Epistles* of Saint Paul were said to be in the houses of women; these women were not simply "hosts" but apparently deacons and overseers of Christian communities.[211]

how the individualism of the Christian message can give rise, in the context of sociocultural upheaval, to new forms of social organization, see David Martin, *Tongues of Fire: The Explosion of Protestantism in Latin America* (Oxford: Basil Blackwell, 1990).

[206] Brown, *The Body and Society*, 31–32; Lynch, *The Medieval Church*, 29–30.

[207] Richard Valantasis, "Porphyry on the Life of Plotinus and the Order of His Books." In *Religions of Late Antiquity in Practice*, ed. R. Valantasis, pp. 50–61 (Princeton, NJ: Princeton University Press, 2000), 56.

[208] John Boswell, *The Kindness of Strangers: The Abandonment of Children in Western Europe from Late Antiquity to the Renaissance* (New York: Pantheon Books, 1988), 178, f. 132; Irah Chase, trans., *The Constitutions of the Holy Apostles* (New York: Appleton & Company, 1848), 94–95.

[209] Judith Butler, *Gender Trouble: Feminism and the Subversion of Identity* (New York: Routledge, 1989).

[210] Meeks, *The First Urban Christians*, 191.

[211] Joan Morris, *The Lady Was a Bishop* (New York: The Macmillan Company, 1973), 1. Kee has pointed out that the "authentic letters" of Paul (e.g., *Romans* 16:1),

The *Acts* of Paul and Thecla (c. 195 C.E.) and the account of Perpetua's martyrdom in Carthage in circa 202 C.E.[212] tell of aristocratic women who defied their patriarchical families for a "new family" centered around Christ. What do these narratives signify? Whereas the rejection of fathers and the procreative family in favor of Christ bespeaks a theological truth (e.g., even women who are so dependent on men find material existence irrelevant once blessed with Holy Spirit), the narratives also hold out the possibility of Christian families and communities on earth where women transcend gender and have expansive leadership roles.[213] Interestingly, Gnostic texts from late antiquity went so far as to cast God as feminine, and they did so using Christian language and imagery, rather than invoking a pagan tradition of mother goddess.[214]

One of the first laws enacted by Constantine in the fourth century abrogated Augustan marriage laws, allowing celibate women to raise children without the guidance of husbands or fathers.[215] Although as early as the second century Christian women found their own *ekklésiae* reverting back to Roman and earlier Jewish paternalism,[216] Christian prohibitions on infanticide and abortion and the condemnation of divorce, incest, marital infidelity, and polygamy empowered Christian women relative to their pagan counterparts.[217] Previously, in Roman society, women as well as slaves were essentially prisoners of their

which probably date to around the mid-first-century C.E., speak of women as deacons, whereas the later, pseudonymous letters of Paul, which date after the first century, speak only of men who were deacons. Howard Clark Kee, "From the Jesus Movement toward Institutional Church." In *Conversion to Christianity*, ed. R. Hefner, pp. 47–63 (Berkeley: University of California Press, 1993), 62.

[212] Musurillo, *Acts of the Christian Martyrs*.

[213] Stevan L. Davies, *The Revolt of the Widows: The Social World of the Apocryphal Acts* (Carbondale: Southern Illinois University Press, 1980); Elizabeth A. Petroff, "Women in the Early Church, St. Perpetua and St. Macrina." In *Medieval Women's Visionary Literature*, ed. E. A. Petroff, pp. 60–69 (New York: Oxford, 1986), 63–64.

[214] Elaine Pagels, "What Became of God the Mother? Conflicting Images of God in Early Christianity." In *Gnosticism in the Early Church*, ed. with an introduction by David M. Scholer, pp. 295–307 (New York: Garland Publishing Company, 1993).

[215] Jo Ann McNamara, *A New Song: Celibate Women in the First Three Christian Centuries* (New York: The Institute for Research and in History, 1983), 127.

[216] Kee, "From the Jesus Movement toward Institutional Church," 61.

[217] Stark, *The Rise of Christianity*, 195–128.

bodies.[218] Aline Rousselle[219] has noted that asceticism in Christianity began with women who vowed to live as virgins; it was not until the end of the third century that men vowed to remain continent. The appeal of renunciation, virginity, and asceticism was as much, if not more, a matter of rebelling against societal forms of domination than a rejection of the body.[220]

Virgins and later monks opted for social disengagement and membership in new communities where mutual service replaced social necessity. Again, if we ask why this disengagement and these new communities appeared in late antiquity, the answer should include disease and its consequences, particularly the disruption of social and familial bonds that kept women and slaves captive.

The Persecution of Christians

Acknowledging disease and its consequences helps explain the spread of Christianity as well as the hostility with which it was greeted by Roman emperors and citizens. In 177 C.E., the city of Lyon witnessed one of the most celebrated martyrdoms of the early Church. Lyon ostensibly was the Roman capital of Gaul and an important center of Roman wealth and power (see Figure 2).[221] The brutal murder of its Christian citizens was described in a letter written by the survivors of the tragedy, which Eusebius included in his *Ecclesiastical History*.

For reasons that are unclear,[222] the mostly Greek-speaking Christian community in Lyon, which had emigrated from Asia Minor, was first banned from appearing in public and then subsequently arrested, tried, and sentenced to death in gladiatorial games ("sacrifices" to the

---

[218] The situation changed little for slaves after Constantine. MacMullen, "What Difference Did Christianity Make?," 325.

[219] Cited in Le Goff, *Medieval Civilization*, 97. See also Susanna Elm, *"Virgins of God": The Making of Asceticism in Late Antiquity* (Oxford: Clarendon Press, 1994).

[220] Brown, *The Cult of the Saints*, 47; McNamara, *A New Song*, "An Unresolved Syllogism"; Markus, *The End of Ancient Christianity*, 82.

[221] Drinkwater, *Roman Gaul*, 21.

[222] See Musurillo, *Acts of the Christian Martyrs*, xx–xxi.

Roman gods). At the time of the persecution, Christians were a much maligned minority throughout the Roman Empire. Christians were seen as religious fanatics and were accused of worshipping a donkey-God and practicing infanticide, cannibalism, and incestuous orgies.[223] This demonization was correlated with Christian refusal to participate in prescribed rituals and sacrifices of Roman state religion.[224] Many Romans, as voiced by Celsus and later Porphyry, believed that the empire had suffered from epidemics and other calamities because of Christian elevation of Jesus to "true God" at the expense of Roman deities.[225] As early as the first century C.E., Luke sought in *Acts* to counter such beliefs by showing that Christianity was not in and of itself disloyal to Rome.[226] Peter and Paul also encouraged Christians to accept and obey Roman authorities.[227] Pagan distrust of Christians, however, not only persisted but also grew. Minucius Felix's dramatic work, *Octavius*, which dates to around 200 C.E., features a pagan protagonist (Caecilius) who articulates quite well the main complaint against Christians:

> Therefore, since all nations unhesitatingly agree as to the existence of the immortal gods, however uncertain may be our account of them or of their origin, it is intolerable that any man [Christians] should be so puffed up with pride and impious conceit of wisdom, as to strive to abolish or undermine [Roman] religion, so ancient, so useful, and so salutary.[228]

[223] Robert L. Wilken, *The Christians as the Romans Saw Them* (New Haven, CT: Yale University Press, 1984), 63.

[224] Burkert, *Homo Necans*; G. Hall, "Ministry, Worship and Christian Life." In *Early Christianity Origins and Evolution to AD 600*, ed. Ian Hazlett, pp. 101–112 (Nashville: Abingdon Press, 1991), 103.

[225] Glover and Rendall, *Tertullian*, 183; James H. and Robert E. A. Palmer, "Minutes of an Act of the Roman Senate." *Hesperia* 24 (1955): 320–349; Robert L. Wilken, *The Christians as the Romans Saw Them* (New Haven, CT: Yale University Press, 1984), 156.

[226] Robert H. Gundry, *A Survey of the New Testament* (Grand Rapids, MI: Academie Books, 1970), 212.

[227] Robert Doran, *Birth of a Worldview: Early Christianity in Its Jewish and Pagan Context* (Boulder, CO: Westview Press, 1995), 10.

[228] Glover and Rendall, *Tertullian*, 333–335.

It has been suggested[229] that Gallo-Roman priests and officials in Lyon, who were responsible at the time for providing a human sacrifice to the gods, took advantage of popular resentment and accused the Christians of godlessness. As Oliver and Palmer[230] noted almost a half-century ago, the Antonine Plague, which began around 165 C.E., certainly was proof that somebody had seriously offended the Roman gods. Shortly after the pandemic began, in 167 C.E., the second-century Christian apologist, Justin "the martyr," was executed for godlessness and immorality.[231] As noted in the previous chapter,[232] various sources indicate or suggest that Gaul was affected by the Antonine Plague, presumably during the years preceding the holocaust at Lyon. Interestingly, Eusebius's account of the martyrdom makes note of the immigrant, merchant character of the Christian community of Lyon.[233] Did Christian merchants unknowingly bring disease to Lyon? Although no one at the time understood precisely how disease spread, it was understood that human beings could somehow carry and spread disease. It is interesting in this regard that Christians in Lyon initially were banned from appearing in public: " . . . we were not only shut out of our houses, the baths, and the public square, but they forbade any of us to be seen in any place whatsoever."[234] Moreover, Christians who apostatized were sacrificed along with Christians who acknowledged and remained true to their faith.[235] This execution of apostatizers largely was unprecedented and suggests that the Christians of Lyon were feared for reasons other than their beliefs; their very bodies seemingly needed to be destroyed. All the bodies were in fact burned and thrown in the Rhone River. Klingshirn[236]

[229] See, for instance, Cohn, *Europe's Inner Demons*, 1–12; W. H. C. Frend, "Town and Countryside in Early Christianity." In *The Church in Town and Countryside*, ed. Derek Baker, pp. 25–42 (Oxford: Basil Blackwell, 1979); Musurillo, *Acts of the Christian Martyrs*, xx–xxi.

[230] "Minutes of an Act of the Roman Senate," 327.

[231] Robert M. Grant, *Greek Apologists of the Second Century* (Philadelphia: Westminster Press, 1988), 74.

[232] See also Drinkwater, *Roman Gaul*, 75.

[233] Frend, "Town and Countryside in Early Christianity," 35, f. 37.

[234] Musurillo, *Acts of the Christian Martyrs*, 63.

[235] Barnes, "Pagan Perceptions of Christianity," 234.

[236] *Caesarius of Arles*, 46.

has pointed out that communities such as Lyon exhibited a strong sense of common self-interest and were quite prepared to defend those interests.

Monasticism and the "Conversion" of Pagan Europe, 315–800 C.E.

Despite tragedies such as occurred in Lyon in 177 C.E., Christianity experienced impressive growth during the late second and third century, particularly in the cities and towns of the Roman Empire. By 300 C.E., about 10 percent of the Roman world was Christian.[237] Pagans continued to be drawn to the Church in significant part by its charity. Because of the threat of persecution, Christian hospitality prior to the third century occurred mostly in private homes. After Constantine's conversion in circa 313 C.E., public hostels were erected with private, church, and public funds.[238] Although the fourth century is known for the large cathedrals and basilicas that were built at this time, the most common foundation was neither cathedral nor basilica; it was a small church or chapel that was part of a monastery or charitable institution for the poor and destitute.[239] Caseau notes that textual evidence suggests that Christians of the fourth century viewed churches more like synagogues, that is, as places to meet, rather than as temples or sacred spaces.[240] It has been suggested that the "Rule of St. Augustine," which was derived from a letter that Augustine wrote in circa 411 C.E. to a group of women seeking guidance, reflects the ubiquity of female religious communities that cared for the sick, aged, and others who required charity.[241] Other sources such as the vita of Caesarius of Arles (470–543 C.E.) imply that

[237] K. S. Latourette, *A History of the Expansion of Christianity. Seven Volumes* (London: Eyre & Spottiswood, 1938–1945), I, 163; Stark, *The Rise of Christianity*, 7.

[238] Hinson, *The Evangelization of the Roman Empire*, 52.

[239] Bryan Ward-Perkins, *From Classical Antiquity to the Middle Ages: Urban Public Building in Northern and Central Italy AD 300–850* (Oxford: Clarendon Press, 1984), 56–57.

[240] Béatrice Caseau, "Sacred Landscapes." In *Late Antiquity: A Guide to the Postclassical World*, ed. G. W. Bowerstock, P. Brown, and O. Grabar, pp. 21–60 (Cambridge: Belknap Press, 1999), 41.

[241] Lucas, *Landmarking*, 62.

the Church devoted considerable resources to infirmaries that cared for the sick.[242]

Although anyone could be a Christian as a matter of accepting the incarnation and a life of charitable giving, the argument that God made himself known through a veil that could only be penetrated by hermeneutics presupposed a select group who could read and interpret scripture.[243] After Constantine embraced Christianity, the Church attracted aristocrats and urban elites who saw the office of bishop as an opportunity to preserve or realize privilege and power as "interpreters."[244] Thus, at the same moment that bishops like John Chrysostom celebrated and implemented works of charity, other bishops squandered their incomes in conspicuous consumption and works of aggrandizement.[245] This abuse of power occurred at a time of continued sociocultural upheaval, coincident with more epidemics and invasions by the Goths and Vandals. Indeed, by the turn of the fifth century many were convinced that the kingdom of God was at hand:

> God made life short, then, so that its troubles might be ended in a brief span of time, since they could not be ended by good fortune. (Maximus of Turin, c. 400 C.E.)[246]

> The final age of the world is full of evils just as old age is full of death. These things have been seen for a long time and continue to be seen

---

[242] J. N. Hillgarth, *Christianity and Paganism, 350–750* (Philadelphia: University of Pennsylvania Press, 1986), 35.

[243] Cameron, *Christianity and the Rhetoric of Empire,* 65.

[244] Under Constantine churches could legally acquire property and bishops were given extensive judicial powers with secular sanctions. The fact that barbarian kings, who became effective military rulers of the empire after the death of Theodosius in 395 C.E., eschewed harming ranking ecclesiastics provided additional reason for Roman nobility to pursue bishoprics. Mathisen, *Roman Aristocrats in Barbarian Gaul,* 144; Paxton, *Christianizing Death,* 66; Stancliffe, *St. Martin and His Hagiographer,* 265–66.

[245] A. B. E. Hood, trans. and ed., *St. Patrick, His Writings and Muirchu's Life* (London: Phillimore, 1978), 2–3; Mathisen, *Roman Aristocrats in Barbarian Gaul,* 95–97. The homilies of John Chrysostom (d. 407), repeatedly emphasized how care of the needy, particularly by the wealthy, was the essence of Christianity. J. H. W. G. Liebeschuetz, *Barbarians and Bishops: Army, Church, and State in the Age of Arcadius and Chrysostom* (Oxford: Clarendon Press, 1990), 176.

[246] Boniface Ramsey, O.P., trans., *The Sermons of St. Maximus of Turin* (New York: Newman Press, 1989), 176.

in this white-haired age: famine, pestilence, destruction, wars, terrors. (Eucherius, c. 430 C.E.)[247]

Eucherius and Maximus of Turin were not alone.[248] As the Roman world spiralled out of control, all the while many bishops flourished,[249] more and more Christians as well as pagans looked for alternative guides to salvation.[250] This search contributed to what Jonathan Smith[251] has described as a "utopian, diasporic or rebellious worldview," manifested in the rise to fame of the rootless holy man at the expense of the cleric and church/temple. Ascetics such as Antony, Hilarion, and Paul the Hermit took to living alone and in small communities in the deserts of Syria and Egypt.[252] Here, as elsewhere, Roman institutions that once seemed ordained by God had declined and men had only each other to turn to.[253]

Part of the holy man's attraction stemmed from his demonstration of God's enduring presence. Although many Christians in 400 C.E. may have believed that Christ's return was imminent, the fact remained that Christ had not been seen for several centuries.[254] The apostles and martyrs also

---

[247] Mathisen, *Roman Aristocrats in Barbarian Gaul*, 44.

[248] Ramsey, *The Sermons of St. Maximus of Turin*, 203–204, 212.

[249] MacMullen, "What Difference Did Christianity Make?," 340–341.

[250] Significant popular disdain for bishops and deacons is evident from the "Apocalypse of Peter," from circa 350 C.E, wherein bishops and deacons are referred to as "waterless canals." See Michael A. Williams, "The Life of Antony and the Domestication of Charismatic Wisdom." *Journal of American Academy of Religion Thematic Studies* 48 (1982): 23–45, 26. See also Michael P. McHugh, trans., *The Carmen de Providentia Dei Attributed to Prosper of Aquitaine* (Washington, DC: Catholic University of America Press, 1964), 293.

[251] *Map is Not Territory* (Leiden: E.J. Brill, 1978), 186–187. See also Phillip Rousseau, *Ascetics, Authority and the Church* (UK: Oxford University Press, 1978).

[252] Holy *women* also emerged in this period but are not represented in the same proactive roles as men. For instance, Mary the Egyptian was a penitent prostitute and Paula was a patroness of holy men. It is not known how representative Mary and Paula were of "holy women" and the extent to which women played a more dynamic role in the early Church. Averil Cameron, "On Defining the Holy Man." In *The Cult of the Saints in Late Antiquity and the Middle Ages*, eds. James Howard-Johnston and Paul Antony Hayward, pp. 27–45 (UK: Oxford University Press, 1999), 40–41.

[253] Peter Brown, *Society and the Holy in Late Antiquity* (Berkeley: University of California Press, 1982), 148–149.

[254] Norman Cohn, "Biblical Origins of the Apocalyptic Tradition." In *The Apocalypse and the Shape of Things to Come*, ed. Francis Carey, pp. 28–42 (Toronto: University of Toronto Press, 1999), 35. Arianism, which challenged Christ's divinity, brought forth

had become historical figures.[255] Theologians such as Eusebius tried to address this absence by writing a history of the Church that demonstrated continuity with the past.[256] But many Christians were illiterate; regardless, Christians required something more tangible than an intellectual argument, particularly in a world whose outward signs suggested that God had lost interest in his creation. The desert saints and their miracles provided just such a proof that God had *not* abandoned his creation.

Details of the ascetic communities organized by Pachomius in Egypt were brought to the West by John Cassian (c. 360–435 C.E.), who became a leading proponent of what was to become western monasticism. Following Cassian's lead, a small but significant number of aristocrats (e.g., Honoratus, Paulinus of Nola) and influential bishops and theologians such as Augustine and the "Cappadocian Fathers" (Basil, Gregory of Nyssa, and Gregory of Nazianzus) established ascetic communities or monasteries in various Mediterranean cities as well as in rural areas (often near sanctuaries to local saints). Cassian, among others, imagined these communities as producing preachers; certainly some (e.g., Lerins) if not most trained clergy to staff the bishoprics of Gaul and elsewhere.[257]

As noted earlier, during the fourth century the Church attracted large numbers of aristocrats who, as bishops, were little concerned with the state of the clergy or the large numbers of Gallo-Roman peasants and "barbarians" who remained ignorant of Christianity. What was largely a Roman and Gallo-Roman episcopacy retained notions that went back to writers such as Strabo and Tacitus, who derided the barbarians or Germanic peoples as primitive.[258] This lack of regard for "rustics" and

---

a strenuous reaction that further obscured Christ's humanity. Hillgarth, *Christianity and Paganism*, 86.

[255] Martyrs perhaps less so, owing to an "explosion" of martyr cults around the mid-fourth century (MacMullen, *Christianity and Paganism*, 120).

[256] Markus, *The End of Ancient Christianity*, 91.

[257] Hood, *St. Patrick*, 2–3.

[258] I. M. Ferris, *Enemies of Rome: Barbarians Through Roman Eyes* (Stroud, UK: Sutton Publishing, 2000); Mathisen, *Roman Aristocrats in Barbarian Gaul*, 27; Nico Roymans, "The Sword or the Plough. Regional Dynamics in the Romanization of Belgic Gaul and the Rhineland Area." In *From the Sword to the Plough: Three Studies on the Earliest Romanisation of Northern Gaul*, ed. N. Roymans, pp. 9–126 (Amsterdam: Amsterdam University Press, 1996), 101; Whittaker, *Frontiers of the Roman Empire*, 196.

barbarians was ameliorated at the end of the fourth century with the appearance of bishops who were inspired by the monastic movement or who were themselves monks.[259] Perhaps the best examples of these influential men were Martin of Tours (336–397 C.E.), Caesarius of Arles (470–543 C.E.), and the monk Columbanus (543–615 C.E.). All three distinguished themselves in different ways by facilitating the expansion of Christianity.

Monastic Exemplars

Martin of Tours was an ascetic monk in Gaul who was acclaimed bishop of Tours in circa 372 C.E.[260] We know a great deal about Martin, relatively speaking, thanks to his disciple, Sulpicius Severus,[261] and Gregory of Tours. Severus's *Life of Saint Martin*, which became perhaps the most influential of all Western hagiographies, detailed Martin's career as bishop, including his choice of a primitive shelter over the bishops' residence, and how Martin traveled about the countryside, winning converts to Christianity among the pagan population of Tours. In highlighting Martin's ascetic life and activism, Severus was neither subtle nor brief in his condemnation of Martin's ecclesiastical peers,[262] many of whom apparently preferred a life of comfort over one of engagement.[263] Importantly, during his quarter-century in office as bishop, Martin established at least two monasteries and trained over one hundred monks who carried on his "missionary agenda" both within and without Tours.[264]

---

[259] Victricius and Patrick were apparently the first bishops in the western empire to propagate the Gospel among barbarians. Chrysostom was unusual among eastern bishops in organizing missionary work among the nomadic Goths along the Danube. Liebeschuetz, *Barbarians and Bishops*, 170–171; Markus, *The End of Ancient Christianity*, 202; Thompson, *Romans and Barbarians*, 231.

[260] Stancliffe, *St. Martin and His Hagiographer*.

[261] It is important to keep in mind that Severus "overstated" Martin's uniqueness or singular contribution to the evangelization of Gaul. Ibid., 339–340.

[262] Hoare, *The Western Fathers*, 43.

[263] Ibid., 6; Raymond Van Dam, *Leadership and Community in Late Antique Gaul* (Berkeley: University of California Press, 1985), 126–127.

[264] Richard Fletcher, *The Barbarian Conversion: From Paganism to Christianity* (Berkeley: University of California Press, 1997), 47; Stancliffe, *St. Martin and His Hagiographer*, 333.

Martin of Tours died in 397 C.E. Although he and his followers greatly accelerated the conversion of rural pagans, a century after Martin's death most Christians still could be found in urban parishes or parishes on the outskirts of cities and towns.[265] These parishes were directly administered by bishops who retained exclusive control of incomes and the right to preach or expound on scripture. In theory, and often in fact, bishops were expected to dispense justice and redistribute wealth by supporting the poor, health care, education, public works, public spectacles, and other "social services."[266] In 527 C.E. and 529 C.E., the former monk Caesarius, who was now the head bishop or metropolitan of Arles, convinced his fellow bishops to relinquish some of their power. Parish priests and deacons for the first time were able to preach and were given control of parish finances.[267] These rights enabled large numbers of priests and deacons in suburban areas to essentially assume the role of missionaries, proactively disseminating and explaining the word of God to their still largely pagan parishioners. Equally important, priests and deacons were now empowered for the first time to use local financial resources in the war against paganism.[268] Caesarius was not only instrumental in empowering priests and deacons, but he armed them with over two hundred sermons (many focused on paganism) that were copied and used by priests in not only Gaul but throughout Europe.[269]

During the fourth and fifth centuries, urban and, to a lesser extent, rural parishes were the chief battleground of monks and clerics. Yet another battleground was large estates or villas under the control of aristocratic

---

[265] During the fourth century, the number of bishoprics in Gaul went from around 26 to almost 100; in northern Italy, the increase was more dramatic: from 5 to 50. Baus et al., *The Imperial Church*, 207; Lynch, *The Medieval Church*, 38.

[266] Baus et al., *The Imperial Church*, 213–217; Fletcher, *The Barbarian Conversion*, 51; Hoare, *The Western Fathers*, x–xv. Many of these responsibilities were spelled out in the *Apostolic Constitutions*, which date to the late fourth century. Chase, *The Constitutions of the Holy Apostles*, 12–78.

[267] Previously priests and deacons only were allowed to read scripture at Mass; they were not allowed to explain or expound on the Bible. Bishops also retained control of tithes and endowments of land or property made to a parish church. In Spain, this was the case until the seventh century.

[268] Klingshirn, *Caesarius of Arles*, 227–230.

[269] A. Ferreiro, "Early Medieval Missionary Tactics: The Example of Martin and Caesarius." *Studia Historica* (1988): 225–238, 228.

landlords who often built oratories or churches for themselves and their peasant following. Although the clerics who serviced these congregations generally were ordained by bishops, the resident clergy served at the behest of the landlord, who decided whether the priest could preach and otherwise evangelize peasants.[270] Not surprisingly, bishops such as Caesarius and Martin of Tours focused considerable effort converting and retaining the faith of these landlords. This much is apparent from a sermon by Maximus of Turin (c. 400 C.E.), where he scolded landlords for looking the other way while their serfs worshipped false gods:

> A few days ago I admonished your charity, brethren, that as devout and holy people you should remove every idolatrous pollution from your possessions and wipe out the entire Gentile error from your fields, for it is not lawful for you who have Christ in your hearts to have the antichrist in your houses or for your servants to worship the devil in shrines while you adore God in church. Nor should anyone consider himself excused, saying: "I didn't order this to take place, I didn't command it," for whoever realizes that a sacrilege is being committed on his property and does not forbid it from taking place has himself ordered it in a certain way.[271]

Perhaps more important than this scolding was the proliferation of monasteries during the fifth and sixth centuries – monasteries that provided trained clergy who staffed villa churches and helped ensure the faith of both aristocrats and their serfs.[272]

At the close of the sixth century, the landowning aristocracy among the northern Franks proactively recruited the Irish monk, Columbanus, and his followers to establish a network of monasteries on their estates.[273] Because the Irish did not share the Gallo-Roman tradition of cities and provincial organization, Columbanus and his fellow monks created a federation of monastic communities, each corresponding to a

---

[270] Klingshirn, *Caesarius of Arles*, 232.

[271] Ramsey, *The Sermons of St. Maximus of Turin*, 236.

[272] Stancliffe, *St. Martin and His Hagiographer*, 335.

[273] Before coming to the continent, from around 530–590 C.E., Celtic-speaking monks had distinguished themselves by leading a religious revival and winning large numbers of converts to Christianity in what is today Ireland, Scotland, Wales, and England.

kin-group and each under the jurisdiction of the "heir" of the founding monk or saint of the region.[274] This Irish "model" appears to have been particularly well suited to the equally nonurban traditions of Germanic peoples.[275] Although the existing Gallo-Roman episcopacy – the heirs of Martin and Caesarius – were suspicious of the Irish interlopers, Columbanus and his monastic following served the interests of northern Frankish aristocrats who embraced Christianity along with their peasants.[276]

The Missionary Challenge: Paganism

Martin, Caesarius, and Columbanus inspired and made possible the work of innumerable other monks and clerics who were the front-line soldiers in the war against paganism. Caesarius empowered priests to preach and provided them with sermons with which to evangelize; Martin and Columbanus established numerous monasteries where hundreds of monks were trained who continued the work of evangelization. Although the three men exemplify the role that religious played in the spread of Christianity, the dynamics of the process are not altogether apparent.[277] This is especially true with respect to the Franks and other Germanic peoples who left little in the way of commentary on how and why they embraced alternative behaviors and beliefs.[278] Even the hagiography of "missionary saints", such as Saint Martin, incorporate only a few chapters that deal with pagan acceptance of Christianity. The lives of the saints, although informative and clearly

---

[274] Patrick Geary, *Before France and Germany: The Creation and Transformation of the Merovingian World* (New York: Oxford University Press, 1988), 174.

[275] Russell, *The Germanization of Early Medieval Christianity*, 158.

[276] Geary, *Before France and Germany*, 177.

[277] Roger Collins, *Early Medieval Europe 300–1000* (New York: St. Martin's Press, 1999) 235, 249–250; Drinkwater, *The Gallic Empire*, 16; Fletcher, *The Barbarian Conversion*, 37; Frend, *Religion Popular and Unpopular*, 9–10; Hen, *Culture and Religion in Merovingian Gaul*, 7; Hinson, *The Evangelization of the Roman Empire*, 38, 277–279; LeGoff, *Medieval Civilization*, 120; James Muldoon, "Introduction: The Conversion of Europe." In *Varieties of Religion Conversion in the Middle Ages*, ed. James Muldoon, pp. 1–10 (Gainesville: University of Florida Press, 1997).

[278] Thompson, *Romans and Barbarians*, 230; Whittaker, *Frontiers of the Roman Empire*.

intended as normative, nevertheless represent a small sample of what were thousands of clerics and monks who effected the Christianization of Europe.[279]

As detailed later, the spread of Christianity entailed accommodation with paganism. Thus, paganism never was entirely "defeated."[280] Still, the fact remains that by the seventh century the majority of Europeans understood themselves as Christians, even if they kept a statue of Ceres or Cybele in their fields.[281] How did Christian monks and clerics realize this partial yet significant victory over paganism? The question is not easily answered, inasmuch as we know relatively little about the religious beliefs and practices of Celtic and Germanic peoples.[282] "Paganism" obscures what undoubtedly were diverse and complex systems of ritual and belief, which are known largely from Christian rather than pagan sources. Medieval hagiography, which is the most abundant literature from the Middle Ages, often incorporates narrative scenes that allude to paganism and its proponents (e.g., "the devil's familiars"). When paganism was discussed in some detail, as in the sermons of Martin of Braga, Caesarius of Arles, or Maximus of Turin, or in the works of Augustine or Isidore, pagan beliefs and ritual invariably were described in derogatory terms. Because most Christians, theologians included, believed that the *malefici* were in fact powerful, Christian writers were hesitant to go into detail with respect to pagan rituals, for fear that some might employ this knowledge for evil ends.[283]

As early as 341 C.E., the emperor Constantius outlawed sacrifice and in other ways curtailed the right of pagans to worship their gods. In 382 C.E., the emperor Gratian all but made Christianity the only imperial religion. Neither decrees nor the proclamations of lesser kings such as Clovis (c. 466–511 C.E.) destroyed paganism, particularly in the

---

[279] Ian Wood, "The Missionary Life." In *The Cult of the Saints in Late Antiquity and the Middle Ages*, eds. James Howard-Johnston and Paul Antony Hayward, pp. 167–183 (Oxford University Press, 1999), 180–181; *The Missionary Life: Saints and the Evangelisation of Europe, 400–1050* (London: Longman, 2001), 7–17, 247–250.

[280] Flint, *The Rise of Magic*.

[281] Amundsen, "The Medieval Catholic Tradition," 66; Brown, *Religion and Society*, 140–141.

[282] Flint, *The Rise of Magic*; Wood, *The Missionary Life*, 254–256.

[283] Flint, *The Rise of Magic*, 69.

countryside.[284] Well into the Middle Ages, pagans retained a belief in what might be described as "the immediate reality of an invisible world."[285] Reality was not simply what could be seen or felt; invisible forces or "spirits" were just as real and often more important, particularly as they were implicated in natural and other calamities. The challenge for pagans was to anticipate, or even better, harness the power of supernatural forces. Mountains and notably springs, unusual trees, and groves were understood by Celtic and Germanic peoples as places to engage the supernatural.[286] During late antiquity, the Celts often constructed simple enclosures and more formal shrines and temples near or at these otherwise sacred places. There votive offerings were made and propitiatory rites were conducted before local and regional Celtic deities (e.g., Lugh, an apparent sun god), who were depicted in various ways, including shape-shifters who assumed animal guises. Germanic peoples shared many aspects of Celtic religion, although they appear not to have had temples and a formal priesthood.[287]

By the fifth century – in the wake of a population collapse and the abandonment or decline of many towns and cities – most Celtic sanctuaries or temples seem to have disappeared or devolved into less formal centers of devotion and pilgrimage (e.g., open-air sites with wooden altars and stone images). As Halsall[288] has pointed out, Gregory of Tours's reference to a temple in the region of Trier is perhaps unique in all the literature from early medieval Gaul. Correspondingly, the Druids and whatever other formal priesthood once existed among the Celts seem to have disappeared by the sixth century. Secular as well as ecclesiastical texts, including penitential literature (manuscript guides used by clergy to mete out penance), imply that pagans had come to rely on diverse religious specialists. Early Christian literature mentions or describes *harioli,*

---

[284] Caseau, "Sacred Landscapes"; Ferreiro, "Early Medieval Missionary Tactics," 232; Stephen McKenna, *Paganism and Pagan Survivals in Spain up to the Fall of the Visigothic Kingdom* (Washington, DC: Catholic University of America, 1938), 42.

[285] I borrow this term from James T. Moore, *Indian and Jesuit* (Chicago: Loyola University Press, 1982).

[286] Pierre Chuvin, *A Chronicle of the Last Pagans*, trans. B.A. Archer (Cambridge, MA: Harvard University Press, 1990).

[287] Wood, *The Missionary Life*, 254–255.

[288] "Social Identities and Social Relationships," 157.

auspices, sortilegi, incantores, and other *malefici* who were accused of practicing witchcraft and sorcery, augury and divination, and astrology.[289] Some of these *malefici* also oversaw cults to the dead and nature, and supervised festivals and rites of the pagan calendar. In a sermon against soothsayers (*aruspex*), Bishop Maximus of Turin described one such group of *malefici* as ascetics who mortified their bodies:

> Let us briefly describe the appearance of a soothsayer of this kind. His head is unkempt, with long hair, his breast is bare, his legs are half hidden by a mantle, and, like a gladiator, he carries a sword in his hands and is prepared to fight. Indeed, he is worse than a gladiator because, while the one is obliged to struggle with someone else, he is compelled to fight with himself;...Judge whether this man, wearing this garb and bloodied with this carnage, is a gladiator or a priest.[290]

Gallic and Germanic communities were in fact well supplied with influential shamans and other mediators of the supernatural who dealt with weather, matters of the heart, prognostication of future events, and perhaps of greatest significance, sickness.[291]

Missionaries and Their Strategies

> Where once barbarian strangers or native brigands dwelt in deserted, equally hazardous areas of forests and shore, now cities, towns, islands and woods with churches and monasteries crowded with people and harmonious in peace, are thronged by revered, angelic choruses of saintly men.[292]

The above quote is from a letter that Paulinus of Nola (355–431 C.E.) wrote in circa 398 C.E. to Victricius, bishop of Rouen, praising Victricius for his missionary work. The quote is suggestive of the vagueness of early medieval sources with respect to how monks supplanted pagan *malefici*

---

[289] Amundsen, "The Medieval Catholic Tradition," 74.
[290] Ramsey, *The Sermons of St. Maximus of Turin,* 237.
[291] Flint, *The Rise of Magic,* 69.
[292] P. G. Walsh, trans., *Letters of St. Paulinus of Nola,* Vol. I, Letters 1–22 (Westminster, MD: Newman Press, 1966), 170.

and effected the spread of Christianity.[293] Victricius founded the first monasteries among barbarians in what is today Belgium and apparently encouraged Patrick to return to Ireland to convert the heathen Irish.[294] Not much more is known about Victricius other than the fact that he was a disciple of Martin of Tours.

In Sulpicius Severus's life of Saint Martin,[295] Martin is described as unabashedly toppling pagan shrines and temples and replacing them with churches. This aggressive approach, which was followed by later missionaries,[296] appears to be corroborated by archaeological evidence from Tours as well as other parts of Gaul.[297] Arguably in a "disease environment," among communities with a recent history of unprecedented calamity, missionaries who toppled idols were administering the *coup de grace* to rituals and beliefs that previously had been called into question by virtue of the failure of pagan religious to prevent, halt, and explain calamity. Medieval "missionaries" often, in fact, followed in the wake of disease, taking advantage of pagan interest in alternative "magic." During the sixth century, for instance, the Sueve king, Charraric, sent pilgrims to the shrine of Martin of Tours hoping to secure a cure for the king's ill son. The pilgrims apparently were successful and afterward the king welcomed a monk named Martin, who went on to become a highly successful missionary and bishop of Braga.[298] In 591 C.E., Pope Gregory sent missionaries to vigorously convert the Lombards, who were dying from the plague. Five years later, the plague prompted Gregory to "at once" organize another mission, this time to Kent, where a small group of monks reportedly baptized ten thousand.[299] According to Bede, "Almost at the same time that this kingdom had accepted the name of

[293] Richard M. Price, "The Holy Man and Christianization from the Apocryphal Apostles to St. Stephen of Perm." In *The Cult of the Saints in Late Antiquity and the Middle Ages*, eds. James Howard-Johnston and Paul Antony Hayward, pp. 215–240 (Oxford, UK: Oxford University Press, 1999), 236–238.

[294] R. P. C. Hanson, trans., *The Life and Writings of the Historical St. Patrick* (New York: Seabury Press, 1983), 23; Hood, *St. Patrick*, 4.

[295] Hoare, *The Western Fathers*, 26–29.

[296] Price, "The Holy Man and Christianization," 221.

[297] Stancliffe, *St. Martin and His Hagiographer*, 335; see also Caseau, "Sacred Landscapes," 32–36.

[298] Ferreiro, "Early Medieval Missionary Tactics," 230.

[299] Frend, *Religion Popular and Unpopular*, 18. On the negative side of the ledger, so to speak, during the Hun invasion of A.D. 451 the "barbarians" beheaded the Bishop

Christ, many of the kingdoms of Britian were attacked by a virulent plague."[300]

The aggressive approach employed by medieval missionaries, be they bishops or monks, often was made possible by pagan elites or kings who were won over with gifts and promises of access to trade.[301] Winning over a king or chief was an effective way for a missionary to ensure his personal success and safety,[302] particularly when the missionary aggressively waged a war on paganism.[303] However, rebuking pagans and destroying their sacred places and things was in any case risky, particularly when monks challenged what were long-established traditions such as the "worship" of trees.[304] Martin of Tours risked his life (he was miraculously saved) when he tried to cut down a pine tree that was considered sacred by a group of pagans.[305] During the early fourth century, some sixty Christians were massacred in reprisal for toppling a statue of Hercules in Sufes, Byzacena.[306] In Maximus of Turin's sermon on the Feast of Saint Alexander, he recounted how the deacon Alexander[307] and two clerics were killed in 397 C.E. when they attempted to build

---

of Rheims because he apparently failed to halt an epidemic of smallpox among the invaders. Hopkins, *Princes and Peasants*, 23.

[300] Colgrave and Mynors, *Bede's Ecclesiastical History*, 377.

[301] James Thayer Addison, *The Medieval Missionary, A Study of the Conversion of Northern Europe A.D. 500–1300* (Philadelphia: Porcupine Press, 1976); Ferreiro, "Early Medieval Missionary Tactics," 229; Lynch, *Christianizing Kinship*, 50–54.

[302] Stancliffe, *St. Martin and His Hagiographer*, 335.

[303] Lawrence G. Duggan, "For Force Is Not of God? Compulsion and Conversion from Yahweh to Charlemagne." In *Varieties of Religious Conversion in the Middle Ages*, ed. James Muldoon, pp. 51–62 (Gainesville: University Press of Florida, 1997); Richard E. Sullivan, "Early Medieval Missionary Activity: A Comparative Study of Eastern and Western Methods." *Church History* 23 (1954): 17–35; Thompson, *Romans and Barbarians*, 246–247. Wood has pointed out that scholars perhaps have been unduly influenced by Bede in emphasizing the role of kings in conversion, particularly to the exclusion of lesser political figures such as Frankish priests or monks who clearly were present in Britain before the Saxon invasion. Wood, *The Missionary Life*, 44–45.

[304] Stephen McKenna, *Paganism and Pagan Survivals in Spain up to the Fall of the Visigothic Kingdom* (Washington, DC: Catholic University of America, 1938), 150–151. Sacred trees were a common feature of Celtic religion, whereas temples with idols were of secondary importance, perhaps because of their Roman origins. Stancliffe, *St. Martin and His Hagiographer*, 337–338.

[305] Hoare, *The Western Fathers*, 28–29.

[306] Hinson, *The Evangelization of the Roman Empire*, 64–65.

[307] At this time, rural churches often were administered by deacons. McKenna, *Paganism and Pagan Survivals*, 26–27.

a church in the Val di Non in the Tyrol ("among whom the Christian name had not been known before").[308]

Destroying pagan sacred places or things did not necessarily induce respect for their Christian replacements.[309] Indeed, the missionary who brashly toppled an idol and, in the process, challenged the religious caretakers of the idol, established a precedent by which the missionary and his own "idols" might subsequently be judged and replaced. It was apparently for these reasons that bishops at the Council of Elvira in 306 C.E. issued a canon instructing wealthy Christians *not* to destroy the pagan idols of their slaves when doing so was likely to arouse the slaves to violence. The same council concluded that individuals killed in the act of destroying pagan images were *not* entitled to the honors usually paid to martyrs of the faith.[310]

Rather than wage an aggressive war on paganism, hagiographic and other sources suggest that many Christian monks and clerics challenged yet tolerated competing magical practices.[311] Martin of Tours toppled pagan shrines but "more often" subdued pagans with his preaching.[312] This more strategic approach was followed by other would-be missionaries,[313] including Martin of Braga, who was instrumental during the sixth century in the spread of Christianity among the Sueves of northwestern Spain.[314] In response to a request from one of his bishops, Polemius from Astorga, who wanted to know how best to reform pagan practices, Martin wrote an influential and much-copied sermon "reforming

---

[308] The three were killed after they rebuked the people for conducting a purification rite ("lustrum") that entailed a procession of sacred objects around a field or village. Ramsey, *The Sermons of St. Maximus of Turin*, 232–234.

[309] Flint, *The Rise of Magic*, 94; see also Price, "The Holy Man and Christianization," 219–225.

[310] McKenna, *Paganism and Pagan Survivals*, 34.

[311] Flint, *The Rise of Magic*, 222.   [312] Hoare, *The Western Fathers*, 29.

[313] Wood, *The Missionary Life*, 256–258.

[314] In circa 550 C.E, Martin founded a monastery at Dumium, not far from the capital of Braga, where he was elected bishop in 556 C.E. By 572 C.E. Martin had been chosen metropolitan and had twelve bishops from the region under him. He is perhaps best known for his sermon on converting the rustics; he also is credited with establishing several monasteries in Galicia, including one near Braga at Dumium. McKenna, *Paganism and Pagan Survivals*, 104–105; Claude W. Barlow, trans., *Iberian Fathers, Volume I: Martin of Braga, Paschasius of Dumium, Leander of Seville* (Washington, DC: Catholic University of America Press, 1969), 3.

the rustics," which reflected both insight into paganism and a noncoercive strategy to combat it.[315] Rather than view pagans as co-conspirators with Satan, Martin saw them as victims:

> Then the devil or his ministers, the demons who had been cast out of heaven, seeing that ignorant men had dismissed God their Creator and were mistaking the creatures, began to appear to them in various forms and speak with them and demand of them that they offer sacrifices to them on lofty mountains and in leafy forests and worship them as God, assuming the names of wicked men who had spent their whole lives in crime and sin, so that one claimed to be Jupiter, ... Another demon called himself Mars, ... Then another demon chose to name himself Mercury.[316]

By tolerating what were powerful shamans, the missionaries retained for difficult times a theological foil (the devil's "familiars") and scapegoat for calamities.[317] It was in fact common during epidemics in the Middle Ages for Christians to vacillate between Christian and pagan claimants to divine power.[318] Missionaries on the frontier met such challenges by shifting the blame for epidemics to the *malefici* and by inventing and reinventing, if necessary, Christian responses to disease and other calamities. Along these lines, whereas Church theologians focused on eternity and represented the sacraments as aids to the next life, missionaries strategically interpreted the liturgy, sacraments, and especially the cult of saints and relics as a means of addressing real-world problems, particularly sickness.[319] Some of the earliest prayer books (*Libri ordinum*) that preserve the rituals of the Visigothic Spanish Church indicate, for instance, that blessings and prayers for the sick were directed primarily toward the health of the body.[320] In the sixth century, in the wake of the plague,

---

[315] Barlow, *Iberian Fathers*, 71–85.   [316] Ibid., 74.

[317] Flint, *The Rise of Magic*, 80–82.

[318] Dalton, *History of the Franks*, II, 461–463.

[319] Amundsen, "The Medieval Catholic Tradition," 73; Flint, *The Rise of Magic*; Russell, *The Germanization of Early Medieval Christianity*, 189; Stancliffe, "From Town to Country," 58–59; Sullivan, "Early Medieval Missionary Activity," 28–30.

[320] Paxton has pointed out that Gallican and Irish prayers differ in that they appear to focus on purifying the soul and ensuring the "health" of eternal salvation. Yet Paxton also notes that there are more surviving witnesses to rites for the sick than to any other ritual of the early Irish church. Paxton, *Christianizing Death*, 70–71, 78–79, 202.

Caesarius of Arles preached that anointing the sick should be offered as an alternative to magical, non-Christian healing practices.[321] It also has been suggested that apocalyptic and millenarian ideas (the impending last judgment) that became popular during the early Middle Ages helped many pagans accept the reality of recurrent disease, particularly the plague.[322]

Flint has persuasively argued that the great popularity during the early medieval period of treatises on the "nature of things" (*De Natura Rerum*), which intertwined scientific and theological explanations for eclipses, earthquakes, and other natural phenomena, were written primarily to provide monks and clerics with insights to counter those of pagan magi (e.g., disease was not the result of elf shot but carried by the wind or clouds and sent by God as chastisement).[323]

Arguably, it was through the cult of the saints and their relics, particularly the complete skeletons of widely known saints,[324] that Christian missionaries gained the upper hand with pagan *malefici*. By moving or "translating" relics to a local church or shrine, which often were built over pagan shrines, the missionaries effectively recouped or appropriated pagan traditions.[325] This transference of emotion apparently was facilitated in part by the Celts' prior personification of supernaturals and the construction of altars and formal shrines under the Romans. Aboriginally, the Celts and other pagan peoples built ossuaries for their revered dead, from whom they apparently sought help when dealing

---

[321] In another of his sermons, Caesarius complained that clerics employed pagan along with Christian practices to deal with "…every kind of infirmity." Sister Mary Magdeleine Mueller, O.S.F., *Saint Caesarius of Arles: Sermons*, Vol. I (1–80) (New York: Fathers of the Church, Inc., 1956), 254.

[322] Biraben and Le Goff, "The Plague in the Early Middle Ages," 60–61.

[323] Valerie I. J. Flint, "Thoughts About the Context of Some Early Medieval Treatises *De Natura Rerum*." In *Ideas in the Medieval West: Texts and Their Contexts*, ed. Valerie I. J. Flint, pp. 1–31 (London: Variorum Reprints, 1988), 28.

[324] Although the skeleton generally was translated in its entirety to a local shrine (usually in the saint's home country), it was not uncommon for the bones to be disarticulated and used to establish subsidiary shrines or churches. Ronald C. Finucane, *Miracles and Pilgrims: Popular Beliefs in Medieval England* (Totowa, NJ: Rowman and Littlefield, 1977), 28–29.

[325] Pamela Berger, *The Goddess Obscured* (Boston: Beacon Press, 1985), 37–76; Howe, "The Conversion of the Physical World," 66.

with life's uncertainties.[326] Although Teutonic traditions are poorly understood, there is some evidence that among the Franks and other Germanic "tribes," cults to Odin and Thor and their shrines and amulets were reimagined in terms of Christ, his loyal saints, and their shrines and relics.[327]

The cult of the saints built upon pagan traditions[328] yet provided pagans with what were touted as new supernatural advocates and protectors, particularly against disease. People were healed of all sorts of ailments at saints' shrines, or so we are told by Gregory the Great, Gregory of Tours, Sulpicus Severus, and other sacred biographers.[329] By the sixth century, a network of shrines with tombs or fragments of dead bodies was established throughout much of the western Roman Empire.[330] The extension of this network continued throughout the Middle Ages and was instrumental in the spread of Christianity to northern Europe.[331]

Alongside the cult of the saints, the monks introduced Christian festivals and a calendar that were consistent with aboriginal experience,

---

[326] James, *Exploring the World of the Celts*; Bruce W. Lincoln, *Myth, Cosmos, and Society: Indo-European Themes of Creation and Destruction* (Cambridge, MA: Harvard University Press, 1986), 12.

[327] Russell, *The Germanization of Early Medieval Christianity*, 189.

[328] Frantisek Graus (cited in Pizarro) points out that one of the most characteristic qualities of relics during the Middle Ages was that they functioned "automatically"; relics exercised their power whether they were in the possession of a thief or a priest, and whether one invoked them with prayer or touched them by accident. This automatism contradicts the doctrine of grace and reflects the extent to which Christianity accommodated pagan thought and practices. Joaquín Martínez Pizarro, *A Rhetoric of the Scene: Dramatic Narrative in the Early Middle Ages* (Toronto: University of Toronto Press, 1989), 202. See also Flint, *The Rise of Magic*, 76; Hinson, *The Evangelization of the Roman Empire*, 64–65.

[329] The analysis of surviving miracle reports from English and European shrines between the twelfth and fifteenth centuries indicates that over nine-tenths of the miracles involved cures of human illnesses. Finucane, *Miracles and Pilgrims: 59*.

[330] Peter Brown, *Society and the Holy in Late Antiquity* (Berkeley: University of California Press, 1982), 6.

[331] Amundsen, "The Medieval Catholic Tradition," 71; Finucane, *Miracles and Pilgrims*, 20; Flint, *The Rise of Magic*, 79; Brown has gone so far as to argue that the cult of the saints is central to explaining the different histories of the Church in the West and Byzantium. *Society and the Holy*, 139–140.

particularly the agricultural cycle.[332] The most important half of the Christian liturgical year corresponded with the time between the winter and summer solstices. The church's emphasis during this period on Christ's cosmic suffering and eventual victory paralleled the day-to-day experiences of pagans, who endured cold and meager food until early summer. The annual Christian feast of Rogation (celebrated for three days before Ascension, the sixth Thursday after Easter) also bespeaks accommodation with the Roman feast of Robigalia and a still earlier Celtic tradition of removing or placating evil spirits. Much like Robigalia, Rogation entailed a procession around the parish perimeter, purifying and blessing the parish and its fields.[333]

The Monastery as Mission: The "Plan of St. Gall"

The monks who effected the spread of Christianity were not "islands unto themselves."[334] They were uniformly associated with monasteries that came to dot the European countryside during the early Middle Ages. Relatively little is known about the size, layout, or functioning of monasteries prior to the ninth century or Carolingian times.[335] In circa 830 C.E., what were probably several monks and scribes drew up a highly detailed architectural plan known as the "Plan of St. Gall." It is not known if this plan was the blueprint for an actual monastery of the same name, which was constructed in the ninth century in what is today Switzerland. Not enough of St. Gall has survived to determine precisely what the monastery looked like and the relationship it bore to the plan.

---

[332] John D. Cox, "Drama, the Devil, and Social Conflict in Late Medieval England." *The American Benedictine Review* 45 (1994): 341–362; Flint, *The Rise of Magic*, 187–188; Le Goff, *Medieval Civilization*, 181.

[333] Cox, "Drama, The Devil and Social Conflict," 348. See also Edward James, ed., *Gregory of Tours: Life of the Fathers* (Liverpool, UK: Liverpool University Press, 1991), 26; John Howe, "The Conversion of the Physical World." In *Varieties of Religious Conversion in the Middle Ages*, ed. James Muldoon, pp. 63–78 (Gainesville: University Press of Florida, 1997).

[334] Fletcher, *The Barbarian Conversion*, 46.   [335] Pickles, *Texts and Monuments*.

Some years ago, Sullivan[336] suggested that the very breadth of the plan, which covered some 3.5 hectares and included forty separate buildings as well as open spaces for gardens and a cemetery/orchard, implied that it served encyclopedic purposes, providing abbots and their patrons with a schematic "menu of options" to choose from when designing or renovating a monastery. Braunfels[337] likewise considered the plan an "ideal model," meant to inspire reflection on monasticism. However, not all agree with Sullivan and Braunfels that the Plan of St. Gall was a "theoretical model." Price has noted that the street pattern and alignment of houses clustering around the present-day church of St. Gall "reflect with amazing accuracy" the boundaries of the monastery as sketched out in the Plan of St. Gall.[338] Riché also has pointed out that the extent and complexity of St. Gall is entirely consistent with what we know of other Carolingian monasteries such as Saint Riquier.[339]

The Plan of St. Gall is striking in that it imagined the monastery as fully engaged with secular society, rather than a world unto itself. The Plan features an integrated set of buildings, courtyards, and gardens where the monks could pursue a communal religious life (Figure 5). This more "contemplative space" articulated with and was intruded upon by courtyards, structures, and use areas that essentially hosted the outside world. Significantly, almost 10 percent of St. Gall was dedicated to health facilities, which were clustered in one quarter of the monastery (infirmary; physicians house with pharmacy and sick ward; house for bleeding; two bath houses; a medicinal herb garden).[340] The fact that the novitiate and infirmary were in identical, adjoining quarters[341] suggests that novices spent a good deal of time caring for the

---

[336] Richard E. Sullivan, "What Was Carolingian Monasticism?" In *After Rome's Fall: Narrators and Sources of Early Medieval History, Essays Presented to Walter Goffart*, ed. A. Callander Murray, pp. 251–289 (University of Toronto Press, 1998).

[337] Wolfgang Braunfels, *Monasteries of Western Europe* (Princeton, NJ: Princeton University Press, 1972), 37.

[338] Lorna Price, *The Plan of St. Gall* (Berkeley: University of California Press, 1982), 87.

[339] Pierre Riché, *Daily Life in the World of Charlemagne*, trans. Jo Ann McNamara (Philadelphia: University of Pennsylvania Press, [1973]1978), 38.

[340] Lorna Price, *The Plan of St. Gall*, 32.   [341] Ibid., 28.

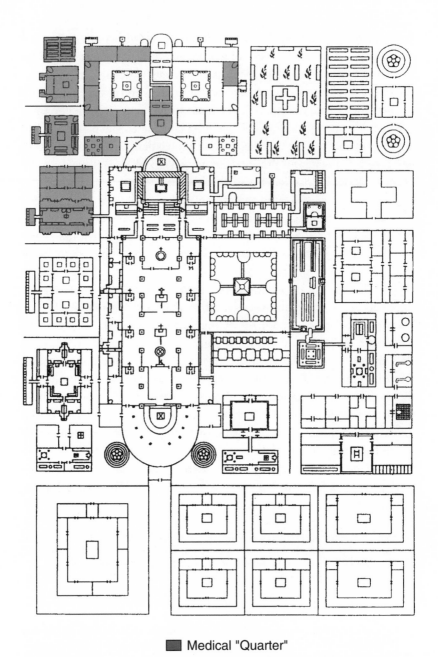

Medical "Quarter"

Figure 5. Plan of St. Gall (After Riché, *Daily Life in the World of Charlemagne*, 19).

sick. The Plan of St. Gall also includes an external school to educate the laity (apparently the children of nobility), and still other structures and facilities to feed and care for pilgrims, paupers, serfs, visiting dignitaries, and people from almost all walks of life, women perhaps excluded.[342] Significantly, rather than being a technological backwater – what one might assume characterizes a "retreat from the world" – the Plan of St. Gall casts the monastery as a repository of cutting-edge knowledge with respect to architecture, horticulture, the use of mechanical devices, milling, metalworking, pottery production, and, again, health care.

What are we to make of the Plan of St. Gall? Was it a new and perhaps radical conception of monastic life, or was it an idealized summation of all that had come before? Monastic historical studies have tended to cast the monastic experience as an exercise in withdrawal, foreign to the mainstream of human endeavor.[343] Scholars often have described early medieval monasticism in terms of isolated communities little concerned with the lives and souls of pagans or fellow Christians. Addison,[344] for instance, stated that it was not until Boniface in the early eighth century that medieval missionaries made conversion of pagans central rather than incidental to their lives. In describing "Bede's monasticism," his exegetes emphasize Bede's concern with the church, the library, and the scriptoria.[345]

The study of monasticism has long focused on the normative writings of its founders,[346] who often extolled the virtues of asceticism and world renunciation.[347] Yet the beginnings of monasticism were surrounded by

---

[342] Sullivan, "What Was Carolingian Monasticism?," 274.

[343] Richard E. Sullivan, *Christian Missionary Activity in the Early Middle Ages* (Brookfield, VT: Variorum [1979]1994), 26, 41–42, f. 5.

[344] "The Medieval Missionary," 6–7, 12–13.

[345] Colgrave and Mynors, *Bede's Ecclesiastical History*, xxv.

[346] Susanna Elm, *"Virgins of God": The Making of Asceticism in Late Antiquity* (Oxford: Clarendon Press, 1994), 8.

[347] Markus, *The End of Ancient Christianity*, 160–161. Walter Daniel's *The Life of Aelred of Rievaulx* (circa 1167 C.E.) offers a particularly good example of what arguably was a long tradition of brevity or silence about how the outside world reached into and articulated with the monastery. See Marsha Dutton, "Introduction to Walter Daniel's *Vita Aelredi.*" In *Walter Daniel: The Life of Aelred of Rievaulx*, trans. F. M. Powicke, pp. 7–89 (Kalamazoo, MI: Cistercian Publications, 1994), 80–81.

debate over Christian perfection.[348] Origen (c. 185–253 C.E.) had argued that contemplation was an important yet preliminary step toward perfection; it helped the individual overcome evil inclinations and then ascend to God through a life of charity. In the fourth century, Evagrius (346–399 C.E.) essentially stood Origen on his head, arguing that Christian perfection presupposed becoming "insensitive" to the world; only then could one concentrate solely on God and love of God.[349]

Evagrius's teachings were brought to the West along with knowledge of Pachomian monasticism by John Cassian and was embraced by later theologians such as Gregory the Great. Although known for uniting action and contemplation, Gregory the Great more frequently celebrated the quiet life:[350]

> For my unhappy soul wounded with worldly business does now call to mind in what state it was, when I lived in my Abbey, and how then it was superior to all earthly matters, far above all transitory and corruptible self, how it did visually think upon nothing but heavenly things.[351]

Sacred biography does indeed emphasize how farmers like Antony and aristocrats like Paulinus of Nola or Benedict of Nursia found God by becoming "dead to the world." Yet these same biographies indicate or suggest that withdrawal from society, while an avenue of *gnosis*, infrequently served the ends of divine providence. With some notable exceptions (e.g., Paul the Hermit), the desert fathers and saints reunited with the secular world.[352] Many rejoined society or were overwhelmed

---

[348] Giles Constable, *Three Studies in Medieval Religious and Social Thought* (Cambridge, UK: Cambridge University Press, 1995), 14–33. Lynch, *The Medieval Church*, 30–31; Stancliffe, *St. Martin and His Hagiographer*, 102; Williams, "The Life of Antony," 32.

[349] Thomas M. Gannon, S.J., and George W. Traub, S.J., *The Desert and the City: An Interpretation of the History of Christian Spirituality* (London: Macmillan, 1969).

[350] Jean Leclerq, O.S.B. *The Love of Learning and the Desire for God* (New York: Fordham University Press, 1982), 28.

[351] D. M. Rogers, ed., *The Dialogues of S. Gregorie: English Recusant Literature 1558–1640*, Vol. 240 (UK: Scolar Press, 1975 [1608]).

[352] Cameron, "On Defining the Holy Man," 38; Alison Goddard Elliott, *Roads to Paradise, Reading the Lives of the Early Saints* (Hanover, NH: University Press of New England, 1987), 178; Le Goff, *The Medieval Imagination*, 56.

by a society seeking them. Antony and his monastic heirs invariably emulated Christ's Galilean ministry – caring for the sick, exorcising demons, and in other ways translating supernatural power into *social* power. The fourth-century historian Sozomen noted that the Syrian monk Hilarion, distinguished himself by fighting demons, curing diseases, bringing relief to the poor and oppressed, chastising tax collectors, and conversing with the emperor.[353] Similarly, Paulinus of Nola (355–431 C.E.), one of the most passionate advocates of "flight," remained committed to the poor and works of charity.[354]

The Evagrian idea that *gnosis* presupposed world renunciation necessarily elicited a rejoinder,[355] inasmuch as the previous history of the Church and indeed Christ's own life were characterized by engagement. In his life of Antony, which presents the earliest and perhaps most celebrated model of ascetic life, Athanasius seemingly went out of his way to point out that one need not be an ascetic or live in the desert to draw close to God.[356] Another of Evagrius's contemporaries, Augustine, also was critical of those who equated world-renunciation with Christian perfection. For Augustine what was critical or essential to monastic life was unspoiled human relationships.[357] In his *City of God*, Augustine

---

[353] Sister Marie Liguori Ewald, trans., "Life of St. Hilarion by St. Jerome." In *The Fathers of the Church, Volume 15: Early Christian Biographies*, ed. Roy J. Deferrari, pp. 241–280 (New York: Fathers of the Church, 1952), 241; Frend, *Religion Popular and Unpopular*, 15.

[354] P. G. Walsh, trans., *Letters of St. Paulinus of Nola*, Vol. I, Letters 1–22 (Westminster, MD: Newman Press, 1966), 13.

[355] Charles F. Keyes, "Charisma: From Social Life to Sacred Biography." *Journal of American Academy of Religion Thematic Studies* 48 (1982): 1–45.

[356] Michael A. Williams, "The Life of Antony and the Domestication of Charismatic Wisdom." *Journal of American Academy of Religion Thematic Studies* 48 (1982): 23–45. See also Henry Chadwick, "Pachomios and the Idea of Sanctity." In *The Byzantine Saint: University of Birmingham Fourteenth Spring Symposium of Byzantine Studies* (San Bernardino, CA: The Borgo Press, 1980), 63–64. McNary-Zak has suggested that this valuing of coenbitic over semi-eremetic practice was not solely because of Athanasius but also disciples of Antony who may have produced a version of the Life of Antony, which Athanasius edited or otherwise revised. Bernadette McNary-Zak, *Letters and Asceticism in Fourth-Century Egypt* (New York: University Press of America, 2000), 97.

[357] It was not that Augustine emphasized engagement with the world through charity but, rather, that life in a brotherhood governed by humility and charity rather than a life of isolation and asceticism mattered most in terms of Christian perfection. Markus, *The End of Ancient Christianity*, 80.

noted such relationships reflected a balance of contemplation and action:

> No man must be so committed to contemplation as, in his contemplation, to give no thought to his neighbor's needs, nor so absorbed in action as to dispense with the contemplation of God.[358]

In his *Conferences*, Cassian essentially imagined the monastery as a brotherhood of love that embraced both contemplative and active lives, with the former emphasizing the study of scripture and the latter preaching. Cassian never implied that monasticism should entail a separation from the rest of society, particularly as he imagined the monastery as producing preachers.[359] In the *Thebaid*, Pachomius established monasteries that were tied economically, socially, and spiritually to nonreligious communities and individuals.[360] As Goehring[361] has noted, Egyptian monasticism – contrary to the literary sources – was neither in its origins nor its subsequent expansion a flight from the inhabited world.

The Monastery as Hospital

> In this utter seclusion he [Abbot Salvius d. 584] lived in greater abstinence than ever; but was careful, in obedience to the law of charity, to give all guests from without his prayers, and with readiest kindliness to offer them bread of oblation, by which many a time sick men were made whole.[362]

The Plan of St. Gall certainly implies a worldly embrace, particularly of the sick. Many early medieval monasteries in the West embraced

---

[358] Vernon J. Bourke, ed., *Saint Augustine: The City of God* (New York: Image Books Doubleday, 1958), 467.

[359] See Markus, *The End of Ancient Christianity*, 188, 192; Boniface Ramsey, O.P., trans., *John Cassian: The Conferences* (New York: Paulist Press, 1997), 22–23.

[360] Phillip Rousseau, *Pachomius: The Making of a Community in Fourth-Century Egypt* (Berkeley: University of California Press, 1985), 149–173.

[361] James E. Goehring, "Withdrawing from the Desert: Pachomius and the Development of Village Monasticism in Upper Egypt." *Harvard Theological Review* 89 (1996): 267–285, 272.

[362] Dalton, *History of the Franks*, II, 285.

the spirit if not the "Rule" of Basil of Caesara, who was perhaps the greatest proponent of linking asceticism and charity and who made care of the sick and poor an imperative for monks.[363] As noted, the "Rule of St. Augustine" (c. 423 C.E.) likewise emphasized a common life of charity devoted to the sick, aged, and others requiring charity.[364] Still later, the much followed, sixth-century Rule of Benedict admonished monks to "take the greatest care of the sick, of children, of guests, and of the poor."[365]

Monk-physicians were common during the early Middle Ages and generally extended care out of charity.[366] As Amundsen[367] has noted, early Christian literature often relates how miraculous healing followed medical failures. This theological emphasis often has been misunderstood and the Church has been seen as hostile to science, especially medicine.[368] However, medicine was a standard part of medieval curriculum and often was pursued by clerics.[369] Monastic *scriptoria* produced more than "religious texts"; they were the major source of medical manuscripts during the Middle Ages. Like Christianity itself, texts such as the Anglo-Saxon *Lacnunga* bespeak accommodation with pagan culture, inasmuch as they are composite medical texts, incorporating knowledge and practices from various traditions (e.g., Greek, Roman, Celtic, Teutonic, Byzantine). Significantly, manuscripts such as the *Lacnunga* speak of "monastic rites" targeted specifically to acute infectious diseases such as smallpox ("*variola*," "the deadly pock").[370]

Peasants who showed up at the monastery were comforted with medicines as well as rituals such as anointing, confession, and even

---

[363] Roberta Gilchrist, *Contemplation and Action: The Other Monasticism* (London: Leicester University Press, 1995); Patricia A. Quinn, *Better Than the Sons of Kings* (New York: Peter Lang, 1989), 17–19.

[364] Lucas, *Landmarking*, 62.

[365] Amundsen, "The Medieval Catholic Tradition," 83.

[366] Flint, *The Rise of Magic*; Paxton, *Christianizing Death*.

[367] "The Medieval Catholic Tradition," 82.   [368] See also Flint, *The Rise of Magic*, 151.

[369] C. H. Talbot and E. A. Hammond, *The Medical Practicioners in Medieval England: A Biographical Register* (London: Wellcome Historical Medical Library, 1965), vi.

[370] J. H. G. Grattan and Charles Singer, *Anglo-Saxon Magic and Medicine* (London: Oxford University Press, 1952), 25, 201–203.

self-flagellation, which became a prescribed means of public penance and provided an immediate, albeit violent, release from guilt, enabling the participants to identify with the suffering of Christ.[371] Whereas the public penance of the early Church often was harsh and humiliating,[372] it appears to have been particularly so for elites, who were made an example of by bishops; the vast majority of Christians atoned for their sins on their deathbed. As the trend toward private as opposed to public penance suggests, early medieval monks and clerics were more likely to have consoled penitents (again, particularly peasants as opposed to elites), reminding them of an omnipotent, inscrutable, and yet beneficent god, who held out the promise of relief in an afterlife. Note that Augustine's rather severe view on predestination was quickly (in 426 C.E.) moderated by monks in Gaul, led by Cassian, and within a decade or so, by Prosper of Aquitaine and Pope Leo the Great. Leo, in particular, argued that God's salvic will was truly universal and responded to human free will.[373] Augustine also found an adversary in Pelagius and his disciple Celestius, who argued in favor of humankind's innate goodness and capacity to emulate a simple and virtuous life.[374] The "guilt trip" laid on everyone by Augustine also was ameliorated by a finely articulated penitential system that emerged during the sixth century and the belief that punishment could be avoided or deflected through prayer and sacrifice.[375]

As previously noted, many monks were champions of the cult of the saints – saints like their own Martin of Tours. By the end of the fifth century, monks throughout Europe had become stewards of monastic

---

[371] Amundsen, "The Medieval Catholic Tradition," 96; M. L. Cameron, *Anglo-Saxon Medicine* (Cambridge, UK: Cambridge University Press, 1993).

[372] Fletcher, *The Barbarian Conversion*, 138–139.

[373] Philip L. Barclift, "Predestination and Divine Foreknowledge in the Sermons of Pope Leo the Great." In *History, Hope, Human Language, and Christian Reality*, ed. Everett Ferguson, pp. 165–182 (New York: Garland Publishing, 1999).

[374] B. R. Rees, ed., *Pelagius, Life and Letters* (Woodbridge, England: Boydell Press, 1998), I, 3, 19; II, 7.

[375] Brown, *Religion and Society in the Age of Saint Augustine*, 135; Peter Brown, "The Decline of the Empire of God." In *Last Things: Death and the Apocalypses in the Middle Ages*, eds. C. W. Bynum and P. Freedman, pp. 41–59 (Philadelphia: University of Pennsylvania Press, 2000); Pierre J. Payer, *Sex and the Penitentials, The Development of a Sexual Code 550–1150* (University of Toronto Press, 1984).

chapels and churches that housed the relics of local martyrs who purportedly cured disease.[376]

The important role played by monks during epidemics is evident in Gregory of Tours's *History of the Franks*, which dates to the end of the sixth century. During an epidemic of plague in 571 C.E., Gregory noted:

> It was at this time that the priest Cato died. Many had fled from this pestilence; but he never left that place, burying the people, and courageously saying his masses. This priest was a man of great humanity and devoted to the poor; and if his character inclined somewhat to pride, this charity tempered it. Bishop Cautinus, after going from place to place in his fear of the pest, died upon Good Friday, the very hour that Tetradius his cousin perished. Lyons, Bourges, Chalon, and Dijon lost much people through this sickness.[377]

A striking aspect of the above quote is the suggestion that bishops like Cautinus fled the plague, rather than tending to the sick and needy, as did the monk, Cato. Gregory went on to discuss another cleric-monk named Julian in the monastery of Radan (in Clermont) who also sacrificed his life caring for the sick.[378] Again, by contrast, Gregory noted how during a devastating epidemic in Marseilles, around 590 C.E., bishop Theodore withdrew to his church "... there throughout the whole calamity he gave himself up to prayers and vigils, imploring God's mercy, that at last the destruction might have end, and peace and quiet be granted to the people."[379]

Although today we might read Gregory's comments on the different responses of monks and bishops as an implied critique of the latter, such a reading would be anachronistic. As de Nie[380] has pointed out, many Christians at the time were convinced that prayer was the most effective way to deal with a crisis, including epidemics.[381] Such reasoning

---

[376] MacMullen, *Christianity and Paganism*, 121.
[377] Dalton, *History of the Franks*, II, 142.   [378] Ibid., II, 141–142.
[379] Ibid., II, 396.
[380] Giselle de Nie, *Views From a Many-Windowed Tower: Studies of Imagination in the Works of Gregory of Tours* (Amsterdam: Rodopi, 1987), 51.
[381] Gregory, who was bishop of Tours, actually imitated Theodore when the epidemic reached his own diocese (as did the new Pope Gregory, who busied himself with prayer when the epidemic reached Rome).

is not difficult to understand, when we keep in mind that this was an age that celebrated God's enduring presence. God was always listening and attentive, and, whereas he may have given the demons license to inflict pain and suffering on sinners, he was not unforgiving or unreceptive toward those who would seek his forgiveness. Although this view was shared by monks and bishops alike, it is significant that monks like Cato and Julian not only prayed but also cared for the sick and needy.

The Monastery as Center of Economic Life

As noted, the Plan of St. Gall includes dormitories, kitchens, storage facilities, and other structures and use areas to feed and accommodate the poor. This aspect of the plan was anticipated by Athanasius in his life of Antony, where Antony recounted how he first depended on others for bread and then with a hoe, axe, and some grain, he became self-sufficient and then refreshed others.[382] Monasticism as it was developed in the east by Pachomios (d. 346) required monks to care for each other as well as the less fortunate. During the tumultuous third and fourth centuries, large numbers of peasants flocked to the Pachomian colonies that sprang up in the Egyptian desert.[383] Here they were fed, housed, and integrated into socioreligious communities where monks "engaged in every sort of handicraft" (including shipbuilding) as well as agriculture,[384] generating enormous surpluses of grain. At times these surpluses were even sent to Libya and Alexandria to feed the needy.[385] Similarly, in the region about Constantinople, there are numerous remains of monasteries from the fifth century that appear to have functioned as centers of Christian charity as well as asceticism.

---

[382] Sister Mary Emily Keenan, S.C.N, trans., "Life of St. Antony by St. Athanasius." In *The Fathers of the Church, Volume 15: Early Christian Biographies*, ed. Roy J. Deferrari, pp. 127–121 (New York: Fathers of the Church, Inc., 1952), 180–181.

[383] Chadwick, "Pachomios and the Idea of Sanctity," 20–22.

[384] Goehring, "Withdrawing from the Desert," 273; Rousseau, *Pachomius: The Making of a Community*, 82–86.

[385] Rene Fulop-Miller, *The Saints that Moved the World* (Salem, NH: Ayer Company, 1945), 75.

Many of these monasteries apparently owed their origins in part to John Chrysostom, bishop of Constantinople. Chrysostom, like Evagrius, first believed that salvation presupposed the life of an ascetic. Later, he abandoned this notion and privileged charity as the essential duty and means of salvation.[386]

Many monasteries in the West came into being during the fifth and sixth centuries when wealthy nobles made gifts of estates to groups of monks. These land grants usually included slaves and nominal freemen[387] who paid "rents" in kind to the monks.[388] Whereas Roman and Gallic nobles commonly exploited and overburdened their slaves and serfs (*coloni*) – channeling surpluses into civic monuments and conspicuous consumption – monastics were encouraged to redistribute their "wealth." Such encouragement was implicit in a communal, nonpropertied existence focused on charity and asceticism. For those abbots who lost sight of these principles, there were often explicit reminders from respected theologians. Thus, Cassiodorus, writing about the mid-sixth century, reminded abbots and monks that:

> The very rustics who belong to your monastery you must instruct in good behaviour, and not increase the load of their legal obligations.... Let a second order of monasticity (*conuersationis*) of the present character be imposed upon them; let them frequently assemble at the holy monasteries; and let them blush to be yours, if they are not recognized to be of your own institute. Let them know that God graciously grants fertility to their lands, if they are in the habit of invoking Him with faith.[389]

Note that, during the early Middle Ages, there were large numbers of "rustics" or laypeople who pursued "a second order of monasticity,"

---

[386] J. H. W. G. Liebeschuetz, *Barbarians and Bishops: Army, Church, and State in the Age of Arcadius and Chrysostom* (Oxford: Clarendon Press, 1990), 180.

[387] These freemen were bound to the land by the Justinian Code and the law of Constantius.

[388] Dom John Chapman, *Saint Benedict and the Sixth Century* (New York: Longmans, Green and Co., 1929), 154.

[389] Ibid., 159.

serving and partaking of life in religious communities, yet continuing to act in a worldly manner.[390]

The earliest monastic communities (Tabennese and Pbow), which were founded by Pachomius in circa 330 C.E., who himself died from plague in 346 C.E., entailed the resettlement of villages that appear to have been depopulated by epidemics.[391] Some if not many monastic communities in the West also owed their existence to small cadres of pioneer monks who homesteaded previously abandoned villas and farms and previously unworked tracts of marsh and forest. Frankly, we do not know a great deal about these monastic foundations. Works like Bede's *Ecclesiastical History* and ruins from Ireland (e.g., Inishmurray) and Scotland suggest a small collection of buildings, generally enclosed by a compound wall, and including a dormitory, refectory, and storage facilities (Figure 6).[392] From what were humble beginnings,[393] the earliest monasteries became sources of stability in what Paxton has described as "a sea of poverty, famine, plague, disorder, and commercial atrophy."[394] This stability was due in part to the "rules" that ordered daily life, which helped ensure regular food surpluses.[395] By the eighth century, many monasteries in the west followed the Rule of St. Benedict. Although Chapters 40 and 50 indicate that monks might harvest crops and do other agricultural work when necessary, Chapter 48 is quite explicit that monks were not expected to engage in agricultural work on a regular basis.[396] It may well be that many monastic communities, particularly after 650 C.E., were successful because the monks stimulated and reorganized local agricultural production, receiving surpluses as income, which were then redistributed or channeled into craft production and

---

[390] Harry Neff Waldron, "Expressions of Religious Conversion Among Laymen Remaining Within Secular Society In Gaul, 400–800 A.D." Ph.D. Dissertation, Ohio State University, Columbus, 1976.

[391] Goehring, "Withdrawing from the Desert," 277.

[392] Colgrave and Mynors, *Bede's Ecclesiastical History*, xxv; Pickles, *Texts and Monuments*, 132–133.

[393] Addison, *The Medieval Missionary*, 78.

[394] Paxton, *Christianizing Death*, 67. See McCormick, *Origins of the European Economy*, for a more in-depth picture of Europe in the early Middle Ages.

[395] Boswell, *Kindness of Strangers*, 251; Quinn, *Better than the Sons of Kings*, 28–31; Wood, *The Missionary Life*, 259.

[396] Chapman, *Saint Benedict and the Sixth Century*, 170–172.

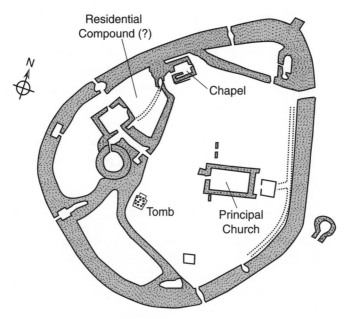

Figure 6. Plan of the Monastic Ruins of Inishmurray (After Heraughty, *Inishmurray, Ancient Monastic Island*, 20).

trade. Although Benedict did not apparently imagine his monks spending their "free time" farming, he did expect them to devote six hours a day working at what were at the time important trades such as carving in wood and stone and working in iron, brass, and ceramics.[397]

With Cassiodorus's example, Benedictine monasteries became sanctuaries of ancient wisdom and centers of new learning. Because many monastic communities could not depend or rely wholly on external sources of labor (slaves or freemen), some of this new learning was channeled into labor-saving devices such as water mills, plows, and other technology, contributing to what Lynn White has called the agricultural revolution of the early Middle Ages. In places like Gaul, the

---

[397] Chapman, *Saint Benedict and the Sixth Century*, 170–172; see also Constable, *Three Studies*, 28; Leclerq, *The Love of Learning*, 12–24; Richard Kieckhefer, "Imitators of Christ: Sainthood in the Christian Tradition." In *Sainthood, Its Manifestations in World Religions*, ed. Richard Kieckhefer and George D. Bond, pp. 1–42 (Berkeley: University of California Press), 17–19.

decline of Gallo-Roman civil administration during the fifth century meant the demise of municipal schools; monks and clerics became the new "teachers" in society at large.[398] Although speaking particularly of the eighth-century monastic foundations of Benedict, Addison's[399] comment that they served the surrounding areas as ecclesiastical, educational, agricultural, and industrial centers may well apply to monastic foundations more generally.[400] It was presumably for this reason that Daniel of Winchester advised Boniface to point out to pagans how much better off Christians were in terms of worldly possessions.[401]

The Monastery and the [Re]Ordering of Social Life

Addison[402] has aptly noted that Celtic monasteries were in a sense tribal institutions – centers of family relation that served as a school and asylum for all who were related by blood to the monastic founder or patron. What was true of Celtic monasteries was probably true of monasteries elsewhere in western Europe, inasmuch as kinship also was a key to social life among Germanic peoples.[403] In this regard, the Plan for St. Gall reflects a centuries-old tradition of providing for the well-being of children. Children were a part of monastic life in many of the earliest cenobitic settlements of Syria and Egypt. They were subsequently welcomed in the monasteries founded and organized under Basil's "rule."[404] Children also were commonplace in the early monastic communities of the West, although it is not clear that this was oblation as opposed to education or fostering.[405] It appears that many if not most children who were reared in monasteries were given to the Church under informal

---

[398] Raymond Van Dam, *Leadership and Community in Late Antique Gaul* (Berkeley: University of California Press, 1985), 133.

[399] *The Medieval Missionary*, 92–93.

[400] See also Lynch, *The Medieval Church*, 33–34; Gilchrist, *Contemplation and Action*.

[401] Sullivan, *Christian Missionary Activity in the Early Middle Ages*, 717.

[402] *The Medieval Missionary*, 76.

[403] Geary, "Barbarians and Ethnicity," 111; Riché, *Daily Life in the World of Charlemagne*, 263–268. Thompson in fact argued that a major reason why Germanic groups such as the Tervingi embraced Arianism was that the notion of a son subordinate to the Father resonated with German social structure. E. A. Thompson, *The Visigoths in the Time of Ulfila* (Oxford: Clarendon Press, 1966).

[404] Quinn, *Better than the Sons of Kings*, 24.   [405] Boswell, *Kindness of Strangers*, 230.

or individual arrangements.[406] Although the Rule of St. Benedict and subsequent canonical legislation resolved, in theory, the status of oblates – donated children became irrevocable wards of the monastery – in practice, parents could reclaim their oblated children and significant numbers left the monastery of their own free will upon reaching adulthood.[407]

In the past, scholars have tended to emphasize particular meanings or functions of oblation, reflecting in part their own predicament of culture.[408] Thus, some have seen it as a religious act rooted in Judeo-Christian theology (e.g., *I Samuel* 1:11; *Mark* 10:4, 14); others have emphasized how it fit the material conditions of life (sociocultural upheaval); still others have emphasized how oblation was an expression of age-old social structures, particularly patron–client relationships and other dependency relationships realized through fictive kinship.

The reception of children in a variety of ways suggests that the assimilation and rearing of children in monasteries fulfilled various functions and was understood to have various meanings.[409] Certainly oblation – or something like it – was rooted in "pagan" experience. In the first century B.C.E., Caesar noted with respect to the Druids:

> ...a great number of young men gather about them for the sake of instruction...many are sent by parents and relatives.... Report says that in the schools of the Druids they learn by heart a great number of verses, and therefore some persons remain twenty years under training.[410]

Given this Celtic tradition, and the profound dislocations resulting from disease, famine, and migration, it makes sense that oblation became institutionalized in early medieval Europe.[411] Most peasant households during this period probably had no more than two children.[412] This

---

[406] Ibid., 251. [407] Ibid., 244.

[408] In this regard, De Jong has unfairly criticized Boswell for reflecting "contemporary sensibilities," as if she or any of us can do otherwise. Mayke De Jong, *In Samuel's Image: Child Oblation in the Early Medieval West* (New York: E.J. Brill, 1996), 5.

[409] Boswell, *Kindness of Strangers*, 228, 235.

[410] Edwards, *Caesar: The Gallic War*, 337–339.

[411] Boswell, *Kindness of Strangers*, 198. [412] Lynch, *Christianizing Kinship*, 206.

was hardly a great "surplus." And yet, in the face of epidemics and famine, many poor parents donated or "exposed" their children, believing monasteries would provide for the children.[413] Because parents often maintained ties to the monasteries where they donated their children, the monasteries were indebted to the parents. Arguably oblation was another form of fictive kinship and coparenthood,[414] which provided social and economic alliances and networks to replace lineage and clan-based systems that were torn apart by epidemics. Children who might have been a drain on their parents – much like the abandoned villas taken over by monks – became productive members of the monastery, and by extension, society.[415] Many children grew up to become monks or clerics,[416] and still others who left the monastery (well disciplined and educated) took up leadership roles in society. In this regard, oblation was perhaps the greatest contributor to the "rise of Christianity" in early medieval Europe. It was always difficult for pagan adults to forgo customs and beliefs that had been passed down over generations. As Caesarius of Arles understood, the key to eradicating pagan "superstitions" was to remove the young people from the process of transmission. Thus, at the Council of Vaison in 529 C.E., Caesarius moved to have young unmarried men leave their homes in his diocese of Arles to receive a Christian upbringing in the homes of local priests. This was already a common practice in Italy[417] and paralleled oblation at monasteries throughout Europe.

Conclusion

Ancient society was unrelentingly brutal and precarious, and the world of Gregory of Tours was no exception. As in modern underdeveloped countries most people had to cope with squalor, misery, and grinding poverty. Senseless violence and cruelty were common. . . . Intemperate

---

[413] Boswell, *Kindness of Strangers*, 256–257.   [414] Lynch, *Christianizing Kinship*.

[415] Boswell, *Kindness of Strangers*, 241.

[416] In Spain and presumably elsewhere a main reason why oblation was adopted was that it held out the promise of creating a corps of missionaries and bishops to win converts to Christianity and combat heresy. Quinn, *Better than the Sons of Kings*, 28.

[417] Klingshirn, *Caesarius of Arles*, 230, 241–242.

weather could easily disrupt agrarian production. An enormous swarm of locust, a late frost, a heavy hailstorm, an extended drought – any of these catastrophes caused local famines that demoted people to the level of animals, forced to eat stalks and grass. Harsh living conditions, inadequate nutrition, and the constant sicknesses and disabilities also reduced people to a subhuman existence.[418]

Life, at a minimum, was difficult during late antiquity and the early Middle Ages. As we have seen, the downturn in human fortunes began during the late second century, coincident with the appearance of new and more virulent forms of infectious disease. Over the course of the next five centuries, smallpox, measles, malaria, and the plague (to name only those of which we are reasonably sure) claimed millions of lives. We know from authors such as Galen that epidemics at times spread "throughout the Roman Empire," affecting Gaul and Spain and presumably more distant provinces such as Britain.

Acute and chronic infectious diseases exacted an enormous toll on Greco-Roman civilization in Rome and other cities of the Mediterranean. Here Christianity won many of its first converts, principally among the underprivileged but also among merchants and aristocrats. Diseases like measles and smallpox do not respect privilege. The nascent Church also was universal, welcoming rich and poor. Although it is obviously difficult to infer what moved countless individuals to accept Christianity, the Christian "message" was conveyed in rhetoric that was highly figural and metaphoric. In keeping with the Gospels, where Christ often spoke in parables, early Christian texts presented religious truth in signs and symbols along with rational argument.[419] Such rhetoric had the advantage that it could be variously interpreted and tailored to different audiences and times. Significantly, during late antiquity and the early Middle Ages, bishops, deacons, and later monks interpreted and popularized Christian sacraments as rituals to heal sick bodies.

Some years back, Ramsay MacMullen[420] posed the question, "What difference did Christianity make?" His answer was, "very little,"

---

[418] Raymond Van Dam, *Saints and Their Miracles in Late Antique Gaul* (Princeton, NJ: Princeton University Press, 1993), 82.

[419] Cameron, *Christianity and the Rhetoric of Empire*, 48, 50.

[420] "What Difference Did Christianity Make?"

particularly when it came to sexual norms, slavery, corruption, judicial violence, and gladiatorial games. Although early Christian literature exaggerates the degree to which deacons, clerics and later monks cured the sick, it does so to make a point that was otherwise valid – Christians were *more* successful than their pagan counterparts in dealing with epidemic disease and other calamities. Christian "missionaries" – those clerics and monks who established Christian communities among pagans – owed their success to what by the fourth century already was a centuries-old tradition of charity and care of the sick and homeless, including young children. The monks who fanned out over Europe during the early Middle Ages offered a whole host of beliefs and practices, everything from formal rites or sacraments to simple prayers, pilgrimages, and religious dramas, which built upon as well as transcended pagan traditions. As was the case with the ritual of Rogation, Christian practices were not simply pagan practices in "new dress," implying that Christian meanings (conveyed through the liturgy) were lost or irrelevant. As Cox[421] has pointed out, what were traditional pagan concerns and ritual – proactively ensuring harmony and negating the power of evil daemons within a bounded area (i.e., a village) – were complemented by narratives that spoke of the life and struggle of Jesus and all Christians who were at war with the daemons of old, now "better" defined by Christian narratives.

Rather than wage a war against idolatry, most successful (and long-lived) monks attracted pagans through charity and benevolence and by living holy lives, worthy of the saints whose relics worked miracles in the here and now.[422] Monks like Martin of Tours, Martin of Braga, and Columbanus offered pagan communities other worldly benefits, including relief from tax collectors[423] and an audience with aristocrats and emperors.[424]

To acknowledge the importance of disease and the material benefits of Christian ritual and clerics/monks is not to discount the "power

---

[421] "Drama, the Devil, and Social Conflict in Late Medieval England," 347–352.
[422] Addison, *The Medieval Missionary*, 80; Finucane, *Miracles and Pilgrims*, 25.
[423] Frend, *Religion Popular and Unpopular*, 15.
[424] Hoare, *The Western Fathers*, 35.

of ideas" or social constructions. Ideas presuppose living (and dying) human beings. The development of Christian theology often followed or was coincident with new realities requiring interpretation and meaning.[425] Too often Christian "ideas" and discourse about charity, virginity, suffering, and so on, have been divorced from daily life. Historically, philosophically idealist theories and strategies – viewing the rise of Christianity in terms of great men and great ideas – has led to the marginalization of historical humans.[426] More recant scholars like Foucault[427] and Le Goff[428] have been "minimalist" in their own right, casting the rise of Christianity in terms of the replacement of "cheerful other worlds" with a preoccupation with purgatory and hell, enforced by "exhaustive and permanent confession." From such a perspective, "the Church" appears as a monolithically sinister regime of power; pagans for the most part lack agency and mimic Greco-Roman stereotypes of "rustics" and "barbarians."[429]

Neither "the Church" nor "pagans" were monolithic. The same Church that brought pain to bear on the human body, paradoxically, showed "obsessive compassion" for the afflicted poor.[430] The same Church that promulgated rules against marriage between close kin to apparently gain control of property used that property to feed and care for orphans, widows, and other faithful.[431] For every bishop who preached of hell and the sin of fornication, there were others such as Martin of Braga who preached of charity and warned of the devil's snares.[432]

---

[425] Lynch, *Christianizing Kinship*, 16.

[426] Russell T. McCutcheon, *Manufacturing Religion: The Discourse on Sui Generis Religion and the Politics of Nostalgia* (Oxford, UK: Oxford University Press, 1997), 22–23.

[427] *The History of Sexuality*, 125.

[428] *Medieval Civilization*, 187.

[429] Relatedly, Goldhill has noted that Foucault's "panoptic vision" of ancient sexuality ignores the agency of ancient readers of erotic narratives. Simon Goldhill, *Foucault's Virginity: Ancient Erotic Fiction and the History of Sexuality* (Cambridge, UK: Cambridge University Press, 1995), 44–45.

[430] Brown, *The Body and Society*, 441.

[431] Jack Goody, *The Development of the Family and Marriage in Europe* (Cambridge, UK: Cambridge University Press, 1983), 46–47.

[432] Even Augustine, who is famous for his doctrine of concupiscence and repression of sex, expected bishops to preach not on sexual sins but *sclera*, violence, fraud, and oppression. Brown, *The Body and Society*, 424–425.

People who were possessed, ill, or otherwise polluted essentially were seen as victims of Satan.[433] Through participation in the sacraments and by enlisting one's guardian angel and a saint(s), the individual, and by extension, the community could negate the devil and his influence. True, the laity's guilt quotient was increased significantly by Augustine (human beings, not Satan, were to blame for sin), but this guilt was ameliorated by the idea that misfortune was a consequence of a *collective* failure to fulfill some promise or covenant with supernaturals. Guilt also was assuaged by a finely articulated penitential system to correct prior imbalances.[434]

The rise of Christianity between 150 and 800 C.E. is the story of millions of pagans who contributed as much as Augustine, Eusebius, and other well-known theologians to Christianity. The "masses" did not get to author the historical record or Christian literature. This silence should not be mistaken for a lack of agency. Lost to history are thousands of pagan converts, many of whom became clerics and monks, who interpreted Christian theology and ritual in accordance with pagan traditions. This is perhaps most apparent in the the cult of the saints, which was central to the Christianity embraced by pagan Europe. The cult of the saints shifted the focus of Christianity from a somewhat distant God to local heroes who once "dead," continued to act as protectors. In significant ways, the cult of the saints represented a continuation of pagan traditions as well as an embrace of the particularly Christian belief in the incarnation. The story of the Gospels is the story of the Holy Spirit alighting in a mere mortal, Mary, who then gives birth to the son of God. Saints are likewise "normal folk" who are filled with the Holy Spirit and who evidence the divine.

The rise of Christianity in Europe is the rise of the cult of the saints, and correspondingly, a Church that was enormously diverse. As Finucane has noted, during the early Middle Ages there was not only French, German, Spanish, and Irish "Churches," but, within each, hundreds of Christian communities that often were led by a semiliterate cleric who was related through kinship (real and fictive) to his peasant congregation – a congregation that embraced Christ's passion and the

---

[433] Flint, *The Rise of Magic*, 153–154.   [434] Brown, *Religion and Society*, 135.

cult of the saints, all the while it "muttered charms over their ploughs and whispered magic words at crossroads."[435] This Church of pre-Carolingian times (prior to 800 C.E.) was quite different from the Church of the later Middle Ages, which better approximates an all-powerful "regime of power" with a [relatively speaking] totalizing discourse.

[435] Finucane, *Miracles and Pilgrims*, 10.

◄◦►

THREE

Disease and the Rise of Christianity in the New World

The Jesuit Missions of Colonial Mexico

It is common knowledge that Latin America is "*muy Católico*," although after a half-century of Protestant missionary work it is perhaps more accurate to say that many or most Latin Americans understand themselves as Christian. In Mexico, urban gangs as well as grandmothers embrace the Virgin of Guadalupe. That they do so for different reasons (just as grandmothers and IRA members in Ireland embrace St. Patrick for different reasons) is less significant than the fact that it is the mother of Jesus who is claimed as a protector.

Of course it was not always so. The "rise of Christianity" in Latin America began some 500 years ago, following Columbus's fateful "discovery." Spanish colonization of the Caribbean and then Mexico featured hundreds of missionaries and clerics who in a relatively short span (c. 250 years) won millions of Indians and mestizos to Christianity. As was the case in early medieval Europe, "conversion" rarely meant the wholesale abandonment of indigenous beliefs and practices. Still, just as most people in sixth-century Iberia or Gaul understood themselves as Christian, so it is today with Mexicans and other "Latin" Americans.

In this chapter, I focus on the rise of Christianity in northern Mexico. Beginning in 1591, the Jesuits over the course of a half-century baptized over four hundred thousand Indians and established dozens of missions across what is today northern Sinaloa, Sonora, southern Chihuahua, and northern Durango. The vast literature produced by the Jesuits, including their annual reports (*anuas*) and published narratives such as the *Historia*, provide an unparalleled commentary on the early colonial period. A critical reading of this commentary reveals that the Indian embrace of the Jesuits and Christianity was coincident with epidemics of the same acute and chronic infectious diseases (e.g., smallpox, measles, malaria) that cast a pall over the lives of the first Christians in the late Roman Empire. Note in this regard that there is little evidence that Native Americans suffered in pre-Columbian times from epidemic diseases that were comparable to those brought to the New World by Europeans.[1] By 1492, after over one thousand years of repeated exposure, Europeans had acquired genetic traits that promoted resistance to *variola* and other pathogens, which devastated Amerindians. The fact that Europeans went unscathed during contact-period epidemics was not lost on surviving Indians, who were left with untold dead and a knowledge base (oral traditions) that had been destroyed or fragmented through the loss of many elders.

The Jesuits followed in the wake of disease, and like early Christian deacons, monks, and clerics in Europe, they reorganized economic, social, and religious life. In doing so, they followed strategies that were over one thousand years old, reconstituting indigenous systems as well as introducing beliefs and practices, especially the cult of the saints, to deal with unprecedented realities.

I begin by briefly surveying the work of the Mendicant orders (Franciscans, Dominicans, Augustinians) who preceded the Jesuits in southern Mexico. The discussion then turns to the Jesuits, who produced a much more voluminous and in many ways insightful literature on how and why Indians took an interest in Christianity and mission ways of life.

---

[1] This may be explained in part by the Indians' relative lack of domesticated animals, particularly chickens, horses, pigs, and cattle. Diseases like measles, smallpox, and influenza are thought to have arisen first among domesticated animals and subsequently became killers of Europeans. Indians did suffer from tuberculosis, trepenomial, and other diseases, which, on occasion may have reached epidemic proportions. John Verano and Douglas Ubelaker, *Disease and Demography in the Americas* (Washington, DC: Smithsonian Institution Press, 1992); Stodder et al., "Cultural Longevity and Biological Stress in the American Southwest." In *The Backbone of History*, eds. R.H. Steckel and J. Rose, pp. 481–505 (Cambridge, UK: Cambridge University Press, 2002).

The "Primitive Church" of the Mendicants

As noted in the Introduction, the Jesuits were conscious that their New World missions paralleled the primitive Church of late antiquity as well as the Church of the early Middle Ages. The Mendicants also drew parallels between themselves and the apostles,[2] yet they infrequently cast themselves in the mold of early medieval saints, who, as we have seen, spread Christianity to the more interior and rural parts of Europe. Arguably the Mendicants' more apostolic view of their mission enterprises reflects in part the more urban-like character of the Mendicants' theater of operations in Mexico.

The first "primitive church" of the Apostles arose in the cities of Mediterranean Europe. Correspondingly, the Mendicants, particularly the Franciscans, who were the most numerous and active of the three orders, worked primarily in the more densely populated, southern third of Mexico.[3] At the time of Cortés's capture of Tenochtitlan, in 1521, southern Mexico was dotted with hundreds of large villages and towns as well as cities such as Tenochtitlan, which had a population of around 200,000. Tenochtitlan and the valley of Mexico (the seat of Mexica power) were to southern Mexico what Rome was to Mediterranean Europe in the second century C.E. The Mexica empire was in significant ways (e.g., economically, politically, militarily, artistically, and scientifically) analogous to the Roman Empire, despite its smaller scale. Some fifty million people were governed/affected by the Roman Empire at its height; perhaps ten million Indians were affected by decisions made by the Mexica in the Valley of Mexico.

---

[2] J.L. Phelan, *The Millennial Kingdom of the Franciscans in the New World*, 2nd ed. (Berkeley: University of California Press, 1970 [1956]); David A. Lupher, *Romans in a New World, Classical Models in Sixteenth-Century Spanish America* (Ann Arbor: University of Michigan Press, 2003).

[3] Beginning in 1546, the Franciscans also established a small number of missions north of Zacatecas, in and along the eastern slopes of the Sierra Madre Occidental. In 1598 they also initiated an extensive missionary enterprise in New Mexico. See William B. Griffen, *Indian Assimilation in the Franciscan Area of Nueva Vizcaya*, Anthropological Papers of the University of Arizona 33 (Tucson: University of Arizona Press, 1979); John L. Kessell, *Kiva, Cross, and Crown* (Albuquerque: University of New Mexico Press, 1987), *Spain in the Southwest* (Norman: University of Oklahoma Press, 2002).

As we have seen, many of the earliest converts to Christianity in Europe came from among the urban poor who suffered through the Antonine Plague (165–185 C.E.) and subsequent dislocations coincident with more epidemics, famine, migration/invasion, and the general failure of Roman sociopolitical systems. Much the same context obtained in southern Mexico coincident with the Spanish invasion of Mexico. Villages and towns throughout southern Mexico initially were devastated by smallpox, which the Spanish brought ashore in Veracruz in 1521.[4] After facilitating Cortés's capture of the Mexica capital, smallpox reached pandemic proportions, affecting southern Mexico, central America, and eventually Peru. Between 1520 and 1525, smallpox killed at least several million Indians in southern Mexico.[5]

Much like the Antonine Plague, the smallpox pandemic of 1520 and 1525 was soon followed by epidemics of other Old World diseases that spread throughout the Mexica Empire and beyond. Between 1530–1534, southern Mexico was besieged by a pandemic of measles, which again, claimed millions of lives. In 1545, typhus made its appearance in Nueva España. The "great matlazahuatl," as it was known in Nahuatl, raged for several years, destroying what some eyewitnesses believed was the bulk of the remaining Indian population.[6] By 1550, the population of southern Mexico also was assailed by chronic infectious diseases, notably malaria, which became endemic along the southeastern and western coasts of Mexico (Figure 7).

Although scholars disagree as to whether the losses numbered as "low" as 5 million or as high as perhaps 15 million, there is a consensus

---

[4] Smallpox was current in Cuba and was brought to Mexico in the form of an infected soldier who was part of an expedition sent by the Governor of Cuba, Velasquez, to arrest Cortés for his unauthorized invasion of Mexico.

[5] These early epidemics were discussed in some detail by Mendieta, and to a lesser extent, by Motolinía. Fray Geronimo de Mendieta, *Historia Eclesiastica Indiana*. 2 vols., ed., Francisco Solano y Perez-lila (Madrid: Ediciones Atlas, 1973 [1585]), II, 97–100; Fray Toribio de Benavente Motolinía, *Historia de los Indios de la Nueva España*, ed. Edmundo O'Gorman (Mexico: Editorial Porrua, 1969 [1541]; For an English-language edition of the latter, see Elizabeth Andros Foster, *Motolinías History of The Indians of New Spain* (Berkeley: The Cortés Society, 1950).

[6] Juan de Grijalva, *Cronica de la Orden de N.P.S. Augustin en las provincias de la Nueva España...de 1533 hasta el de 1592* (Mexico: Imprenta Victoria, 1924 [1624]), 214.

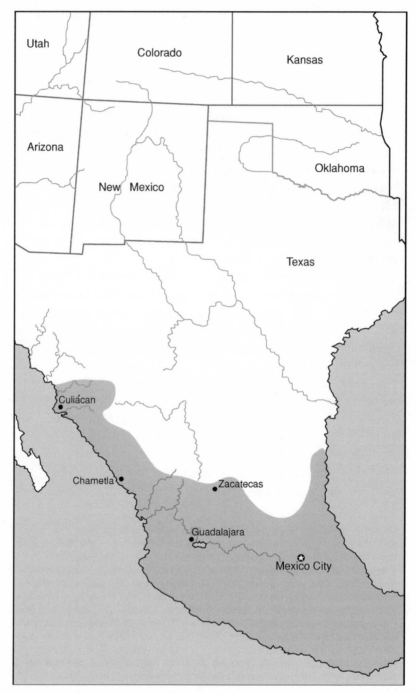

Figure 7. Area of Mexico Affected by Disease by 1550.

that by 1575, Spanish-introduced diseases had destroyed half or more of the Indian population of southern Mexico. During the third quarter of the sixteenth century, Mexico as a whole enjoyed a respite of sorts from major contagions. However, during this time the development of the Spanish mining frontier to the north enlarged the pool of susceptibles, setting the stage for another round of epidemics, which beginning around 1575, regularly began to affect northern as well as southern Mexico. By 1600, the Indian population of southern Mexico had been reduced by close to 90 percent, to a little more than one million.[7]

In colonial Mexico, then, as in early medieval Europe, the rise of Christianity was coincident with a population collapse. Only a few short years after this collapse began, in 1524, the first of many contingents of friars reached Mexico. The "Friars minor" or Franciscans concentrated their efforts in the Valley of Mexico, Puebla, and later, in Michoacan to the west. They were soon joined by the Dominicans, who worked primarily in and around Mexico city and in Oaxaca, among the Mixtec and Zapotec. The Augustinians, who were relative "late comers" (arriving in Mexico in 1533), established several strings of convents radiating out of the Valley of Mexico, most notably to the north and east of Tenochtitlan, among the Otomí and Huaxteca (Figure 8).

Between 1524 and 1572, the Mendicants baptized at least several million Indians – many of whom died – and established over 150 convents, monasteries, and lesser religious "houses" where they attended to the spiritual needs of the Indians and a rapidly emerging mestizo population. In the wake of disease, the friars reorganized the remnants of indigenous pueblos into Christian communities that now paid tribute,

---

[7] Woodrow Borah and Sherburne F. Cook, *The Aboriginal Population of Central Mexico on the Eve of the Spanish Conquest*, Ibero-Americana 45 (Berkeley: University of California Press, 1963); Nobel David Cook, *Born to Die, Disease And New World Conquest, 1492–1650* (Cambridge, UK: Cambridge University Press, 1998); Sherburne F. Cook and W. W. Borah, *The Indian Population of Central Mexico: 1530–1610*, Ibero-Americana 44 (Berkeley: University of California Press, 1960); Charles Gibson, *The Aztecs Under Spanish Rule* (Stanford, CA: Stanford University Press, 1964), 138; Daniel T. Reff, *Disease, Depopulation and Culture Change in Northwestern New Spain, 1518–1764* (Salt Lake City: University of Utah Press, 1991), 97–119; Verano and Ubelaker, *Disease and Demography*.

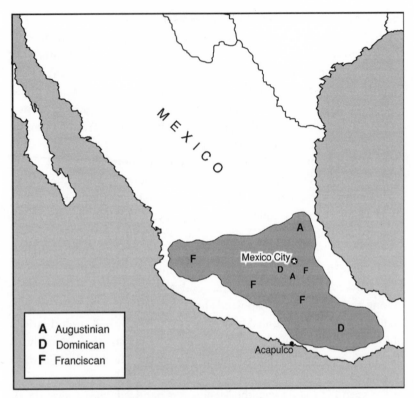

Figure 8. Areas of Mendicant Missionary Activity to 1570 (After Ricard, *The Spiritual Conquest of Mexico*, 62–63).

both symbolic and material, to new lords and deities.[8] As was true of the first "primitive church," Indians from all walks of life, particularly the poor, embraced the friars and their offer of a ritual cleansing of the soul. In imitation of the apostles, the friars preached and conducted baptisms in "open chapels," later erecting single-nave churches.[9] Although the Mendicants were tied to the political establishment – quite the

---

[8] Influential scholars such as Ricard said next to nothing about the role of disease in the "spiritual conquest" of Mexico. Phelan acknowledged disease and its demographic consequences, but ignored the sociocultural consequences of disease and its role in the Franciscan's "millennial kingdom." Robert Ricard, *The Spiritual Conquest of Mexico* (Berkeley: University of California Press, 1966 [1933]); Phelan, *The Millennial Kingdom*, 92–96, 155.

[9] Phelan, *The Millennial Kingdom*, 49–50.

opposite of the leaders of the first primitive church, who were oppressed by the Roman government – the friars emulated early Christians in their often fierce opposition to government policies and the efforts of Spanish civilians to exploit the Indians. Because many friars emulated Christ and the desert saints, embracing asceticism and works of charity, many Indians were persuaded the friars were truly men of God. Indian acceptance of the friars was enhanced by the latter's measured respect for Indian customs, which followed from the friars' mastery and use of indigenous languages.[10] The continuation of native traditions was further encouraged by Mendicant reliance on Indian catechists to nurture and sustain Indian conversion. As late as 1560, there were relatively few regular or secular priests in southern Mexico.[11] Like the semi-literate deacons and clerics of early medieval Europe, Indian catechists or *fiscales*, together with their Indian charges, took considerable latitude interpreting and re-imagining Christian beliefs and ritual.

By the friars' own admission, their "primitive church" lasted little more than forty years. In 1562, Fray Mendieta publicly lamented how the asceticism and unselfish efforts of the first generation of friars had given way to a bureaucratic routine, and worse yet, discouragement.[12] To make matters worse, the friars, who were previously united in their praise and devotion to the Indians, now were divided into pro- and anti-Indian factions. Friars who once shunned comfort, preferring to redistribute the wealth generated by their neophytes, increasingly were accused by secular bishops of sinking vast fortunes in ostentatious churches and monasteries.[13] Alarmed at reports of Mendicant abuses and infighting, Philip II in October of 1571 issued a royal cedula effectively terminating the Mendicant monopoly in Mexico. The following year the first contingent of Jesuits sailed from Spain to Mexico.

---

[10] Ricard, *The Spiritual Conquest*, 46, notes that he himself compiled a list of 109 linguistic works on indigenous languages authored by the friars during the period 1524–1572.

[11] In 1559 there were in all Mexico 380 Franciscans divided among 80 convents; 210 Dominicans in 40 convents; 212 Augustinians, also in 40 convents. Ricard, *The Spiritual Conquest*, 23.

[12] Phelan, *The Millennial Kingdom*, 57; Ricard, *The Spiritual Conquest*, 58.

[13] Ricard, *The Spiritual Conquest*, 168, 239.

The Jesuits

The Mendicant experience in the south differed in degree not kind from the Jesuit experience in northern Mexico. As we pursue the latter, there will be an extended opportunity to reflect on the Indian embrace of Christianity. Toward this end, it is useful to provide some background on the Society of Jesus and then the Indians of northern Mexico.

> Of obscure origin and mean education, tainted by a career as a common soldier, ill-dressed, unkempt, practicing unfamiliar forms of devotion under the patronage of a bishop himself somewhat turbulent and unconventional, all the while occupying no regular position in the functional hierarchy of the Church – at every point he contrasted with the average Gallic bishop of his day, who tended to be well heeled, well connected, well read and well groomed.[14]

This concise description of Saint Martin of Tours (d. 397 C.E.), the most famous medieval "missionary-saint," applies equally well to Saint Ignatius Loyola, the founder of the Society of Jesus, who was canonized in 1622. Both Martin and Loyola were soldiers with checkered backgrounds who experienced a radical transformation, subsequently dedicating their lives to God. Each man embraced a life of austerity, if not asceticism, inspiring countless others to turn to God and then humankind, particularly the disadvantaged. Unlike many of their ecclesiastical contemporaries, Martin and Ignatius privileged preaching and works of charity. Both men also shared a deep conviction that God and Satan were constants in human affairs. Victory over Satan presupposed God's grace, which was understood as not only ubiquitous, but also mysteriously cooperative with human free will. Human beings could and should do a lot to improve their lives and the lives of others.

In 1540, while the Mendicants were busy in southern Mexico, Pope Paul III officially recognized the Society of Jesus. The Jesuits, as they came to be known, were led by Loyola and included a handful of like-minded men who had been inspired by the Augustinian revival and devotionalism that swept Europe during the Renaissance. Augustine held

---

[14] Richard Fletcher, *The Barbarian Conversion, From Paganism to Christianity* (Berkeley: University of California Press, 1999), 42.

that God's presence and design were everywhere to be seen, including in the laws of nature. Paradoxically, it was the very regularity and predictability of God's creation, implying a designer and engineer, that lulled humankind into a stupor with respect to God's enduring presence. In this regard, miracles were not really a violation of God's laws, but a reaffirmation of their existence; they were God's way of reminding humankind that he remained very much involved with his creation.[15]

Loyola's vision for the Society of Jesus was predicated on a belief in God's enduring presence.[16] Contrary to popular opinion, Loyola and his followers did not conceive of themselves as a militia called to arms to battle Luther and other "heretics." Likewise, the first Jesuits were not bent on reforming the Church; they eschewed becoming involved in "normal" ecclesiastical activities such as serving as parish priests, vicars, or bishops. Loyola's vision was more mystical, yet pragmatic.[17] He was inspired by the immediacy of the New Testament and particularly the *Acts of the Apostles*. As made explicit in the Jesuit "formula," which is analogous to the "rules" followed by monastic orders, Loyala imagined the Jesuits as a true missionary order that reproduced the lives of Jesus's disciples. Rather than reside in a monastery with a distinctive garb and fixed routine centered around the Divine Office, the Jesuits were to be mobile, adaptable (e.g., wear whatever is appropriate; pray when appropriate), and focused on helping others in need. The ministries emphasized by Loyola were spreading the word of God (e.g., preaching and engaging individuals in devout conversation) and helping those suffering from spiritual and physical ailments.[18] Consistent with the life of Christ and the Apostles, this was all to be done without recompense.

---

[15] Marcus Dods, ed., *The City of God by Saint Augustine*, 2 Vols. (New York: Hafner, 1948), I, 219.

[16] John W. O'Malley, *The First Jesuits* (Cambridge, MA: Harvard University Press, 1993), 84.

[17] There is tendency to think of the Jesuits as more pragmatic or rational (e.g., eschewing asceticism and poverty) as compared with say the Franciscans. See, for instance, Phelan, *The Millennial Kingdom*, 109. Although there may be some truth to this perception, particularly as the Jesuits became more of a teaching rather than missionary order (often living in comfortable, urban residences), Jesuit missionaries who served on the frontier were every bit as "mystical" and ascetic as their Franciscan counterparts.

[18] During just one outbreak of plague in Lisbon in 1569, as many as seventeen Jesuits died caring for the sick. So many Jesuits died during the period 1550–1575 that the Jesuit Father General attempted to limit priestly ministries to the sick and dying.

Significantly, while Loyola valued asceticism – it figured in his own radical transformation – he did not see it as requisite for a religious life. If mortifying one's body worked, fine; someone else might find humility caring for lepers or bathing the infirm. What mattered most was drawing near to God, which Loyola believed was best effected through charity.[19]

Upon entering the Society of Jesus, all novices undertake the "Spiritual Exercises," a mystical retreat of sorts that Loyola mandated for fellow Jesuits.[20] The Exercises generally require a month and involve a stepwise progression of prayer and reflection on one's life and relationship with God. During this retreat and the entire two-year novitiate, the Jesuit novice endeavors to enter into a devout conversation with God – a conversation that ideally continues to evolve with regular infusions of grace.[21] Again, what is particularly significant about this training is that it was geared to public ministries. Thus, the "Contemplation for Love," which is the last meditation of the Spiritual Exercises, ends with "love ought to manifest itself in deeds rather than words."

As part of the Spiritual Exercises, Ignatius Loyola had his followers meditate at length on how Satan and his legion of demons set snares throughout the world, enticing people to sin.[22] This theme was a constant of Loyola's writings[23] and reflected in significant measure the teachings of Thomas Aquinas,[24] whose works were specifically recommended by the Jesuit Constitutions.[25] In his *Summa Contra Gentiles* and *Summa Theologica*, Aquinas detailed how the devil and his army of demons were capable of creating innumerable illusions that were observable to

[19] O'Malley, *The First Jesuits*, 85.
[20] In 1606 the Sixth General Congregation of the Society of Jesus made it mandatory for every member of the Society to undertake the Exercises each year for at least a week. O'Malley, *The First Jesuits*, 360.
[21] George E. Ganss, ed., *Ignatius Loyola: The Spiritual Exercises and Selected Works* (New York: Paulist Press, 1991); O'Malley, *The First Jesuits*, 37–50.
[22] Ganss, *Ignatius Loyola*, 155.
[23] Malachi Martin, *The Jesuits* (New York: Touchstone Books, 1987), 159.
[24] J. B. Russell, *Lucifer: The Devil in the Middle Ages* (Ithaca, NY: Cornell University Press, 1984), 107, f.206; H. R. Trevor-Roper, *The European Witch-Craze of the 16th and 17th Centuries* (Harmondsworth, England: Penguin Books, 1967), 17–18.
[25] George E. Ganss, *The Constitutions of the Society of Jesus* (St. Louis: The Institute of Jesuit Sources, 1970), 219.

the senses, including assuming or possessing a body – all in an effort to promote sin.[26] Such ideas were reworked and given new emphasis during the Counter-Reformation.[27] Works of demonology such as the *Malleus Maleficarum*[28] and Martin del Rio's *Disquisitionum Magicarum Libri Sex in Tres Tomos Pariti* (Six Books of Research on Magic Divided into Three Volumes) transformed these teachings into "useful manuals" that contributed further to a Jesuit preoccupation with Satan.

As noted in the Introduction, shortly after the founding of the Society of Jesus, the Jesuits came to disagree amongst themselves over Ignatius's vision of the Society as a missionary order. The Jesuits as a whole were some of the best-educated men in Europe and, by 1600, many had chosen to become teachers rather than missionaries. This shift in vocations, which is discussed in the next chapter, had profound consequences for New World missionaries. Here what I wish to emphasize is that the Jesuits who were sent to the northern frontier of Nueva España, beginning in 1591, personified Loyola's vision of the Society of Jesus as a missionary order.

Letters written by Jesuits to superiors, requesting assignment to the New World, often speak of a desire to emulate the apostles.[29] Those

---

[26] St. Thomas Aquinas, *Introduction to St. Thomas Aquinas*, ed. A. C. Pegis (New York: Modern Library, 1945).

[27] Pilar G. Aizpuru, *La Educación Popular de los Jesuitas* (Mexico: Universidad Iberoamericana, 1989), 98; Michel de Certeau, *The Mystic Fable, Volume One, The Sixteenth and Seventeenth Centuries*, trans. Michael B. Smith (University of Chicago Press, 1992), 261; Fernando Cervantes, "The Idea of the Devil"; John D. Cox, "Drama, the Devil, and Social Conflict in Late Medieval England." *The American Benedictine Review* 45 (1994): 341–362; Anne J. Cruz and Mary E. Perry, eds., *Culture and Control in Counter-Reformation Spain* (Minneapolis: University of Minnesota Press, 1992); Henry O. Evennett, *The Spirit of the Counter-Reformation* (Notre Dame, IN: Notre Dame Press, 1968); J. B. Russell, *Lucifer, The Devil in the Middle Ages* (Ithaca, NY: Cornell University Press, 1984), *Mephistopheles* (Ithaca, NY: Cornell University Press, 1986).

[28] Heinrich Kramer and James Sprenger, *The Malleus Maleficarum*, trans. Montague Summers (New York: Dover Publications, 1971 [1489]).

[29] This was particularly true after 1590. The normal procedure was for a Jesuit to petition his provincial superior for a mission assignment; particularly zealous Jesuits often wrote the Father General in Rome. Joseph de Guibert, *The Jesuits, Their Spiritual Doctrine and Practice, A Historical Study* (Chicago: Loyola University Press, 1964), 287; A. Lynn Martin, *The Jesuit Mind, The Mentality of an Elite in Early Modern France* (Ithaca, NY: Cornell University Press, 1988); W. E. Shiels, S.J., "The Critical Period in Mission History." *Mid-America* (new series) 10 (1939): 97–109.

who petitioned for assignments in Mexico, Peru, and the Río de la Plata were disenchanted with trends back home in Europe, especially the Reformation and the popularization of mechanistic philosophy, both of which distanced God from his creation. At a minimum, the choice of a missionary vocation in America was a conscious decision in favor of a difficult life, not to mention martyrdom. Most Jesuits who came to the New World could have stayed in Europe and pursued the comfortable and secure life of an educator.[30] This point was made on more than one occasion by Pérez de Ribas in the *Historia*. Perhaps the most powerful instance entailed his quotation of a letter in which a fellow missionary, Father Pedro de Velasco, pleaded with the Jesuit provincial *not* to be recalled from the frontier and assigned to a prestigious position at the Jesuit University of San Pedro y San Pablo in Mexico City. Velasco was the son of the former governor of Nueva Vizcaya and was also the nephew of the viceroy of Nueva España. Velasco's powerful family apparently pressured the Jesuit provincial to have the younger Velasco reassigned. Like other missionaries, Velasco knew the chances were excellent that he would die a martyr on the frontier, yet Velasco still opposed his transfer to Mexico City:

> My father provincial, I feel tenderly and most eagerly about helping these poor little ones. I am inclined to this ministry and am adverse, for my part, to the Spaniards' pretenses. . . . It occurs to me to point out that a consequence of my transfer would be the loss of a great amount of glory to Our Lord. This can be deduced from the thousands of souls who have been baptized in this place, among whom in the first three years more than three hundred people died who had just been baptized or had just received the sacraments. It seems to me that as a result, more glory will have been rendered to God than would be in the same amount of time required for me to teach a course in the literary arts. There are still a great number of gentiles to be baptized and many dry-boned elderly people scattered among those peaks who must be brought down from the mountains, gathered together, and given spiritual life. It seems that this must be done through the voice and

---

[30] Marcelin Defourneaux, *Daily Life in España in the Golden Age*, trans. Newton Branch (Stanford, CA: Stanford University Press, 1979), 106–108.

tongue of some prophet, and while I may not be the one, I have been the first priest and minister among them. There are three languages spoken in these pueblos, and I did everything possible to learn two of them and am now learning the third. The position of reader and lecturer can be filled much more satisfactorily by other ministers in Mexico City. When I think of leaving this ministry, my remorse returns, thinking that I have to exchange the book of the Gospel of Christ and His apostles for one written by Aristotle. This is all due to my own faults, for not having known how to read the book of the Holy Gospel with the necessary willingness and reverence. Going to live near my relatives will only serve for lesser calm, so I trust that the lord viceroy, who is so pious and prudent, will allow me to remain here. That would be of great service to Our Lord and to the welfare of these peoples, who are so defenseless, as I will write to His Excellency. May Our Lord keep Your Reverence, into whose holy sacrifices and prayers I commend myself, requesting with the resignation that I must that you please consider my proposal if possible.[31]

Father Velasco got his wish,[32] as did several dozen other Jesuits who helped effect the rise of Christianity among the Indians of northern Mexico.

The Indians of Northern Mexico

We know a good deal about the Jesuits but relatively little about the Indians of northern Mexico. There are no pre-Hispanic or post-Conquest texts by Indians that detail what life was like in northern Mexico when the first Spaniards came ashore in Veracruz in 1519. Europeans, not Indians, are our principal source of textual information on native life during the colonial period. The Jesuits, in particular, compiled a voluminous literature on the northern frontier. At a time when most *criollos* and Europeans had become convinced that Indians were fundamentally

---

[31] Andrés Pérez de Ribas, *History of the Triumphs of Our Holy Faith Amongst the Most Barbarous and Fierce Peoples of the New World*, trans. D.T. Reff, M. Ahern, and R. Danford (Tucson: University of Arizona Press, 1999 [1645]), 181.

[32] Velasco spent over thirteen years on the northern frontier (1607–1621) before finally leaving for Mexico City, where he taught scripture and moral theology.

flawed or irrevocably lost to Satan,[33] the Jesuits assumed that the Indians were indeed redeemable and their customs fundamentally sound, albeit misguided.[34] At the outset of the *Historia,* in Book I, Pérez de Ribas depicted Sinaloa as a land that had been blessed by God's grace, as reflected in the relative abundance and variety of foodstuffs and the way nature (e.g., trees and birds' nests) reflected Christian truths such as the Trinity. Pérez de Ribas went on to suggest that God's grace extended to the Indians and their culture. Thus, he noted the Indians' productive farming and fishing methods and the rather ingenious way in which they dealt with floods. With respect to the Indians' "barbarous" customs, Pérez de Ribas suggested that they reflected an ignorance of the word of God, not a lack of reason. It is significant in this regard that the Jesuits in the late 1500s remained strong advocates of a native clergy, even when other regular and secular priests took no stand or actively opposed an Indian priesthood.[35]

The Jesuits went further than many of their European contemporaries in their understanding of native peoples, explaining in part their success as missionaries. However, although remarkable, the Jesuits never escaped the predicament of their Spanish-Jesuit culture, particularly their understanding of themselves as on a mission from God. The Jesuits were convinced that Satan was everywhere setting snares, but particularly in America, where he had frightened away the holy angels and had ruled for millennia.[36] Jesuits like Pérez de Ribas agreed with Acosta and Sahagún

---

[33] Fernando Cervantes, "The Idea of the Devil and the Problem of the Indian: the case of Mexico in the Sixteenth Century," *Research Papers, University of London, Institute of Latin American Studies* 4 (1991).

[34] Pérez de Ribas and fellow Jesuits had much in common with Las Casas, who wrote a century earlier when many missionaries were still optimistic about the Indian and the rebirth of the Church in the New World.

[35] As the sixteenth century drew to a close, the Jesuits as a whole retreated from this position of favoring admission of Indians to the priesthood. Ernest J. Zubillaga, ed., *Monumenta Mexicana, Vol. III: (1585–1590)* (Rome: Institum Historicum Societatis Iesu, 1968), 328–338.

[36] Aizpuru, *La Educación Popular de los Jesuitas,* 98; Peter M. Dunne, *Andrés Pérez de Ribas* (New York: United States Catholic Historical Society, 1951), 129; Sabine Mac-Cormack, *Religion in the Andes, Vision and Imagination in Early Colonial Peru* (Princeton, NJ: Princeton University Press, 1991); Antonio Ruiz de Montoya, *Conquista Espiritual hecha por los religiosos de la Compañía de Jesus en las provincias del Paraguay, Parana, Uruguay y Tape* (Bilbao: Corazon de Jesus, 1892 [1639]), 32.

that it was necessary to understand and describe native beliefs to dethrone Satan.[37]

The Jesuits readily questioned native informants and spied on clandestine rites, recording their observations for the benefit of other missionaries. Such observations, when coupled with the accounts of Spanish explorers, archaeological data, and recent works by Native Americans, provide a collage that captures some of the complexity of native life in 1492.[38]

Native Life on the Eve of the Conquest

... like the Romans, these Indians have a large number of deities, including some for illnesses, war, and bountiful harvests from their fields. Their idols take the form of animals and each deity is honored on a particular day with dances, drunkenness, body painting, and other vices that commonly accompany such festivities.[39]

The Indians of northern Mexico were perceived by the Jesuits as similar in a number of significant ways to the "Romans," that is, the pagan population of the late Roman Empire. The Jesuits took the similarities as an indication of the Indians' backwardness. However, native life in northern Mexico was anything but retarded. Cultural relativism dictates that we forgo judgments of whether one culture is "better" or more advanced than another. However, as early modern Europeans

[37] Jóse de Acosta, *Historia Natural y Moral de las Indias*, 2 vols. (Madrid, 1894[1590]), II, 137; Fray Bernardino de Sahagún, *Historia General de las Cosas de Nueva España*, 2nd ed. (Mexico: Editorial Porrua, 1969), 27.

[38] See for instance: Vine Deloria, *God Is Red* (Golden, CO: North American Press, 1992); *The Metaphysics of Modern Existence* (San Francisco: Harper and Row, 1979); Paula Gunn Allen, ed., *Spider Woman's Granddaughters* (New York: Fawcett Columbine, 1989), *The Sacred Hoop* (Boston: Beacon Press, 1986); Edmund J. Ladd, "Zuni on the Day the Men in Metal Arrived." In *The Coronado Expedition to Tierra Nueva: The 1540–1542 Route Across the Southwest*, eds. Richard and Shirley Flint, pp. 225–233 (Niwot: University Press of Colorado, 1997); Lawrence E. Sullivan, *Native Religions and Cultures of North America* (New York: Continuum, 2000); George Tinker, *Missionary Conquest* (Minneapolis: Fortress Press, 1993).

[39] "Anua del año de mil seiscientos y dos," Historia 15, Archivo General de la Nación, Mexico City.

were not the least bit hesitant about making such judgments, and invariably did so, it is necessary to point out that the Indians in northern Mexico lived at least as well as contemporary Europeans. In his overview of native life, Pérez de Ribas noted that Indian houses were sparse but clean; their food was relatively abundant and rarely denied strangers; Indian children played as children should; theft and murder were rare; women did not have to fear being raped; and democracy, which the Jesuits misunderstood as "no government," characterized public decision making.[40] Warfare was common among native peoples, but it was not conducted in northern Mexico in the "total" fashion of early modern Europe or Mesoamerica. The Jesuits often spoke of Indian cannibalism, infanticide, and intoxication, but all were known in Europe. Archaeologists and Euro-Americans more generally seem fascinated with Indian cannibalism, yet they ignore their own long history of the same. For instance, immediately following the Saint Bartholomew's Day Massacre in France in 1572 (about as savage and insane a moment as imaginable), Huguenot body parts were sold and eaten in Paris and Lyon.[41]

In 1492, the Indian population of northern Mexico[42] numbered close to one million (Figure 9). This is at best a "good guess," owing to the limited observations of early Spanish explorers and missionaries.[43] Sadder still is the admission that we know next to nothing about entire communities or "tribes" such as the Baciroa, Zoe, Tubar, and Macoyahui. Because of their proximity to Spanish mines, and thus infectious disease, many mountain peoples, including major groups such as the Tepehuan, Acaxee, and Xixime, were all but wiped out by 1625, before the Jesuits or other observers had a chance to comment on the complexities of life in the Sierras. The rapid spread of disease was alluded to

---

[40] Pérez de Ribas, *History of the Triumphs*, 87–101.
[41] Kirkpatrick Sale, *Conquest of Paradise* (New York: Penguin Books, 1991), 134n.
[42] Northern Mexico here refers to what is today northern Sinaloa (north of the Rio Mocorito), Sonora, Chihuahua, and Durango.
[43] Peter Gerhard, *The Northern Frontier of New Spain* (Princeton, NJ: Princeton University Press 1982); Reff, *Disease, Depopulation, and Culture*; Carl O. Sauer, *Aboriginal Population of Northwest Mexico*. Ibero-Americana 10 (Berkeley: University of California Press, 1935).

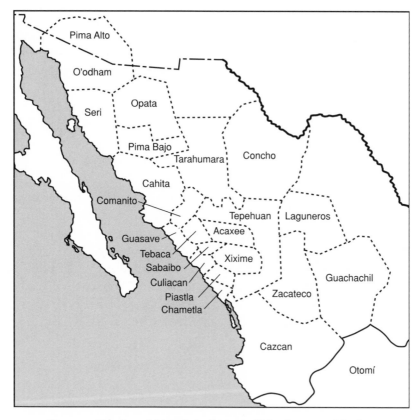

Figure 9. Ethnic and Linguistic Groups of Northwestern Mexico.

by a Franciscan missionary who worked among the Tarahumara in the eighteenth century:

> What is certain is that the Tarahumara nation was very numerous in the past; in every part of the mountain one encounters caves full of human remains. Some of these sepulchers are not that old because they contain the remains of wool cloth. These Indians did not get wool until shortly before the Holy Word [meaning missionaries] came into these mountains.[44]

[44] Thomas E. Sheridan and Thomas Naylor, eds., *Rarámuri, A Tarahumara Colonial Chronicle 1607–1791* (Flagstaff, AZ: Northland Press, 1979), 115.

The million or so Indian inhabitants of northern Mexico were distributed among innumerable *rancherías*, each with upward of a dozen
houses,[45] and several hundred villages and pueblos, ranging in size from
several dozen to over a thousand households. Permanent settlements
were chiefly along the many rivers that originate in the Sierra Madre
Occidental.[46] Some of these rivers flow eastward down across the central plateau; more numerous are rivers that flow westward, descending swiftly through canyons and foothills and then across the Sonoran desert and the sub-tropical coastal plain of northern Sinaloa and
Sonora.

With the exception of coastal groups such as the Seri, the Indians of
northern Mexico primarily were farmers. Using a variety of agricultural
techniques, ranging from simple floodwater farming to canal irrigation,
many communities were able to exceed subsistence requirements, supporting craft production and trade.[47] The archaeological and historical
records indicate that native peoples in northern Mexico as well as the
American Southwest were involved in the exchange of maize, turquoise,
buffalo robes, cotton, feathers, pottery, raw and finished shell, salt,
obsidian, peyote, and labor itself.[48] Archaeologists disagree about the

---

[45] Native structures, particularly in lowland areas, generally consisted of round structures with dome shaped roofs, constructed of reeds and reed matting. See George P.
Hammond and Agapito Rey, trans. and eds., *Obregon's History of 16th Century Exploration in Western America* (Los Angeles: Wetzel Publishing Company, 1928), 84;
Basil C. Hedrick and Carroll L. Riley, trans., *Documents Ancillary to the Vaca Journey*, University Museum Studies 5 (Carbondale: Southern Illinois University Museum,
1976). This lowland house-type was strikingly similar to the homes of the late Neolithic Celts. Indian structures with walls of wattle and daub or adobe were common in the foothills and mountains, where they apparently offered greater warmth in
winter.

[46] Ralph L. Beals, *The Comparative Ethnology of Northern Mexico Before 1750*, Ibero-
Americana 2 (Berkeley: University of California Press, 1932); William E. Doolittle,
Cultivated Landscapes of Native North America (New York: Oxford University Press,
2000), *Canal Irrigation in Prehistoric Mexico* (Austin: University of Texas Press, 1990);
Peter Gerhard, *The Northern Frontier of New Spain*; Reff, *Disease, Depopulation and
Culture Change*; Carroll L. Riley, *The Frontier People* (Albuquerque: University of New
Mexico Press, 1982); Sauer, *Aboriginal Population of Northwest Mexico*.

[47] Doolittle, *Cultivated Landscapes, Canal Irrigation*.

[48] Ricard Ford, "Inter-Indian Exchange in the Southwest." In *Handbook of North American Indians Volume 10: Southwest*, ed. Alfonso Ortiz, pp. 711–722 (Washington, DC:
Smithsonian Institution Press, 1983); Riley, *The Frontier People*.

Figure 10. Floodplain along the Rio Sonora near Baviacora.

precise nature of the relationship,[49] but it is clear that native peoples in what is today northern Mexico and the U.S. Southwest were involved in long-distance exchanges with one or more Mesoamerican civilizations in southern Mexico (e.g., Mexica, Tarascans).

[49] The arguments range from ephemeral relationships to actual colonization of the northern frontier by Mesoamericans, who anticipated the "Spanish model" of mixing religious conversion with an extractive economy based on mining. Although there is evidence for the latter in the southern Sierra Madre Occidental (e.g., in Zacatecas) and in west Mexico, archaeologists disagree about other purported colonies further to the north (e.g., Paquime/Casas Grandes, Chaco Canyon, the Hohokam). Charles C. DiPeso, "Prehistory: Southern Periphery." In *Handbook of North American Indians Volume 9: Southwest*, ed. Alfonso Ortiz, pp. 152–161 (Washington, DC: Smithsonian Institution Press, 1979); Jonathan E. Reyman, ed., *The Gran Chichimeca: Essays on the Archaeology and Ethnohistory of Northern Mesoamerica* (Sydney: Avebury, 1995); Phil Weigand, "Minería y Intercambio de Minerales en Zacatecas Prehispánica." In *Zacatecas III, Anuario de Historia*, ed. C. Esparanza Sanchez, pp. 138–195 (Zacatecas, Mexico: Universidad Autónoma de Zacatecas, 1981), "Evidence for Complex Societies During the Western Mesoamerican Classic Period." In *The Archaeology of West and Northwest Mexico*, eds. Michael Foster and P. C. Weigand, pp. 47–92 (Boulder, CO: Westview Press, 1985); Anne I. Woosley and John C. Ravesloot, eds., *Culture and Contact, Charles C. Di Peso's Gran Chichimeca* (Dragoon, AZ: Amerind Foundation, 1993).

Most Indian groups in northern Mexico were hunter-gatherers as well as farmers. Jesuit missionaries were schooled in Renaissance humanism, which reified Aristotelian notions such as the idea that one had to live in a town or city to be civilized.[50] Indeed, the Jesuit mission enterprise was predicated on a maxim articulated by classical authors such as Cassiodorus: "Men ought to draw together into cities."[51] Not surprisingly, the missionaries had great difficulty appreciating hunting and gathering, either as a complement to sedentary life or as the bases of life itself. And yet, by the Jesuits' own admission, the Indians lived remarkably well from their pursuit of plants and animals. Many early observers commented on the relative abundance of deer and all types of wild game and fish in Sinaloa and Sonora.[52]

The Jesuits had as much difficulty with native political systems as they did hunting and gathering, again because of the privileged views of Aristotle and the weight of Western tradition, which held that humanity was "naturally" divided into rulers and ruled. The Jesuits and other Europeans saw the universe as ordered from the top down; the benefit of every doubt was enjoyed by persons of authority, in whom both religious and secular authority were invested with a sacral character.[53] It was difficult in this regard for the Jesuits to appreciate the relatively egalitarian

---

[50] Joan Corominas, *Diccionario critico etimologico castellano e hispanico*, 5 vols. (Madrid: Editorial Gredos, 1980), IV, 598; Helen Nader, *Liberty in Absolutist Spain, The Hapsburg Sale of Towns, 1516–1700* (Baltimore, MD: Johns Hopkins University Press, 1990); Antony Pagden, *The Fall of Natural Man* (Cambridge, UK: Cambridge University Press, 1982); Angel Rama, *The Lettered City* (Durham, NC: Duke University Press, 1996).

[51] Thomas Hodgkin, *The Letters of Cassiodorus* (London: H. Frowde, 1886), 31.

[52] Among groups such as the Yoeme (Yaqui), often entire communities would undertake communal hunts. Obregon, who accompanied Ibarra's expedition in 1563–1565, recounted one hunt in which two thousand Yoeme surrounded and then advanced on a marsh, driving large numbers of deer, rabbits, and quail into the hands of the pursuers. Hammond and Rey, *Obregon's History*, 87, 102, 257–259. See also Ralph Beals, *The Aboriginal Culture of the Cahita Indians*, Ibero-Americana 19 (Berkeley: University of California Press, 1943), 14; Hedrick and Riley, *Documents Ancillary to the Vaca Journey*, 45, 52; Campbell W. Pennington, *The Pima Bajo of Central Sonora, Mexico, Volume I: The Material Culture* (Salt Lake City: University of Utah Press, 1980), 207; Ignaz Pfefferkorn, *Sonora: A Description of the Province*, trans. Theodore E. Treutlein (Albuquerque: University of New Mexico Press, 1949), 106.

[53] Johan Huizinga, *The Waning of the Middle Ages* (New York: St. Martin's Press, 1967 [1919]), 46–55; John W. O'Malley, *The First Jesuits* (Cambridge, MA: Harvard University Press, 1993), 353.

and democratic nature of Indian sociopolitical systems. Indeed, throughout the *Historia*, Pérez de Ribas seemed to deny that the Indians had any "government."[54] The Jesuits nevertheless described what clearly were complex organizations. Among the Yoeme (Yaqui) as well as other Cahita-speakers (e.g., Mayo, Zuaque, Ocoroni), and also the Nébome, Opata, Acaxee, and Xixime, native settlements were organized in terms of localized descent groups headed by senior males. It was primarily *"principales"* and caciques who were polygamous and enjoyed differential access to material possessions such as cotton *mantas*. The Jesuits also indicated that caciques functioned as religious leaders, conducting rites and ceremonies for the community as a whole; individual concerns were more the charge of shamans.[55]

Many Indian communities in northern Mexico were integrated into larger sociopolitical systems or chiefdoms headed by what the Jesuits referred to as "principal chiefs." Principal chiefs alone decided matters of war and peace and often raised armies numbering in the thousands, which were drawn from the settlements of lesser caciques. The principal chiefs also were powerful by virtue of their production and redistribution of surpluses. Pérez de Ribas noted that the principal chiefs had the largest fields, which were cultivated with the assistance of their subordinates.

During the initial Jesuit *entrada* to the Mayo, Father Pedro Méndez noted in a letter that he was welcomed by the principal cacique and what apparently were fifteen lesser caciques, all of whom represented over nine thousand Indians in seven pueblos and numerous rancherías.[56] Some of the earliest Jesuit accounts of the Yoeme, before they were missionized and felt the full brunt of introduced disease, mention two or three principal chiefs (Anabailutei, Conibomeai, Hinsemeai) who represented many thousands of followers spread up and down the Río Yaqui.[57] During an *entrada* beyond the mission frontier in 1619, Pérez de Ribas had a chance

---

[54] See for instance, Pérez de Ribas, *History of the Triumphs*, 92.
[55] Ibid., 97.
[56] "Anua del año de mil seiscientos catorce," *Historia* 15, Archivo General de la Nación, Mexico City.
[57] For instance, "Anua del año de mil seiscientos y diez," *Historia* 15, Archivo General de la Nación, Mexico City; Pérez de Ribas, *History of the Triumphs*, 327–344.

encounter with the principal cacique of the Sisibotari Opata of the Río Sahuaripa drainage. The chief's name was Gran Sisibotari:

> He was still young, and he was very good-natured. He wore a long manta tied at the shoulder like a cloak. He also wore another manta tied tightly around the waist, as do other Indians of this nation. For protection when shooting arrows he had a beautiful martin pelt wrapped around his left wrist, which holds the bow [381] while the right hand snaps the bowstring.... Others use pelts of common animals for this purpose.... This principal cacique's bow and quiver of arrows were carried by another Indian who was like his squire. Both pieces were beautifully carved in their fashion. The cacique brought with him a good number of his vassals, who looked upon and treated him with great respect and reverence.... He welcomed me at a place near his lands and settlements. Although we did not visit them, they could be seen in the distance. He showed us his valley and pueblos and invited us to visit, expressing his desire for priests to come to his lands to teach them the word of God.[58]

In 1620, an unnamed Jesuit working among the Nébome, who were neighbors of the Sisibotari, also met Gran Sisibotari. The priest reported that the Sisibotari were divided among some seventy *rancherías*. A Jesuit report from 1628 indicates that these *rancherías* had between twenty and thirty structures of adobe.[59] Gran Sisibotari, in effect, "ruled" over a population of close to nine thousand.[60]

There is considerable archaeological evidence, principally in the form of hilltop forts and retreats, which indicate that warfare was common during the protohistoric period (c. 1400–1600 C.E.) in northern Mexico.[61] The relative ease with which caciques assembled well-organized armies numbering in the thousands, including armies that defeated or seriously challenged Spanish-led forces, is testimony to the prevalence of warfare. The Jesuits stated or implied that the Indians went

---

[58] Pérez de Ribas, *History of the Triumphs*, 409–410.
[59] "Missiones de San Ygnacio en Mayo, Yaqui, Nevomes, Chinipas, y Sisibotaris, 1628," Historia 15, Archivo General de la Nación, Mexico City.
[60] Reff, *Disease, Depopulation and Culture Change*, 220–222.
[61] Ibid., Steven A. LeBlanc, *Prehistoric Warfare In The American Southwest* (Salt Lake City: University of Utah Press, 1999), 44.

to war almost at the drop of a hat ("for no other reason than the desire for human flesh"). However, they also noted that murder and other acts of violence were rare among the Indians. On various occasions in the *Historia*, Pérez de Ribas attributed warfare to competition over land, access to salt deposits and hunting territories, and, in one instance, to a dispute that arose over the rules for playing a native game, *correr el palo* (running-stick game).

It would seem that population growth and competition for resources during late prehistory were the principal causes of warfare among the Indians of northern Mexico as well as the American Southwest. Interestingly, during the late Neolithic in Europe (centuries before Christianization), Celtic population growth apparently lead to increased warfare and the building of fortified retreats and hilltop fortifications, similar to those found in northern Mexico almost two thousand years later.[62] Correspondingly, the Celts and Germans afforded warriors positions of power and influence. As noted earlier, caciques and principal chiefs among the Indians of northern Mexico were respected at least in part for their military prowess.

Whereas native elites in Sinaloa had differential access to wives and certain material possessions, the accumulation of wealth was ameliorated by a cacique's responsibility to redistribute rather than hoard or consume goods and services, as was the case with early modern Europe's aristocracy and emerging middle class. Similarly, a cacique's power, although perhaps derived in the first instance by membership in a particular clan or lineage, ultimately depended on his (and sometimes her) demonstrated leadership in battle and/or forming a consensus. Pérez de Ribas often recounted how native caciques met in council or addressed entire pueblos, endeavoring through speeches to create a consensus with respect to public policy on matters such as baptism, war, or peace:

> On these occasions, the old principales and the sorcerers would meet at the house or ramada of the cacique. They would be seated around a torch, where they would proceed to light some of their tobacco-filled

---

[62] Regarding the Celts, see Simon James, *Exploring the World of the Celts* (London: Thames and Hudson, 1993), 60–62; Bruce Lincoln, *Myth, Cosmos, and Society, Indo-European Themes of Creation and Destruction* (Cambridge, MA: Harvard University Press, 1986); J. M. Wallace-Hadrill, *Early Medieval History* (Oxford: Basil Blackwell, 1975), 19–30.

reeds, which they would then pass around to smoke. Then the Indian who held the greatest authority would stand up, and from his standing position, he would chant the beginning of his sermon. He would start by walking very slowly around the plaza of the pueblo, continuing his sermon and raising the tone of his voice, shouting so that the entire pueblo could hear him from their bonfires and houses. This circling of the plaza and sermon would take more or less half an hour, depending on the preacher. When this was done, he would return to his seat, where his companions would welcome him with great acclaim. Each one would express this individually, and if the preacher was an old man, which they usually are, the response went like this: "You have spoken and advised us well, my Grandfather. My heart is one with yours." If the person congratulating him were an old man, he would say, "My older or younger brother, my heart feels and speaks what you have said." Then they would honor him with another toast and round of tobacco. Next, another orator would get up and give his sermon in the same manner, spending another half an hour circling the plaza.[63]

It took Europeans and Anglo-Americans another hundred years to grasp and hesitatingly embrace democracy. We should not be surprised that Jesuits such as Pérez de Ribas, although he might adequately describe democracy in action, ultimately was frustrated that caciques did not simply order their people to do as they (or the missionary) wished.

The Immediate Reality of the Invisible World

Predictably, the Jesuits and Europeans more generally had enormous difficulty understanding Indian "religious" beliefs and practices. The Jesuits were not prepared to recognize nor engage the likes of an Indian Augustine, nor were they willing to engage oral traditions, which they assumed, a priori, were defective. The Jesuits tended to dismiss Indian reflections on the other-than-empirical world with comments like "the Indians spoke confusingly about the other world." Such "confusion"

---

[63] Pérez de Ribas, *History of the Triumphs*, 97–98.

invariably was attributed to Satan. Of course, more often it was the Jesuits and not the Indians who were confused.[64]

Juxtaposing Jesuit observations with other sources, including recent Indian and Chicana/o commentaries,[65] one can perceive considerable overlap and yet profound differences in the way Europeans and Indians viewed the world in which they lived out their lives. The Judeo-Christian origin myth, *Genesis*, posits an all-powerful God who created human beings in his own image; human beings alone have souls and consciousness of being and they are otherwise superior to other life forms (the great chain of being). And yet, because of "the fall," God decreed that humankind would have a difficult time wresting a living from an uncooperative earth (e.g., drought, floods). Indeed, the earth became "paradise lost"; Jews and Christians look not to the earth but to the heavens, for Heaven. Jews and Christians likewise understand that everything – individual lives, the fate of nations, the seasons, and so on – is a function of God's plan, a plan that promises an eventual restoration of paradise lost, albeit for some, not all.

The origin myths of native peoples such as the Pueblos often begin with an unpleasant, primordial underworld, which human forbearers flee, climbing a tree or otherwise making their way to the earth's surface. There they are greeted by kindred spirits who engage humankind in the job of bringing other life forms into being. The result is an empirically beautiful and also mysteriously wonderful, earthly existence.[66] Whereas Judeo-Christians imagine paradise as lost and seemingly far removed from earth (in the "heavens"), Indians see the earth as paradise gained!

---

[64] See Donald Bahr, "Bad News: The Predicament of Native American Mythology." *Ethnohistory* 48 (2001): 587–612.

[65] Some of the more enlightening of these "commentaries" include recent analyses of contemporary beliefs and practices among groups such as the Yoeme as well as novels and poetry that bespeak enduring Indian traditions. Lawrence Evers and Felipe S. Molina, *Yaqui Deer Songs/Maso Bwikam* (Tucson: Sun Tracks and The University of Arizona Press, 1987); Muriel Painter, *With Good Heart: Yaqui Beliefs and Ceremonies in Pascua Village* (Tucson: University of Arizona Press, 1986); Graciela Limon, *Song of the Hummingbird* (Houston: Arte Publico Press, 1996); Luci Tapahonso, *Blue Horses Rush In* (Tucson: University of Arizona Press, 1998).

[66] John Bierhorst, *The Mythology of North America* (New York: William Morrow, 1985); Ramon Gutiérrez, *When Jesus Came: The Corn Mothers Went Away* (Stanford, CA: Stanford University Press, 1991), 3–7; Alfonso Ortiz, *The Tewa World* (Chicago: University of Chicago Press, 1969), 13–16.

It should perhaps be noted that such a perspective is entirely reasonable even by scientific standards; decades of searching the Milky Way and nearby galaxies have disclosed nothing even remotely comparable to earth.

The origin myth of the Pueblos and other Indians cast human beings as co-creators and potentially divine, rather than God's dependent and often wayward children. The human potential for divinity was realized "in the beginning" through human participation in making the world come to life, so to speak. Subsequently, in what non-Indians understand as historical time, Indians used ritual and prayer/song to communicate with and enlist the support of invisible forces/spirits that are coterminous with life itself. Deer, for instance, are not simply "game animals," but fellow beings who evidence awe-inspiring, mysterious qualities. Rather than dismiss these qualities because they can not be fully apprehended using our five senses, native peoples acknowledge the ineffable, treating deer and other life forms with not only respect, but also as gifted others who can mysteriously know and change the course of events. In this regard, Indians shared with Judeo-Christians the ideal of "do unto others as you would have them do unto you." However, for Indians, the category of "others" went far beyond human beings; all living things (e.g., deer, a spring, a gnarled mesquite tree, a mountain) were understood as related and dependent on each other. Whereas Christians talk of grace, seeing it as a gift from God, who can extend or withhold it as he pleases, Indians talk of a "great spirit" or spiritual energy that is coterminous with life itself. This energy can be used for good or bad purposes (there is no Satan at war with God, enticing humans to sin) and again, is realized through meaningful relationships with other life forms whose own identity and agency presuppose reciprocity with humans.[67]

Like the Neolithic Celts, the Indians of northern Mexico viewed mountains, springs, and distinctive trees as instances of the in-breaking of the divine, and thus appropriate points of engagement with the forces/spirits of nonordinary reality. This view of nature may have crystallized in Mexico during the millennium preceding the Conquest,

---

[67] Kenneth M. Morrison, "Sharing the Flower: A Non-Supernaturalistic Theory of Grace." *Religion* 22 (1992): 207–219. Jill McKeever Furst, *The Natural History of the Soul in Ancient Mexico* (New Haven: Yale University Press, 1995).

when prehistoric Indian populations became increasingly sedentary and more reliant on agriculture.[68] With agriculture and sedentarism, large areas of the physical and natural environment that formerly were experienced on a regular basis by the entire community now were frequented only occasionally. The world beyond the village was, in a sense, returned to nature and became a logical repository of the supernatural. Accordingly, groups such as the Yoeme equate the "spirit world" or *Huya Aniya* with the desert scrubland (*monte*) beyond the village or pueblo.[69]

Individuals or groups such as hunting parties or traders who ventured into the *Huya Aniya* did so always mindful of the possibility of unsolicited contact with beings from other dimensions, again reflecting the fact that these "spirits" were as interested in human beings as the latter were spirits. The spirits of the *Huya Aniya* that were encountered or solicited by individuals often were described by the Jesuits in rather abstract terms, as if the spirits were shape-shifters and could assume various forms.[70] The Jesuits at the same time reported that groups such as the Guasave, Mayo, Yoeme, and Acaxee recognized a variety of seemingly anthropomorphic supernaturals, who had dominion over arenas such as warfare, agriculture, hunting, carnal delights, and the discovery of lost or stolen items.[71] Again, this is how the Jesuits described native religion, implicitly seeing Indian deities as functionally distinct (e.g., "war gods"). Perhaps, like the Celts of pagan Europe or the Christian cult of the saints, the Indians saw their "deities" as having certain behavioral attributes that dictated their engagement under certain circumstances. Among pagan Europeans, Hercules's strength might be invoked by warriors as well as

[68] Di Peso, "Prehistory: Southern Periphery."

[69] Beals, *Aboriginal Culture of the Cahita Indians*, 18; Evers and Molina, *Yaqui Deer Songs*; Edward H. Spicer, *The Yaquis: A Cultural History* (Tucson: University of Arizona Press, 1980), 65–67. Note that Spicer in his *Cycles of Conquest* (Tucson: University of Arizona Press, 1962) suggested that the concept of the *Huya Aniya* was a postcontact phenomenon, resulting from Jesuit settlement of the Yaqui in villages and towns. This inference is not supported by empirical data, which indicate the Yaqui were living in large settlements aboriginally. It is clear as well from Jesuit sources that the concept of the *Huya Aniya* was well developed among the Yaqui and many other groups at the time of Spanish contact.

[70] Ralph Beals, *The Acaxee, a Mountain Tribe of Durango and Sinaloa*. Ibero-Americana 6 (Berkeley: University of California Press, 1933), 22ff.

[71] Pérez de Ribas, *History of the Triumphs*, 245–246.

those struggling with illness.[72] The Christian cult of the saints, which built upon this pagan tradition, also cast particular saints as having certain behavioral attributes rather than functional specializations (even though over time saints like Sebastian became known for his ability to halt disease, or saints like Antony became the saint of choice when dealing with lost items).

Indian supernaturals at times were represented by idols of stone and wood, which were kept in caves or secluded areas outside Indian villages.[73] Presumably some of these idols and their associated deities were introduced between 800 and 1350 C.E. by the Aztatlan and Chalchihuities cultures, which spread northward from Mesoamerica along the west coast of Mexico and up through the southern Sierra Madre Occidental, respectively.[74] Among the various deities worshipped by the Ahome and Guasave was one who provided good harvests, health, and success in war, and who was represented by an idol of stone approximately a meter in height, "in the form of a pyramid with certain characters carved in it that were unintelligible."[75] The Jesuits also reported Mesoamerican-like idols among the Tepehuan, including one that was described as a meter in height, made of stone, with a realistic depiction of a man's head and a column for a body (Figure 11). The idol was kept at a shrine of sorts at the summit of a hill, along with a smaller idol in the shape of a caracole, which is highly suggestive of the Mesoamerican deity Quetzalcoatl. Similarly, the Jesuits related one occasion when a priest surprised a group of Acaxee who were engaging an idol that may have been related to Xochipilli – the Mesoamerican god of flowers, music, games, and all

[72] Ton Derks, *Gods, Temples and Ritual Practices: The Transformation of Religious Ideas and Values in Roman Gaul* (Amsterdam: Amsterdam University Press, 1998), 78–79.

[73] F. J. Alegre, S.J., *Historia de la Provincia de la Compañia de Jesus de Nueva España*. 4 vols. New ed. E. J. Burrus and F. Zubillaga (Rome: Bibliotecha Instituti Historici S.J., 1956–1960), II, 81; Hammond and Rey, *Obregon's History*, 68.

[74] Di Peso suggested that the prehistoric peoples associated with the Chalchihuities, Aztatlan, and Casas Grandes "cultures" all worshipped in some way the Mesoamerican deity, Quetzalcoatl. Di Peso, "Prehistory: Southern Periphery," 159; see also Gordon F. Ekholm, *Excavations at Guasave, Sinaloa, Mexico*. Anthropological Papers of the American Museum of Natural History 38 (Part II) (New York: American Museum of Natural History, 1942).

[75] "Anua del año de mil quinientos noventa y seis," Historia 15, Archivo General de la Nación, Mexico City.

*" In one pueblo the priests found an idol that was highly
renowned among these people [Tepehuan]. It was made of
stone and was forty inches tall. It had the head of a man,
and the rest was like a column."*

Pérez de Ribas, *History of the Triumphs*, 586

Figure 11. Stone Idol from Northern Mexico (After Ganot and Peschard, "The
Archaeological Site of El Canon del Molino, Durango, Mexico," 167).

aesthetic pursuits.[76] The idol was "in the shape of a man" and was on one of the two terraces of a *batei* or ballfield where the Acaxee were playing the semisacred ball game. On the opposite terrace the Acaxee had peyote, which apparently was consumed during the ritual performance of the ball game.[77]

The Jesuits noted that the sun and moon often were spoken of as mates and the supreme source of power and life.[78] The Acaxee and Cahita reportedly recognized a creator God or "lord of life and death...the most venerated of all."[79] It is not clear if this creator god was distinct from the sun, or whether it was a different "aspect" of the sun, perhaps analogous to "God the Father" of the Christian trinity.

All members of native society apparently were privy to the spirit world. The Jesuits nevertheless indicated or implied that certain individuals, often referred to as "sorcerers" (*hechiceros*), acted as intermediaries for other members of the community. As noted in the previous chapter, early Christian authors were reluctant to elaborate on the "sorcery" of European shamans or *magi*, owing to their conviction that doing so was potentially dangerous. The Jesuits were similarly uncomfortable

[76] Fray Bernardino de Sahagún, *Primeros Memoriales*, Paleography of Nahuatl. Text and trans. Thelma Sullivan, Completed by H. B. Nicholson et al. (Norman: University of Oklahoma Press, 1997), 139–140, f.15; Jacques Soustelle, *Daily Life of the Aztecs* (Stanford, CA: Stanford University Press, 1961), 22.

[77] Pérez de Ribas, *History of the Triumphs*, 504. Note that there is considerable less tangible evidence of Mesoamerican influence. The Opata, for instance, were reported to have had a version of the "flying pole dance," which is associated with the worship of Tlaloc – the Mesoamerican god of thunder, rain, and lightning. Fray Diego Duran, *Book of the Gods and Rites and The Ancient Calendar*, trans. Fernando Horcasitas and Doris Heyden (Norman: University of Oklahoma, 1971 [c.1580]), 161–166; Charles Lange and Carroll L. Riley, eds., *The Southwestern Journals of Adolph Bandelier* (Albuquerque: University of New Mexico Press, 1970), 236, 242; Pfefferkorn, *Sonora: A Description of the Province*, 182–183; Theodore E. Treutlein, trans. and ed., *Missionary in Sonora, the Travel Reports of Joseph Och, S.J., 1755–1767* (San Francisco: California Historical Society, 1965), 163–164. Father Juan Nentvig also reported that the Opata had a ceremony ("plea to the clouds") that was invoked to bring rain and that may have been directed at Tlaloc or Xípe Totec. Juan Nentvig, S.J., *Rudo Ensayo*, trans. Alberto F. Pradeau and Roberto R. Rasmussen (Tucson: University of Arizona Press, 1980 [1764]), 59.

[78] See, for instance, "Estado de la provincia de Sonora,...segun se halla por el mes de Julio de este año de 1730, escrito por un padre misionero de la provincia de Jesus de Nueva España, 1730," *Documentos para la Historia de Mexico*, 1853–57, Serie IV, 628.

[79] Alegre, S.J., *Historia de la Provincia*, II, 81; Beals, *Aboriginal Culture of the Cahita Indians*, 59.

talking about Indian shamanism, which was understood as more than hocus-pocus. When a missionary was called to an Indian home because a *hechicero* purportedly had made the house tremble, the priest did not scoff at the messenger but quickly grabbed his prayer book and hastened to do battle with Satan. The Jesuits believed that God, in his infinite wisdom, allowed Satan supernatural powers, which could be tapped by sorcerers or those duped by "the evil one."

Although the *hechicero's* or shamans' particular "arts" and knowledge were rarely discussed by the Jesuits, the latter spoke at great length of their power and influence over fellow Indians. Some *hechiceros* were solicited to deal with a variety of personal misfortunes, for which they received payments of food or other material items. The calamity most often mentioned by the Jesuits was sickness, which some shamans reportedly treated using sleight of hand, curing by blowing and sucking, and other forms of sympathetic magic.[80] Because some *hechiceros* were said to cause illness or misfortune, they were indeed more like sorcerers than shamans.[81]

It is apparent that some *hechiceros* and Indian caciques functioned as priests of sorts, caring for idols and arranging public rituals to placate or enlist the support of deities.[82] Among the Xixime, the Jesuits spoke of "priests" who also were "petty kings," clearly linking political and religious offices.[83] In some cases, caciques appear to have inherited their idols and positions and may have formed a priestly hierarchy as among the Zuni.[84] It is clear that some native religious were as important in death as they were in life. Shortly after Fathers Martin Azpilcueta and Lorenzo de Cárdenas began working among the Ayvinos and Batucos,

---

[80] Arguably phrases like "sleight of hand" and "blowing and sucking" do not do justice to the complexity of shamanism. Among the Tohono O'Odham, for instance, "blowing" on patients is a religious gesture predicated on a complex cosmology and theology of spirit helpers who assist with the diagnosis and curing of the sick. See David L. Kozak and David I. Lopez, *Devil Sickness and Devil Songs: Tohono O'Odham Poetics* (Washington, DC: Smithsonian Institution Press, 1999), 72–73.

[81] Beals, *Aboriginal Culture of the Cahita Indians*, 57ff.

[82] Ibid., 58–59; Beals, *The Acaxee*, 29–31; "Carta del Padre Nicolás de Arnaya Dirigida al Padre Provincial Francisco Baez el año de 1607," *Documentos para la Historia de Mexico, 1853–57, Serie IV*, 71–72, 78–79.

[83] "Anua del año de mil seiscientos y diez," Historia 15, Archivo General de la Nación, Mexico City; Pérez de Ribas, *History of the Triumphs*, 546.

[84] Beals, *Aboriginal Culture of the Cahita Indians*, 61, 69.

two branches of the Eudeve Opata, the priests discovered that the natives had shrines where they left offerings and petitioned for help from deceased "sorcerers" and "*principales*":

> On one occasion, [Father Cárdenas] learned that some of his Indian parishioners, [particularly] those who were the greatest principales and had most recently been converted to our holy faith, still maintained and preserved a certain sepulchre as a type of altar in a woods outside the pueblo. There (as if they were still gentiles), they continued to perform their former superstitions, tendering various offerings to the ancient bones of a sorcerer. They venerated him as if he were divine, believing that it was from him that they received the blessing of rain.[85]

In this instance, and presumably others, the Indian "sorcerer" probably had earned the respect of the people for his ability to perform various public rites associated with the worship of a deity such as Tlaloc, the god of thunder, rain, and lightning.

Native Religion and Christianity Compared

In sum, native life in northern Mexico on the eve of Columbus's fateful voyage was anything but simple. Spanish explorers did not find cities of gold but they did find permanent villages and towns, some with ball courts, platform mounds, altars, and plazas. From hunting and gathering and a variety of agricultural techniques, ranging from floodwater farming to canal irrigation, many communities were able to realize surpluses and support craft production and exchange. Like Celtic and Germanic peoples who assimilated and reinterpreted Roman culture during the late Neolithic (before Caesar's invasion of Gaul in the first century B.C.E), the Indians of northern Mexico during prehistory assimilated various aspects of Mesoamerican culture, including religious beliefs. Again, like

---

[85] Andrés Pérez de Ribas, *Coronica y Historia Religiosa de la Provincia de la Compañia de Jesus de Mexico*, 2 vols. (Mexico: Sagrado Corañon, 1896 [1653]), 502. Note that these and other "shrines" may have been an outgrowth of the seated burial tradition at Casas Grandes in Chihuahua; seated burials in caves also were reserved for elites in contact-period Nayarit. Matias de la Mota Padilla, *Historia de la Conquista del Reino de la Nueva Galicia* (Guadalajara: Tallers Graficos de Gallardo y Alvares del Castillo, 1924 [1742]), 325.

the Celts and Germans of late Neolithic Europe, the Indians of northern Mexico were organized sociopolitically on the bases of kinship, governed by elites with differential access to and control of production and organizational strategies. Many Indian communities were organized at the supra-village level into chiefdoms.

With respect to "religion," the Indians of northern Mexico differed considerably from sixteenth-century Iberians, particularly in viewing good and evil in relative rather than absolute terms. From an Indian perspective, evil was anything that undermined or ignored the reciprocity and respect due all life forms, human and otherwise. Humans were not understood as inherently sinful, but simply imperfect creatures prone to mistakes. Correspondingly, Indians had no notion of a quintessentially evil being, Satan, who went about making trouble. The idea of "Hell" or of sin as an affront to God, rather than a human failing, also was foreign to Indians. Despite these important differences, there was a good deal that the Indians had in common with Christians, particularly from Mediterranean Europe. Indeed, with some tinkering (e.g., substitution of spirits for saints), William Christian's characterization of religion in sixteenth-century Spain readily describes indigenous beliefs and practices in northern Mexico:

> As in all Christendom, Iberian villages and towns had their special places, times, and techniques for getting in touch with saints. Each has a set of particular saints they were accustomed to call on for help, and who sometimes called on them. . . .

> The rural shrines, most of which survive today, were situated in particularly striking locations: near holy springs; on the sites of old castles; in parish churches of abandoned towns; or at fords in rivers. . . .

> Communities contacted their saints most in times of crisis. . . .

> Village relations with saints, then, were a series of obligations, many of them explicit and contractual, not unlike their obligations to secular lords. . . .

> Apparitions were one of the ways that new saints were brought into this system or devotions to old saints were revived. Community pantheons were always in a state of flux. . . .

Even without appearing, saints constantly communicated their availability and benevolent interest through the obscure language of signs.[86]

Both Indians and Iberians, including the Jesuits, believed that the empirically known world was populated/visited by spirits who were active participants in human affairs. Some supernaturals "spoke" through anthropomorphic idols and fetishes – a stone idol in the case of the Indians; for the Jesuits it was likely a relic. Both Indians and Iberians believed that their respective spirits and saints required regular sacrifices and devotion, to ensure the health and well-being of kindred spirits. Similarly, both believed that drought, floods, sickness, hail, and other calamities were a sign of some imbalance and alienation of supernaturals. Through dreams and vision quests, Indians sought to identify appropriate sources of power to aid with life and its uncertainties. Although the Church in Europe never was comfortable with the laity pursuing God on their own, dreams and vision quests (e.g., Loyola's *Spiritual Exercises*) were central to the spirituality of saints like Antony, Teresa de Avila, or Ignatius Loyola.

Indians whose own efforts proved unsuccessful could turn to shamans/sorcerers, who, much like Catholic priests, were respected and renumerated for their demonstrated expertise in dealing with matters of jealousy, the heart, or sickness. Similarly, the community as a whole relied on caciques and principal chiefs and, in some instances, perhaps a priestly class, to act as intermediaries with supernaturals. Through public rituals, regular offerings were made to supernaturals to ensure the continuity of the community. Interestingly, among groups such as the Opata some native shamans/priests remained important conduits to the supernatural after death, paralleling the Christian cult of the saints.

The Jesuit Missions of Northern Mexico, 1591–1660

The Jesuits and other Europeans were not willing and in many cases able to see the above parallels. Indian "religions" might in some ways be comparable to Christianity, but that was because Satan always sought

---

[86] William A. Christian, *Apparitions in Late Medieval and Renaissance Spain* (Princeton, NJ: Princeton University Press, 1981), 13–14.

to be revered as the true God. From a Jesuit perspective, Indian religion at best was misguided and at worst, idolatry.

When given the opportunity in 1591, the Jesuits hastened to the northern frontier to unseat Satan. However, neither the Jesuits nor the Spanish Crown were interested solely in Indian souls. Prior to the Spanish invasion of the New World, the mostly Nahuatl-speaking Indians of the south had looked to northern Mexico for turquoise, peyote, and other prized resources. Cortés and his contemporaries quickly picked up on the allure of the north. As early as 1529, the infamous Nuño de Guzman led an invasion up the west coast of Mexico, hoping to find another Tenochtitlan. Other explorers followed, and by 1541 Spaniards had made their way up into the American Southwest (Figure 12). The explorers were looking for gold but found very little of it. However, in 1546 their persistence paid off. That year vast deposits of rich silver ore (some "tainted" with gold) were discovered in the Sierra Madre Occidental, near what was to become the city of Zacatecas, several hundred miles to the north of the valley of Mexico.

During the third quarter of the sixteenth century, hundreds of Spaniards and thousands of their black slaves and Indian workers[87] flocked to the north, where mines were opened in the mountains and along the eastern slope of the Sierra Madre Occidental (Figure 13). Many of these mines were in the lands of the Chichimeca Indians.[88] At the time of the Spanish conquest, the Mexica were celebrating in song and dance the bravery of the Chichimeca, who had courageously resisted Mexica incursions during the fifteenth century. In keeping with their reputation, the Chichimeca wasted no time attacking Spanish wagon trains moving to and from the northern mining frontier and Mexico City. The financial losses were staggering, and during the third quarter of the sixteenth century the Spanish Viceroy tried unsuccessfully to subdue the Chichimeca.[89] In the wake of colony-wide reforms and the failure of

---

[87] Most Indians were legally free laborers but often were effectively enslaved by Spaniards through debt relationships; Indian laborers often relied on Spaniards for food, clothing, tools, and so on.

[88] Chichimeca is the Nahuatl term for various semisedentary groups, who were mostly Otomí speakers, to the northwest of the Valley of Mexico.

[89] P. J. Bakewell, *Silver Mining and Society in Colonial Mexico: Zacatecas 1546–1700* (Cambridge, UK: Cambridge University Press, 1971); Thomas B. Naylor and Charles W. Polzer, S.J., eds., *The Presidio and Militia on the Northern Frontier of New Spain,*

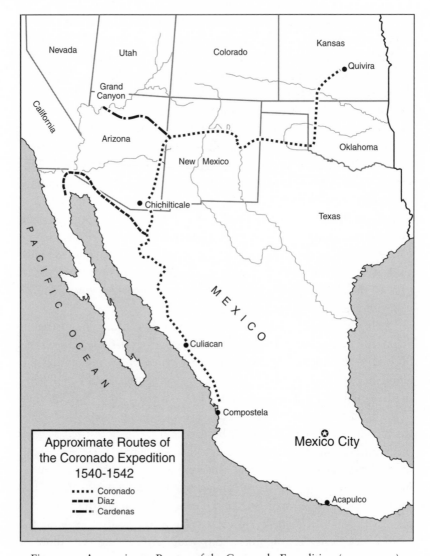

Figure 12. Approximate Routes of the Coronado Expedition (1540–1542).

military means, Viceroy Don Luis de Velasco turned to the Jesuits for help. The Jesuits had come to Mexico in 1572 and had distinguished

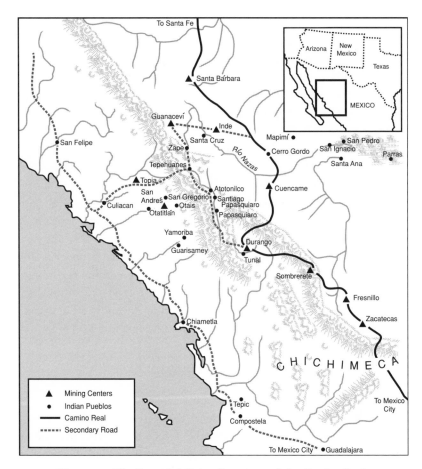

Figure 13. The Spanish Mining Frontier and the *Camino Real*.

themselves in mastering the Otomí language, which was the principal language spoken among the Chichimeca.[90]

The Jesuits enjoyed considerable success with the Chichimeca, and within a few years wagon trains were moving with relative safety to and from Mexico City and the mining frontier to the north. Even before Jesuit success was apparent, the recently appointed governor of

[90] Ernest J. Burrus, S.J., "The Language Problem in Spain's Overseas Dominions." Neue Zeitschrift fur Missionswissenschaft, *Nouvelle revue de science missionaire* 35 (1979): 161–170.

the northernmost province of Nueva Vizcaya, Rodrigo del Río y Losa, asked the Jesuit provincial in Mexico City for priests to be sent to the very limits of the northern frontier. Mineral paints worn by Indians in Sinaloa and in the Sierra Madre Occidental hinted at the possibility of yet undiscovered silver deposits. The Indians, however, were said to be wilder than the Chichimeca. It was nevertheless hoped that the Jesuits could civilize the Indians and create a labor force to mine the rich ore deposits that everyone believed would be found.

In the spring of 1591, Fathers Martin Pérez and Gonzalo de Tapia reached the frontier outpost of the Villa de San Félipe in northern Sinaloa, thus initiating the Jesuit mission enterprise. About the same time, Jesuit superiors in Mexico instructed Fathers Juan Augustín de Espinosa and Gerónimo Ramírez to begin missionary work on the eastern side of the Sierra Madre Occidental, among the Laguneros and Zacateco Indians about the Río Nazas. From these humble beginnings, the Jesuits over the course of the next seventy-five years slowly extended the mission frontier ever northward, establishing dozens of missions and baptizing over four hundred thousand Indians in the process (Figure 14).

The Jesuit Mission

When we speak of the Jesuit "mission," what we are referring to are individual priests who took up residence in what was usually the largest Indian pueblo in a region or river-valley segment. Often these Indian pueblos, which became "head missions" (*cabeceras*), had in excess of one hundred Indian households. Nearby there usually were smaller villages or *rancherías* of related Indians, called *visitas*, which were part of a priest's responsibility.

Because infectious diseases have their greatest impact on large, nucleated settlements, epidemics continually threatened Indian settlement-systems such that the main or largest Indian settlements occasionally were depopulated from death and flight. Priests generally followed in the wake of disease, and so often the first proposals made by a recently arrived missionary was that the Indians "reduce themselves" or resettle in what previously was their largest or main settlements.

During the early Middle Ages, missionary-saints gained innumerable converts by working miracles among the sick and dying. For instance,

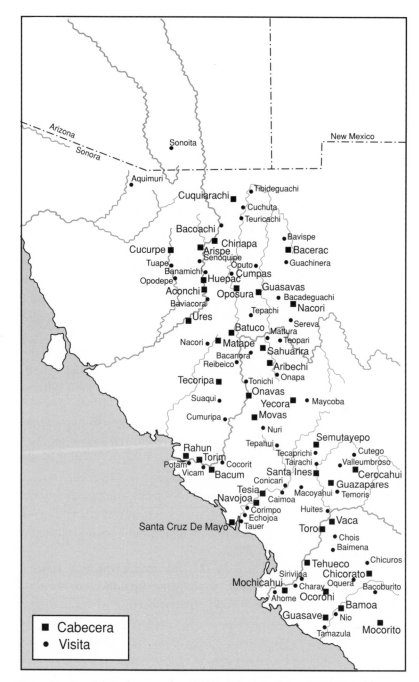

Figure 14. Jesuit Missions to 1660 (After Polzer, *Rules and Precepts of the Jesuit Missions*, 35).

the *vita* of Saint Severin (d. 482) – "the apostle of Noricum" (a Roman province in the eastern Alps or what is today Austria) – relates how he healed a Rugian boy, prompting the Rugians and "other races" to seek out the soldier of Christ.[91] Similarly, many advances of the Jesuit mission frontier occurred during or immediately following epidemics, when gentile groups beyond the mission frontier sent delegations, often headed by caciques, to petition for priests and baptism. Caciques and other elites ordinarily would be expected to balk at any encroachment on their power and influence. However, elites who survived epidemics were under considerable pressure from their following to at least listen to the Jesuits, especially because the missionaries and their ritual cleansing of the soul were perceived as a means of preventing or curing sickness.

There were never enough Jesuits to accommodate Indian requests for missionaries and baptism. Accordingly, many groups often had to wait years and, in some cases, a decade before getting a resident padre. The Jesuits in the meantime paid the Indians occasional visits and often encouraged their ever-dwindling numbers to resettle in established missions. Often gentiles agreed to such proposals, even when resettlement meant residing in a pueblo where the people spoke a different language.

When a priest did finally come to reside permanently among a group, the missionary followed a tradition that went back to the third century,[92] immediately baptizing infants and children under seven, with their parents' consent. Older children and adults were baptized if they were in danger of dying, which was not uncommon. Ideally, adults were baptized after they had mastered the catechism and demonstrated a willingness to live as Christians (e.g., refrain from drinking, adultery, and aboriginal religious practices, in particular).

The Jesuits understood that by the time an individual is an adult he or she usually has assimilated "truths" that are difficult to abandon. Like their clerical and monastic counterparts in early medieval Europe,[93]

[91] Ludwig Beiler, trans., *Eugippius: The Life of Saint Severin*, The Fathers of the Church: A New Translation, Volume 55 (Washington, DC: Catholic University of America, 1965), 64.

[92] Joseph H. Lynch, *Godparents and Kinship in Early Modern Europe* (Princeton, NJ: Princeton University Press, 1988), 122.

[93] Clare Stancliffe, *St. Martin and His Hagiographer* (Oxford: Clarendon Press, 1983), 335.

the Jesuits focused their initial efforts at conversion on Indian elites, who were expected to put pressure on their adult following to embrace Christian truths. Caciques often were recruited with gifts (e.g., clothes, horses). Once cooperation was ensured, the caciques and other native leaders were allowed to retain power and authority, which were exercised through the offices of *gobernador* (governor), *alcalde* (justice of the peace), and *fiscal* (church superintendent).[94] The *gobernador* was given a cane of office and other trappings and was expected to help implement decisions and policy set by the resident missionary.[95] Not insignificantly, once baptized, caciques were afforded the rare privilege of partaking of the Holy Eucharist, which was represented by the Jesuits as a mystical meal of supernatural power. Aboriginally, the Indians had a comparable ritual ("cannibalism") in which they consumed the physical remains of a deceased warrior who had demonstrated superhuman qualities.

The importance of having a cacique as an ally is well illustrated by a report from 1653 from the mission of San Francisco Xavier, in northern Sonora. The report relates how a *hechicero* in a Suma *ranchería* had convinced many people that baptism was responsible for a recent epidemic. One of those who became ill during the epidemic was a "principal" who had been baptized but who was cured after seeing a vision of the Virgin Mary. After the *principal* sided with the local missionary, who claimed that the epidemic was the *hechicero's* doing, the natives rallied to the priest's side, silencing the *hechicero* with the threat of decapitation.[96]

With the support of the cacique and other elites, the Jesuits were able to proceed with the baptism of the remaining adults and adolescents. As suggested, the Jesuits in significant ways followed the catechumenate model of the early Church, which meant that adult Indians desiring baptism had to first demonstrate that they could lead a Christian life. As

---

[94] The right to appoint *gobernadors* and *alcaldes* actually was reserved for civil authorities, but often in fact the local Jesuit missionary guided the appointment process.

[95] Peter M. Dunne, S.J., *Pioneer Black Robes on the West Coast* (Berkeley: University of California Press, 1940), 103; Charles W. Polzer, S.J., *Rules and Precepts of the Jesuit Missions of Northwestern New Spain, 1600–1767* (Tucson: University of Arizona Press, 1976), 39 ff; Spicer, *Cycles of Conquest*, 288 ff; Theodore E. Treutlein, "The Economic Regime of the Jesuit Missions in the Eighteenth Century." *Pacific Historical Review* 8 (1939): 284–300; Pfefferkorn, *Sonora, A Description of the Province*, 266.

[96] "Puntos de annua del año de 1653 del collegio y misiones de Cinaloa," Missiones 26, Archivo General de la Nación, Mexico City.

Figure 15. Ruins of the Mission of Nuestra Señora del Pilar y Santiago de Cocóspera.

was the case with the primitive Church, Jesuit neophytes were encouraged to attend Mass, but were dismissed during the celebration of the Eucharist. Again, as during late antiquity and the early Middle Ages,[97] the Jesuits used the season of Lent (the weeks leading up to Easter or Pentecost) to prepare catechumens for baptism. As we have seen, during the early Middle Ages the baptism rite took on important social functions, inasmuch as baptized infants and adults, as well as their immediate relatives, received new, often fictive kin. The Jesuits continued this tradition among the Indians, who, like the Celts, had their own preconquest traditions of fictive kinship and ceremonial sponsorship. As discussed later, the fragmentation of lineages and communities as a result of epidemics made ritual coparenthood an effective means of reconstituting social relations.

When a Jesuit missionary took up residence in an Indian settlement, it was usually in a one- or two-room structure made from reed mats.

---

[97] F. R. Hoare, trans. and ed., *The Western Fathers, Being the Lives of SS. Martin of Tours, Ambrose, Augustine of Hippo, Honoratus of Arles and Germanus of Auxerre* (New York: Sheed and Ward, 1954), xv; Lynch, *Christianizing Kinship*, 92–93.

The Jesuits imitated the apostles and conducted religious services and instruction outdoors, under large ramadas. Once the baptism of adults largely was completed, the resident padre proposed to his congregation the construction of a "permanent" (built of adobe) church to house the most prized possession of a mission community, namely, one or more holy relics and the consecrated host (Figure 15). Jesuit churches, some of which survive to this day, required a considerable investment of time, labor, and love. Still the Jesuits kept their churches relatively simple, favoring the single-nave variety, which was characteristic of the Apostolic Church.[98] Often agricultural and other surpluses generated by mission Indians were sold and the money used to beautify the churches with statuary, tapestries, and paintings.

Paul's missionary strategy, as evidenced in his letters and *The Acts of the Apostles*, was to establish Christian communities in select cities, whence knowledge of Christ's teachings were spread by Paul and his neophytes to outlying settlements. The Jesuits followed this Pauline pattern. Each Jesuit missionary was required to make the rounds of his mission district or *partido*, visiting the sick and otherwise seeing to the spiritual and corporal needs of Indians in outlying settlements (*visitas*), allied to his pueblo of residence or *cabecera*. Mass and feastdays (e.g., Nativity, Lent, Corpus Christi) usually were celebrated by the priest in the *cabecera* Church and were attended by Indians from the *visitas*, which usually were within walking distance (an hour or two away by foot). Sunday and other religious days were the occasion for celebration, including feasts at which Indians from an entire mission district would be fed with cattle provided by the resident padre from the mission herd.

The above description of the Jesuit mission is far from complete. A visitor to a *cabecera* would on occasion witness a public whipping, when an adulterous Indian bared his back for a dozen lashes. The Jesuits were under strict orders to never administer corporal punishment. Still, they often sought out sinners and dictated public penance, staying the hand of an Indian *fiscale* when the resident padre was sure the penitent and the onlooking crowd understood the gravity of offending God and his ministers. In this regard, Jesuit missionaries emulated priests in early

---

[98] Phelan, *The Millennial Kingdom*, 49–50.

medieval Europe, who, prior to the eighth century (when private confession and penance became widespread), required their neophytes to confess publicly on their knees.

The history of the early Church in Europe and the history of the Jesuit missions are replete with rebellion and apostasy. On the occasion of a rebellion or a threat to a priest, the Jesuits along the western slopes of the Sierra Madre, in Sinaloa and southern Sonora, had recourse to a small detachment of Spanish soldiers who were stationed in the Villa de San Félipe and later relocated to Fort Montesclaros. Missionaries in the Sierras and on the eastern slopes of the mountains called upon Spanish militia in Durango and Parral. Rebellious Indians were not tolerated on theological grounds[99] and because they set an untenable precedent. Indian communities that spawned apostates often had the rebels returned for public execution. On one such occasion, which seems to have even shocked Spaniards in Mexico City, the Jesuits condoned the execution of thirty-three Suaqui apostates.

It is hard to gauge the extent to which the Jesuits ruled with an "iron hand." Jesuit missionaries purportedly followed the model established by Francis Xavier, who argued that the missionary should be flexible and deal with people in a tender fashion; missionaries were not to control others by instilling servile fear.[100] Rules drawn up specifically for the mission frontier by Jesuit Father Visitors echoed such principles, instructing missionaries to "show the Indians all love and charity . . ." and to "avoid as much as possible all forms of strictness and harshness."[101] One could ask, however, whether such rules bespeak effective safeguards against abuse or point to a problem of abusive priests.

The Jesuit materials hold out various possibilities, including priests who were respected for their kindness.[102] Father Pedro Méndez, who spent perhaps more time on the frontier than any other missionary (over

---

[99] Jesus is quoted in *Luke* 12:10 as saying that blasphemy against the Holy Spirit could never be forgiven. Because the Holy Spirit was with the apostles and by extension, the Jesuits, apostates generally were executed.

[100] O'Malley, *The First Jesuits*, 81.   [101] Polzer, *Rules and Precepts*, 68.

[102] Kessell, *Spain in the Southwest*, 394f.7, notes that the documentary record from New Mexico indicates that the Franciscans also were a diverse group that included abusive priests. The record does not suggest, however, that sexual impropriety or cruelty were the norm among Franciscan missionaries.

twenty years), paints a picture in one of his letters that seems anything but repressive:

> It is amazing to see toddlers three or four years old sitting in small groups and saying their prayers as best they can. When the older children are tardy in the morning they come to excuse themselves by saying, "Pardon me, Father, I overslept," or, "It was so cold that I waited before coming." A name has been coined for these children. It is [246] *Paretabuseme*, which means "the priest's guard" (because they see me walking accompanied by them). Although the Mayo use this term in jest because they see that I have no other guard or escort, I take it in the way that it should be taken – that through them the Lord is protecting me. Although such matters may seem insignificant, these children are not.[103]

Disease and the Mission Frontier

Whatever the reality with respect to Jesuit reliance on violence, it did not stop many thousands of Indians from seeking baptism and missionaries. By 1660, when the Indian population was still relatively large and the missions were at their height,[104] the Jesuits had baptized over four hundred thousand Indians. Neither pagan Europeans nor Indians embraced Christianity whole-heartedly. Still, by any measure, but particularly the Indians' own understanding of themselves as Christians, the Jesuits enjoyed remarkable success.

What prompted and sustained Indian interest in Christianity and mission ways of life? As was the case in Europe during late antiquity, epidemics of acute and chronic infectious disease paved the way for the Jesuits in Mexico. As noted earlier, Cortés's invasion of Mexico ushered in a half-century of disease episodes that devastated the Indian population of southern Mexico. After a respite of sorts, in 1575, southern Mexico experienced a new round of epidemics that regularly began to make their way northward to the Spanish mining and Jesuit mission frontiers.

---

[103] Pérez de Ribas, *History of the Triumphs*, 293.

[104] After 1660 the Jesuit mission system continued to expand in northern Sonora, Baja California, southern Chihuahua, and finally, southern Arizona. However, this expansion was largely anticlimactic, because of a continuing decline in the Indian population of northern New Spain.

In January 1593, some eighteen months after Fathers Pérez and Tapia had established the first Jesuit missions in and around the Villa de San Félipe, the priests wrote to superiors in Mexico of a dreadful epidemic of smallpox that claimed the lives of thousands of Indians in northern Sinaloa (Figure 16).[105] According to the *anua* of 1593, smallpox and measles first appeared in the Villa de San Félipe and then spread rapidly to what were a dozen or so Jesuit missions along the Río Sinaloa. Gentile pueblos as much as forty miles from San Félipe also were reportedly stricken with smallpox or measles. Almost everyone became ill, leaving many communities unable to care for the sick and dead. Father Martín Pérez offered a particularly graphic account of the epidemic, noting that smallpox and measles spread from village to village, leaving many houses filled with people burning with fever and covered from head to foot with repulsive sores.[106]

The Jesuits responded to the disaster by turning their residence in the pueblo of Cubiri into a hospital. Those who were able to reach the hospital were fed and cared for by Brother Francisco de Castro, who months before had come north with two additional priests. While Brother Castro attended to the sick and dying at Cubiri, Fathers Tapia and Pérez, and the recently arrived priests, Fathers Velasco and Santiago, made the rounds of the dozen or so mission pueblos, working day and night, attending to both the spiritual and corporal needs of their neophytes. It was impossible, however, for the five Jesuits to attend to all the sick and dying, particularly as many Indians fled their villages in fear and horror. By the Jesuits' own admission, many Indians died during the epidemic who never saw a priest.[107] Those who fled the missions later were found

---

[105] "Puntos sacados de las relaciones de Antonio Ruiz, P. Martin Perez, P. Vincente del Aguila, P. Gaspar Varela, Juan de Grixalva, Capitan Martinez, y otras," Misiones 25; "Anua del año de mil quinientos de noventa y tres," Misiones 25; "Anua del año de mil quinientos noventa y quatro," Historia 15, Archivo General de la Nación, Mexico City; Juan E. Nieremberg, S.J. (with Andrade Cassini), *Varones Illustres de la Compañia de Jesus.* 3 vols. (Bilbao, 1889 [1666]); Alegre, *Historia de la Provincia,* I, 391–394; W. E. Shiels, S.J., *Gonzalo de Tapia (1561–1594): Founder of the First Permanent Jesuit Mission in North America* (New York: United States Catholic Historical Society, 1934); Dunne, *Pioneer Black Robes.*

[106] "Puntos sacados," Misiones 25, Archivo General de la Nación, Mexico City.

[107] Alegre, *Historia de la Provincia,* I, 392; "Anua del año de mil quinientos noventa y quatro," Historia 15, Archivo General de la Nación, Mexico City, 36.

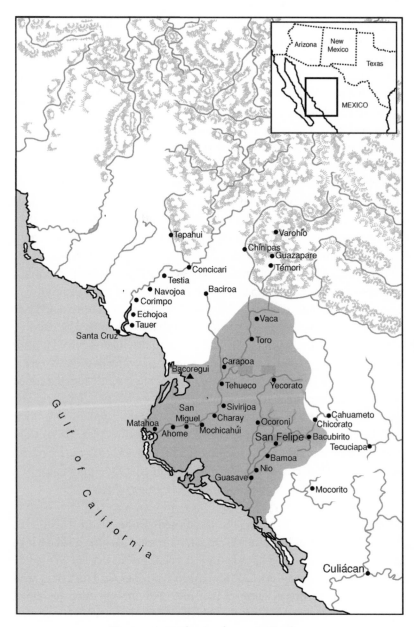

Figure 16. Epidemic of 1593 in Sinaloa.

lying under trees in the scrubland along the coast. So great were the losses that many bodies were left where they lay for want of someone to bury them. Ironically, the priests, and more precisely, their native assistants, unknowingly helped spread disease. Father Velasco wrote of one occasion when Father Tapia visited a pueblo that had escaped the epidemic but where many subsequently became ill and died.

During the summer of 1594, about the time smallpox and measles subsided in Sinaloa, the Jesuits working on the other side of the Sierra Madre reported that smallpox also had reached epidemic proportions among the Laguneros and Zacateco Indians (Figure 17). We know little about the epidemic and its consequences, beyond the fact that the Jesuits were visited by a group of caciques who begged for priests to visit their lands because many of their children were dying from smallpox. Significantly, in Father Juan Augustín's letter describing a visit to one of the afflicted villages he made no mention of sick adults; Augustín mentioned eighteen boys and girls who were sick.[108] Because of their proximity to the Spanish mining frontier, the Laguneros and Zacateco apparently had suffered on previous occasions from smallpox, explaining why children were sick rather than adults (the adults apparently had survived a prior bout with smallpox and acquired resistance to *variola* in the process).

The epidemic of 1593–1594 was the first of many epidemics described by the Jesuits that affected the Indians of northern Mexico. Jesuit reports mention or discuss epidemics of smallpox, measles, typhus, and other maladies that swept through the mission system at regular five to eight year intervals (e.g., 1593, 1601–1602, 1607–1608, 1611–1612, 1617, and 1623–1625). This temporal pattern reflects in part the appearance of a new generation of susceptibles, particularly young children.[109]

As was the case in 1593–1594, most epidemics spread well beyond the mission frontier. In 1614, the Jesuits sent Father Pedro Méndez to the Río Mayo to establish the first missions among the Mayo. The Mayo had petitioned for over a decade for a resident priest. Letters written by Father Méndez as well as Captain Diego Martínez de Hurdaide, who accompanied the priest, indicate that one or more maladies, including typhus, were current among the Mayo and had spread well up into

---

[108] Alegre, *Historia de la Provincia*, I, 423; Pérez de Ribas, *History of the Triumphs*, 661.
[109] Reff, *Disease, Depopulation and Culture Change*, 132–179.

Figure 17. Epidemic of 1594 in northern Durango and southern Chihuahua.

central Sonora. In a letter copied by Pérez de Ribas, Captain Hurdaide recounted how he had been visited by delegations from the interior who pleaded for priests because they were disappearing:

> I experienced their good nature and docility and their great willingness to receive the Holy Gospel, especially the Nébome, who with demonstrations of great regret said to me, "We will all be gone before a priest comes to baptize us."[110]

In his own letter describing the *entrada*, Méndez wrote that during his first fifteen days among the Mayo he baptized thirty-six hundred infants and adults, five hundred of whom died "...going quickly to be with Our Lord."[111] Later that year, in December, Méndez again wrote his superiors: "It is a thing of great consolation that frequently when I am out visiting all the [Mayo] pueblos, baptizing the sick, I find on my return that Our Lord has taken most if not all of them."[112]

In 1608, shortly after the Jesuits had established missions on the eastern slopes of the Sierras, among the Laguneros, the missions of Laguna and Parras were devastated by an epidemic of smallpox, which affected native peoples throughout much of the northern frontier. Among the many who suffered and died was a delegation of gentile Indians who happened to be visiting Parras when the epidemic began. Tragically, the gentiles fled Parras for their homes in the mountains, taking smallpox with them:

> Returning to the people from the mountains, who fled the illness, it not only overtook them along the way, but also spread to their lands and distant rancherías in the mountains. It attacked them with such fury that barely one or two people survived in rancherías that previously had a hundred or more people. The few survivors came to give word of what was happening, and as a result many were disabused of the erroneous belief preached by their sorcerers, namely that the illness had struck and killed them because they had been baptized.... There were gentiles who, once they were disabused, brought their sick children

---

[110] Pérez de Ribas, *History of the Triumphs*, 290.
[111] Alegre, *Historia de la Provincia*, II, 255; Pérez de Ribas, *History of the Triumphs*, 288.
[112] "Anua del año de mil seiscientos catorce," Historia 15, Archivo General de la Nación, Mexico City; Pérez de Ribas, *History of the Triumphs*, 294.

down from the mountains to be baptized. They arrived half-dead, and upon receiving the water of Holy Baptism, they went to heaven. God did not grant them any more life than what they needed to make it to Parras and from there to be taken to His glory.[113]

The Demographic and Cultural Consequences of Disease

The rise of Christianity in Europe was coincident with a demographic collapse that began in late antiquity and continued well into the Middle Ages.[114] The Indian embrace of Christianity in southern and northern Mexico was likewise coincident with a population collapse. Comparison of population figures given by Spanish explorers (before the introduction of disease) with Jesuit baptismal and census data suggest that native populations in northern Mexico were reduced by 30 to 50 percent prior to sustained contact with the Jesuits. Within a few decades of incorporation into the mission system, native populations uniformly were reduced by 75 percent or more.[115]

The rate and extent of population decline is reflected in Jesuit reports on baptisms and mission population. In 1638 the Jesuits reported that, although three hundred thousand Indians had been baptized, only a third of that number were still alive. In the Sierra Madre Occidental, where Spaniards and disease appeared rather early (c. 1575), only 10 percent of the Indians baptized by the Jesuits survived in 1638.[116] In 1678, when the number of Indians baptized exceeded four hundred thousand, the mission population totaled only sixty-three thousand.[117] At the time of

[113] Pérez de Ribas, *History of the Triumphs*, 682.
[114] N. J. Pounds, *An Historical Geography of Europe* (Cambridge, UK: Cambridge University Press, 1990), 52–53.
[115] Reff, *Disease, Depopulation, and Culture Change*; Robert H. Jackson, *Indian Population Decline: The Missions of Northwestern New Spain, 1687–1840* (Albuquerque: University of New Mexico Press, 1994).
[116] "Memorial al Rey para que no se recenga la limosna de la Misiones y consierva al Senor Palafox en las relaciones a la Compañia, Andrés Pérez de Ribas, 12 de Septiembre 1638," Temporalidades 2009-1, Archivo Historico de Hacienda, Mexico City; C.W. Hackett, *Historical Documents Relating to New Mexico, Nueva Vizcaya, and Approaches Thereto, to 1773*, Collected by Adolph and Fanny R. Bandelier, 3 vols. (Washington, DC: Carnegie Institution of Washington, 1937).
[117] "Relacion de los Missiones que la Compañia tiene en el Reyno y Provincias de la Nueva Viscaya en la Nueva España echa el año de 1678 con ocasion de la Visita

the expulsion of the Jesuit order from the New World (1767), the mission population had declined to approximately thirty thousand.[118]

Numbers only begin to tell the story with respect to the consequences of disease on the northern frontier. As we have seen, the Jesuits noted that often during outbreaks of disease almost entire settlements became infected, incapacitating entire households and leaving a fraction of the population to care for the sick. This situation often was made worse by the tendency for those who were unaffected or who were in the incuba-tion stage of disease to flee with the first signs of illness. Communities that suddenly were abandoned or that lost a large number of people from sickness or flight necessarily suffered shortages of food and other neces-sities. Outbreaks of disease often occurred during the cooler months of the year, in spring and fall. Epidemics in the spring made it difficult to prepare fields or sow crops; those in the fall interrupted or curtailed harvests. The fall was also when native peoples secured their main meat supply (deer) for the year. Both the hunt, which was largely limited to the rutting season, and the drying of meat were imperiled by sickness. With-out surpluses, it was difficult or impossible to support craft production or trade. Because native groups often relied on each other (e.g., coastal groups supplied salt to interior groups who reciprocated with maize), many more people suffered than those who were directly affected by an outbreak of measles or some other malady.

The collapse of productive and organizational strategies, particularly the loss of surpluses and trade goods, necessarily undermined the power and influence of native caciques, who were responsible for accumulating and redistributing surpluses. This is of course assuming that the caciques themselves survived encounters with smallpox, measles, and so on. In 1619, when Pérez de Ribas met the principal cacique of the Sisibotari Opata, "Gran Sisibotari," the chief was said to be "still young." Nine years later, when the first Jesuit priest took up residence among the Sisibotari, the chief was dead.[119] The chief apparently died during the

General dellas que por orden del Padre Provincial Thomas Altamirano hizo el Padre Visitador Juan Hortiz Zapata de la misma Compañia," Misiones 26, Archivo General de la Nación, Mexico City.

[118] Reff, *Disease, Depopulation and Culture Change*, 210–203.

[119] "Missiones de San Ygnacio en Mayo, Yaqui, Nevomes, Chinipas, y Sisibotaris, 1628," Historia 15, Archivo General de la Nación, Mexico City, 345.

epidemic of 1623–1625, which reportedly killed over eighty-six hundred Indians, not counting those like Gran Sisibotari who died without the sacraments.[120]

The power and influence of native caciques, whose duties often included functioning as priests, were undercut by their failure to explain and prevent epidemics. Unlike the Jesuits, who had knowledge of and experience with epidemic disease, native elites had little experience to draw from to explain, never mind halt the unprecedented suffering wrought by smallpox and other maladies. As noted, Native Americans had never experienced diseases like those brought to the New World by Europeans.

Jesuit materials indicate that native shamans and priests initially broached existing deities or attempted to manipulate demonstrated repositories of mana to prevent or counteract disease. At the outset of the epidemic of 1607–1608 in the missions of Laguna and Parras, a comet appeared in the sky. An unnamed Jesuit wrote the following account of how the Laguneros interpreted and responded to the conjunction of the comet and epidemic. Interestingly, the Indians broached the events in much the same terms as pagans and medieval Christians.[121] As the quote speaks to many issues, I have cited it at length:

A comet appeared at the outset of an epidemic, and some Indians from another nation who had been reduced to this pueblo [Mapimí] were afraid that the sickness would affect them here. Therefore, they decided to hold a mitote, their very well-known traditional dance, to favorably dispose the comet, or Satan, whose trickery was encouraging them. The dance was celebrated in the following fashion: First, they came forward in pairs – women and men of all ages, from seven to a hundred years old. All of them carried little baskets in their right hands; in their left hand they each held an arrow with the flint point pressed against their heart. Some of their little baskets were full of the dates that they have in this land. Others were full of prickly pears, while still others had the fruit they call mescal or mezquitamal.[122] Some

---

[120] "Carta Annua de la Provincia de la Compañia de Jesus de Nueva España, Juan Lorencio," Misiones 25, Archivo General de la Nación, Mexico City.
[121] Valerie I.J. Flint, The Rise of Magic in Early Medieval Europe (Princeton, NJ: Princeton University Press, 1991), 135–138.
[122] Roasted buds of the century plant.

of them brought field mice, pocket gophers, rabbits, and snakes, all of them dead. At the end of the procession came four old men, all of them painted and each with a leather whip in his hand.

The end of the comet (some of them said) was in the form of plumage; others said it had the form of an animal's tail. For this reason, some came with feathers on their heads and others with a lion's or fox's tail, each of them mimicking the animal he represented. In the middle of the plaza there was a great bonfire into which they threw their baskets along with everything in them. They did this so that by burning up and sacrificing these things, they would rise up as smoke to the comet. As a result, the comet would have some food during those days and would therefore do them no harm....

Once this diabolical dance was concluded, the rabble dispersed to their various rancherías. Some of them returned to the pueblo of Mapimí, where the illness finally arrived. This was because God did not want them to believe that the superstitious and diabolical sacrifice in which they had placed their trust would free them from this illness.... Later, the epidemic worsened in such a way that so many of these savages died that they had to dig pits in which they were buried in heaps. Some of those who were fleeing further inland were dying in the countryside. Thus, as I was responding to a call to baptize a sick young man who was nine leagues away, along a stretch less than a quarter of a league long I encountered eleven people dead in the countryside. This was the course that the epidemic ran among these unfortunate people, and a great number of sick Indians died.[123]

The above letter was written at roughly the same time that fellow Jesuits working several hundred miles to the west, along the Río Fuerte, reported that the Tehueco Indians were found to be worshipping a god "of life and death" who was associated with lightning and to whom offerings were made to stop the spread of disease.[124] Father Martín Azpilcueta seems to have encountered a similar set of beliefs among the Eudeve-Opata of Batuc.[125] The linking of smallpox to deities associated with lighting is reminiscent of the smallpox cults that emerged among the

[123] Pérez de Ribas, *History of the Triumphs*, 675–676.
[124] Ibid., 245–246.
[125] "Carta del Padre Martin de Azpilcueta al Padre Ignacio de Cavala, 3 de Deciembre 1630," Misiones 25, Archivo General de la Nación, Mexico City.

Dahomey in west Africa during the nineteenth century. The Dahomey cults believed that earth deities – Big Brother and Little Brother – used smallpox and lighting, respectively, to punish people for transgressions, including sorcery. To prevent epidemics, the smallpox cults built shrines and made offerings to Big Brother as well as instituted behavioral reforms and punishment.[126]

Had the Jesuits not followed closely upon the heels of smallpox and other diseases, the Tehueco and other groups in northern Mexico undoubtedly would have developed a wholly native response to disease, perhaps replete with smallpox cults. The Indians of northern Mexico were not so ethnocentric, however, as to deny the utility of alternative beliefs and rituals. As we have seen, there is considerable evidence that they embraced significant aspects of Mesoamerican religion prior to the European invasion. The Indians of northern Mexico were similarly responsive to the Jesuits, giving rise to a "folk Catholicism" that bespeaks an Indian, Spanish, and in some ways wholly "Mexican" worldview.

The Dynamics of Conversion

Many Yoeme (Yaqui) today understand Jesus Christ as a curer who once preached and performed miracles in the Yoeme homeland (Hiakim).[127] Jesuit missionaries were likewise perceived by the Indians as shamans or sorcerers with knowledge and rituals to "cleanse the soul" and provide protection from or cure for disease.[128] Shortly after the epidemic of 1593 in Sinaloa subsided, the Suaqui of the Rio Fuerte experienced a

---

[126] Geoffrey Parrinder, *West African Religion* (Epworth Press, London, 1949); Frederick Quinn, "How Traditional Dahomian Society Interpreted Smallpox." *ABBIA*, Revue Culturelle Camerounaise 20 (1967): 151–166.

[127] Thomas Sheridan, "The Yoemem (Yaquis), An Enduring People." In *Paths of Life, American Indians of the Southwest and Northern Mexico*, eds. Thomas Sheridan and Nancy J. Parezo, pp. 35–40 (Tucson: University of Arizona Press, 1996), 36.

[128] See, for instance, Alegre, *Historia de la Provincia*, II, 470; Gerard Decorme, S.J., *La Obra de los Jesuitas Mexicanos durante la Epoca Colonial, 1572–1767*, 2 vols. (Mexico: Jose Porrua e Hijos, 1941), 360–361; Sheridan and Naylor, *Rarámuri*, 36; see also Martin Dobrizhoffer, *An Account of the Abipones, an Equestrian People of Paraguay*, 2 vols. (New York: Johnson Reprint Corporation, 1970), 79; Luis Necker, *Indios Guaranies Y Chamanes Franciscanos, Las Primeras reducciones del Paraguay (1580–1800)*, Biblioteca Paraguaya de Antropología, Vol. 7 (Asuncion: Centro de Estudios Antropológicos, Universidad Católica, 1990).

frightening earthquake. Some Suaqui suspected that Father Gonzalo de Tapia, the local Jesuit superior, was responsible for the earthquake and had punished the Suaqui for their hostility toward the Jesuits. To appease Tapia, the Suaqui brought corn, beans, and other presents and extended an invitation to Tapia to visit their lands.[129]

In Mexico as in early medieval Europe, the line between priests and sorcerers was very thin.[130] Indian perceptions of the Jesuits as shamans, and baptism as a shamanistic rite, is reflected in a report from 1639, recounting the establishment of a mission among the Opata of the Sonora Valley. The report noted that, much to Jesuit dismay, many parents of baptized children asked that their children be rebaptized at the first sign of illness.[131]

The Jesuits offered rituals as well as a complex theology that had evolved over the course of a millennium in part to explain as well as deal with epidemic disease. The forty-hours' devotion, for instance, initially was a response to an epidemic of plague that besieged Milan in 1345. The thrust of the Jesuit explanation for why the Indians were suffering from disease was that God sent the Indians not only disease but also missionaries! The combination of the two represented a "wonderful" opportunity for the Indians to exercise their free will. It was not entirely or largely the Indians' fault, given that they had never been exposed to the Gospel, that they were deceived by their shamans and Satan. But now that they were hearing the word of God, they were being given the opportunity to choose God over Satan and salvation over damnation. Those who elected baptism – no matter they died – could be assured of heaven. Many could also expect that baptism would cure them of sickness. Other Holy Sacraments, together with the cult of the saints, offered the possibility of miracles and transcendence.

From an Indian perspective, what was particularly attractive about the Jesuit worldview was that it shifted the burden of guilt from the Indians to Satan. At the outset of an epidemic, the Indians naturally questioned themselves and how they may have offended the spirit world.

---

[129] Pérez de Ribas, *History of the Triumphs*, 123.

[130] Peter Brown, *Religion and Society in the Age of Saint Augustine* (New York: Harper & Row, 1972), 129; Necker, *Indios Guaranies*.

[131] "Puntos de Anua de la nueba mission de San Francisco Jabier, año de 1639," Misiones 25, Archivo General de la Nación, Mexico City. See also Necker, *Indios Guaranies*.

The offense was not really theirs; they were simply caught in a cosmic struggle between God and Satan. So argued the Jesuits. Significantly, in advancing this argument the Jesuits invoked a conception of Satan and human sin that harkened back to late antiquity and the early Middle Ages. With the exception of Indian shamans, who from the Jesuit perspective consciously entered into a pact with Satan, the Jesuits cast the Indians as victims rather than co-conspirators.

The fact that shamans perished during epidemics while the Jesuits went unscathed made Jesuit "theories" and finger pointing (at the shamans) all the more plausible:

> ... it was also noted that God took the lives of other principal Indians who were obstacles to the teaching of the Gospel. He finished them off, to the amazement of others. But at the same time these nations have seen and noticed that the [Jesuit] priests among them live long lives.[132]

Native interest in baptism and the Jesuits presupposed the failure of native priests and shamans to adequately explain, prevent, and cope with the unprecedented suffering caused by smallpox and other maladies. Shamans who did not themselves perish often were discredited and sometimes killed because their pharmacology and rituals failed to prevent illness or restore health.[133] Part of the shamans' undoing was that after they pronounced a person as dying, the shaman as well as the patient's relatives apparently abandoned the sick.[134] At times, the shamans went to other extremes that offended their own people:

> There was a deep-rooted abuse that was more common among these people [Laguneros] than among other barbarians. When an important person became sick, they would sacrifice a newborn child so that the older person would regain his health. ... The devil persuaded another faction of these peoples that if they were present when a sick person died, they would all die as well. The fear caused by this superstition

---

[132] Pérez de Ribas, *History of the Triumphs*, 374.

[133] "Puntos de annua del año de 1653 del collegio y misiones de Cinaloa," Misiones 26, Archivo General de la Nación, Mexico City; Beals, *Aboriginal Culture of the Cahita Indians*, 63.

[134] Pfefferkorn, *Sonora, A Description of the Province*, 219–220; Treutlein, *Missionary in Sonora, Travel Reports of Joseph Och*.

and abuse led people to bury the sick before they were dead in order to avoid being present at the hour of death.[135]

There are many documented cases of magical death – instances where sorcery victims fail to respond to medical treatment.[136] A shaman's diagnosis that a patient was unlikely to recover often may have proved to be a self-fulfilling prophecy.

In the previous chapter I quoted a letter by Bishop Dionysius, recounting how early Christians " . . . took charge of the sick, attending to their every need . . . ," while pagans " . . . fled from their dearest, throwing them into the roads before they were dead."[137] Jesuit missionaries went to great lengths to comfort the sick with food and water as well as emotional and spiritual support.[138] The fact that each Jesuit missionary was part of a much larger network of missions meant that individual priests, including those recently arrived at a new mission, had access to food surpluses and material support from other missions, which could be "borrowed" to aid those afflicted by an epidemic. To give but one example, during the epidemic of 1623–1625, which claimed over eighty-six hundred Indian lives, priests throughout the northern frontier assisted each other for days and weeks on end, attending to the sick and moving food and medicines wherever needed.[139]

The Jesuits treated the sick by bleeding patients (standard European practice at the time) and more commonly by administering medicines and herbs that were imported from Mexico or that were suggested by their neophytes.[140] In 1711, a Jesuit lay brother, Juan de Esteyneffer, compiled the *Florilegio Medicinal*, a three-volume source book on how to diagnose and treat various illnesses.[141] Esteyneffer gathered much

---

[135] Pérez de Ribas, *History of the Triumphs*, 667.

[136] Ann M. McElroy and Patricia A. Townsend, *Medical Anthropology in Ecological Perspective* (North Scituate, MA: Duxbury Press, 1979), 288.

[137] G. A. Williamson, trans., *Eusebius: The History of the Church from Christ to Constantine* (Harmondsworth, Middlesex, England: Dorset Press, 1965), 305–306.

[138] Pérez de Ribas, *History of the Triumphs*, 673.

[139] "Carta annua de la Provincia de la Compañia de Jesus de Nueva España, Juan Lorencio, 16 de Mayo 1624," Misiones 25, Archivo General de la Nación, Mexico City.

[140] Margarita A. Kay, "The Florilegio Medicinal: Source of Southwestern Ethnomedicine." *Ethnohistory* 28 (1977): 251–259; Nentvig, *Rudo Ensayo*, 43; Pfefferkorn, *Sonora: A Description of the Province*, 60–78.

[141] Kay, "The Florilegio Medicinal."

of his information from priests who had worked on the frontier, who, in turn, acquired substantial information from native "apothecaries." The *Florilegio* parallels in many ways the *Lacnunga* and other medical manuscripts that were compiled by medieval monks and used to treat their pagan neophytes.

The Jesuits also imitated their medieval counterparts in their use of "sympathetic magic" and the cult of the saints and their relics. In one instance, for example, the Jesuits gathered up the remains of a painting of the Virgin that had been burned during an Indian revolt and used the ashes, which were mixed with holy water, to treat the ill.[142] The annual reports compiled by Jesuit missionaries often speak of Indian women who were aided during childbirth by medals, relics, specialized prayers, and basic care. The *anua* of 1621, for instance, related how a woman who had been in labor for three days finally gave birth to a healthy child after the resident priest placed a medal of Saint Ignatius around her neck. The *anua* tells of another women who was near death who gave birth to a healthy child ("without any lesions") upon receiving the last rites and a medal of Saint Ignatius.[143] Similar "edifying cases" involving pregnant women can be found in many Jesuit reports.[144] Anzures y Bolaños notes that there are 153 saints mentioned in the *Florilegio Medicinal* who were said to intercede with God on behalf of the sick.[145]

It is an article of faith rather than reason or even Christian theology that baptism, relics, or medals can "cure disease."[146] However, the very fact that the sacraments were used and combined with basic clinical

---

[142] Pérez de Ribas, *History of the Triumphs*, 633.

[143] "Anua del año de mil seiscientos y veinte y uno," Historia 15, Archivo General de la Nación, Mexico City.

[144] See, for instance: "Anua del año de mil seiscientos y veinte," Historia 15, 253; AGN "Missiones de San Ygnacio en Mayo, Yaqui, Nevomes, Chinipas, y Sisibotaris," Historia 15, 344; "Puntos para el Anua del año de 1635, destas misiones de San Ignacio Nuestro Padre en la Provincia de Cinaloa, Tomas Basilio, 26 de Marzo 1636," Misiones 25, 264; "Puntos para el Anua del año de 1636 destas misiones de San Ignacio Nuestro Padre en la Provincia de Cinaloa, Tomas Basilio, 9 de Abril 1637," Misiones 25, 2. Archivo General de la Nación, Mexico City.

[145] Juan de Esteyneffer, *Florilegio Medicinal*, ed. Ma. Carmen Anzures y Bolanos (Mexico: Academia Nacional de Medicina, 1978 [1711]), 70–71.

[146] Christian theology invariably has asserted that rosaries or medals have no intrinsic power. What power obtains from their use stems from their facilitation of desires to be one with God, which can attract the Holy Spirit and its beneficial effects.

care meant that many survived who otherwise would have died.[147] The Jesuits as well as Franciscans[148] realized very early in the colonial period that clinical care dramatically lowered the mortality rate during epidemics.

There were other important respects in which the Jesuits filled a void left by the failure of native priests and shamans. Epidemics were amenable to Christian beliefs and practices such as retribution for sin, pilgrimages, and processions. In scenes that were reminiscent of Europe during the Middle Ages,[149] the Jesuits organized public processions that often involved scourging. Processions of this kind were common throughout Mexico during the colonial period and apparently were quite therapeutic.[150] In one of his early letters describing the founding of missions among the Mayo, Father Pedro Méndez provided a graphic account of how his neophytes – young and old, caciques and servants – made switches of maguey fiber, on the ends of which were balls of wax in which cactus thorns were embedded. Méndez noted that entire villages gathered with their switches and readily took part in scourging processions, apparently venting their fears and frustration.[151] During the epidemic of 1606 and 1607, upwards of one thousand Acaxee participated in scourging processions in the hope of halting the epidemic.[152]

Processions to halt epidemics were common in Europe during the Middle Ages and the early modern period.[153] Gregory of Tours's *Life of*

---

[147] Jean-Pierre Peter, "Disease and the Sick at the End of the Eighteenth Century." In *Biology of Man in History*, eds. R. Forster and O. Ranum, trans. R. Forster and P. Ranum, pp. 81–94 (Baltimore, MD: Johns Hopkins University Press, 1975), 123.

[148] Francisco de Florencia, S.J., *Historia de la Provincia de la Compañia de Jesus de Nueva España* (Mexico: Editorial Academia Literaria, 1955[1694]), 260; Fray Gerónimo de Mendieta, *Vidas Franciscanas*, ed. Juan B. Iguiniz (Mexico: Universidad Nacional Autónoma, 1945), 174.

[149] J.N. Biraben and Jacques Le Goff, "The Plague in the Early Middle Ages." In *Biology of Man in History*, eds. E. Forster and O. Ranum, trans. R. Forster and P. Ranum, pp. 48–80 (Baltimore, MD: Johns Hopkins University Press, 1975), 61.

[150] Donald B. Cooper, *Epidemic Disease in Mexico City, 1761–1813* (Austin: University of Texas Press, 1965).

[151] Dunne, *Pioneer Black Robes*, 150–151; Pérez de Ribas, *History of the Triumphs*, 291–292.

[152] Pérez de Ribas, *History of the Triumphs*, 517.

[153] William A. Christian, *Local Religion in Sixteenth-Century Spain* (Princeton, NJ: Princeton University Press, 1981).

the Fathers (592 C.E.), which recounts the saintly lives and accomplishments of some twenty holy men (bishops, monks, recluses) in sixth-century Gaul, also speaks of processions to end drought and ensure ample harvests:

> ...One day a great drought desolated the countryside of the Auvergene, and the grass dried up so that there was no pasture for the animals. Then the saint of God [Bishop Quitianus] piously celebrated the Rogations, which are done before Ascension.... And before they arrived at the gate of the town, a heavy rain fell upon the whole land, so that they were lost in admiration, and said that it was due to the prayers of His holy man.[154]

Jesuit missionaries emulated medieval holy men, directing public rites that were geared toward calamities other than disease:

> On one occasion, during a great drought, the fields belonging to the [Yoeme] pueblo of Torim began to dry up. This prompted the children to hold a scourging procession to a shrine of Our Lady that they had erected on a little hill near their pueblo. Because of these little innocents' prayers, and in honor of His Most Blessed Mother, Our Lord let abundant rain fall on the fields of the pueblo; no rain fell on the fields of other nearby pueblos. The Indians were amazed and the neighboring pueblos became fond of imitating the people of Torim in their devotion to the Most Holy Virgin.[155]

The Mission as Center of Economic Life

The Jesuits were cast by Enlightenment philosophers such as Voltaire as instruments of right reason, and by recent scholars as the source of thousands of innovations that revolutionized Indian life.[156] The missions, in Bolton's words, were like a "great industrial school," with shops for shoemakers, carpenters, tailors, blacksmiths, weavers, and other artisans who worked and trained native apprentices.[157]

---

[154] Edward James, ed., *Gregory of Tours: Life of the Fathers* (Liverpool, UK: Liverpool University Press, 1991), 26–27.
[155] Pérez de Ribas, *History of the Triumphs*, 367.
[156] Spicer, *Cycles of Conquest*, 58, 292, 295–297, *The Yaquis*, 32, 86.
[157] Herbert E. Bolton, "The Mission as a Frontier Institution in the Spanish-American Colonies." *American Historical Review* 23 (1917): 42–61, 57. See also John F. Bannon,

Jesuit sources indicate or suggest that most Spanish or Jesuit "innovations" were of little consequence during the seventeenth century. The Jesuits had difficulty, for instance, propagating many Old World plants that were brought to the arid, northern frontier.[158] Of the many "innovations" introduced by the Jesuits, cattle clearly had the most significant impact on aboriginal culture. The Jesuits established their first cattle ranch near San Félipe shortly after they arrived in Sinaloa in 1591. During October or November of each year, a portion of the Jesuit herd was slaughtered and the meat jerked and then apportioned among priests in outlying missions.[159] As the missions increased in number and distance from Jesuit headquarters, it became more efficient for each priest to take thirty or more head of cattle with him when he began a mission.[160] These herds often flourished and became an important food source for the Indians. Note, however, that cattle were not an "improvement" over the wild game that the Indians relied on traditionally. As noted, the Indians enjoyed both a wide variety and relative abundance of hunted animals. If cattle were desired and became highly valued, it was because domesticated animals were a more readily available source of nourishment in a disease environment. This point was made by Pérez de Ribas in a report he wrote in 1638 while Jesuit provincial: " . . . were it not for the cattle the Indians would have died during times of sickness."[161]

Although the Jesuits were not the vanguard of civilization imagined by the philosophes and modern researchers, they emulated medieval missionary-saints and abbots and were exceptional at organizing, and more precisely, reconstituting Indian subsistence and organizational strategies. Knowledge of Indian ways was acquired by mastering the language of the Indians.[162] Indeed, no other skill was demanded of the

---

S.J., *The Mission Frontier in Sonora, 1620–1687* (New York: United States Catholic Historical Society, New York, 1955), 196.

[158] Reff, *Disease, Depopulation, and Culture Change,* 254–260; "The Jesuit Mission Frontier in Comparative Perspective: The Reductions of the Rio de la Plata and the Missions of Northwestern New Spain, 1588–1700." In *Contested Ground*, eds. Donna Guy and Thomas Sheridan, pp. 16–31 (Tucson: University of Arizona Press, 1998).

[159] Pfefferkorn, *Sonora: A Description of the Province*, 99.

[160] Hackett, *Historical Documents*, 122–123.

[161] Ibid., 100.

[162] Acosta argued at length on this subject in his *De Procuranda*, which was perhaps the most influential "guide" to missionary work for Jesuits. Jóse de Acosta, *De Procuranda*

Jesuit missionary more than knowledge of Indian languages.[163] Interestingly, the most celebrated missionaries of early medieval Europe were "outsiders" who mastered the language of their neophytes. This is true of Martin of Tours, who hailed from Romania but worked in Gaul; Martin of Braga, who was from Greece and missionized the Sueve of northwestern Iberia; Patrick, who was a Briton and converted the Irish; and Ulfila, who was from Anatolia and evangelized the Goths.

Because Jesuit missionaries were required to learn and use the language of their Indian neophytes, they necessarily came face-to-face with the logic and complexity of the Indians' behaviors and beliefs.[164] Indeed, in a letter by Father Pedro Méndez, copied by Pérez de Ribas, Méndez remarked that he had discovered that the Mayo Indians were familiar with atomistic theory. Méndez obviously discussed more than the catechism, in Cáhita, with his Mayo converts. The earliest *artes* and *vocabularios* of native languages produced by the Jesuits clearly reflect more than a concern with Christian doctrine. Thus, one reads in a Jesuit *vocabulario*

Indorum Salute (Predicación el Evangelio en las Indias), trans. Francisco Mateos, S.J. (Madrid: I.G. Magerit, 1952 [1588]), 361–366.

[163] Although scholars have questioned whether the Jesuits were unique among New World missionaries in their mastery of Indian languages, there is abundant evidence from northern Nueva España that the Jesuits learned and used native languages more than their Franciscan counterparts. Griffen, *Indian Assimilation*, 55; Felix Zubillaga, *Monumenta Mexicana, Vol. V (1592–1596)* (Rome: Institum Historicum Societatis Iesu (1973), 21, 219. Polzer, *Rules and Precepts*, 56–57, has suggested that the Franciscan practice of moving their missionaries at regular intervals often made it difficult or impossible for priests to master native languages. Jesuit reports, rules, and correspondence repeatedly emphasize that priests should become proficient in the native language of their assigned mission. See, for instance, Rodrigo de Cabredo, "Ordenaciones del Padre Rodrigo de Cabredo para las Missiones, January 1, 1611, Durango," Latin American Manuscripts, Mexico II, Lily Library, Indiana State University. Figures compiled by the Jesuits further testify to the mastery of Indian languages. Burrus, "The Language Problem in Spain's Overseas Dominions," 169, f.50. Peter Dunigan, "Early Jesuit Missionaries: A Suggestion for Further Study." *American Anthropologist* 60 (1958): 725–732.

[164] Talal Asad, "The Concept of Cultural Translation in British Social Anthropology." In *Writing Culture: The Poetics and Politics of Ethnography*, eds. James Clifford and George Marcus, pp. 141–164 (Berkeley: University of California Press, 1986), 158–159; Burrus, "The Language Problem in Spain's Overseas Dominions"; Christopher Herbert, *Culture and Anomie: Ethnographic Imagination in the Nineteenth Century* (Chicago: University of Chicago Press, 1991).

of Tehuima, which was the principal dialect spoken by the Opata of central and northern Sonora, a term for "canal of wood" (*cuvabot*), and a verb form of *cuvabot, cuvalotam*, "to make a canal of wood."[165] What is perhaps the earliest guide to the Cahita language, which was compiled by Father Juan de Velasco around 1600, lists sixteen terms for trees with edible fruit.[166] In keeping with the prevalence and complexities of disease, one of the longest entries in the earliest Jesuit *vocabulario* for the Nébome language is for *enfermo*.[167]

In point of fact, Jesuit success founding and administering missions was as much a profane as a sacred undertaking. In this regard, the Jesuit mission functioned much like early monastic communities in Europe, organizing economic and social life within and without the religious community or mission. Under the terms of the *Patronato Real*, each Jesuit missionary received a modest annual stipend of around three hundred pesos, much of which was spent on relatively expensive items imported from southern Mexico for religious functions (e.g., wine, oil, medicine, candle wax, rosaries). Each missionary was forced to meet the larger and more costly operating expenses of his assigned mission.[168] To do so, most missionaries essentially assumed the more important rights and responsibilities of caciques, particularly "principal chiefs." Father Gaspar Varela wrote a brief description of the daily routine of the missionary that reflects well the responsibilities of a resident padre:

> In the morning after Mass the padre goes back to his house, where he receives the *alcaldes* and *fiscales*, come to report on persons in the pueblo who are sick. The padre instructs them what is to be done, both as to the bodily needs of the sick but more especially as regards their spiritual needs. ... After the sick have been cared for, the padre's next task is to settle disputes and differences which have arisen among the Indians concerning their lands and other petty matters. ... These two duties done, the whole pueblo, grown-ups and youngsters, turn out to

---

[165] "Copia de un fragmento de vocabulario de alguna lengua indigena Opata de Mexico." Temporalidades 333–141, Archivo Historico de Hacienda, Mexico City, 21.

[166] Eustaquio Buelna, *Arte de la lengua Cáhita* (Mexico, 1891), 138.

[167] Campbell W. Pennington, *The Pima Bajo, Volume II: Vocabulario en la Lengua Nevome* (Salt Lake City: University of Utah Press, 1979)

[168] Polzer, *Rules and Precepts*; Theodore E. Treutlein, "The Economic Regime of the Jesuit Missions in the Eighteenth Century." *Pacific Historical Review* 8 (1939): 284–300, 289.

work at their daily tasks. During the season of sowing and harvesting no other work is done but that in the fields. Thus the whole year is portioned out...[169]

In each mission and its outlying visitas the Jesuits organized and supervised the division of Indian labor as well as the production, exchange, and redistribution of goods and services. Writing in 1673, Father Daniel Marras noted that each missionary generally had two or three pueblos under his care, and in each pueblo there was a field of wheat and another larger field of maize, beans, and cotton. Father Marras explained that the fields were cleared, sown, and harvested by mission converts, who received two meals per day in exchange for their labor. The meals consisted of a stew made from maize and one or two cattle that were slaughtered for the purpose. Marras noted it was not uncommon for three hundred or four hundred people to participate in fieldwork. Each Sunday and on holy days the resident missionary hosted a feast that featured cattle that were slaughtered and consumed.[170]

The principles of sharing and reciprocity espoused by Jesus and embraced by the early Church were basically those upon which the Jesuits founded their mission systems. By requiring their neophytes to work approximately three days a week on communal lands, the Jesuits were able to realize surpluses to support native artisans and specialized activities, from tortilla makers and cattle herders to butchers and wine (mescal) producers.[171] The surpluses also served as a bulwark against food shortages, which the Jesuits themselves noted were correlated with disease.[172] Father Marras noted that during one four- to five-month period, as many as five cattle a day were slaughtered and consumed in his mission. During a famine in 1655, the resident priests in the Yoeme

---

[169] Bannon, *The Mission Frontier in Sonora*, 61.

[170] See capitulo 22 of "Apologetico Defensorio y Puntual Manifesto que los Padres de la Compañia de Jesus, Missioneros de las Provincias de Sinaloa y Sonora, Francisco Xavier de Faria," Historia 316, Archivo General de la Nación, Mexico City; Luis Navarro Garcia, *Sonora y Sinaloa en el Siglo XVII* (Sevilla: Escuela de Estudios Hispano-Americanos, 1967), 208–210.

[171] Navarro Garcia, *Sonora y Sinaloa en el Siglo XVII*, 208–210.

[172] "Missiones de San Ygnacio en Mayo, Yaqui, Nevomes, Chinipas, y Sisibotaris," Historia 15, Archivo General de la Nación, 340.

missions of Raum and Pótam distributed six thousand daily food rations over a four-month period.[173]

As with native chiefdoms, surpluses that were not invested locally or consumed during emergencies were sold to acquire items (e.g., statuary, chalices, bells, tapestries) that brought prestige and honor to a missionary, native church officials, and the mission community as a whole. Still other trade items (e.g., chocolate, rosary beads, ponies, knives) were redistributed by the missionary among his loyal followers.[174] Like the desert saints (e.g., Hilarion) and early medieval monks (e.g., Saint Martin of Tours) who protected commoners from tax collectors, Jesuit missionaries blocked Spanish miners and land owners from exploiting or enslaving mission converts.[175] Of course, natives who worked for other Spaniards were a drain on the Jesuits' own labor pool and were likely to be corrupted by gambling, alcoholism, and a preoccupation with material possessions, which was particularly threatening to the communal principles of mission life.

The Mission and the Reordering of Social Life

As noted, aboriginally most native groups in northern Mexico were organized on the bases of lineages and clans. Communities so organized do not fare well in a disease environment, characterized by sudden, random, and significant reductions in population – reductions that often meant the elimination of entire households and the scattering of kin. It is difficult under such circumstances to follow alliance rules governing marriage or postmarital residence. Those who tried to keep to the rules were likely to have no men or women to receive or exchange in marriage; households that relied solely on lineage members would have had been at a loss for kin with whom to work, raise children, or bury the dead.[176]

---

[173] "Anua del año de mil seiscientos cincuenta y siete," Historia 15, Archivo General de la Nación, Mexico City.

[174] Ibid., 30.

[175] This was true of northern Mexico as well as sixteenth-century Brazil and Paraguay. John Hemming, *Red Gold: The Conquest of the Brazilian Indians* (Cambridge, MA: Harvard University Press, 1978), 139–160; Necker, *Indios Guaraníes*, 50.

[176] Carol R. Ember and Melvin Ember, "The Conditions Favoring Multilocal Residence." *Southwestern Journal of Anthropology* 28 (1972): 382–400; Elman R. Service, *Primitive Social Organization* (New York: Random House, 1962), 137.

During the early Middle Ages, when the fabric of social life also was rendered by epidemic disease, fictive kinship became essential to the ordering of social life. The same was true in the Jesuit missions of Nueva España, and indeed in much of colonial Latin America. The Jesuits ordered social relations around the monogamous, patriarchical Christian family. Through fictive kinship, particularly coparenthood, which was initiated through the sponsorship of a child at baptism, Indian couples were able to establish significant yet fluid alliances with other families. What was a "religious act," namely baptism, created a spiritual kin group as well as social network, consisting of child, the child's natural parents, the sponsoring godparent, the baptizing clergy, and all their respective spouses and children. Because both boys and girls were baptized and came to have godparents, the system was both expansive and flexible. Significantly, as was the case in medieval Europe,[177] Indian coparents did not refuse each other, whether it was help with sowing a field or borrowing money.

Fictive kinship made it possible not only for lineages or families to reorder their social lives but also for entire communities to reimagine their future as kin. Pérez de Ribas recounts several instances in which native groups who were once enemies, merged, with one "adopting" the other. Such was the case with the numerically larger Sinaloa Indians, who assimilated hundreds of Zoe and Huite Indians:

> Three hundred individuals, young and old, left their cliffs to come live with the Sinaloa, who received them in their pueblo and homes with such great displays of affection and kindness that they took the adornments from their own children and placed them on the children of their new guests, just as we noted they had done with the Zoe. For his part the priest also celebrated their arrival, showing much paternal affection to these little children whom God was bringing to his home.[178]

Through ritual coparenthood the Jesuits created one, big, bilateral family, with the resident padre functioning both spiritually (the administrator of baptism) and politically as the head of the new kinship

---

[177] Joseph H. Lynch, *Godparents and Kinship in Early Modern Europe* (Princeton, NJ: Princeton University Press, 1988), 187.

[178] Pérez de Ribas, *History of the Triumphs*, 263.

system. In this regard, the Jesuit missionary enjoyed rights and responsibilities not unlike those enjoyed by the abbots of Irish monasticism, which spread to the European continent in the sixth century.

In the previous chapter, it was noted that the dislocations of the second and third centuries C.E. created a window of opportunity for women who sought new opportunities by assuming leadership roles in the Church. These opportunities were undermined by the post–Constantine Church, which denied women access to the clergy and largely restricted women to the convent or home, both of which ultimately were under male control. At the same time, women found agency in Gospel accounts of Christ acquiescing to whatever his mother asked of him. *Luke* I: 46–49 ("... from now onwards all generations will call me [Mary] blessed,...") and Chapter 12 of the *Book of Revelations* implied that Mary was elevated to an all-powerful deity.[179] The cult of the saints, particularly saints like Catherine of Alexandria, also held out the possibility of Christian women who transcended restrictive gender roles, albeit suffering martyrdom in the process.

In northern Mexico, Indian women experienced a similar rollercoaster ride that ended in much the same ambivalent status for women on earth and in heaven. It must be admitted that the historical record, meaning ostensibly Jesuit narratives, is far from opaque with respect to the rights and responsibilities of women, prior to or following missionization. The often cryptic comments of Spanish explorers as well as the Jesuits suggest that aboriginally women were respected but their sphere of influence was restricted to the home or village.[180] With one exception, an Indian caciquess named Luisa among the Ocoroni, Indian men invariably were described by the Jesuits as decision makers, particularly when it came to "external affairs," which in late prehistory became preeminent, owing to an increase in intertribal warfare.

In his much celebrated yet controversial book, *When Jesus Came the Corn Mothers Went Away*, Ramon Gutiérrez attributed the friars' success

---

[179] Elizabeth Johnson, "Marian Devotion in the Western Church." In *Christian Spirituality, High Middle Ages and Reformation*, ed. Jill Raitt, pp. 392–414 (New York: Crossroad, 1987), 411.

[180] Women may have enjoyed more rights and responsibilities among Cáhita-speakers such as the Ocoroni, Suaqui, and Mayo, who appear to have been matrilineal.

in part to their coopting of Pueblo women, who took an interest in the priests in part because the friars protected women's rights. In a context of great uncertainty, Indian women appear to have been particularly attracted to Christianity and mission life. Many undoubtedly were not happy with Franciscan and Jesuit privileging of male authority. However, many women may have seen this authority as the cost of assuaged fears and grief over dying children, aborted infants, and death during pregnancy and childbirth. It was women, and over time, girls who were just barely able to conceive, who suffered most during epidemics and who bore the burden of replacing an ever-diminishing population during the colonial period. Writing in the mid-eighteenth-century, Father Joseph Och noted that he often was asked to marry thirteen-year-old girls, who promptly became pregnant.[181]

Like women in early medieval Europe, who also died prematurely trying to halt a population collapse, Indian women were especially attracted to the mother of the Christian God. Mary knew the experience of childbirth and motherhood, including the heartbreak of watching her son die. Mary was also a deity, a deity the Indians were perhaps already familiar with, in some instances equating her with the moon.[182] Such was the case in late antique Europe, where the cult of Mary sprang in part from pagan traditions of a female deity.[183] The rapid spread of Saint Brigit's cult in early medieval Europe also has been linked to a prior, Celtic deity named Brigit, who was especially associated with fertility and the arts of women.[184] The Jesuits did mention or allude to Indian belief in what appear to have been female deities. The Indians of northern Mexico may well have had myths and oral traditions like those found among the Pueblos, who speak of "Yellow Woman,"

[181] Treutlein, *Missionary in Sonora*, 135.
[182] It was not uncommon in colonial Mexico for Indians and mestizos to perceive the Virgin Mary as part of the Trinity (God the Father, Mary, Christ). Taylor, *Magistrates of the Sacred*, 294–295.
[183] Stephen Benko, *The Virgin Goddess: Studies in the Pagan and Christian Roots of Mariology* (London: E.J. Brill, 1993); Pamela Berger, *The Goddess Obscured* (Boston: Beacon Press, 1985); Elaine Pagels, "What Became of God the Mother? Conflicting Images of God in Early Christianity." In *Gnosticism in the Early Church*, ed. with an introduction by David M. Scholer, pp. 295–307 (New York: Garland Publishing Company, 1993).
[184] Stephen C. McCluskey, *Astronomies and Cultures in Early Medieval Europe* (Cambridge, UK: Cambridge University Press, 1998), 64–65.

"Iyatiku," "Thought Woman," and other givers of life and restorers of health.[185]

In his discussion of the conversion of the Zuaque Indians of the Río Fuerte, Pérez de Ribas, who was their first missionary, recalled how the Zuaque women warmly embraced his proposal for a new church when he pointed out that, "this house was for Mary, the Mother of God." Continuing he noted:

> The Zuaque women were so spirited in the construction of their principal church that they decided to also build a small chapel to the Most Holy Virgin. It was erected next to the pueblo at the top of a pretty little pinnacle of rock, the base of which was bathed by a river.[186]

Significantly, Pérez de Ribas went on to note that the Suaqui, prior to "conversion," left offerings to an Indian deity (female?) at this "pretty little pinnacle." On the occasion of an earthquake:

> The blind and ignorant Zuaque cast into this water [at the base of the pinnacle] large quantities of mantas, blue-green stones, beads, and other things that they valued, thinking that this would placate whomever was the cause of these tremendous horrors.[187]

Following the lead of Ignatius Loyola, who had a vision of Mary and the infant Jesus on the night of his conversion, the Jesuits were, and still remain especially devoted to Mary.[188] As Pérez de Ribas tells it, the Indians thought it a great honor to receive Communion and celebrate Mary's feastdays:

> On the afternoon preceding such feast days, as soon as they return from their fields, they assemble in church to hear a sermon by the priest about the mystery [pertaining to that particular feast day]. They are already in church before sunrise, where they remain to hear the

---

[185] Gunn Allen, *Spider Woman's Granddaughters*, 210–218; Gutiérrez, *When Jesus Came*, 3–7.

[186] Pérez de Ribas, *History of the Triumphs*, 225.

[187] Ibid., 123.

[188] Joseph N. Tylenda, S.J., *Jesuit Saints & Martyrs* (Chicago: Loyola University Press, 1984), 109–111.

singing of her Mass and to receive Communion. Afterward they say her Rosary.[189]

Unless one reads the Jesuit *anuas*, it is hard to appreciate just how great was the Indians' devotion to Mary; again, this was especially true of women. The anuas are filled with accounts of women who clung to a rosary or a medal of Saint Ignatius (himself a devotee of Mary) during childbirth or in the throes of death.

As discussed in the previous chapter, nothing was more important to the "rise of Christianity" in early medieval Europe than the tens of thousands of children who were given to monasteries to be fed, clothed, educated, and formed as Christians. Large numbers of these children, upon reaching adulthood, left the monastery and assumed influential positions, sometimes as clerics, but more generally as Christians rather than pagans. The Franciscans and Jesuits likewise understood that the real hope for a Christian future in Mexico lay with native children, who, unlike their parents, were still impressionable. As Pérez de Ribas noted:[190]

A maxim repeated by all the ancient and modern writers is that the rearing of children with the catechism and good habits is fundamental to the welfare of a republic. For one thing, childhood is an impression-able period; youth, like a soft, malleable material, can be imprinted with virtues. Childhood is also the beginning, when the foundation is laid for the rest of a man's life, and a building erected on this [proper] foundation is more durable and lasting. If this is the case and has been verified in the youth of the civilized nations and republics of the world, then an even stronger argument can be made with respect to the necessity [of educating the youth] among people like those we have discussed here, who were totally destitute of catechism and civil order. Accordingly, to ensure that the Faith and good customs of these

---

[189] Pérez de Ribas, *History of the Triumphs*, 250.

[190] For the Franciscans see Richard C. Trexler, "From the Mouths of Babes: Christianiza-tion by Children in 16th Century New Spain." In *Religious Organization and Religious Experience*, ed. J. Davies, pp. 115–135 (New York: Academic Press, 1982). Gutiérrez, *When Jesus Came*, 122, has persuasively shown that Franciscan "success" in New Mexico also was predicated on the friars undermining the power and influence of elites by effectively placing children under their tutelage and making young people indebted to the priests for rights and responsibilities.

nations would persevere, our evangelical ministers were particularly concerned with the education of the young people.[191]

The "ancient writers" mentioned by Pérez de Ribas undoubtedly included Caesarius of Arles, Basil of Caesaria, and Benedict of Nursia, all of whom wrote of the importance of rearing children with the catechism and "good habits."

Because of their perceived effectiveness as religious and "principal chiefs," and by situating themselves through baptismal sponsorship at the top of Indian social organization ("the father of all"), the Jesuits became fountains of justice and wisdom for children as well as adults. This much is apparent from the previously quoted letters of Father Gaspar Varela and Father Pedro Méndez, both of whom spoke of the close relationship and affection that obtained between missionaries and children.[192] Within a few years of their arrival on the northern frontier, the Jesuits established what were essentially boarding schools in the Villa de San Félipe and Durango. Already in 1602, there were thirty boys "from all these nations" at the Jesuit "seminary" in San Félipe.[193] At this time there was an epidemic that prompted many Indians to flee the missions. The success that the Jesuits had with native children is exemplified by an account of a group of sixteen Ocoroni children who refused to accompany their parents when the parents sent word that they were abandoning their village for the mountains.[194]

Jesuit boarding schools were mainly for the sons of caciques and particularly bright children. The *anua* of 1610 indicates that the young men were taught not only Christian doctrine but also reading and writing,

---

[191] Pérez de Ribas, *History of the Triumphs*, 168.

[192] This concern with children was recognized in Pope Paul III's bull of 1540 approving the Jesuit order: "Above all things let them have at heart the instruction of boys and ignorant persons in the knowledge of Christian doctrine, ... " Francesco C. Cesareo, "Quest for Identity: The Ideals of Jesuit Education in the Sixteenth Century." In *The Jesuit Tradition in Education and Missions*, ed. Christopher Chapple, pp. 17–33 (Scranton, PA: University of Scranton Press, 1993), 19. The Franciscans also made children a central focus and means of evangelization in central Mexico. See Trexler, "From the Mouths of Babes."

[193] "Anua del año de mil seiscientos y dos," Historia 15, Archivo General de la Nación, Mexico City.

[194] Pérez de Ribas, *History of the Triumphs*, 168–169.

music, singing, and other "good habits."[195] Because most Indian groups often had to wait years for a resident priest, it was common for an Indian group in the meantime to send some of their children to the schools to be educated. The children often returned as young (Christian) adults to their nation, where they assumed positions of authority and assisted the resident priest. Indeed, the Jesuits sometimes used the young men as "quasi-priests:"

> ... some of these young men who were being reared in the seminary turned out to be so skilled and devoted that, confident in their excellent intellectual capacity and virtue, the priest sometimes entrusted them to give speeches to the pueblo under his supervision. They did this in church, appropriately dressed and standing on the steps of the altar. This means was extremely effective because the same catechism taught by the minister of the Gospel was received with special pleasure and had a greater affect and impact, becoming more ingrained in their hearts, when it came from the mouths of their sons and relatives in their own style and language.[196]

It was with the children that the Jesuits enjoyed their greatest and most lasting success as agents of culture change. By 1660 most Indian pueblos in northern Mexico were governed by Indians who had been instructed as children in Christian ways.

Persistence and Accommodation of Indian Behaviors and Beliefs

The argument could well be made that the Jesuits largely had their way with native peoples, particularly the children. Correspondingly, the Christianity that emerged in northern Mexico during the colonial period was more imposed than negotiated. Jesuit narratives certainly parallel early medieval literature in suggesting that Indian religious beliefs and practices were wholly destroyed and replaced by Christianity. The passage below from Pérez de Ribas's *Historia* reads very much like the

---

[195] "Anua del año de mil seiscientos y diez," Historia 15, Archivo General de la Nación, Mexico City.
[196] Pérez de Ribas, *History of the Triumphs*, 169.

sixth-century *Vita Sanctae Radegundis* and other saints' lives,[197] which relate the wholesale destruction of pagan temples:

> One day Father [Cárdenas] asked me to accompany him on this pilgrimage. He did not reveal his plans to the Indians, but he intentionally took along all those who were members of the brotherhood devoted to that sanctuary. As soon as we arrived, this good priest began to preach to them (from his mule, which served as a pulpit). On one hand, he condemned those abominations, and on the other he tried to persuade them that our God was the true Lord of the rain and of all creation. He did this so effectively and became so energetic that he could bear to wait no longer, and dismounting in a single move, he destroyed that sepulchre with his fists. Like someone full of fire, this priest took out steel and flint and set a flame to all the bones and ruins of that Mahommedan sepulchre. As it turned to ashes, he made a cross, which he then erected in order to sanctify that place. We all knelt at the foot of that holy cross and prayed the Creed out loud with those who had recently been baptized. Because *diligentibus Deum omnia cooperant in bonum*,[198] our Lord deigned to allow this priest's fervent deed to have such a good effect that the neophytes reformed in such a way that they have never returned to these types of superstitions.[199]

The Jesuits in northern Mexico did indeed engage in "search and destroy" missions. Given the importance attached by all Christians to the first commandment (no worshipping of false gods and idols), it is hard to imagine missionaries doing anything other than destroying Indian idols and temples. However, the destruction of places or things did not necessarily mean the end of indigenous beliefs and rituals. As was the case in early medieval Europe, retention of indigenous beliefs and practices was an unavoidable consequence of missionary efforts to retain Indian belief in an activist God(s), while at the same time discrediting indigenous practices, places, and things. This paradoxical situation is evident from a letter written by Father Martin Pérez in 1593, two years after he and Gonzalo de Tapia founded the first Jesuit missions in Sinaloa. In

---

[197] See Flint, *The Rise of Magic*, 72.
[198] "All things turn out well for those who love God."
[199] Pérez de Ribas, *Coronica y Historia Religiosa*, 502.

the letter, Pérez recounted how the priests purportedly convinced their neophytes to abandon a rite of ceremonial sponsorship (referred to as an "adoption ceremony") in favor of a Christian ritual:

These Indians used to hold a celebration for adopted children, during which all the orphans in their nation were placed with their respective relatives, who received them as their own children in a solemn celebration. They held just such a celebration the year the priests arrived [1591], in the following manner. First, the Indians searched out and gathered together the orphans who were to be adopted. Then they erected two houses made of petates, or mats, similar to those in which they resided. The two houses matched one another and were separated by a distance of a hundred paces. In one house they placed the orphaned children, who remained there for eight days, during which time they were fed atole, which is the same as maize gruel. In the other house (which was larger) they sprinkled loose sand in the middle of the floor, creating a circle two and one half varas [six feet] in diameter. The Indians moved in and out of this circle, singing and dancing, adorned or painted, with rods in their hands. At times they sat on the sand and painted different figures with loose sand of varying colors, which they placed within lines they traced with a thin reed. They painted mainly two figures that appeared to be human; one they called Viriseva. The other was called Vairubi, who was said to be the mother of the first figure. They spoke with much confusion about what these figures represented, like the blind who lack divine light. It even seemed that they spoke of them with a glimpse of God and His Mother, for they referred to them as the first beings from whom the rest of mankind was born. Nevertheless, everything they said was confusing. . . .

Mention must also be made of the results of the religious instruction that was imparted to the Indians who participated in the aforementioned celebration. Subsequently, during the Feast of the Nativity, which was being celebrated with much solemnity and joy in another pueblo, the priests noticed that the Indians had another ramada similar to those used in the ceremony for the adopted children. Within it they found another circle of sand paintings of a river, lions, tigers, serpents and other poisonous creatures. Now instead of the two figures of Variseva and Vairubi, however, the Indians had painted something different. One figure was of a man, another of a woman, and another of a child. When the priests asked what it all meant, the Indians responded that one figure was God and the other His Mother; the figure of the child was Jesus Christ, Their Son, all of whom they asked to safeguard them from those wild animals and the rivers that flooded their planted fields. The Indians added, "We are teaching this to our children so that they will do likewise from now on."

The priests praised the Indians' worthy efforts to recognize God and His Most Holy Son as the authors of all our well-being, as well as the Virgin, who intercedes to achieve it. They told them that they should take recourse in them during times of need and tribulation, but since it seemed that this ceremony touched too closely upon their former celebrations, the priests wished to remove it from their memory. Therefore, they ordered that one day during Christmastide (having abandoned those figures) the Indians should enter the church dancing and ask God and the Virgin (whose image was there with Her Son in Her arms) for the same things they had formerly sought through their worthless superstitions. They were thus instructed and content.[200]

What the above quote reveals is that the Jesuits and Indians accommodated each other. The Indians apparently abandoned their makeshift ramadas and ephemeral sandpaintings for a more enduring Christian church with its more permanent depictions of what nevertheless remained anthropomorphic supernaturals, who lorded over yet responded to their creation. The Jesuits for their part essentially condoned the conflation of indigenous deities (Viriseva, Vairubi) with the Christian holy family. By allowing the Indians "to enter the church dancing," which was hardly considered appropriate in Europe,[201] the Jesuits further accommodated an Indian tradition that insisted on the inseparability of songs, prayers, dances, drums, ritual movements, and dramatic address.[202]

In her book *The Rise of Magic in Early Medieval Europe*, Valerie Flint convincingly showed how medieval texts, while they often highlight direct assaults on paganism by Christian clerics and monks, also bespeak

---

[200] Pérez de Ribas, *History of the Triumphs*, 116–118.
[201] J. C. Schmitt, "The Rationale of Gestures in the West: Third to Thirteenth Centuries." In *A Cultural History of Gesture*, ed. J. N. Bremmer and H. Roodenburg, pp. 59–70 (Oxford: Oxford University Press, 1991).
[202] Gunn Allen, *The Sacred Hoop*, 62; Spicer, *The Yaqui*, 96.

toleration of paganism and the shamans (*magi*) who acted as intermediaries of the supernatural. As Sulpicius Severus noted in his biography
of Martin of Tours, Martin toppled pagan shrines but "more often"
subdued pagans with his preaching.[203] Jesuit texts such as the *Historia*
or Ruiz de Montoya's *Conquista Espiritual*[204] likewise reveal that Jesuit
missionaries often tolerated Indian shamans, particularly when it was
clear that they could essentially beat the shamans at their own game:

> On one occasion [during an epidemic in 1620], a pueblo was stricken
> with smallpox, which for them is like the plague. The priest ordered a
> very famous sorcerer to be brought before him. This Indian had
> boasted that he had brought on this illness and that it would not
> end until he desired and commanded it to do so. With these [boasts
> and threats], he was able to collect from the fearful residents whatever
> gifts they had, which are the wages of these diabolical liars. The priest
> subsequently made inquiries and discovered other similar [beliefs] re-
> garding the devil and how he adopted the form of various animals,
> speaking to them and teaching them how to kill their enemies. This is a
> fitting and longstanding pretense of the father of lies, who encourages
> acts of vengeance and rage. The priest asked some sorcerers: "Why
> don't you kill me?" A famous sorceress answered: "We do not have the
> power to kill you because you say Mass." Many others confirmed this
> statement. When the same priest went to preach, the good Christians
> came to him and said: "Father, we love you very much because you do
> us a lot of good. However, because you always reprimand the sorcer-
> ers in your sermons, revealing their tricks, they hate you and would
> like to kill you with spells, but they cannot do so because you say
> Mass.[205]

The above quote masks the vulnerability of Jesuit priests and the like-
lihood that missionaries accommodated Indian traditions out of fear
for their lives. It did not take the Indians long to realize that saying
Mass, and more precisely, consecration and consumption of the Holy
Eucharist, *did not* render missionaries safe from arrows and clubs. In the

---

[203] Hoare, *The Western Fathers*, 29.
[204] Clement J. McNaspy, S.J., trans., *The Spiritual Conquest of Ruiz de Montoya* (St. Louis:
Institute of Jesuit Sources, 1993 [1639]), 23.
[205] Pérez de Ribas, *History of the Triumphs*, 368–369.

wake of continuing population losses from disease, most every Indian group in time became suspicious that Christianity was not "the answer." Between 1591 and 1660, a dozen Jesuit missionaries were killed during what were frequent Indian uprisings and apostasy.[206] The Jesuits proudly acknowledged this fact, believing it offered yet another proof that the Jesuit mission enterprise was a reiteration of the life of Christ and the primitive Church. After all, Christ was rejected and crucified and the pre-Constantine Church had more than its fair share of martyrs. The history of the early medieval Church also is replete with missionaries such as Alexander (d. 397) and Boniface (d. 754) who were martyred. Still, while Jesuit authors may have professed "peace of mind,"[207] missionaries clearly at times were intimidated and feared for their lives. After many years on the frontier, Father Pedro Méndez noted in one of his letters:

> I certainly confess that one of the greatest difficulties of coming here [the Rio Mayo], which it was mentioned I might find, was the noise – the all-night drumming and dancing – which disturbed me for several years in similar districts. It seemed to me that these things, which the infidels do, are a thing from hell. But Our Lord has decided to confound my faintheartedness, and due to your Reverence's holy assistance, I have not found any trace of what I had feared; rather, at night there is only the sweet sound of prayer.[208]

Missionaries in the late nineteenth and twentieth centuries embraced, often intuitively, the anthropological concept of culture. Because cultures were understood to be indivisible wholes with integrated behaviors and beliefs, missionaries often felt compelled to make a clean sweep of native life.[209] The Jesuits had no such concept of culture and, accordingly,

---

[206] Susan Deeds, "Indigenous Rebellions on the Northern Mexican Mission Frontier: From First-Generation to Later Colonial Responses." In *Contested Ground, Comparative Frontiers on the Northern and southern Edges of the Spanish Empire*, eds. D. Guy and T. Sheridan, pp. 32–52 (Tucson: University of Arizona Press, 1998); Charlotte M. Gradie, *The Tepehuan Revolt of 1616* (Salt Lake City: University of Utah Press, 2000); Daniel T. Reff, "The 'Predicament of Culture' and Spanish Missionary Accounts of the Tepehuan and Pueblo Revolts." *Ethnohistory* 42 (1995): 63–90.

[207] Pérez de Ribas, *History of the Triumphs*, 364.

[208] Ibid., 293.

[209] Christopher Herbert, *Culture and Anomie, Ethnographic Imagination in the Nineteenth Century* (Chicago: University of Chicago Press, 1991).

they focused on things that they found objectionable; Indian customs that were deemed harmless or "without offense" often were ignored. This selective approach resulted in the continuation of strictly indigenous practices as well as indigenous practices whose outward appearance rather than substance was changed. Indians who for generations prayed and left offerings at the base of a Zapote tree or a "pretty little pinnacle" (as in the case of the Suaqui mentioned above) presumably entertained similar thoughts and emotions when the tree was replaced with a wooden cross or the pinnacle was invested with a statue of Mary. Jesuit letters and reports, and even the churches that survive to this day in northern Mexico, admit numerous examples of such multiple realities, everything from "black" Christs and madonnas to crosses bearing feathers.[210]

In Beowulf and other early medieval texts, pagan terms for secular lord, king, or judge often were used as referents for God and Christ.[211] The same lexicosemantic phenomenon occurs in Jesuit linguistic materials, including grammars in which "sin" was translated as ritual pollution and "God" as "headman."[212] Such "hybridization" was not peculiar to Jesuit enterprises.[213] The 1528 pictorial catechism of Pedro de Gante, who was among the very first Franciscans in Mexico, refers to "God the Holy Spirit" through a depiction of a hummingbird (a sign of the Aztec deity, Huitzilopochtli) rather than a dove![214]

Gospel stories about the Cross and the Virgin did not necessarily erase or preclude thoughts and emotions nourished by Indian oral traditions. One of the best examples of Jesuit failure to "remove it from their memory" is the dance of the *matachíns*, which today is understood as a sacred ritual and devotion to the Virgin Mary and sometimes Joseph and the

---

[210] The Indian practice of attaching foliage or feathers to crosses has a parallel among medieval converts to Christianity, who as late as the ninth century attached foliage to stone crosses, much to the dismay of bishops.

[211] Giles Constable, *Three Studies in Medieval Religious And Social Thought* (Cambridge, UK: Cambridge University Press, 1995), 158.

[212] David L. Shaul, "The State of the Arte: Ecclesiastical Literature on the Northern Frontier of New Spain." *The Kiva* 55 (1990): 167–175.

[213] Kenneth Mills, *Idolatry and Its Enemies, Colonial Andean Religion and Extirpation, 1640–1750* (Princeton, NJ: Princeton University Press, 1997), 247.

[214] Barbara DeMarco, "The Semiotic Catechism." *Interdisciplinary Journal for Germanic Linguistics and Semiotic Analysis* 6 (2001): 257–264.

Holy Family.[215] Father Ignaz Pfefferkorn, who observed the dance of the *matachíns* being performed by the Opata in the eighteenth century, was of the opinion that the dance originated in Mesoamerica in precontact times.[216] In the late 1800s Bandelier was told by Opata informants that the dance was called *Da-ui* and that the women participants wore a medal of the moon while the men wore one symbolizing the sun.[217] At contact, the Opata venerated the sun and moon as mates, a fact that reportedly was hidden from the Jesuits.[218] The historical record, in effect, suggests that the dance of the *matachíns* originally was a celebration of the "holy family" of the sun and moon (and presumably other celestial "relatives" such as Venus), which was rephrased in terms of the Christian Holy Family. One sees the same mixing of traditions or "border epistemolgies"[219] in the ceremonial year as it is experienced and celebrated by surviving Indian groups such as the Yoeme. Among the Yoeme, the ceremonial year follows a Christian calendar but also corresponds to a precontact Indian emphasis on ceremonial dualism.[220]

Although it is difficult to demonstrate (it is not something Jesuits would have acknowledged), Jesuit missionaries may have "gone [significantly] native," contributing further to the persistence of indigenous beliefs and practices. The Jesuit order went out of its way to insure that members did not stray from the Church's and Society of Jesus's teachings and practices. Jesuit superiors, in particular, were charged with keeping constant tabs on subordinates.[221] However, it was difficult for Jesuit superiors to maintain scrutiny of missionaries on the frontier. Because of a shortage of priests, most Jesuit missionaries worked by themselves, often for years, during which time they only occasionally saw another priest, never mind a Jesuit superior. Physical separation as well

---

[215] Spicer, *The Yaqui*, 101.

[216] Pfefferkorn, *Sonora, A Description of the Province*, 182–183.

[217] Lange and Riley, *Southwestern Journals of Adolph F. Bandelier*, 236–242.

[218] "Estado de la provincia de Sonora," 628.

[219] Walter Mignolo, *Local Histories/Global Designs: Coloniality, Border Thinking, and Subaltern Knowledges* (Princeton, NJ: Princeton University Press, 2000).

[220] Spicer, *The Yaqui*, 61; see also Thomas Sheridan, "The Yoemem (Yaquis), An Enduring People." In *Paths of Life, American Indians of the Southwest and Northern Mexico*, eds. Thomas Sheridan and Nancy J. Parezo, pp. 35–40 (Tucson: University of Arizona Press, 1996).

[221] O'Malley, *The First Jesuits*, 355.

as slow and imperfect communication meant that priests on the frontier often made decisions on their own.[222] As we saw in the previous chapter, there was a very similar situation in early medieval Europe, where deacons and clerics in rural areas often were free of episcopal scrutiny and, as a consequence, interpreted Christian theology rather "loosely," accommodating paganism.

Jesuit missionaries may never have escaped the confines of their Spanish-Catholic culture and particularly Jesuit worldview. This seems to have been particularly true of Jesuits such as Acosta, who was a "man of letters" more than a missionary. In this regard, it is somewhat misleading to suggest that missionaries paid little attention to what Amerindians had to say about nature, cosmology, or other systems of meaning.[223] Missionaries who lived out their lives on the frontier could not afford to ignore their neophytes. What the Indians had to say – a world of alternative possibilities – became inescapable as a consequence of the Jesuit imperative that all missionaries master the language of their Indian neophytes. In his history of the Jesuit missions of Paraguay, which was published in 1639, Father Ruiz de Montoya alluded to the cultural relativism that often seems to have followed the mastery of an Indian language:

> They [the Guaraní] knew of God's existence, and even in a certain way of his unity. This is gathered from the name they give him, *Tupá*. The first syllable, *tu*, expresses wonder, while the second, *pá*, is an interrogative; thus it corresponds to the Hebrew word *Man-hu*, "What is this?," in the singular.[224]

It is significant that Ruiz de Montoya authored a grammar and eight-hundred-page dictionary of the Guaraní language.

Jesuit acknowledgment of otherness is suggested by Jesuit use of native terms (or native terms alongside Spanish lexical items) as well as passages in which authors such as Pérez de Ribas essentially afforded

---

[222] Ibid., 354.
[223] Walter Mignolo, "Introduction and Commentary." In *Natural and Moral History of the Indies* [1590] by José de Acosta, ed. Jane E. Mangan and trans. Frances Lopez-Morillas, pp. xvii–xxviii, 451–518 (Durham, NC: Duke University Press, 2002), 475.
[224] McNaspy, *The Spiritual Conquest*, 49.

Indians an opportunity to express views on a subject such as abortion that a Spaniard could or would never express:

> Another abuse found among the Mayo that it was necessary to correct was that pregnant women could easily abort their infants. There was some of this in other nations, particularly when a pregnant woman already had a nursing infant. When they were reproached for this abuse and cruelty, the response of the Indian woman was, "Can't you see that I am looking out for the life of this child that I'm holding in my arms?," thus making it clear that she was killing one child to raise another.[225]

Jesuits who talked with their Indian converts – and obviously many did, and not simply about "religious matters" – may well have discovered that they had more in common with the Indians than with fellow Europeans. Early Jesuit missionaries were defined by a belief in God's enduring presence; this belief was shared by their Indian converts. Jesuit missionaries could hardly have been excited about a Jesuit-trained philosopher named Descartes (1596–1650), who captured the imagination of Europe with "proof" that God did indeed exist but not in the manner of Augustine's meddling parent; instead, it was in the manner of a distant observer, long separated from his creation.[226] Jesuit missionaries and Indians may have disagreed about who or what was responsible for miracles, but neither doubted the in-breaking of the divine, as evidenced by reports of flying shamans, talking stones, or altar cloths that mysteriously began to bleed.[227]

The Jesuits shared with the Indians a commitment to communal, nonpropertied living and ceremonial and ritualistic labor, which were prescribed by the Jesuit Constitutions.[228] The Jesuit "formula for living" was at odds with the individualism, materialism, and the "buyer beware" attitude of emergent capitalism back in Europe. Jesuit celebration of obedience to superiors (senior males), personal poverty, and charity were entirely consistent with principles of seniority, reciprocity, and redistribution that governed native economic, sociopolitical, and

---

[225] Pérez de Ribas, *History of the Triumphs*, 290.
[226] Russell, *Mephistopheles*, 82–83.   [227] Reff, "Predicament of Culture."
[228] O'Malley, *The First Jesuits*; Ganss, *The Constitutions of the Society of Jesus*.

religious systems.[229] Of course, the Jesuits, like their European contemporaries, were not on the whole prepared to consider the idea of
cultural parity.[230] However, missionaries naturally invoked their own
cultural experience and categories during encounters with native beliefs
and practice. In so doing, they necessarily were confronted, if only at a
subconscious level,[231] with the parallels between Indian and their own
Jesuit beliefs and behavior.[232] Such conflation of self and other presumably contributed to an acceptance of "Indian" expressions of Christianity, particularly as the Enlightenment drew near and Jesuit missionaries
found themselves at odds with their European contemporaries.

Conclusion

The previous chapter showed how the rise of Christianity in Europe was
coincident with a demographic collapse and profound sociocultural upheaval, caused in significant part by epidemics of acute and chronic
infectious disease. It is apparent that the rise of Christianity in colonial
Mexico also was coincident with a disease-induced population collapse
and the fragmentation of native societies. Pagans in late antique and
early medieval Europe embraced Christianity because it entailed an extensive and compelling discourse about mysterious yet compassionate
deities (God and his saints), and offered rituals (e.g., baptism, the Mass,
pilgrimages, processions) to restore harmony to a world upended by
Satan and disease. In this chapter we have seen that early Mendicant
and later Jesuit missionaries employed the same or similar rituals and
spoke in terms reminiscent of the early Church, including (in the case
of the Jesuits) casting the Indians as victims rather than co-conspirators
with Satan. The Jesuit mission was in significant ways analogous to the
earliest *ekklésiae* and post-Constantine institutions (e.g., monasteries,

---

[229] Palacios y Zoffoli, *Gloria y Tragedia*, 185; Reff, *Disease, Depopulation and Culture Change*, 265.
[230] J.H. Elliott, *Spain and Its World, 1500–1700* (New Haven, CT: Yale University Press, 1989), 42.
[231] Consciously acknowledging the parallels may have been unnerving. Thomas A. Abercrombie, *Pathways of Memory and Power* (Madison: University of Wisconsin Press, 1998), 18.
[232] Pagden, *The Fall of Natural Man*, 97–98,161.

convents, hospitals, orphanages), in that it reorganized economic and social life. Like Saint Martin and other "missionary-monks" of the early Middle Ages, the Jesuits introduced new beliefs and rituals as well accommodated Indian traditions, chiefly through a celebration of miracles and the cult of the saints and their relics.

Sacred biographers and historians of late antiquity and the early Middle Ages described the pagan embrace of Christianity in terms of the mysterious cooperation of invisible forces (e.g., Holy Spirit, angels, saints) and faithful monks, deacons, and bishops. As discussed in the next chapter, Spanish missionary authors, particularly the Jesuits, embraced much the same teleological framework to describe their mission enterprise in colonial Mexico.

FOUR

The Relevance of Early Christian Literature to Jesuit Missionaries in Colonial Mexico

To this point I have emphasized the cultural–historical parallels in the rise of Christianity in the late Roman Empire and colonial Mexico. Jesuit authors often were aware of the parallels, explaining in part why they relied on early Christian literature as a source of literary models and rhetoric to represent their New World mission enterprises. In this chapter, I elaborate on the similarities between early Christian and Jesuit literatures. At the same time, I will show how the lives of Jesuit missionaries, including their political/institutional context, resembled the lives of early Christian martyrs and saints. The larger argument advanced is that the "reality" of the mission frontier is, paradoxically, both constituted and reflected in Jesuit missionary texts.

Jesuit "borrowing" ranges from metaphors and epithets – references to the mission frontier as "the Lord's vineyard" or to Satan as a "demonic kinsman" – to long passages that appear to have been suggested by early Christian literature. In a sermon on drinking, which dates to the early sixth century, Bishop Caesarius of Arles complained:

It is said that some of the rustici, when they have either gotten wine or made other drinks for themselves, invited their neighbors and kin for a drinking party as though it were a wedding feast. They keep their guests for four or five days and overwhelm them with excessive drinking.[1]

[1] William E. Klingshirn, *Caesarius of Arles: The Making of A Christian Community in Late Antique Gaul* (Cambridge, UK: Cambridge University Press, 1994), 197.

One encounters much the same complaint in Jesuit texts:

> The most widespread vice among nearly all these peoples was drunk-
> enness. They were intoxicated for days and nights on end. Instead
> of drinking alone in their houses, their drinking occurred in con-
> tinuous, well-publicized festivities that were held for the purpose of
> inebriation.[2]

Not only pagans and Indians were similarly described but so, too,
were early Christian saints and Jesuit missionaries. In early Christian
sacred biographies, saints are yoked to God, who watches over and
protects his missionaries. Late antique and medieval accounts of the
lives of saints such as Paul the Hermit, Brendan, Antony, and Cuthbert
are filled with divine intercession, including food delivered from on high:

> While they were discoursing about such matters, they noticed a fleet
> raven alight upon a branch of a tree. Gently swooping down, to their
> amazement, it deposited a whole loaf of bread between them. "Ah,"
> said Paul when the bird had flown away, "God has sent us our dinner,
> God truly good, truly merciful." (Jerome's *Life of St. Paul the Hermit*,
> c. 376 C.E.)[3]

> They were making their way along a river, talking about such things,
> when they suddenly saw the eagle settling down on the bank, "There,"
> said the saint, "is the servant I was telling you about. Run and see
> what God has sent and bring it back quickly." The boy brought back
> a big fish which the bird had just caught. (Bede's *Life of Cuthbert*,
> c. 730 C.E.)[4]

In a letter from 1632, written almost one thousand years after Bede's life
of Cuthbert, Jesuit missionary Juan de Ardeñas recounted how he, too,

---

[2] Pérez de Ribas, *History of the Triumphs*, 89–90.
[3] Sister Marie Liguori Ewald, trans., "Life of St. Hilarion by St. Jerome." In *The Fathers of the Church, Volume 15: Early Christian Biographies*, ed. Roy J. Deferrari, pp. 241–280 (New York: Fathers of the Church, 1952), 233.
[4] J. F. Webb, trans., *The Lives of the Saints* (Baltimore, MD: Penguin Books, 1965), 87.

had been saved from starvation by an eagle bearing dinner:

> As we were all travelling together along a narrow path between steep mountains, God willed that we should find a half-dead hare, laying on the ground. I told my Indians to pick it up and take it along. We had barely walked another one hundred paces when an eagle dropped another large hare from above; it landed so close to me that the mule I was riding bolted. I told the Indians to grab what God had sent us to eat.[5]

Perhaps most significantly, God and his saints were a constant source of help in the struggle to win and retain converts to Christianity. Again, what is striking is that early Christian and Jesuit authors conveyed this "fact" in such similar terms. Compare, for instance, the following passages from Bede (writing about early medieval Britian) and Pérez de Ribas (writing about northern Mexico):

> At this time [c. 683 C.E.] there was a little boy of the Saxon race in the monastery who had been lately converted to the faith and who had been afflicted by disease and confined to his bed for a long time.... Suddenly, by divine dispensation, the most blessed chiefs of the apostles deigned to appear to him. The apostles greeted him with holy words and said, "Son, do not let fear of death trouble you, for we are going to take you today to the heavenly kingdom." ... The boy asked for the priest and told him all these things.... Soon after this, on the same day, the boy died, proving by his own death the truth of what he had heard from Christ's apostles.[6]

> There was an Indian, one of the first to be baptized, who lived a good life. He had been ill for many days and feared that he had been bewitched.... When the priest arrived the sick man said to him, "Father, you should know that a priest like yourself has appeared to me, in your habit, together with four other priests who were his companions.

---

[5] Pérez de Ribas, *History of the Triumphs*, 364–365.
[6] Colgrave and Mynors, *Bede's Ecclesiastical History*, 379–381.

They were bathed in light,[7] and with a serious look on his face the first one asked me why I did not confess as often as I used to." ... The son told his father, the priest who had come to hear confession, that the saint who had appeared to him had said, "Confess, for in a few days you will find yourself in heaven. I will take you there." ... after having received the Holy Sacraments, the sick man died and was taken to Our Lord, as can be expected given the circumstances surrounding his death.[8]

Finally, in life as well as death God was one with his missionaries. In Ruiz de Montoya's *Spiritual Conquest* (1639) the longtime missionary recounted how apostate Indians in Paraguay killed two fellow Jesuits. The Indians tried to destroy the priests' corpses, including the heart of Father Roque González, which had been ripped from his body. In keeping with the lives of Christian martyrs and saints (and God's presence in those lives),[9] the heart of Father González would not burn: "To dispose of every trace of the martyrs, they lit a huge fire and threw the two bodies and heart [of Father Roque] into it. The latter, however, remained intact."[10]

As noted in the previous chapter, Jesuit authors were not alone in casting themselves as a reiteration of the lives of early Christian martyrs and saints.[11] One of the more striking woodcut images in Fray Jeronimo de Mendieta's *Historia Eclesiastica Indiana*, which recounts the history of the early Franciscan missions of Mexico, is of a friar preaching to Indians who are depicted as Romans.[12]

---

[7] Presumably these five saints were Ignatius Loyola and four other Jesuits who had been canonized as saints (Francis Xavier, Luis de Gonzaga, Stanislas Kotska, and Jean Berhmans).

[8] Pérez de Ribas, *History of the Triumphs*, 247–248.

[9] Ronald C. Finucane, *Miracles and Pilgrims, Popular Beliefs in Medieval England* (Totowa, NJ: Rowman and Littlefield, 1977), 30.

[10] Ruiz de Montoya, *The Spiritual Conquest*, trans. Clement J. McNaspy, S.J. (St. Louis: Institute of Jesuit Sources, 1993 [1639]), 154.

[11] Mendicant acknowledgment of the parallels was most explicit during the half-century following Cortés's conquest (e.g. Las Casas [c. 1550] 1967), when missionaries were still optimistic about the Indians' acceptance of Christianity. Sabine MacCormack, *Religion in the Andes* (Princeton, NJ: Princeton University Press, 1991), 239–240.

[12] See Volume I of Fray Jeronimo de Mendieta, *Historia Eclesiastica Indiana*, 2 vols., ed. Francisco Solano y Perez-lila (Madrid: Ediciones Atlas, 1973 [1596]). See also J. L.

During the Counter-Reformation, the Vatican, episcopacy, and various religious orders, especially the Society of Jesus, encouraged and supported new editions of the lives and teachings of the Church Fathers (*Vitae Patrum*).[13] The Council of Trent went so far as to rule that patristic sources carried the same authoritative weight as the Bible. The lives of the saints, which were at the heart of devotionalism during the Renaissance, also were promoted by the Church and Jesuit order.[14] At the same time that the Church and Society of Jesus were privileging early Christian literature, both sought to block or limit the publication of "heretical discourse." In the wake of Erasmus and Luther, the Council of Trent in 1564 required Church approval of all manuscripts before they were printed.[15] The Society of Jesus also sat in judgment of its own, Jesuit authors. This is apparent from the letters of approbation from Jesuit superiors that precede published narratives. Jesuit censors were not the least bit hesitant about suppressing texts by Jesuits that were deemed "offensive."[16]

Phelan, *The Millennial Kingdom of the Franciscans in the New World*, 2nd ed. (Berkeley: University of California Press, 1970 [1956]), 44–58.

[13] Henri-Jean Martin, *Print, Power, and People in 17th-Century France*, trans. David Gerard (Metuchen, NJ: The Scarecrow Press, 1993), 78–80; A. D. Wright, *The Counter-Reformation: Catholic Europe and the Non-Christian World* (London: Weidenfeld and Nicolson, 1982), 9.

[14] The Church embraced patristic sources in part to defend itself from charges that it had deviated from the values and beliefs of the early Church. Hippolytus Delehaye, S.J., *The Legends of the Saints, An Introduction to Hagiography*, trans. V. M. Crawford (London: Longmans Green Company, 1907), Henri-Jean Martin, *Print, Power, and People*, 88, 101, 103.

[15] The council followed a precedent established in 1502 by the Spanish Crown, which required the acquisition of a license before a book could be published. The council also called for the appointment of inspectors to visit bookshops and to levy fines on booksellers who were caught dealing in prohibited texts. Philip II welcomed such regulations and promoted still others, including an expurgatory index that excised passages from otherwise orthodox books. Henry Kamen, *Inquisition and Society in Spain in the Sixteenth and Seventeenth Centuries* (Bloomington: Indiana University Press, 1985), 79, 183, Henri-Jean Martin, *Print, Power, and People*, 3–5.

[16] In 1640 or thereabouts Jesuit censors denied permission for the publication of a history of the Paraguay missions, written by Father Juan Pastor. Magnus Morner, *The Political and Economic Activities of the Jesuits in the La Plata Region; The Hapsburg Era* (Stockholm: Library and Institute of Ibero-American Studies, 1953), 2. In 1653 Pérez de Ribas completed a sequel to the *Historia*. Although the *Corónica* had been written at the suggestion of the Jesuit Father General, once completed it was deemed offensive in part by Jesuit superiors and was denied publication rights. Andrés Pérez de Ribas,

Jesuit authors certainly had to be mindful of the institutions that in significant ways defined and governed their lives. Indeed, it could be suggested that Jesuit authors borrowed from early Christian literature, and liberally so, because they essentially were required to do so, particularly if they wanted their narratives published. Does this then mean, however, that the story told by Jesuit authors has more to do with their "institutional context" and the lives of early Christian martyrs and saints, than Jesuit missionary lives as lived? How should we understand, for instance, the very similar comments at the outset of this chapter by Pérez de Ribas and Caesarius of Arles regarding the heathen penchant for intoxication? One could argue that both complaints had more to do with prior texts, in particular, the Bible, than any pagan and Indian "reality." Along these lines, both Caesarius and the Jesuits were schooled in the Old Testament *Book of Daniel*, which implied/dictated ("Belshazzar's feast") that gentiles, idolatry, and alcohol all went "hand-in-hand."[17] Did Caesarius and the Jesuits "see" and complain about something that was there by virtue of scripture, or is it the case that Celts and Indians, "in reality," regularly became intoxicated to access the sacred?

In pursuing such questions (for which there are answers, although they are never simple or given *a priori*), I have taken an essentially "constructivist" stance.[18] I have assumed that each performance of cultural heritage, and in particular, the writing of Jesuit narratives, is more than a copy of prior performances (early Christian literature) because of new cultural–historical contingencies. Pursuit of these institutional, epistemological/theological, and historical contingencies suggest that Jesuit authors did in fact employ rhetoric, conventions, and type scenes from early Christian literature because this literature was privileged by the Jesuit order, the Church writ large, and the Hapsburg Court. However, it is also the case that sacred biography and history gave voice to values, beliefs, and real-world experiences that Jesuit missionaries shared with their late antique and early medieval counterparts.

Corónica y Historia Religiosa de la Provincia de la Compañia de Jesus de Mexico, 2 vols. (Mexico: Sagrado Corazon, 1896 [c. 1653]).

[17] *The New Jerusalem Bible* (Garden City, NY: Doubleday, 1985), 1480–1481.

[18] For an exemplification of constructivism and a critique of alternative approaches, see Edward M. Bruner, "Abraham Lincoln as Authentic Reproduction: A Critique of Postmodernism." *American Anthropologist* 96 (1994): 397–415.

The Institutional/Political Context of Jesuit Missionary Discourse

Scholars often speak of "the Church" as if it was a monolithic institution with one voice. Yet the clerics and religious as well as the Papacy and secular elite (e.g., kings, princes) who made up "the Counter-Reformation Church" often disagreed amongst themselves over what was conveyed in the Bible, the *Vitae Patrum*, the lives of the saints, and other privileged texts. The Council of Trent, which ceased its deliberations in 1563, spent twenty years debating Church teachings. Most everyone may have agreed that early Christian literature should be read and cited, but not everyone agreed as to why. The deliberations of the Council of Trent, competition between religious orders and between secular and regular priests,[19] and debates over issues such as how to distinguish communication with God versus the devil, all testify to the contested nature of the Church and its teachings.[20] Moreover, the Society of Jesus – like societies and cultures writ large – was itself dynamic and contested. Almost from its official recognition in 1540, Jesuits carried on a lively and sometimes acrimonious debate about their "way of proceeding."[21]

One cannot equate Jesuit use of early Christian literature with some unidimensional, Counter-Reformation discourse, however that is defined (e.g., normative pronouncements on the Eucharist, the role of the clergy, husband–wife relationships, etc.). Jesuit missionary authors often used, and one might say, deployed, early Christian literature for a variety of reasons, but particularly to promote and defend their mission enterprises.

The Crown, the Episcopacy, and Other Religious Orders

Today as in the past, the members of the Society of Jesus are divided among numerous "provinces" spread around the world. During the

---

[19] Regular priests are members of a religious order (e.g., Dominicans, Jesuits); secular priests are under the authority of bishops.
[20] John W. O'Malley, *The First Jesuits* (Cambridge, MA: Harvard University Press, 1993), 371; A. D. Wright, *Catholicism and Spanish Society Under the Reign of Philip II, 1555–1598, and Philip III, 1598–1621* (Lewiston, Australia: Edwin Mellen Press, 1991).
[21] Malachi Martin, *The Jesuits* (New York: Touchstone Books, 1987).

colonial period, there were a handful of Jesuit provinces in the Americas. Jesuits in the province of Nueva España competed for resources with Jesuits in Peru and the Río de la Plata as well as with other religious (e.g., Franciscans) – all of whom were beholding to the Spanish Crown. Through a series of papal concessions known as the *Patronato Real*, Spain's Hapsburg rulers controlled the appointment and financing of missionaries and clerics who were sent to the New World. Importantly, by the early 1600s, missionary enterprises throughout the Spanish empire had reason to doubt the continued support of the Spanish monarchy. Spain's economy was in crisis, because of population decline back home in Spain, a shrinking Iberian economy, and the loss of American silver to Dutch and English pirates.[22] By 1600, missionary orders also were competing for what were fewer and fewer recruits, owing to a decline in religious vocations in Spain and a need for more priests to deal with the Reformation and mounting social ills in Europe.[23]

New World Jesuits competed not only with fellow religious but also with secular clergy.[24] The papal bull *Regimini* of 1540, which officially recognized the Society of Jesus, largely freed the Jesuits from the control of episcopal hierarchy. Bishops and other secular clergy in Europe and the New World often resented the Jesuits' independence and their perceived "holier-than-thou" attitude. Because of their activism and many

---

[22] Marcelin Defourneaux, *Daily Life in España in the Golden Age*, trans. Newton Branch (Stanford, CA: Stanford University Press, 1979), 91–96; J. H. Elliott, *Spain and Its World, 1500–1700* (New Haven, CT: Yale University Press, 1989), 125–133; Jóse A. Maravall, *Culture of the Baroque: Analysis of a Historical Structure* (Minneapolis: University of Minnesota Press, 1986), 149.

[23] John F. Bannon, *The Mission Frontier in Sonora, 1620–1687* (New York: United States Catholic Historical Society, 1955), 118–127; John Correia-Afonso, S.J., *Jesuit Letters and Indian History, 1542–1773*, 2nd ed. (New York: Oxford University Press, 1969); Henry Kamen, *Inquisition and Society in Spain in the Sixteenth and Seventeenth Centuries* (Bloomington: Indiana University Press, 1985), 200; Maravall, *Culture of the Baroque*, 149; W. E. Shiels, "The Critical Period in Mission History." Mid-America (new series) 10 (1939): 97–109; P. Francisco Zambrano, S.J., *Diccionario bio-bibliografico de la Compania de Jesus en Mexico*, 16 vols. (Mexico: Editorial JUS, 1961–77), VI (1966), 572.

[24] Regular clergy were those governed by a "rule," such as the Jesuits, Franciscans, and Dominicans, and largely were free of the control of the episcopacy. Secular priests were under the direct authority of bishops, who, in turn, were appointed by the king and his deputies.

public ministries, the Jesuits often attracted the laity to their churches. This did not sit well with secular priests who insisted that Catholics should receive the sacraments in (and support financially) their parish church.[25] The Jesuits did not make things easier for themselves by criticizing secular priests for a lack of education and pursuit of payment for preaching and clerical services.[26] With rare exceptions, the Jesuits refused salaried positions or *benefices*, which often provided secular clergy in the Americas with comfortable, if not, lavish, lifestyles.[27] The Jesuits, however, did accept gifts of money and property (e.g., houses, ranches, farms), which yielded considerable sums that supported Jesuit colleges and residences.[28] Of course, a gift made to a Jesuit residence or college was a gift that might otherwise have gone to a bishop and his diocese.

As we have seen, Jesuit missionary texts had to be approved by Church officials before they could be published. An Augustinian friar, a Franciscan censor appointed by the Spanish Crown, and an episcopal vicar from Madrid, all signed off on Pérez de Ribas's *Historia*. That all did so is testament to Pérez de Ribas's skill at casting the Jesuit missions of Mexico in the best and least offensive light. Who better to enlist in such a cause than the apostles and early Christian martyrs and saints (and by extension, almighty God). Jesuit missionary authors knew that accounts of priests who were favored by God in life and death would resonate with their religious and lay Catholic audience, including young men who might be weighing a decision to pursue a Jesuit vocation, particularly as a missionary in the New World. Note that there was considerable precedent for using hagiography as a literary model to increase religious vocations. In the late medieval period religious orders regularly produced works celebrating the heroic and saintly accomplishments of

---

[25] The struggle between regular and secular priests is evidenced by approximately one hundred pamphlets that were published in Paris between 1625 and 1636 arguing for and against secular versus regular priests (Martin, *Print, Power, and People*, 120–121).

[26] A. Lynn Martin, *The Jesuit Mind: The Mentality of an Elite in Early Modern France* (Ithaca, NY: Cornell University Press, 1988), 208; Felix J. Zubillaga, S.J., ed., *Monumenta Mexicana*, III (1585–1590) (Rome: Institum Historicum Societatis Iesu, 1968), 336.

[27] O'Malley, *The First Jesuits*, 286.

[28] At times Jesuit wealth became quite extensive. See Nicholas P. Cushner, *Lords of the Land: Sugar, Wine, and Jesuit Estates of Coastal Peru, 1600–1767* (Albany: State University of New York, 1980).

their members to attract new recruits.[29] Of course, the more it could be shown that a mission enterprise benefited from divine intercession, the more that mission enterprise would be esteemed and supported materially by the Jesuit order, the Church as a whole, and the Spanish Crown. It is worth emphasizing that Spain's Hapsburg rulers were as concerned with saving souls, including their own, as they were realizing a profit on their New World investments. In 1633, in the midst of bankruptcy, Philip IV approved three hundred thousand ducats for wine and oil to celebrate Mass in the monasteries of the New World.[30]

Jesuit missionary narratives abound in rhetoric from early Christian literature such as "plenteous harvests of souls" and "abundant fruits of the vineyard." Such rhetoric, together with accounts of miracles, which were considered a characteristic feature of the apostolic Church,[31] helped to establish an essential unity between the Jesuit experience in Mexico and the nascent Church. Jesuit missionary authors often bolstered this connection with Latin quotes from early Christian literature. Latin quotes not only strengthened, substantively, Jesuit missionary arguments, but also established a Jesuit author's learnedness as well as his orthodoxy. The passage below from Pérez de Ribas's *Historia* exemplifies this use of Latin quotes to make the point that the Jesuits essentially were no different from the apostles, particularly in enjoyment of God's grace and an ability to work miracles:

> Let us now examine in detail what was experienced in the conversions of these peoples and the type of miracles that were promised by God's Son to those who are new in the Faith. As He was about to ascend [to heaven], He charged the apostles with preaching the Holy Gospel to the entire world: *Signa autem eos, qui crediderint, haec sequentur: Daemonia eijciunt, linguis loquentur nouis, serpentes tollent, & si quid mortiferum bibent non eis nocebit, super aegros, manus*

---

[29] Michael Goodich, *Vita Perfecta: The Ideal of Sainthood in the Thirteenth Century* (Stuttgart: Anton Hiersemann, 1982).

[30] C. H. Haring, *The Spanish Empire in America* (San Diego: Harcourt Brace Jovanovich, 1947), 172.

[31] Phelan, *The Millennial Kingdom*, 50; M. O'Meara, "Planting the Lord's Garden in New France: Gabriel Sagard's *Le Grand Voyage* and *Histoire du Canada*." *Rocky Mountain Review* 46(1992):11–25.

imponent, & bene habebunt.[32] I refer anyone interested in learning about which of these wonders has occurred in these missions to the entire course of this history. One will find a great number of clear cases in which demons were expelled, although not so much from bodies as from, more importantly, the souls of innumerable sorcerers who had intimate and familiar dealings with these enemies of the human race.[33]

Pérez de Ribas went on to note that the Jesuits in northern Mexico not only drove out demons but also approximated or surpassed the apostles in all other miracles promised by the risen Christ, including speaking in tongues (mastering Indian languages), handling serpents ("domesticating" the Indians), drinking poisons (surviving Indian use of poisonous herbs), and curing the sick.

In contrast to the Jesuits, the Mendicants infrequently claimed that miracles were a significant part of their success in southern Mexico. To quote Mendieta, "In this land of Nueva España Our Lord has not wanted to make or work public miracles."[34] Although Mendieta was of the opinion that miracles were unnecessary, given the Indians' ready embrace of the faith, his comment is still surprising given his confident portrayal of the early Mendicant experience as another "primitive church" (Jesus and the apostles worked an abundance of miracles).[35] The absence of miracles not withstanding, Franciscan-missionary authors nevertheless did draw parallels between themselves and the apostolic Church.[36] In Motolinía's *History of The Indians of New Spain* (1541), he equated preconquest Mexico with Old Testament Palestine.[37] Elsewhere he likened the preconquest Mexicans to "...the Romans of old," apparently

---

[32] Mark 16:17–18: "Where believers go, these signs shall go with them; they will cast out devils in my name; they will speak in tongues that are strange to them; they will take up serpents in their hands, and drink poisonous draughts without harm; they will lay their hands upon the sick and make them recover." Ronald A. Knox, *The Holy Bible: A Translation from the Latin Vulgate* (New York: Sheed and Ward, 1956), 52.

[33] Pérez de Ribas, *History of the Triumphs*, 455.

[34] *Historia Eclesiastica Indiana*, II, 148.

[35] See Phelan, *The Millennial Kingdom*, 50–51.

[36] Ibid., 44–47.

[37] Elizabeth A. Foster, ed. and trans., *Motolinía's History of The Indians of New Spain* (Berkeley: The Cortés Society, 1950 [1541]), 191, 205, 227, 234–235, 269.

meaning in the age of Augustus.[38] Mendieta employed similar rhetoric, casting Cortés, for instance, as another Moses who freed the Mexica from servitude in Egypt.[39] Correspondingly he cast the Franciscans' New World enterprise as a new Israel.[40] Later Franciscans such as Torquemada and Vetancurt continued this tradition of preconquest Mexico as another "Reign of King Saul," liberated as it were by New World apostles.[41]

Mendicant rhetoric of another "primitive church" was, in part, dictated by the same institutional and political constraints as confronted the Jesuits, particularly a need to ensure support from the Crown and the Church. The Hapsburg Court, the Council of the Indies, and the ecclesiastical and religious hierarchy all presumably took solace in what today we perceive as a "positive spin" on a destructive, colonial enterprise. Significantly, mendicant invocation of antiquity and the primitive Church

---

[38] Ibid., 208. Although Foster observed that Motolinía's *Historia* makes only thirteen references to the Bible, the *Historia* was derived from Motolinía's earlier *Memoriales*, which frequently quotes the Bible as well as classical literature. Indeed, a comparison of Motolinía's *Historia*, Book I, Chapter I, with the corresponding chapter (2) in the *Memoriales*, reveals a long paragraph absent from the *Historia* and present in the *Memoriales* that makes explicit references to Egypt of the Old Testament, quoting the Books of *Wisdom* and *Exodus*. Foster, *Motolinía's History*, 14; Fray Toribio de Benavente Motolinía, *Historia de los Indios de la Nueva España*, ed. Edmundo O'Gorman (Mexico: Editorial Porrua, 1969), 13–18; *Memoriales e Historia de los indios de la Nueva España*, ed. with an introduction by Fidel de Lejarza (Madrid: Ediciones Atlas, 1970), 10–16.

[39] *Historia Eclesiastica*, I, 107. See also II, 61, 108–109, 121–124, 129.

[40] Mendieta (II, 92–93) also speaks of parallels with the primitive church, as when he laments how the Indians were not treated as true Christians by Spaniards, just as many Jewish Christians in the primitive church looked down on or objected to gentiles becoming Christians. He likewise casts the friars as apostles and speaks of their work in comparison with the primitive church (e.g., I, 151), Phelan, *The Millennial Kingdom*, 11.

[41] See, for instance, Fray Juan de Torquemada, *Monarquia Indiana*, 3 Vols. (Mexico: Editorial Porrua, 1969 [1615]), I, 579–583. Explicit parallels between the Franciscan experience and the Old and New Testaments is perhaps most evident in Books 20 and 21, which deal with the lives of Franciscans in Mexico (III, 389–634). In the second volume of *Teatro Mexicano*, titled Chronica de la Provincia del Santo Evangelio de Mexico (1697), Vetancurt drew parallels between the Franciscans and the pre-Constantine Church, as when he casts the original twelve friars in the mould of Saints Peter and Paul and draws a parallel with the Apostle Philip and *Acts* 8. A further example is Chapter XL on the life of Father Andrés de Olmos; the margin notes are to the Gospels of *John* and *Luke*, *Acts*, *I Corinthians*, *Exodus*, *Isaiah*, and *Psalms*. Fray Agustin de Vetancurt, *Teatro Mexicano, Descripción Breve De Los Sucesos Ejemplares, Históricos Y Religiosos Del Nuevo Mundo De Las Indies* (Mexico: Editorial Porrua, 1970 [1697–98]), 5, 9.

was used to critique as well as value the Spanish colonial enterprise. The Dominican friar, Bartolomé de Las Casas, argued that the parallels between the Indians of the New World and the Greeks and Romans of antiquity implied that the Indians had a complex civilization and thus every right to manage their own lives and destiny.[42] In pursuing the parallels between Indian America and pre-Christian Europe, Las Casas also pointed out that contemporary Europe retained many Greco-Roman beliefs and practices; what right did Spaniards (professing concern for Indian souls) have to seize Indian lands when the Spaniards themselves were still significantly pagan?

The Jesuit Order

Missionary-authors such as Ruiz de Montoya and Pérez de Ribas wrote particularly for fellow Jesuits, including superiors who authorized the publication of Jesuit narratives. By 1600, there were some two hundred Jesuit residences and colleges spread throughout the world.[43] In each, dinner was followed every night with a reading from a book chosen by the master of novices or rector. Missionary accounts, which were first made popular by the letters of Francis Xavier from India, were particularly popular after-dinner reading.[44]

There are many ways in which the Jesuit narratives speak particularly to a Jesuit audience, including the ubiquitous metaphor of the Lord's vineyard, which was used as a referent for missions in Mexico and elsewhere. Similarly, Jesuit authors often gave voice to the particular Jesuit ideal of unquestioning obedience to superiors, often using metaphors and similes (e.g., obedience should be blind; like a corpse) drawn from the writings of Ignatius Loyola.[45] Expressions such as "love poverty

---

[42] *Apologética Historia Sumaria, by Fray Bartolomé de Las Casas. 2 Vols*, ed. Edmundo O'Gorman (Mexico: Universidad Nacional Autonoma de México Instituto de Investigaciones Históricas, 1967 [c. 1558]), I, 598, II, 296. See also David A. Lupher, *Romans in a New World: Classical Models in Sixteenth-Century Spanish America* (Ann Arbor: University of Michigan Press, 2003).

[43] A. Lynn Martin, *Plague? Jesuit Accounts of Epidemic Disease in the 16th Century* (Kirksville, MO: Sixteenth Century Journal Publishers, 1996), 201.

[44] de Guibert, *The Jesuits*, 217; O'Malley, *The First Jesuits*, 358.

[45] O'Malley, *The First Jesuits*, 353.

as a mother" abound in the *Historia* and were taken from the Jesuit Constitutions.[46] Additionally, the Jesuits whose careers are recounted in the *Historia* or Montoya's *Spiritual Conquest* are exemplary in part because of their adherence to their vows as well as particular Jesuit customs and rules governing such things as the timing and frequency of daily prayer.

Although Jesuit missionary authors embraced Jesuit ideals and signifying practices, Jesuit discourse and thinking has never been unidimensional. The biggest point of contention for early modern Jesuits was Ignatius Loyola's ideal of itinerant ministry. As noted, the Jesuit world view owed much to Augustine. At the same time, the "Formula" or plan of the Jesuit order that was developed by Ignatius Loyola was Thomistic in its activism. Whereas Augustine tended to see human beings enfeebled by original sin, and thus dependent on God for salvation, Aquinas believed that human beings could compensate through reason for Adam's sin and thus endear themselves to God through a Christian life. Ignatius followed Augustine in seeing God everywhere but he embraced Aquinas's prescription for actually drawing close to God, again principally through good deeds or charity.

Almost from its inception the Society of Jesus, particularly in Spain, struggled with the tendency to abandon Ignatian activism in favor of a more contemplative life, realized as educators.[47] This struggle is reflected in the *Ratio Studiorum* or plan of study designed for Jesuit novices. As noted in the introduction, the *Ratio* lists many works of early Christian literature. However, this is not the entirety of the reading list; it also includes more than a fair share of contemplative works by authors such as John Cassian (d. 435), Peter Damian (d. 1072), Bernard of Clairvaux (d. 1153), and Richard of St. Victor (d. 1173). Significantly, each of these authors celebrated life within the monastery, arguing that spiritual development was a supremely individual affair between God and the person; little or no mention was made by these authors of venturing beyond the cloister to help others.[48]

---

[46] Ganss, *Ignatius Loyola*, 292.   [47] Lynn Martin, *Plague*, 40.

[48] Michael Casey, *A Thirst for God: Spiritual Desire in Bernard of Clairvaux's Sermons on the Song of Songs* (Kalamazoo: Cistercian Publications, 1998); Patricia McNulty, trans. and ed., *St. Peter Damian: Selected Writings on the Spiritual Life* (London: Faber and Faber,

As early as 1575, the Jesuit Father General became alarmed about the growing number of Jesuits who were drawn to a contemplative rather than apostolic vocation. Indeed, a key reason for implementing the *Ratio Studiorum* was to limit the exposure of Jesuit novices and scholastics to contemplative works and ideas.[49] As part of the struggle to strike more of a balance between a contemplative life and one of activism, Catherine of Sienna (1347–1380 C.E.) appears on the reading list. The saint, in the midst of several years of retreat and solitude, had a mystical experience that led her to forgo her life of contemplation for one of service to others.[50]

Despite the efforts of Jesuit superiors, by 1600 most Jesuits had come to prefer life as a teacher in a Jesuit college to life as an itinerant missionary.[51] This was true not only in Europe but also in colonial Mexico. The first Jesuits sent to the New World (in 1567) were a group of nine missionaries who were killed by the Indians of "La Florida" shortly after they came ashore in what is today southern Georgia.[52] The tragic loss of life as well as the huge investment that the Society had made in the martyred priests and brothers prompted the Father General of the order, Francis Borja, to rethink the Jesuit presence in the New World. When a new group of Jesuits were dispatched to Nueva España in 1572, they were assigned to Mexico City and essentially were told *not* to initiate risky missionary work.[53] The Jesuits promptly (1574) founded the Colegio de San Pablo y San Pedro and within a decade opened similar schools for the children of Spanish and criollo elites in Guadalajara, Vallodolid, Puebla, and Oaxaca. During this same period the Jesuits founded schools for Indian children in and around Mexico City, namely the Colegio of

---

1959); Boniface Ramsey, O.P., *John Cassian: The Conferences* (New York: Paulist Press, 1997); Grover A. Zinn, trans., *Richard of St. Victor* (New York: Paulist Press, 1979).

[49] Joseph de Guibert, *The Jesuits: Their Spiritual Doctrine and Practice, A Historical Study* (Chicago: Loyola University Press, 1964), 219; Wright, *The Counter-Reformation*, 16.

[50] See *The Letters of Catherine of Siena*, trans. Suzanne Noffke, O.P. (Binghamton, NY: Center of Medieval and Renaissance Studies, 1988).

[51] O'Malley, *The First Jesuits*, 239, 375; *Religious Culture in the Sixteenth Century* (Brookfield, VT: Variorum, 1993), 483–485.

[52] Felix Zubillaga, S.J., ed., *Monumenta Antique Florida (1566–1572), Monumenta Missionum Societatis Jesu*, Vol. 3 (Rome: Institum Historicum Societatis Jesu, 1946); Pérez de Ribas, *History of the Triumphs*, 718–722.

[53] Felix Zubillaga, ed., *Monumenta Mexicana, Vol. I (1570–1580)* (Rome: Institum Historicum Societatis Iesu, 1956), 26.

San Martin at Tepotzotlan (1580), for Otomí children, and the Colegio of San Gregorio in Mexico City (1586), which educated the children of Nahuatl elites.[54]

Although Ignatius Loyola (1491–1556) valued and indeed supported the ministry of education,[55] he certainly did not imagine the Society of Jesus becoming a teaching order. And yet a half-century after Loyola's death, most Jesuits were educators, serving in close to three hundred colleges spread around the world.[56] True, Jesuits as a whole enjoyed reading or hearing about the exploits of Francis Xavier, but many apparently saw missionary work as less demanding intellectually.[57]

During the generalships of Everard Mercurian (1573–1580) and Claudio Aquaviva (1581–1615), particularly the latter, the Jesuit hierarchy sought to recapture Loyola's original vision of the Society of Jesus as apostles, particularly in places like Mexico.[58] Aquaviva in 1590 appointed a Jesuit Visitor, Diego de Avellaneda, who, over the objection of Mexican Jesuits,[59] initiated the Jesuit missions of northern Nueva España. In the years that followed, the Father General, with the support of the Spanish Crown, dispatched increasing numbers of Jesuit priests and brothers to the northern frontier. There, as we have seen, the

[54] Francisco Gonzalez de Cossio, ed., *Relacion Breve de la Venida de los de la Compañia de Jesus, Año de 1602*, Manuscrito anónimo del Archivo Histórico de la Secretaría de Hacienda (Mexico: Imprenta Universitaria, 1945).

[55] In 1548 Loyola approved the opening of the first Jesuit school in Messina, Italy. By the time of his death, in 1556, he had personally approved thirty-nine colleges and universities. Following Loyola's death the number of schools mushroomed; by 1607 there were 293 colleges. By 1750 the number of institutions peaked at 669. Francesco C. Cesareo, "Quest for Identity: The Ideals of Jesuit Education in the Sixteenth Century." In *The Jesuit Tradition in Education and Missions*, ed. Christopher Chapple, pp. 17–33 (Scranton, PA: University of Scranton (PA) Press, 1993), 17.

[56] Cesareo, "Quest for Identity," 17; de Guibert, *The Jesuits*, 288, f.21; O'Malley, *The First Jesuits*, 200–242.

[57] T. V. Cohen, "Why the Jesuits Joined." *Historical Papers/Communications Historiques*, 237–259 (Toronto: Canadian Historical Association, 1974).

[58] Agustín Churruca Peláez, S.J., *Primeras Fundaciones Jesuitas En Nueva España 1572–1580* (Mexico, DF: Editorial Porrúa, 1980), 348–349; Zubillaga, *Monumenta Mexicana* I, 513.

[59] Many Mexican Jesuits, like their Mendicant contemporaries, had come to question the Indians' "capacity" for Christianity. Jesuits in Mexico who opposed missions were mentioned and alluded to by Avellaneda in letters to the father general. Felix J. Zubillaga, S.J., ed., *Monumenta Mexicana*, Vol. IV (1590–1592) (Rome: Institum Historicum Societatis Iesu, 1971), 62–64, 282–284.

Jesuits realized one of the most successful mission enterprises in the New World.

The struggle over ministries and the profound shift in the orientation of the Jesuit order during the late sixteenth and early seventeenth centuries posed a clear threat to Jesuit missionaries in the New World, who depended on the Society for recruits as well as support in dealings with the Spanish Crown and the Council of the Indies. Again, given the privileged status of early Christian literature, authors such as Ruiz de Montoya and Pérez de Ribas understandably exalted their respective mission enterprises, casting them as a reiteration of the primitive and early medieval Church, staffed as it were by missionaries who emulated early Christian martyrs and saints. Sacred history and biography provided a dramatic narrative framework as well as rhetoric and type scenes (e.g., faith healing the blind) that riveted the reader to the fact of missionary sacrifice and divine election:

> They trooped off to the hut where Father Alonso was. At the shouts of the mob, he and his death came simultaneously to the threshold. An evil cacique seized him and commanded one of his servants to kill him. They rained blows upon him. The mastiff who held him, fearful of being hit by a stray blow himself, let go of him. With filial love Father Alonso moved towards the corpse of his already dead father [superior, Roque González], saying over and over: "Sons, why are you killing me? Sons, what are you doing?"[60]

Note that Ruiz de Montoya's quoting of Father González's final words, which echo the words of Christ, was a characteristic literary convention of medieval hagiography.[61]

The heroes of the early Christian literature included martyrs as well as saints who died a thousand deaths, daily sacrificing their lives for others until such time as God saw fit to call them to their eternal reward. Correspondingly, Jesuit texts recount the lives of priests who sacrificed their lives in the manner of Saint Antony and Saint Martin of Tours. Significantly, because many Jesuits had come to perceive a teaching position as superior to ministries to the poor and humble, authors such as

---

[60] Ruiz de Montoya, *The Spiritual Conquest*, 151.
[61] Heffernan, *Sacred Biography*, 78–79.

Pérez de Ribas embraced every opportunity to highlight the careers of priests such as Juan de Ledesma, who was both a scholar and "father" to the Indians. A university professor and intellectual giant, whose writings and opinions were respected in Mexico as well as Europe, Ledesma devoted years of his life to the spiritual and corporal needs of the Indians of Mexico City who flocked to the Jesuit church of San Gregorio:

> In the title of this excellent man's vita, I state why I have included here the life and admirable examples of virtue of this teacher, who held university professorships, expertly taught the sciences, and filled posts that are ordinarily considered to be more lofty and illustrious than the ministry of laboring among poor Indians. Even though this history records the lives of those whose principal occupation was among nations of poor and humble Indians, I include Father Juan de Ledesma because this was precisely how he demonstrated his excellent virtues. In this man, one observed the unusual combination of that which is divine and lofty and that which is humble and less illustrious. While the former of these virtues might beg to have this outstanding man included in their history, the latter beg for his vita to be recorded here. He devoted his life most sincerely to ministering to the humble, as will be seen in the account I will provide, which has been summarized from the records concerning this highly respected teacher that were printed at the request of important people in Mexico City. For this reason, I will be obliged to write more extensively than usual about this matter. The esteem in which the sons of the Company hold the ministry to the Indians (a point that is discussed throughout this Book) will also be demonstrated and confirmed.[62]

Early Medieval Institutional Parallels

The fact that Mendicant and Jesuit authors consciously "deployed" hagiographic rhetoric to defend and promote their missionary enterprises is entirely consistent with the experience of early Christian authors. As discussed in the previous chapter, with the Edict of Milan of 313 C.E.,

---

[62] Pérez de Ribas, *History of the Triumphs*, 472.

Constantine freed the Church from persecution, contributing to a rapid expansion of Christianity. Corruption within the now institutionalized Church helped give rise to the ascetic and monastic movements. Large numbers of commoners and would-be clerics opted for monasteries or isolated hermitages where they endeavored to realize religious perfection. Arguably, the monastic movement raised an important issue within the Church that has resurfaced throughout its history, particularly when confronted with large numbers of gentiles. What is the appropriate life for a Christian cleric or religious? Is it forgoing this world to become one with God through prayer and contemplation, or is it heeding Christ's call to venture into the world, proclaiming through word and deed the message of the Gospel?

During the early medieval period, the Church wrestled with this question as well as the issue of whether missions were worthwhile, particularly among "simple" peasants (*rustici*) and German-speaking "barbarians." As was the case one thousand years later with the Indian, ecclesiastics shared popular fear and contempt for "barbarians."[63] Many Bishops and apparently many monks were content and, indeed, convinced that a contemplative life, free from worldly distractions, was the true path to religious perfection.[64] Note that prayer was seen as having the power to effect change; one could pray for the conversion of pagans because, following Augustine, it is God ultimately who chooses who is saved. Prayer, if it moved God, could count for much more than the efforts of one hundred missionaries.

Even Gregory the Great (c. 540–604 C.E.), who was noted for his missionary zeal, more frequently extolled the virtues of the quiet life:

For my unhappy soul wounded with worldly business does now call to mind in what state it was, when I lived in my Abbey, and how then it was superior to all earthly matters, far above all transitory and

---

[63] W. H. C. Frend, *Religion Popular and Unpopular in the Early Christian Centuries* (London: Variorum Reprints, 1976), 17.

[64] Duncan Robertson, *The Medieval Saints' Lives: Spiritual Renewal and Old French Literature* (Lexington, KY: French Forum Publishers, 1995), 76; Raymond Van Dam, *Leadership and Community in Late Antique Gaul* (Berkeley: University of California Press, 1985), 136.

corruptible self, how it did visually think upon nothing but heavenly things.[65]

There additionally were many clerics who simply did not care about either their own faith or that of others![66]

Early Christian missionaries such as Saint Patrick and Saint Martin of Tours had to deal with much the same institutional opposition that confronted Jesuit missionaries one thousand years later. To promote and defend the missionary vocation, early sacred biographers such as Sulpicius Severus emphasized Saint Martin's Christlike ministries, including Martin's many miracles, which provided testament to God's support of his vocation:

> At Paris he was passing through the city gates accompanied by a great crowd when, to everybody's horror, he kissed the pitiable face of a leper and gave him his blessing. The man was at once cleansed from all trace of his affliction, and coming to the cathedral the next day with a clear skin he gave thanks for his recovered health.[67]

Because the Church as an institution was decentralized during the early Middle Ages, as compared with the Counter-Reformation, early Christian authors such as Sulpicius Severus and Saint Patrick could celebrate the missionary calling as well as condemn those who opposed it. Saint Patrick in his *Confessions* was none too subtle rebuking his ecclesiastical contemporaries who opposed his mission to Ireland:

> ... for many tried to prevent this mission and talked among themselves behind my back and said: "Why is this fellow walking into danger among enemies who do not know God?" Not that they were being malicious, but they did not like the idea, as I myself can confirm – take it from me, it was because of my lack of education; and I was not

---

[65] *The Dialogues of S. Gregorie, 1608/ St. Gregory* (Ilkley, England: Scolar Press, 1975 [1608]), 2.

[66] Klingshirn, *Caesarius of Arles*, 146; Van Dam, *Leadership and Community*, 154.

[67] F. R. Hoare, ed. and trans., *The Western Fathers, Being the Lives of SS. Martin of Tours, Ambrose, Augustine of Hippo, Honoratus of Arles and Germanus of Auxerre* (New York: Sheed and Ward, 1954), 32.

quick to recognize the grace which was then in me; now I appreciate that I should have done so before.[68]

Jesuit missionary authors could not explicitly attack detractors within or without the Jesuit order, particularly as they sat in judgment of Jesuit narratives and enterprises. However, Jesuit authors could emulate Patrick and Severus by emphasizing God's enduring presence in the lives of Jesuit missionaries:

> Geróniomo de Acosta himself recounted one occasion when Father Pedro [Gravina} was supposed to visit the pueblo of Coapa. He was preparing to walk, but then it happened that a mule came by and kicked him twice, knocking him to the ground. Those who were there thought he was dead. When they went to help him he got up, saying "I don't need any help. Thanks to God, it was nothing." This is the extent to which he remained free from harm, which those present thought had taken his life.[69]

Jesuit narratives such as the *Historia* and the *Conquista Espiritual* relate numerous miracles reminiscent of medieval hagiography, such as the remains of martyred Jesuits – be it a heart or arm – that refused to burn, or faithful missionaries and their neophytes who were saved from starvation by an eagle bearing dinner. In the context of the Counter-Reformation, and stiff competition among Jesuits (educators vs. missionaries) as well as between Jesuits and other religious and clerics, it made great sense to tell a story that most everyone valued.

The Immediate Reality of an Invisible World

Jesuits were formed as religious through a reading of early Christian literature, but it should not be assumed that they remained "prisoners" of this literature or some singular interpretation of it, imposed as it were by Jesuit superiors. As we have seen, Jesuit superiors struggled,

---

[68] A. B. E. Hood, ed. and trans., *St. Patrick: His Writings and Muirchu's Life* (London: Phillimore, 1978), 51.
[69] Pérez de Ribas, *History of the Triumphs*, 571.

unsuccessfully, to keep faith with Loyola's vision of the Society of Jesus as apostles rather than educators. Loyola's vision was predicated on an epistemology and theology that was as difficult to mandate as the missionary vocation. By the early 1600s, European Jesuits and their students (e.g., Descartes) were at the vanguard of the Enlightenment, embracing deism, mechanistic philosophy, and inference based on empirical observation (hardly the message of early Christian literature). Significantly, Jesuit missionaries in the New World were reluctant to partake of this profound shift in epistemology, which distanced God from his creation. Well into the seventeenth century New World Jesuits held fast to what was largely a medieval worldview.[70]

Missionaries on the northern frontier of Nueva España or the Río de la Plata believed as much in divine providence and miracles as did early medieval monks and bishops. And why not? Arguably the actual experience of the "new world" – a world where sights, sounds, and other human beings did not conform to prior conceptions – strengthened Jesuit belief in the mysterious workings of almighty God. In this regard, it is doubtful that Descartes would have written his meditations if he had lived in Mexico and been trained by *criollo* rather than French Jesuits. The New World was far too taxing experientially to engender feelings of certainty. This was particularly true for Jesuit missionaries who lived out their lives in Indian rather than European communities, speaking Indian languages. Jesuit missionaries were reminded on a daily basis by their Indian neophytes that the world was as medieval Europeans had imagined – a place of mystery where supernaturals both made and defied the laws of nature.

Early Christian sacred biography and history resonated with Jesuit missionaries (and Indians) precisely because this literature celebrated the immediate reality of an invisible world. It was not by accident that Ruiz de Montoya and Pérez de Ribas titled their respective histories as they did; one alluded to the primacy of the Holy Spirit in Paraguay (*Conquista Espiritual*) whereas the other equated Jesuit success in Mexico with

---

[70] Giles Constable, *Three Studies in Medieval Religious And Social Thought* (Cambridge, UK: Cambridge University Press, 1995), 254; Sabine MacCormack, *Religion in the Andes: Vision and Imagination in Early Colonial Peru* (Princeton, NJ: Princeton University Press, 1991); James T. Moore, *Indian and Jesuit* (Chicago: Loyola University Press, 1982).

"the triumphs of our Holy Faith." Acknowledgment of God's primacy was a time-honored tradition of sacred historians and biographers.[71] Indeed, as Heffernan has pointed out, there are no heroes or heroines in sacred biography and history as we understand the terms today, that is, self-made men or women.[72] The heroes of early Christian literature were chosen and "made" by God through the operation of the Holy Spirit. If martyrs and saints worked miracles it was God's doing, not their own. Significantly, the essence of a Jesuit's religious formation, particularly as Loyola imagined it, was to cultivate a relationship with God that resulted in God moving in and through the Jesuit.[73] Although one might think that this was the norm for religious, many Catholic theologians of the Counter-Reformation repudiated or looked askance at Jesuit attempts to engage God in "devout conversation." For many, religion consisted of unquestioning acceptance of dogma, strict practice of morality and discipline, and stern legislation and sanctions to guarantee right thinking and practice.[74]

Jesuit missionaries in the New World were as convinced as Loyola and early Christian authors that Satan as well as God were actively involved in human affairs. Again, life as lived on the mission frontier – a place where strange cries could be heard at night, or where Indian informants insisted that shamans flew to convocations on distant mountains – gave credence to the idea of Satan as a real adversary:

> This nation was so entombed in darkness that a woman who had been enlightened by the teaching of the Gospel declared and so stated to one of the priests who preached the Gospel: "Father, look across the river; do you see all those hills, mountains, peaks, and heights there? Well, we revered all of them and there we practiced and celebrated our superstitions." The old women certified that the devil appeared to them in the form of dogs, toads, coyotes, and snakes – forms that correspond to what he is. Indian principales and fiscales declared as

---

[71] Sister Mary Emily Keenan, S.C.N, trans., "The Life of St. Antony by St. Athanasius." In *The Fathers of the Church, Volume 15, Early Christian Biographies*, ed. Roy J. Deferrari, pp. 127–216 (New York: Fathers of the Church, Inc., 1952), 140.

[72] *Sacred Biography*, 63–64.

[73] George E. Ganss, ed., *Ignatius Loyola, The Spiritual Exercises and Selected Works* (New York: Paulist Press, 1991).

[74] O'Malley, *The First Jesuits*, 371.

a fact widely accepted among them that at night the sorceresses used to attend certain dances and gatherings with demons and that they returned through the air.[75]

In early sacred biography and history, Satan is no symbol or metaphor of evil, but a fallen angel who readily assumes human and other guises, always intent upon obstructing God's unfolding plan.[76] In early Christian literature, Satan seems capable of almost anything:

> During the bubonic plague of which we have spoken [in 572 C.E.], the devil, falsely appearing as St. Martin, had wickedly brought to a woman named Leubella offerings which would, he said, save the people.[77]

Jesuit narratives such as the *Spiritual Conquest* speak of an equally ingenious devil:

> Seeing his unbelieving followers now turned into devout Christians, he aimed his shafts at deceiving them with specious devotions. In the reduction of San Ignacio, five devils appeared. Four were dressed like ourselves in black cassocks, trimmed with tinselly bands, their faces very handsome. The fifth appeared in the form in which the Blessed Virgin is portrayed.[78]

During the Counter-Reformation, many Christians believed that the misfortune caused by the devil largely was a result of a pact (the "devil's letter") forged between the devil and human beings at the latter's instigation. The assumption that human beings were Satan's "familiars" rather than his victims explains in part the burning of witches and the torture meted out to defendants brought before the "Holy Office."[79]

---

75 Pérez de Ribas, *History of the Triumphs*, 368.
76 Glenn F. Chestnut, *The First Christian Histories: Eusebius, Socrates, Sozomen, Theodoret, and Evagrius* (Paris: Editions Beauchesne, 1986), 106; Giselle de Nie, *Views From a Many-Windowed Tower: Studies of Imagination in the Works of Gregory of Tours* (Amsterdam: Rodopi, 1987), 31; Hoare, *The Western Fathers*, 36; Herbert Musurillo, ed. and trans., *The Acts of the Christian Martyrs* (Oxford: Clarendon Press, 1972), 63–85.
77 Edward James, ed., *Gregory of Tours: Life of the Fathers* (Liverpool, UK: Liverpool University Press, 1991), 8.
78 Ruiz de Montoya, *The Spiritual Conquest*, 64.
79 Cervantes, *The Idea of the Devil*; Michel de Certeau, *The Mystic Fable* (Chicago: University of Chicago Press, 1992), 261; J. B. Russell, *Lucifer, The Devil in the Middle*

Importantly, this *un*sympathetic view of human participation in sin was a late medieval development (post–seventh century) that "blossomed" with horrible consequences during the Early Modern period.[80] During late antiquity and the early Middle Ages (before Augustine's rather severe views gained wide acceptance), human beings were seen more as victims than familiars of the devil.[81] Neither holy men (e.g., Saint Antony) nor peasants are portrayed in early Christian literature as "looking for trouble."

Jesuit missionaries in the New World had more in common with early medieval Christians than with their modern European contemporaries, who tended to blame women or Indians for conspiring with Satan.[82] With some notable exceptions (e.g., Acosta), Jesuit missionaries such as Pérez de Ribas and Ruiz de Montoya saw the Indian as a victim rather than a familiar of the devil.[83] It was the Indian shaman rather than Indians in general who conspired with Satan:

> The Devil universally attempts to mimic the worship of God with fictions and frauds. The Guaraní nation has been unsullied by idols or idol worship; by heaven's grace they are unencumbered by lies and ready to receive the truth, as long experience has taught us. Despite this, the devil has found fraudulent means for enthroning his ministers, the magicians and sorcerers, to be the pestilence and ruin of souls.[84]

In 1616, the northern frontier of Nueva España was rocked by the Tepehuan revolt, one of the most destructive uprisings in the New World.[85] According to Pérez de Ribas, who passed through the Tepehuan

---

Ages (Ithaca, NY: Cornell University Press, 1984), *Mephistopheles* (Ithaca, NY: Cornell University Press, 1986).

[80] For instance: Fray Martín de Castañega, *Tratado de las supersticiones y hechicerías* (Madrid: Gráficas Ultra, 1946 [1529]); Heinrich Kramer and James Sprenger, *The Malleus Maleficarum*, trans. with introductions and notes by Montague Summers (New York: Dover Publications, 1971 [1487]).

[81] Peter Brown, *Religion and Society in the Age of Saint Augustine* (New York: Harper & Row, 1972), 136; Flint, *The Rise of Magic.*

[82] Cervantes, *The Idea of the Devil.*

[83] Daniel T. Reff, "The 'Predicament of Culture' and Spanish Missionary Accounts of the Tepehuan and Pueblo Revolts." *Ethnohistory* 42 (1995): 63–90.

[84] Ruiz de Montoya, *The Spiritual Conquest*, 85.

[85] Charlotte M. Gradie, *The Tepehuan Revolt of 1616* (Salt Lake City: University of Utah Press, 2000); Reff, "The 'Predicament of Culture'."

missions only weeks before the revolt, the uprising had been the work of Satan and his familiars "the diabolical sorcerers":

> Before writing about the fierce, barbarous, and infidel decision made by this nation, I must explain the motive and cause of this – one of the greatest uprisings, disturbances, and ravages of war in Nueva España.... There was only one cause of what happened here – it was a scheme invented by Satan and welcomed by these blind people. It enraged their spirits to take up arms against the Faith of Christ and all things Christian. They demonstrated this in the many deeds that they executed during their destructive attack. This was demonstrated even more clearly by the principal instigators and authors of the uprising – the diabolical sorcerers who had familiar dealings with the devil.[86]

The Similar Lives of Early Saints and Jesuit Missionaries

The lives of the saints often end with an explicit recognition that they were written for the edification of monks. The didactic nature of hagiography was conveyed largely through *exempla* (narrative scenes with a morale) and explicit "lessons" on values such as industriousness:

> A few days later, as he [Saint Antony] was busy at his work – *for he was careful to work hard* – someone stood at the door and pulled the plait he was making, for he was weaving baskets, which he gave visitors in exchange for what they brought. (*emphasis mine*)[87]

Jesuit texts evidence much the same narrative conventions and reflect a similar concern with describing for novices the difficult life of a missionary on the frontier. Jesuit letters recounting the lives of deceased missionaries (*cartas necrologias*), as well as published narratives such as the *Historia* or Juan Nieremberg's *Varones Illustres* (1666), are replete with passages about Jesuits who lived out their lives in tattered robes, slept on boards in one-room huts, practiced self-mortification (e.g., wearing

---

[86] Pérez de Ribas, *History of the Triumphs*, 594.
[87] Keenan, "Life of Saint Antony," 182.

studded-belts or "hair shirts" like Saint Antony), and subsisted on little more than corn gruel:

> He [Father Juan del Valle] spent eight months of the year in the desert, traveling fifty leagues inland to convert gentiles and living under a tent. In Indian pueblos he stayed in little xacales or cramped and flimsy huts that were made of branches and straw and which had only a mat covering the window and doorway, allowing the cold and wind to enter freely. Some called these blessed priests [del Valle and other Jesuit missionaries to the Tepehuan] the hermits of Thebaid [a great monastic settlement in fourth century Egypt], and not without good reason.[88]

Jesuit authors clearly drew from the lives of the desert fathers and medieval saints for language and literary conventions to describe Jesuit asceticism. This borrowing, however, was consistent with life on the mission frontier. For instance, most Jesuit missionaries knew the poverty of a Saint Antony or Hilarion. Under the terms of the *Patronato Real*, Jesuit and other New World missionaries received a very modest stipend from the Spanish Crown. This money, which was to be used for clothing and other personal items, often was spent by Jesuit missionaries on rosaries, medals, statuary, and items for their respective mission churches.

Jesuits who served in Mexico largely were volunteers. Their request for a missionary assignment in the New World was a conscious decision to forego a life of relative comfort back home in Spain in favor of martyrdom. Between 1591 and 1660, over a dozen Jesuits died on the northern frontier at the hands of apostate Indians; almost every priest who served in the north was threatened at one time or another by Indians who opposed or re-canted their conversion. In point of fact, the lives of early Christian martyrs and saints were more than abstractions for priests on the mission frontier.

Along with martyrdom and a life of relative poverty, Jesuit missionaries embraced a life of relative isolation reminiscent of the "desert saints." Indeed, lack of contact with other Jesuits and Europeans reached the point where Jesuit superiors in Mexico had to mandate that

---

[88] Pérez de Ribas, *History of the Triumphs*, 642.

missionaries in adjoining districts meet at an absolute minimum of once a year.[89] During these convocations each Jesuit was supposed to make the Spiritual Exercises, which, ironically, is a mental journey that parallels the spiritual retreat of the desert saints.[90]

As we have seen, the Jesuit missionary was also like desert and medieval saints in that he often was called upon to cure the sick. Miraculous cures are common in both Jesuit and early Christian literature:

> First the children, then their elders, began to succumb to a swelling in their throats that brought death after an illness of less than three days. His congregation was being wiped out as if they were being slaughtered by the sword. No human measures brought any relief.... Immediately he blessed some oil and, at its touch, the internal swelling went down and a passage was thereby opened for breathing and swallowing. The heavenly remedy effected a cure as rapidly as the onslaught of the disease had brought death. (Constantius of Lyon's *Life of Saint Germanus of Auxere*, 478 C.E.)[91]

> Another Indian from the same pueblo was suffering from a constriction of the throat that was causing him a lot of pain. I had some holy water brought and, making two Crosses over the place where it hurt, I told him to trust in the Lord who had died on the Cross. Through this divine remedy (for there are few human remedies in this land) he and other sick people were healed. (Jesuit *anua* of 1601)[92]

Again, there is certainly some truth to the idea that both medieval and Jesuit authors emphasized miraculous cures because such cures were the essence of Christ's Galilean ministry, and thus imparted value and authority to missionary lives and the authors and texts that represented

---

[89] Rodrigo de Cabredo, "Ordenaciones del Padre Rodrigo de Cabredo para las Missiones, January 1, 1611, Durango," Latin American Manuscripts, Mexico II, Lily Library, Indiana State University.

[90] Ganss, *Ignatius Loyola*.

[91] F. R. Hoare, trans., "Constantius of Lyon, The Life of Saint Germanus of Auxerre." In *Soldiers of Christ, Saints and Saints' Lives from Late Antiquity and the Early Middle Ages*, eds. Thomas F. X. Noble and Thomas Head, pp. 75–106 (University Park: Pennsylvania State University Press, 1995), 83.

[92] "Anua del año de mil seiscientos y uno," Historia 15, Archivo General de la Nación, Mexico City.

those lives. The miraculous cure also had theological significance; it was an assertion of the most fundamental of all Christian beliefs, namely that through Christ's sacrifice and his gift of the sacraments, Christians could mobilize God to intercede on their behalf.[93] However, as detailed in Chapters 2 and 3, the popularity of the miraculous cure also reflects the prevalence of epidemic disease, which was coincident with the spread of Christianity in Europe and the New World. Medieval hagiographers and Jesuit authors talked a lot about sickness and miraculous cures because both were central to the missionary experience.

Conclusion

Jesuit authors self-consciously drew from sacred biography and history, knowing that their "institutional" audience would be moved by metaphors, similes, and type scenes that equated the Jesuit missionary with a long line of martyrs and saints, going back to Christ. Jesuit authors embraced early Christian literature because it was a privileged discourse, but they did so for particular reasons, especially to defend and promote their mission enterprises. This was nothing new; some of the earliest sacred biographies were written to defend the missionary calling.

In representing their missionary experience, Jesuit authors focused on those aspects or events from their own lives and the lives of fellow missionaries that had analogues in early Christian literature. Jesuit authors did not simply "lie," nor are their texts simply reiterations of early Christian narratives. Jesuit missionary authors selectively recalled what were real-life parallels between the Jesuit missionary experience and the experience of monks and clerics in the late Roman Empire. Importantly, Jesuit missionaries in the New World thought much like early medieval monks and clerics. At a time when many Europeans, including fellow Jesuits, relegated God to the status of a distant observer, Jesuit missionaries in the America remained convinced of God's enduring presence. This conviction was bolstered by the actual experience of a mysterious and troubling New World – a world where the Holy Spirit, Satan, and miraculous cures were seemingly commonplace. Significantly, woven

---

[93] Heffernan, *Sacred Biography*, 28–29.

into the fabric of the *Life of Saint Martin* or the works of Gregory of Tours are narrative scenes that recount a very real struggle between Christian missionaries and pagan priests and shamans. Early sacred biography and history is replete with accounts of monks and clerics who struggled with many of the same "heathen" practices (e.g., ceremonial intoxication, "tree worship") that the Jesuits confronted one thousand years later. Arguably, many Jesuits who read or recalled early Christian sacred biography and history saw their own lives flash before them. It is not surprising then that Jesuit missionaries-turned-authors would use early Christian literature to help tell their own story.

Conclusion

A surprising number of saints – the Apostle Paul, Hildegard of Bingen, Saint Francis of Assisi, Saint Teresa, to name but a few – were touched by God during a bout of illness.[1] It was not just the privileged who reported encountering God while ill.

Beginning in the second century C.E., infectious disease regularly besieged the population of the Roman Empire. Epidemic disease claimed inumerable lives and undermined everyday life and the constitution of subjectivity (e.g., being pagan, a woman, a citizen of the state). In an age of anxiety and "cosmic pessimism,"[2] pagans embraced new beliefs and rituals that promised protection from Satan and the diseases he unleashed on the Roman world. Converts to Christianity acquired a new "family" and social relations to replace those devastated by smallpox, measles, malaria, and plague. Christian communities of Roman antiquity responded to epidemics with not only prayer and healing rituals but also awe-inspiring charity.

The monks and clerics who fanned out over Europe during the early Middle Ages were agents of charity and "soldiers of Christ," armed with rituals and relics to combat and appease supra-human agents who

---

[1] Rene Fulop-Miller, *The Saints That Moved The World* (Salem, NH: Ayer Company, 1945), 340.

[2] E. R. Dods, *Pagan and Christian in an Age of Anxiety* (Cambridge, UK: Cambridge University Press, 1968), 21–22; Jonathan Z. Smith, *Map Is Not Territory* (Leiden: E.J. Brill, 1978), 186–187.

bestowed plague and malaria on humankind. The strategy employed by the apostles and later articulated by Gregory the Great and medieval hagiographers was largely one of reimagining rather than destroying "pagan" religiosity. Missionary saints unabashedly toppled pagan shrines, but just as often tolerated competing magical practices. Through the introduction of relics, particularly of widely known saints, Christian missionaries were able to provide communities with what were touted as new supernatural advocates and protectors. By translating the relics to a local church or shrine, which invariably was built over pagan shrines, the missionaries effectively recouped prior passions and traditions. This mixing and transference of emotion was facilitated by the pagans' prior personification of supernaturals and the construction of altars and formal shrines under the Romans.[3]

Early Christian sacred biography and history are replete with mention of roadside cairns, flying "witches," ceremonial intoxication, and numerous other "heathen" practices that the Jesuits encountered in the New World one thousand years later. In colonial Mexico, as in early medieval Europe, the Mendicants and Jesuits worked with native societies that experienced profound dislocations coincident with invasions, migrations, epidemics, and conquest. Beginning in 1593, the annual reports compiled by the Jesuits mention epidemics of smallpox, measles, typhus, and other maladies, which swept through the northern missions and beyond at regular five- to eight-year intervals. As was the case in early medieval Europe, epidemics of infectious disease not only contributed to a population collapse but also undermined the structure and functioning of Indian societies. Enter the Jesuits who emulated medieval abbots and monks by reconstituting native subsistence practices and sociopolitical organization, with the resident priest now functioning as "principal chief." This assumption of authority was facilitated by the introduction of Christian beliefs and rituals that had evolved over the course of a millennium in the Old World to deal in part with epidemic disease. Although one might question the intrinsic value of relics, rosaries, confession, or a blood procession, they can nevertheless have positive benefits for individuals and communities confronting unprecedented suffering. Because

---

[3] Simon James, *Exploring the World of the Celts* (London: Thames and Hudson, 1993).

the Jesuits coupled prayer with clinical care of the sick, they had an advantage over Indian shamans, who had little or no experience with acute infectious disease.

Early Christian monks and clerics and the later Jesuits understood that reorienting the lives of pagan and Indian adults was difficult at best. Through oblation and boarding schools, respectively, medieval monks and the Jesuits worked closely and intensely with children, making sure that they acquired few of their parents' "sinful" ways. Arguably, this focus on children was of paramount importance in the rise of Christianity in both Europe and America.

The conclusion that disease played a dynamic role in the rise of Christianity in the Old World and the New is inferable from early Christian and Jesuit narratives, and yet, paradoxically, early Christian and Jesuit authors infrequently acknowledged that epidemics contributed significantly to pagan and Indian interest in Christianity. Disease was analogous to Indian "government" insofar as the Jesuits documented disease episodes but rhetorically ignored or denied their importance. Often disease and epidemics appear as *punctum* – unplanned narrative details that reflect an irreducible reality obscured by an author's understanding of what is important. Early Christian and Jesuit authors thought God was important, certainly more so than the proximate causes (e.g., epidemics, sociocultural upheaval) of pagan and Indian interest in Christianity.

As we have seen, Jesuit missionary authors cast their New World experience largely in terms of a battle between the Jesuits, favored and aided by God, and the devil and his Indian "familiars," the shamans. Using metaphors (e.g., devil's snares, the Lord's vineyard), type scenes (e.g., exorcisms, miracles), and rhetorical strategies (e.g., direct discourse) from early Christian literature, authors such as Ruiz de Montoya and Pérez de Ribas sought to show how the Jesuit experience was not simply in keeping with the history of the early Church but also was ordained and directed by God. The representation of the Jesuit and Franciscan mission enterprises as a reiteration of God's plan (prophecized in the Old Testament and fulfilled in the Gospels, *Acts of the Apostles*, and the lives of medieval saints) reflects political and institutional contingencies, which weighed heavily on the minds of missionary authors. Jesuits and Mendicants clearly described their New World experience as another primitive Church to ensure continued funding and support from the Spanish Crown and the Church. However, the fact that most Jesuit missionaries chose a missionary vocation, thus inviting martyrdom, suggests that missionaries such as Ruiz de Montoya and Pérez de Ribas truly believed the "story" they fabricated. Today, in the wake of the Enlightenment, many people find the story surreal, particularly as it emphasizes invisible forces. Not insignificantly, there is reason to believe that as the Enlightenment "dawned" during the seventeenth century, Jesuit missionaries in Mexico also became disenchanted with what was essentially their medieval worldview. This shift in Jesuit thinking (reflected in the writings of Descartes) had significant implications for the Jesuits as well as the Indians of northern Mexico.

The Enlightenment and the Demise of the Jesuit Missions

The literature of mysticism provides a path for those who "ask the way to get lost...."[4]

The Bibliothéque Nationale catalog of 1742 shows religious books dwindling in numbers after 1680, a sense of anti-climax, of disenchantment. There are no more devotions. The Age of Enlightenment (i.e. Rationalism) is at hand.[5]

In 1643 – at the very height of Jesuit success in northern Mexico – Jesuit superiors in Mexico wrote for the first time of a troubling development: "There diminishes constantly among us the knowledge of Indian languages."[6] Despite the issuance of rules to rectify this situation, the linguistic skills of Jesuit missionaries continued to decline. This decline was nourished by a general European disregard for Indian languages, which was made explicit in the revised laws of the Indies of 1681. The eighteenth law held that it was not possible even in the most perfect Indian language to correctly explain or convey the mysteries of

---

4 Michel de Certeau, *Heterologies, Discourse on the Other*, trans. B. Massumi (Minneapolis: University of Minnesota Press, 1986), 80.
5 Henri-Jean Martin, *Print, Power, and People in 17th-Century France*, trans. David Gerard (Metuchen, NJ: The Scarecrow Press, 1993), 528.
6 Peter M. Dunne, *Andrés Pérez de Ribas* (New York: United States Catholic Historical Society, 1951), 143.

the Catholic Faith, and thus the Indians were to be instructed in Spanish.[7] In 1744, the Jesuit Father Visitor Juan Antonio Baltasar noted in a report that many of the twenty-seven missionaries stationed in Sonora did not know the native language of their assigned mission.[8]

The decline in Jesuit mastery and use of Indian languages was coincident with what David Shaul has noted was a simplification of the robust grammars and other linguistic materials that were first produced by pioneer Jesuit missionaries.[9] As the seventeenth century unfolded, the once robust *artes* and *vocabularios*, which were copied and handed down from one priest to the next, lost many abstract concepts. Shaul has suggested that these changes in Jesuit linguistic materials were part of a much larger process of linguistic compartmentalization. Where once the Jesuit missionary and his neophytes conversed in the Indians' language about a large number and variety of subjects, by the mid-1600s many priests were using Indian languages in formulaic speeches or in the confessional, where they were employed in a rote fashion.

Jesuit missionaries stopped talking to their Indian neophytes. But why? Certainly by 1650 it was not *necessary* for Jesuit missionaries to master and use native languages. By this date, the actual administration of most Indian communities was handled by bilingual Indian governors, *alcaldes*, and *fiscales*. These elites, who were supervised by resident Jesuit missionaries, often had been educated as children in Jesuit boarding schools.

A perhaps more significant reason why the Jesuits stopped talking to the Indians was that the Jesuits and Indians no longer were in agreement about what previously had united them: the immediate reality of an invisible world. The Enlightenment, in particular, distanced God from his creation and made Europeans in general less accepting of the idea of an "activist" God.[10] Whereas the Jesuits and other Europeans increasingly

---

[7] Pagden, *The Fall of Natural Man*, 183.

[8] Ernest J. Burrus, S.J., and Félix Zubillaga, S.J., *El Noroeste de México, Documentos Sobre Las Misiones Jesuíticas 1600–1769* (México, DF: Universidad Nacional Autónoma de México, 1986), 197–209.

[9] Shaul, "The State of the Arte: Ecclesiastical Literature on the Northern Frontier of New Spain." *The Kiva* 55 (1990): 167–75.

[10] See MacCormack, *Religion in the Andes*, 434–455.

harbored doubts about God's (and Satan's) enduring presence,[11] the Indians of northern Mexico remained convinced that God was one with his creation. This is at once apparent from both ethnohistorical and ethnographic studies of native peoples and cultures.[12]

The gulf that came to separate Indians and Jesuits is apparent in the works of eighteenth-century Jesuit missionary-authors such as Joseph Och, Ignaz Pffeferkorn, and Juan Nentvig. All three priests spoke of the Indians as inherently and irrevocably savage.[13] The same priests complained of the Indians' misguided Christianity as well as the persistence of wholly aboriginal rituals and beliefs.[14] Indeed, in their frustration, some Jesuits went so far as to condone the destruction of recalcitrant groups such as the Seri.[15] Genocidal proposals were unheard of one hundred years previous, when the Jesuits were still talking to the Indians. As with other "final solutions,"[16] an enormous chasm had opened between Jesuit and Indian. In many ways, the Jesuit mission enterprise had hit rock bottom. Coincidentally[17] (it was not that the Spanish Crown cared about the Indians), in 1767 the Jesuit order was suppressed and expelled from Nueva España. Franciscan missionaries and clerics took over and then disbanded what was once a flourishing Jesuit mission system. What remained of the Indian population of northern Nueva España, some thirty thousand Indians, saw their future go from difficult to bleak. With the exception of the Yoeme and Mayo and groups such

---

[11] The fear of budding Deism led to a spate of Jesuit publications between 1598 and 1643 that critiqued the idea of a disinterested God. Martin, *Print, Power, and People*, 114–15.

[12] For instance: Bahr, "Bad News"; Richard S. Felger and M. B. Moser, *People of the Desert and Sea, Ethnobotany of the Seri Indians* (Tucson: University of Arizona Press, 1985); Kozak and Lopez, *Devil Sickness*; Painter, *With Good Heart*; Stacy Schaefer and Peter T. Furst, *People of the Peyote* (Albuquerque: University of New Mexico Press, 1996); Spicer, *The Yaquis*; Sheridan, *Empire of Sand*.

[13] Nentvig, *Rudo Ensayo*; Pfefferkorn, *Sonora, A Description of the Province*; Treutlein, *Missionary in Sonora*.

[14] For instance: "Estado de la provincia de Sonora," 631–632; Nentvig, *Rudo Ensayo*, 59–62; Treutlein, *Missionary in Sonora*, 133.

[15] Sheridan, *Empire of Sand*, 169.

[16] Zygmunt Bauman, *Modernity and the Holocaust* (Ithaca, NY: Cornell University Press, 1989).

[17] As noted, during the sixteenth and seventeenth centuries, the Jesuits were favored by Spain's Hapsburg rulers. Shortly after the Bourbons took power they came to see the Jesuits as a threat or obstacle to their rule and so they pressured the Vatican to have the Jesuit order suppressed during the third quarter of the eighteenth century.

as the Seri and Tarahumara, who withdrew to the most inhospitable and inaccessible regions of Mexico, respectively, the Indians of northern Nueva España disappeared, merging into a Mestizo culture that is at once rich and lacking for reasons of history. Central to this process of ethnogenesis were plagues and priests; the former broke the bonds of once thriving communities, while the latter brought fragmented communities and identities together in communities that were both Christian and Indian.

The Myth of One Christianity

During the past half-century, scholars seemingly have struggled as much as Jesuit missionaries with the realization that Indian "converts" to Christianity retained pre-Christian beliefs and practices. The expectation that Indians or medieval Europeans should have either accepted or rejected Christianity may well reflect the Christian upbringing of most scholars. Christians understand conversion as an all-or-nothing proposition, effected by the Holy Spirit. The West's other religion, science – particularly cognitive dissonance theory – assumes that human beings sooner or later resolve whatever conflict arises over matters of belief. And yet unresolved cognitive dissonance – harboring what are often conflicting feelings and thoughts – would seem just as human as conflict resolution.[18]

The expectation of a synthesis also may stem from the idea of religion *sui generis*.[19] Because religion is always something else, it never is likely to be homogeneous. Moreover, even if we allow for heuristic purposes that religion is a subsystem of culture, it is still dynamic and contested; there are no steady states. Certainly the Christianity that arose in early medieval Europe and that was introduced to America was varied and remained so following the embrace of Indians. The Vatican and Council of Trent may have insisted that Mary was a saint, but most Iberians treated

---

[18] N. Ettlinger, "Cultural Economic Geography and a Relational and Microspace Approach to Trusts, Rationalities, Networks, and Change in Collaborative Workplaces." *Journal of Economic Geography* 3 (2003): 145–171.

[19] Russell T. McCutcheon, *Manufacturing Religion, The Discourse on Sui Generis Religion and the Politics of Nostalgia* (Oxford, UK: Oxford University Press, 1997).

Mary as a deity.[20] Similarly, while the Jesuits may have advocated engaging God in "devout conversation," many fellow religious and clerics believed it was dangerous (given Satan's powers of deception) engaging God one-on-one.

The Christianity introduced and "legislated" by the Jesuits and other Iberians was not only heterogenous, but orthodoxy of any type was hard to legislate on the mission frontier, which lacked cathedrals, universities, and other policing institutions and officers. The Jesuits as well as the Franciscans relied heavily on Indian *temachtianos* and *fiscales* who took a proactive role interpreting Christianity. Much the same situation obtained in early medieval Europe, where countless clerics and deacons not under the control of bishops interpreted Christian theology, accommodating pagan traditions in the process.

Christianity in Europe and Mexico arose in a similar cultural–historical context, prospering by embracing local indigenous traditions while announcing a new covenant and understanding of the divine. Casting this process as syncretism suggests reconciliation of diverse beliefs and practices; hybridity is perhaps preferable inasmuch as it implies a heterogenous mixing of traditions, with certain categories and paradigms privileged, depending on local circumstances. The rise of Christianity in both the Old World and the New bespeak "border epistemologies,"[21] which have persisted precisely because they are more than a timeless and otherworldly set of propositions.

[20] William B. Taylor, *Magistrates of the Sacred: Priests and Parishioners in Eighteenth-Century Mexico* (Stanford, CA: Stanford University Press, 1996), 55–56.
[21] Walter D. Mignolo, *Local Histories/Global Designs: Coloniality, Border Thinking, and Subaltern Knowledges* (Princeton NJ: Princeton University Press, 2000).

Bibliography

Manuscripts

Archivo General de la Nación, Mexico City

n.d.   Misiones 25. "Puntos sacados de las relaciones de Antonio Ruiz, P. Martin Perez, P. Vincente del Aguila, P. Gaspar Varela, Juan de Grixalva, Capitan Martinez, y otras.

1593   Misiones 25. "Anua del año de mil quinientos de noventa y tres."

1594   Historia 15. "Anua del año de mil quinientos noventa y quatro."

1596   Historia 15. "Anua del año de mil quinientos noventa y seis."

1601   Historia 15. "Anua del año de mil seiscientos y uno."

1601   Historia 15. "Carta del Padre Juan Bautista Velasco del año de mil seisceintos uno."

1602   Historia 15. "Anua del año de mil seiscientos y dos."

1604   Historia 15. "Anua del año de mil seiscientos quatro."

1610   Historia 15. "Anua del año de mil seiscientos y diez."

1612   Historia 15. "Anua del año de mil seiscientos doze."

1614   Historia 15. "Anua del año de mil seiscientos catorce."

1615   Historia 15. "Carta del Padre Diego de Guzman al Padre Provincial de Septiembre de mil seiscientos veinte y nuebe." (Note: Despite the title, internal evidence indicates that this letter was written in 1615.)

1616   Historia 15. "Carta del Padre Martin Perez, del año de mil seiscientos diez y seis."

1619   Historia 15. "Anua del año de mil seiscientos diez y nueve."

1620   Historia 15. "Anua del año de mil seiscientos y veinte."

1621   Historia 15. "Anua del año de mil seiscientos y veinte y uno.

1622   Misiones 25. "Carta Annua de la Provincia de la Compañia de Jesus en Nueva España, 15 de Mayo 1623."

1623   Misiones 25. "Carta annua de la Provincia de la Compañia de Jesus de Nueva España, Juan Lorencio, 16 de Mayo 1624."

1624   Misiones 25. "Carta Annua de la Provincia de la Compañia de Jesus de Nueva España, Juan Lorencio, 20 de Mayo 1625."

1625   Misiones 25. "Carta Annua de la Provincia de la Compañia de Jesus de Nueva España, Juan Lorencio."

1627   Misiones 25. "Carta Annua de la Provincia de la Compañia de Jesus de Nueva España, Juan Lorencio, 20 de Mayo 1627."

1628   Historia 15. "Missiones de San Ygnacio en Mayo, Yaqui, Nevomes, Chinipas, y Sisibotaris."

1628   Misiones 25. "Carta annua de la Provincia de Nueva España del año de 1628, Geronimo Diaz, 25 de Mayo 1629."

1628   Historia 15. "Missiones de San Ygnacio en Mayo, Yaqui, Nevomes, Chinipas, y Sisibotaris."

1630   Misiones 25. "Carta del Padre Martin de Azpilcueta al Padre Ignacio de Cavala, 3 de Diciembre 1630."

1630   Misiones 25. "Carta del Padre Martin de Azpilcueta al Padre Ignacio de Cavala, 3 de Diciembre 1630."

1635   Misiones 25. "Puntos para el Anua del año de 1635, destas misiones de San Ignacio Nuestro Padre en la Provincia de Cinaloa, Tomas Basilio, 26 de Marzo 1636."

1636   Misiones 25. "Puntos para el Anua del año de 1636 destas misiones de San Ignacio Nuestro Padre en la Provincia de Cinaloa, Tomas Basilio, 9 de Abril 1637."

1638   Misiones 25. "Copia de una carta del Padre Gaspar de Contreras al Padre Provincial, Santiago Papasquiaro, 5 de Agosto 1638."

1639   Misiones 25. "Puntos de Anua de la nueba mission de San Francisco Jabier, año de 1639."

1639   Misiones 25. "Puntos de Anua de la nueba mission de San Francisco Jabier, año de 1639."

1653   Missiones 26. "Puntos de annua del año de 1653 del colegio y misiones de Cinaloa."

1656   Jesuitas. "Catalogo de la gente de confession, que se halla en estas provincias, año de 1656."

1657   Historia 15. "Anua del año de mil seiscientos cincuenta y siete."

1657   Historia 316. "Apologetico Defensorio y Puntual Manifesto que los Padres de la Compañia de Jesus, Missioneros de las Provincias de Sinaloa y Sonora, Francisco Xavier de Faria."

Archivo Historico de Hacienda, Mexico City

n.d.   Temporalidades 333–141. "Copia de un fragmento de vocabulario de alguna lengua indigena Opata de Mexico."

1638   Temporalidades 2009–1. "Memorial al Rey para que no se recenga
        la limosna de la Misciones y consierva al Senor Palafox en las
        relaciones a la Compañia, Andrés Pérez de Ribas, 12 de Septiembre
        1638."
1678   Misiones 26. "Relacion de los Missiones que la Compañia tiene en
        el Reyno y Provincias de la Nueva Viscaya en la Nueva España echa
        el año de 1678 con ocasion de la Visita General della que por orden
        del Padre Provincial Thomas Altamirano hizo el Padre Visitador
        Juan Hortiz Zapata de la misma Compañia."

Bancroft Library, University of California, Berkeley

1617   Bancroft Collection, "Carta del Padre Andres Perez al Padre Provincial,
        13 de Junio 1617."

Lily Library, Indiana State University

1611   L. A. Manuscripts, Mexico II, "Ordenaciones del Padre Rodrigo de
        Cabredo para las Missiones, January 1, 1611, Durango."

Newberry Library, Chicago

1616   Ayers Collection, "Carta annua de la provincia de Nueva España del
        año de 1616. Nicolás de Arnaya, 18 May 1617."
1702   Ayers Collectoin, "Arte de la lengua teguima, llamada vulgarmente
        Opata, Natal Lombardo" (published in Mexico in 1702).
1753   Graff Collection, "Vida y heroycas virtudes del vble. Padre de Velasco,
        Provincial que fue de la Compañia de Jesus de Nueva España, Francisco
        Xavier de Faria, Mexico."

Published Sources

Abercrombie, Thomas A. *Pathways of Memory and Power*. Madison: University
    of Wisconsin Press, 1998.
Abrahamse, D. *Hagiographic Sources for Byzantine Cities, 500–900 AD*. Ann Arbor:
    University Microfilms, 1967.
Acosta, Jóse de. *De Procuranda Indorum Salute* (Predicación el Evangelio en las
    Indias). Trans. with an introduction and notes by Francisco Mateos, S.J.
    Madrid: I. G. Magerit, 1952 [1588].
———. *Historia Natural y Moral de las Indias*. 2 vols. Madrid, 1894 [1590].

Addison, James Thayer. *The Medieval Missionary, A Study of the Conversion of Northern Europe A.D. 500–1300*. Philadelphia: Porcupine Press, 1976.

Adorno, Rolena. "Reconsidering Colonial Discourse For Sixteenth- and Seventeenth-Century Spanish America." *Latin American Research Review* 28 (1993): 135–145.

Ahern, Maureen. "Visual and Verbal Sites: The Construction of Jesuit Martyrdom in Northwest New Spain in Andrés Pérez de Ribas' *Historia de los Triumphos de nuestra Santa Fee* (1645)." *Colonial Latin American Review* 8 (1999): 7–33.

Aizpuru, Pilar G. *La Educación Popular de los Jesuitas*. Mexico: Universidad Iberoamericana, 1989.

Alegre, Francisco Javier, S.J. *Historia de la Provincia de la Compañia de Jesus de Nueva España*, 4 vols. New edition by E. J. Burrus and F. Zubillaga. Rome: Bibliotecha Instituti Historici S.J. 1956–1960 [1780].

Alter, R. *The Art of Biblical Narrative*. New York: Basic Books, 1981.

Althusser, L. "Ideology and Ideological State Apparatuses." In *Reading Popular Narrative: A Source Book*. Ed. Bob Ashley. London: Leicester University Press, 1997 [1971].

Amundsen, Darrel W. "The Medieval Catholic Tradition." In *Caring and Curing: Health and Medicine in the Western Religious Tradition*, pp. 65–108. ed. R. Numbers and D. Amundsen. London: Macmillan, 1986.

Aquinas, St. Thomas. *Introduction to St. Thomas Aquinas*. Edited by A. C. Pegis. New York: Modern Library, 1945.

Arenal, Electra, and Powell, Amanda, eds. and trans. *Sor Juana Ines de la Cruz, The Answer/La Repuesta*. New York: Feminist Press. 1994.

Asad, Talal. "The Concept of Cultural Translation in British Social Anthropology." In *Writing Culture: The Poetics and Politics of Ethnography*, pp. 141–164. Ed. James Clifford and George Marcus. Berkeley: University of California Press, 1986.

———. *Genealogies of Religion: Discipline and Reasons of Power in Christianity and Islam*. Baltimore, MD: Johns Hopkins University Press, 1993.

Ashburn, P. M. *The Ranks of Death*. New York: Coward-McCann, 1947.

Aspurz, Lazaro de, O.F.M. *La aportacion extranjera a las misiones espanoles del Patronato Regio*. Madrid: Consejo de la Hispanidad, 1946.

Austin, Alfredo López. *The Rabbit on the Face of the Moon: Mythology in the Mesoamerican Tradition*. Salt Lake City: University of Utah Press, 1996.

Badone, Ellen, ed. *Religious Orthodoxy and Popular Faith in European Society*. Princeton, NJ: Princeton University Press, 1990.

Bagnall, Roger S., and Frier, Bruce W. *The Demography of Roman Egypt*. Cambridge, UK: Cambridge University Press, 1994.

Bahr, Donald. "Bad News: The Predicament of Native American Mythology." *Ethnohistory* 48 (2001): 587–612.

Bailey, Gauvin Alexander. *Art on the Jesuit Missions in Asia and Latin America, 1542–1773*. Toronto: University of Toronto Press, 1999.

Bakewell, P. J. *Silver Mining and Society in Colonial Mexico: Zacatecas 1546–1700.* Cambridge, UK: Cambridge University Press, 1971.

Bakhtin, M. M. *The Dialogic Imagination: Four Essays.* Trans. C. Emerson and M. Holquist. Austin: University of Texas Press, 1981.

Bakhtin, M. M., and Volosinov, V. N. *Marxism and the Philosophy of Language.* Trans. by L. Matejka and I. R. Titunik. Cambridge, MA: Harvard University Press, 1986.

Bandelier, Adolph F. "Final Report of Investigations Among the Indians of the Southwestern United States, Carried on Mainly in the Years from 1880 to 1885," Vol. 2. *Papers of the Archaeological Institute of America,* American Series 3 and 4. Cambridge, 1890–1892.

Bannon, John Francis, S.J. *The Mission Frontier in Sonora, 1620–1687.* New York: United States Catholic Historical Society, New York, 1955.

Barclift, Philip L. "Predestination and Divine Foreknowledge in the Sermons of Pope Leo the Great." In *History, Hope, Human Language, and Christian Reality,* pp. 165–182. Ed. Everett Ferguson. New York: Garland Publishing, 1999.

Barlow, Claude W., trans. *Iberian Fathers, Volume I, Martin of Braga, Paschasius of Dumium, Leander of Seville.* Washington, DC: Catholic University of America Press, 1969.

Barnes, T. "Pagan Perceptions of Christianity." In *Early Christianity Origins and Evolution to AD 600,* pp. 231–244. Ed. Ian Hazlett. Nashville: Abingdon Press, 1991.

Barthes, Roland. *S/Z.* Trans. R. Miller. New York: Hill and Wang, 1977 [1970].

———. *Camera Lucida.* Trans. Richard Howard. New York: Hill and Wang, 1981.

Bauman, Zygmunt. *Modernity and the Holocaust.* Ithaca, NY: Cornell University Press, 1989.

Baus, Karl, Beck, Hans-George, Ewig, Eugen, and Hermann, Josef Vogt. *The Imperial Church From Constantine To The Early Middle Ages.* Trans. Anselm Biggs. New York: Seabury Press, 1980.

Beals, Ralph L. *The Comparative Ethnology of Northern Mexico Before 1750.* Ibero-Americana 2. Berkeley: University of California Press, 1932.

———. *The Acaxee, a Mountain Tribe of Durango and Sinaloa.* Ibero-Americana 6. Berkeley: University of California Press, 1933.

———. *The Aboriginal Culture of the Cahita Indians.* Ibero-Americana 19. Berkeley: University of California Press, 1943.

Bekker-Nielsen, Tonnes. *The Geography of Power: Studies in the Urbanization of Roman North-West Europe.* BAR International Series 477. Oxford, UK: Oxford, 1989.

Bellah, Robert. "Religious Evolution." In *Sociology of Religion,* pp. 262–292. Ed. R. Robertson. Baltimore, MD: Penguin Books, 1969.

Benavides, Fray A. *The Memorial of Fray Alonso de Benavides.* Trans. E. Ayers. Chicago: Privately Published, 1916 [1630].

Benko, Stephen. *The Virgin Goddess: Studies in the Pagan and Christian Roots of Mariology*. London: E. J. Brill, 1993.

Berger, Pamela. *The Goddess Obscured*. Boston: Beacon Press, 1985.

Beverley, John. *Subalternity and Representation*. Durham, NC: Duke Univeristy Press, 1999.

Bieler, Ludwig, trans. *Eugippius, The Life of Saint Severin*. The Fathers of the Church: A New Translation, Volume 55. Washington, DC: Catholic University of America Press, 1965.

_____. *The Mythology of North America*. New York: William Morrow, 1985.

Biraben, J. N., and LeGoff, Jacques. "The Plague in the Early Middle Ages." In *Biology of Man in History*, pp. 48–80. Ed. E. Forster and O. Ranum and trans. E. Forster and P. Ranum. Baltimore, MD: Johns Hopkins Press, 1975.

Blinkoff, Jodi. "Francisco Losa and Gregorio López: Spiritual Friendship and Identity Formation on the New Spain Frontier." In *Colonial Saints*, pp. 115–128. Ed. Allan Greer and Jodi Blinkoff. New York: Routledge, 2003.

Boak, A. E. *Manpower Shortage and the Fall of the Roman Empire in the West*. Ann Arbor: University of Michigan Press, 1955.

Bodenstedt, Sister Mary Immacualte, S.N.D., A.M. *The Vita Christi of Ludolphus The Carthusian*. Washington, DC: Catholic University of America Press, 1944.

Bolton, Herbert E. "The Mission as a Frontier Institution in the Spanish-American Colonies." *American Historical Review* 23 (1917): 42–61.

Boone, Elizabeth H., and Mignolo, Walter D., eds. *Writing Without Words: Alternative Literacies in Mesoamerica and the Andes*. Durham, NC: Duke University Press, 1994.

Borah, Woodrow, and Cook, Sherburne F. *The Aboriginal Population of Central Mexico on the Eve of the Spanish Conquest*. Ibero-Americana 45. Berkeley: University of California Press, 1963.

Borges Moran, Pedro. *Metodos misionales en la cristianizacion de America, Siglo XVI*. Madrid: Departamento de Misionologia Espanola, 1960.

_____. *El envio de misioneros a America durante la epoca espanola*. Salamanca: Universidad Pontificia, 1977.

Boswell, John. *The Kindness of Strangers: The Abandonment of Children in Western Europe from Late Antiquity to the Renaissance*. New York: Pantheon Books, 1988.

Bourdieu, Pierre. "Legitimation and Structured Interest in Weber's Sociology of Religion." In *Max Weber, Rationality, and Modernity*, pp. 119–136. Ed. Samuel Whimster and Scott Lash. London: Allen and Urwin, 1987.

_____. *In Other Words: Essays Toward a Reflexive Sociology*. Stanford, CA: Stanford University Press, 1990.

Bourke, Vernon J., ed. *Saint Augustine: The City of God*. New York: Image Books Doubleday, 1958.

Boyd, Mark F. "Epidemiology of Malaria: Factros Related to the Intermediate Host." In *Malariology*, Vol. 1, pp. 551–607. Ed. Mark F. Boyd. Philadelphia: W.B. Saunders, 1949.

Bradshaw, P., ed., *The Canons of Hippolytus*. Nottingham: Grove Books, 1987.

Braunfels, Wolfgang. *Monasteries of Western Europe*. Princeton, NJ: Princeton University Press, 1972.

Breisach, Ernst. *Historiography: Ancient, Medieval & Modern*. Chicago: University of Chicago Press, 1983.

Brown, Peter. *The World of Late Antiquity*. London: Thames and Hudson, 1971.

———. *Religion and Society in the Age of Saint Augustine*. New York: Harper & Row, 1972.

———. *The Making of Late Antiquity*. Cambridge, MA: Harvard University Press, 1978.

———. *The Cult of the Saints*. Chicago: University of Chicago Press, 1981.

———. *Society and the Holy in Late Antiquity*. Berkeley: University of California Press, 1982.

———. *The Body and Society*. New York: Harper & Row, 1988.

———. "The Decline of the Empire of God." In *Last Things: Death and the Apocalypse in the Middle Ages*, pp. 41–59. Ed. C. W. Bynum and P. Freedman. Philadelphia: University of Pennsylvania Press, 2000.

Bruner, Edward M. "Abraham Lincoln as Authentic Reproduction: A Critique of Postmodernism." *American Anthropologist* 96 (1994): 397–415.

Bruyn, George W. *An Illustrated History of Malaria*. New York: Parthenon Publishing Group, 1999.

Buelna, Eustaquio. *Arte de la Lengua Cahita*. Mexico, 1891.

Burkert, Walter. *Homo Necans: The Anthropology of Ancient Greek Sacrificial Ritual and Myth*. Trans. Peter Bing. Berkeley: University of California Press, 1983.

———. *Ancient Mystery Cults*. Cambridge, MA: Harvard University Press, 1987.

Burkhart, Louise M. *The Slippery Earth: Nahua-Christian Moral Dialogue in Sixteenth Century Mexico*. Tucson: University of Arizona Press, 1989.

Burn, A. R. "*Hic Breve Vivitur*: a Study of the Expectation of Life in the Roman Empire." *Past and Present* 4 (1953): 2–31.

Burrus, Ernest J., S.J. "The Language Problem in Spain's Overseas Dominions." Neue Zeitschrift fur Missionswissenschaft. *Nouvelle revue de science missionaire* 35 (1979): 161–170.

Burrus, Ernest J., S.J., and Zubillaga, Félix, S.J. *Misiones Mexicanas de la Compañia de Jesus (1618–1745): Cartas e informes conservados en la "Colección Mateu."* Madrid, 1982.

———. *El Noroeste de México, Documentos Sobre Las Misiones Jesuíticas 1600–1769*. México, DF: Universidad Nacional Autónoma de México, 1986.

Busvine, J. R. *Insects, Hygiene and History*. London: Athlone Press, 1976.

Butler, Judith. *Gender Trouble: Feminism and the Suversion of Identity*. New York: Routledge, 1989.

Bynum, Caroline W. *Fragmentation and Redemption: Essays on Gender and the Human Body in Medieval Religion*. New York: Zone Books, 1991.

———. "Images of the Resurrection Body in the Theology of Late Antiquity." *The Catholic Historical Review* LXXX (1994): 179–237.

———. *The Resurrection of the Body in Western Christianity, 200–1336*. New York: Columbia University Press, 1995.

Cameron, Averil. *Christianity and the Rhetoric of Empire: The Development of Christian Discourse.* Berkeley: University of California Press, 1991.
———. *The Later Roman Empire.* Cambridge, MA: Harvard University Press, 1993.
———. "On Defining the Holy Man." In *The Cult of the Saints in Late Antiquity and the Middle Ages,* pp. 27–45. Eds. James Howard-Johnston and Paul Antony Hayward. Oxford, UK: Oxford University Press, 1999.
Cameron, M. L. *Anglo-Saxon Medicine.* Cambridge, UK: Cambridge University Press, 1993.
Cardiel, José. *Breve relacion del régimen de las misiones del Paraguay.* Madrid: Gráficas Nilo, 1989 [1767].
Carmack, Robert M. "Chapter 3, Mesoamerica at Spanish Contact." In *The Legacy of Mesoamerica,* pp. 80–121. Eds. R. M. Carmack, Janine Gasco, and Gary H. Gossen. Upper Saddle River, NJ: Prentice Hall, 1996.
Caseau, Béatrice. "Sacred Landscapes." In *Late Antiquity: A Guide to the Post-classical World,* pp. 21–60. Eds. G. W. Bowerstock, P. Brown, and O. Grabar. Cambridge: Belknap Press, 1999.
Casey, Michael. *A Thirst for God: Spiritual Desire in Bernard of Clairvaux's Sermons on the Song of Songs.* Kalamazoo: Cistercian Publications, 1988.
Castañega, Fray Martín de. *Tratado de las supersticiones y hechicerías.* Madrid: Gráficas Ultra, 1946 [1529].
Celli, Angelo. *The History of Malaria in the Roman Campagna from Ancient Times.* Ed. and enlarged by Anna Celli-Fraentzel. London: J. Bale, Sons & Danielsson, 1933.
Certeau, Michel de. *Heterologies: Discourse on the Other.* Trans. B. Massumi. Minneapolis: University of Minnesota Press, 1986.
———. *The Mystic Fable, Volume One, The Sixteenth and Seventeenth Centuries.* Trans. Michael B. Smith. Chicago: University of Chicago Press, 1992.
Cervantes, Fernando. *The Idea of the Devil and the Problem of the Indian: the Case of Mexico in the Sixteenth Century.* Research Papers, University of London, Institute of Latin American Studies 4. London: Institute of Latin American Studies, 1991.
Cesareo, Francesco C. "Quest for Identity: The Ideals of Jesuit Education in the Sixteenth Century." In *The Jesuit Tradition in Education and Missions,* pp. 17–33. Ed. Christopher Chapple. Scranton, PA: University of Scranton Press, 1993.
Chadwick, Henry. "Pachomios And The Idea Of Sanctity." In *The Byzantine Saint, University of Birmingham Fourteenth Spring Symposium of Byzantine Studies.* San Bernardino, CA: Borgo Press, 1980.
Chapman, Dom John. *Saint Benedict and the Sixth Century.* New York: Longmans, Green and Co., 1929.
Charles-Edwards, T. M. "Palladius, Prosper, and Leo the Great: Mission and Primal Authority." In *Saint Patrick AD 493–1993,* pp. 1–12. Ed. David N. Dumville and Contributors. Woodbridge, UK: Boydell Press, 1999 [1993].

Chase, Irah, trans. *The Constitutions of the Holy Apostles*. New York: Appleton & Company, 1848.

Chestnut, Glenn F. *The First Christian Histories: Eusebius, Socrates, Sozomen, Theodoret, and Evagrius*. Paris: Editions Beauchesne, 1986.

Christian, William A. *Local Religion in Sixteenth-Century Spain*. Princeton, NJ: Princeton University Press, 1981.

―――. *Apparitions in Late Medieval and Renaissance Spain*. Princeton, NJ: Princeton University Press, 1981.

Churruca Peláez, Agustín, S. J. *Primeras Fundaciones Jesuitas En Nueva España 1572–1580*. Mexico, DF: Editorial Porrúa, 1980.

Chuvin, Pierre. *A Chronicle of the Last Pagans*. Trans. B. A. Archer. Cambridge, MA: Harvard University Press, 1990.

Clendinnen, Inga. *Ambivalent Conquests*. Cambridge, UK: Cambridge University Press, 1987.

Clifford, James. "Introduction, Partial Truths," In *Writing Culture, The Poetics and Politics of Ethnography*, pp. 1–26. Eds. J. Clifford and G. Marcus. Berkeley: University of California Press, 1986.

―――. *The Predicament of Culture*. Cambridge, MA: Harvard University Press, 1988.

Clifford, James, and Marcus, George, eds. *Writing Culture, The Poetics and Politics of Ethnography*. Berkeley: University of California Press, 1986.

Cloudsley-Thompson, J. L. *Insects and History*. New York: St. Martin's Press, 1976.

Cohen, T. V. "Why the Jesuits Joined." *Historical Papers/Communications Historiques* (1974): 237–259. Toronto: The Canadian Historical Association.

Cohn, Norman. *Europe's Inner Demons: An Enquiry Inspired by the Great Witch-Hunt*. New York: Basic Books, 1975.

―――. "Biblical Origins of the Apocalyptic Tradition." In *The Apocalypse and the Shape of Things to Come*, pp. 28–42. Ed. Francis Carey. Toronto, Canada: University of Toronto Press, 1999.

Colgrave, Bertram, and Mynors, R. A. B., eds. *Bede's Ecclesiastical History of the English People*. Oxford: Clarendon Press, 1969.

Collins, Roger. *Early Medieval Europe 300–1000*. New York: St. Martin's Press, 1999.

Comaroff, Jean. *Body of Power Spirit of Resistance. The Culture and History of a South African People*. Chicago: University of Chicago Press, 1985.

Constable, Giles, ed. *The Letters of Peter the Venerable, Volume II*. Cambridge, MA: Harvard University Press, 1967.

―――. *Three Studies in Medieval Religious and Social Thought*. Cambridge, UK: Cambridge University Press, 1995.

Cook, Nobel David. *Born to Die, Disease And New World Conquest, 1492–1650*. Cambridge, UK: Cambridge University Press, 1998.

Cook, Sherburne F., and Borah, W. W. *The Indian Population of Central Mexico: 1530–1610*. Ibero-Americana 44. Berkeley: University of California Press, 1960.

Cooper, Donald B. *Epidemic Disease in Mexico City, 1761–1813*. Austin: University of Texas Press, 1965.

Corominas, Joan. *Diccionario critico etimologico castellano e hispanico*. 5 vols. Editorial Gredos, Madrid, 1980.

Correia-Afonso, John, S. J. *Jesuit Letters and Indian History, 1542–1773*. 2nd ed. New York: Oxford University Press, 1969 [1955].

Cossio, Francisco Gonzalez de, ed. *Relacion Breve de la Venida de los de la Compañia de Jesus, Año de 1602* (Manuscrito anónimo del Archivo Histórico de la Secretaría de Hacienda). Mexico: Imprenta Universitaria, 1945.

Cousins, Ewert. "The Humanity and Passion of Christ." In *Christian Spirituality, High Middle Ages and Reformation*, pp. 375–391. Ed. Jill Raitt. New York: Crossroad, 1987.

Cox, John D. "Drama, the Devil, and Social Conflict in Late Medieval England." *The American Benedictine Review* 45 (1994): 341–362.

Cramer, Peter. *Baptism and Change in the Early Middle Ages c. 200–c. 1150*. Cambridge, UK: Cambridge University Press, 1993.

Crosby, Alfred W. *The Columbian Exchange*. Westport, CT: Greenwood Press, 1972.

———. *The Measure of Reality, Quantification and Western Society, 1250–1600*. Cambridge, UK: Cambridge University Press, 1997.

Cruz, Anne J., and Mary E. Perry, eds. *Culture and Control in Counter-Reformation Spain*. Minneapolis: University of Minnesota Press, 1992.

Cushner, Nicholas P. *Lords of the Land: Sugar, Wine, and Jesuit Estates of Coastal Peru, 1600–1767*. Albany: State University of New York, 1980.

Dalton, O. M., trans. *The History of the Franks, by Gregory of Tours*. 2 vols. Oxford: Clarendon Press, 1927.

Davidson, H. R. Ellis. *Gods and Myths of Northern Europe*. Baltimore, MD: Penguin, 1964.

Davies, Jon. *Death, Burial and Rebirth in the Religions of Antiquity*. London: Routledge, 1999.

Davies, Stevan L. *The Revolt of the Widows: The Social World of the Apocryphal Acts*. Carbondale: Southern Illinois University Press, 1980.

de Guibert, Joseph. *The Jesuits: Their Spiritual Doctrine and Practice, A Historical Study*. Chicago: Loyola University Press, 1964.

De Jong, Mayke. *In Samuel's Image: Child Oblation in the Early Medieval West*. New York: E.J. Brill, 1996.

de Nie, Giselle. *Views From a Many-Windowed Tower: Studies of Imagination in the Works of Gregory of Tours*. Amsterdam: Rodopi, 1987.

Dean, M. *Critical and Effective Histories: Foucault's Methods and Historical Sociology*. London: Routledge, 1994.

Decorme, Gerard. S.J. *La obra de los Jesuitas Mexicanos durante la época colonial, 1572–1767*. 2 vols. Mexico: Jose Porrúa, 1941.

Deeds, Susan. "Rural Work in Nueva Vizcaya: Forms of Labor Coercion on the Periphery." *Hispanic American Historical Review* 69 (1989): 425–449.

_____. "Double Jeopardy: Indian Women in Jesuit Missions of Nueva Vizcaya." In *Indian Women of Early Mexico*, pp. 255–272. Ed. S. Schroeder, S. Wood, and R. Haskett. Norman: University of Oklahoma Press, 1997.

_____. "Indigenous Rebellions on the Northern Mexican Mission Frontier: From First-Generation to Later Colonial Responses." In *Contested Ground, Comparative Frontiers on the Northern and Southern Edges of the Spanish Empire*, pp. 32–52. Ed. D. Guy and T. Sheridan. Tucson: Univesity of Arizona Press, 1998.

Deferrari, Roy J., ed. *The Fathers of the Church, Volume 15: Early Christian Biographies*. New York: Fathers of the Church, 1952.

_____, trans. *Paul Orosius: The Seven Books of History Against the Pagans*. Washington, DC: Catholic University of America Press, 1964.

Defourneaux, Marcelin. *Daily Life in España in the Golden Age*. Trans. Newton Branch. Stanford, CA: Stanford University Press, 1979.

Delehaye, Hippolytus, S.J. *The Legends of the Saints: An Introduction to Hagiography*. Trans. V. M. Crawford. London: Longmans Green Company, 1907.

Deloria, Vine. *The Metaphysics of Modern Existence*. San Francisco: Harper and Row, 1979.

_____. *God Is Red*. Golden, CO: North American Press, 1992.

DeMarco, Barbara. "The Semiotic Cathechism." *Interdisciplinary Journal for Germanic Linguistics and Semiotic Analysis* 6 (2001): 257–264.

Derks, Ton. *Gods, Temples and Ritual Practices: The Transformation of Religious Ideas and Values in Roman Gaul*. Amsterdam: Amsterdam University Press, 1998.

Derrida, Jacques. *On Grammatology*. Trans. G. Spivak. Baltimore, MD: Johns Hopkins University Press, 1976 [1967].

_____. *Writing and Difference*. Trans. A. Bass. London: Routledge and Kegan Paul, 1978 [1967].

Di Peso, Charles C. "Prehistory: Southern Periphery." In *Handbook of North American Indians, Volume 9 (Southwest)*, pp. 152–161. Ed. Alfonso Ortiz. Washington, DC: Smithsonian Institution Press, 1979.

Dixon, C. W. *Smallpox*. London: J. and A. Churchill Ltd, 1962.

Dobrizhoffer, Martín. *An Account of the Abipones, an Equestrian People of Paraguay*. 2 vols. New York: Johnson Reprint Corporation, 1970.

Documentos para la Historia de Mexico, Cuarta Serie, Mexico 1857

1596   "Anua del año de 1596."
1598   "Anua del año de 1598."
1600   "Testimonio juridico de las poblaciones y conversiones de los serranos Acaches, hechas por el Capitan Deigo de Avila y el venerable padre Hernando de Santarén por el ano 1600 (written by Martín Duarte)."

1601   "Carta del Padre Nicolás de Arnaya Dirigida al Padre Provincial
        Francisco Baez el año de 1601."
1618   "Carta de Alonso del Valle al Padre Provincial, 9 de Mayo de 1618."
1730   "Estado de la provincia de Sonora, . . . segun se halla por el mes de Julio
        de este año de 1730, escrito por un padre misionero de la provincia de
        Jesus de Nueva España."
Dods, E. R. *Pagan and Christian in an Age of Anxiety*. Cambridge, UK: Cambridge
    University Press, 1968.
Dods, Marcus, trans. and ed. *The City of God by Saint Augustine*. 2 vols. New
    York: Hafner, 1948.
Donalson, Malcolm Drew, trans. *A Translation of Jerome's Chronicon with His-
    torical Commentary*. Lewiston, NY: Mellen University Press, 1996.
Donini, Guido, and Ford, Gordon B., Jr., trans. *Isidore of Seville's History of the
    Kings of the Goths, Vandals, and Suevi*. Leiden: E.J. Brill, 1966.
Doolittle, William. *Canal Irrigation in Prehistoric Mexico*. Austin: University of
    Texas Press, 1990.
———. *Cultivated Landscapes of Native North America*. New York: Oxford
    University Press, 2000.
Doran, Robert. *Birth of a Worldview: Early Christianity in Its Jewish and Pagan
    Context*. Boulder, CO: Westview Press, 1995.
Dowden, Ken. *European Paganism: The Realities of Cult from Antiquity to the
    Middle Ages*. London: Routledge, 2000.
Drinkwater, J. F. *Roman Gaul: The Three Provinces, 58 BC–AD 260*. London:
    Croom Helm, 1983.
———. *The Gallic Empire*. Stuttgart: Franz Steiner Verlag Wiesbaden GMBH,
    1987.
Duffy, Eamon. *The Stripping of the Altars: Traditional Religion in England c. 1400–c.
    1580*. New Haven, CT: Yale University Press, 1992.
Duggan, Lawrence G. "For Force Is Not of God"? Compulsion and Conver-
    sion from Yahweh to Charlemagne. "In *Varieties of Religious Conversion in the
    Middle Ages*, pp. 51–62. Ed. James Muldoon. Gainesville: University Press of
    Flordia, 1997.
Duncan-Jones, Richard. *Structure and Scale in the Roman Economy*. Cambridge,
    UK: Cambridge University Press, 1990.
Dunigan, Peter. "Early Jesuit Missionaries: A Suggestion for Further Study."
    American Anthropologist 60 (1958): 725–732.
Dunne, Peter Masten, S.J. *Pioneer Black Robes on the West Coast*. Berkeley: Uni-
    versity of California Press, 1940.
———. *Pioneer Jesuits in Northern Mexico*. Berkeley: University of California
    Press, 1944.
———. *Andrés Pérez de Ribas*. New York: United States Catholic Historical
    Society, 1951.
Dutton, Marsha. "Introduction to Walter Daniel's *Vita Aelredi*." In *Walter Daniel:
    The Life of Aelred of Rievaulx*, pp. 7–89. Trans. and anno. F. M. Powicke.
    Kalamazoo, MI: Cistercian Publications, 1994.

Edwards, H. J., trans. *Caesar The Gallic War*. London: William Heinemann, 1916.

Ekholm, Gordon F. *Excavations at Guasave, Sinaloa, Mexico*. Anthropological Papers of the American Museum of Natural History 38 (Part II). New York: American Museum of Natural History, 1942.

Eliade, Mircea. *Ordeal by Labrynth*. Chicago: University of Chicago Press, 1982.

Elliott, Alison Goddard. *Roads to Paradise: Reading the Lives of the Early Saints*. Hanover, NH: University Press of New England, 1987.

Elliott, J. H. *Spain and Its World, 1500–1700*. New Haven, CT: Yale University Press, 1989.

Elm, Susanna. *"Virgins of God": The Making of Asceticism in Late Antiquity*. Oxford: Clarendon Press, 1994.

Elsner, J. *Art and the Roman Viewer*. Cambridge, UK: Cambridge University Press, 1995.

Ember, Carol R., and Ember, Melvin. "The Conditions Favoring Multilocal Residence." *Southwestern Journal of Anthropology* 28 (1972): 382–400.

Esteyneffer, Juan de. *Florilegio Medicinal*. Ed. Ma. Carmen Anzures y Bolanos. Mexico: Academia Nacional de Medicina, 1978 [1719].

Ettlinger, N. "Cultural Economic Geography and a Relational and Microspace Approach to Trusts, Rationalities, Networks, and Change in Collaborative Workplaces." *Journal of Economic Geography* 3 (2003): 145–171.

Evers, Lawerence, and Molina, Felipe S. *Yaqui Deer Songs/Maso Bwikam*. Tucson: Sun Tracks and The University of Arizona Press, 1987.

Ewald, Sister Marie Liguori, trans. "Life of St. Hilarion by St. Jerome." In *The Fathers of the Church, Volume 15: Early Christian Biographies*, pp. 241–280. Ed. Roy J. Deferrari. New York: Fathers of the Church, 1952.

Fajardo, Jose del Rey, S.J. *Bio-Bibliografia de los Jesuitas en la Venezuela colonial*. Caracas: Instituto de Investigaciones Historicas, Universidad Catolica "Andres Bello," 1974.

Falk, Marcia. *Love Lyrics from the Bible*. Sheffield: Almond Press, 1982.

Farris, Nancy. *Maya Society under Colonial Rule: The Collective Enterprise of Survival*. Princeton, NJ: Princeton University Press, 1984.

Felger, Richard S., and Moser, M. B. *People of the Desert and Sea: Ethnobotany of the Seri Indians*. Tucson: University of Arizona Press, 1985.

Ferreiro, A. "Early Medieval Missionary Tactics: The Example of Martin and Caesarius." *Studia Historica* (1988): 225–238.

Ferris, I. M. *Enemies of Rome: Barbarians through Roman Eyes*. Stroud, UK: Sutton Publishing, 2000.

Finucane, Ronald C. *Miracles and Pilgrims: Popular Beliefs in Medieval England*. Totowa, NJ: Rowman and Littlefield, 1977.

Fletcher, Richard. *The Barbarian Conversion: From Paganism to Christianity*. Berkeley: University of California Press, 1999.

Flint, Valerie I. J. "Thoughts About the Context of Some Early Medieval Treatises *De Natura Rerum*." In *Ideas in the Medieval West: Texts and Their Contexts*. Ed. Valerie I. J. Flint, pp. 1–31. London: Varirum Reprints, 1988.

_____. "The Early Medieval 'Medicus,' the Saint – and the Enchanter." *Social History of Medicine* 2 (1989): 127–145.

_____. *The Rise of Magic in Early Medieval Europe.* Princeton, NJ: Princeton University Press, 1991.

Florencia, Francisco de, S.J. *Historia de la Provincia de la Compañia de Jesus de Nueva España.* Mexico: Editorial Academia Literaria, 1955 [1694].

Ford, Richard. "Inter-Indian Exchange in the Southwest." In *Handbook of North American Indians (Volume 10), Southwest,* pp. 711–722. Ed. Alfonso Ortiz. Washington, DC: Smithsonian Institution Press, 1983.

Foster, Elizabeth Andros, ed. and trans. *Motolinías History of The Indians of New Spain.* Berkeley: Cortés Society, 1950 [1541].

Foucault, Michel. *The Archaeology of Knowledge.* Trans. A. Sheridan. New York: Vintage Books, 1969.

_____. *The Order of Things.* Trans. A. Sheridan. New York: Vintage Books, 1970 [1966].

_____. *The History of Sexuality I An Introduction.* Trans. R. Hurley. New York: Random House, 1978.

_____. "What is an Author?" In *Textual Strategies: Perspectives in Post-structuralist Criticism,* pp. 141–160. Ed. J. Harari. Ithaca, NY: Cornell University Press, 1979.

_____. "Politics and Reason." In *Michel Foucault, Politics, Philosophy, Culture.* Ed. L. D. Kritzman, trans. A. Sheridan and others. New York: Routlege, 1988.

_____. "Sexuality and Power." In *Religion and Culture Michel Foucault,* pp. 115–130. Ed. Jeremy R. Carrette. New York: Routledge, 1999 [1978].

Fox, Robin L. *Pagans and Christians.* New York: Knopf, 1987.

Frankfurter, David. "Ameletic Invocations of Christ for Health and Fortune." In *Religions of Late Antiquity in Practice,* pp. 340–343. Ed. R. Valantasis. Princeton, NJ: Princeton University Press, 2000.

Frend, W. H. C. *Religion Popular and Unpopular in the Early Christian Centuries.* London: Variorum Reprints, 1976.

_____. "Town and Countryside in Early Christianity." In *The Church in Town and Countryside,* pp. 25–42. Ed. Derek Baker. Oxford: Basil Blackwell, 1979.

Fulop-Miller, Rene. *The Saints that Moved the World.* Salem, NH: Ayer Company, 1945.

Furst, Jill Leslie McKeever. *The Natural History of the Soul in Ancient Mexico.* New Haven, CT: Yale University Press, 1995.

Gadamer, Hans-Georg. *Truth and Method.* New York: Crossroad Press, 1975 [1960].

Gade, Daniel. *Nature and Culture in the Andes.* Madison: University of Wisconsin Press, 1999.

Gannon, Thomas M., S.J., and Traub, George W., S.J. *The Desert and the City; An Interpretation of the History of Christian Spirituality.* London: Macmillan, 1969.

Ganot, Jaime, and Peschard, Alejandro A. "The Archaeological Site of El Canon del Molino, Durango, Mexico." In *The Gran Chicchimeca: Essays on the Archaeology and Ethnohistory of Northern Mesoamerica*, pp. 146–178. Ed. J. Reyman. Sydney: Avebury, 1995.

Ganss, George E., S.J. *The Fathers of the Church, Volume 17: Saint Peter Chrysologus, Selected Sermons, and Saint Valerian, Homilies.* New York: Fathers of the Church, 1953.

———. ed., *The Constitutions of the Society of Jesus.* St. Louis: The Institute of Jesuit Sources, 1970.

——— ed. *Ignatius Loyola, The Spiritual Exercises and Selected Works.* New York: Paulist Press, 1991.

Gardner, Edmund G., ed. *The Dialogues of Saint Gregory.* London: Philip Lee Warner, 1911.

Geary, Patrick. *Before France and Germany: The Creation and Transformation of the Merovingian World.* New York: Oxford University Press, 1988.

———. "Barbarians and Ethnicity." In *Late Antiquity: A Guide to the Postclassical World*, pp. 107–130. Ed. G. W. Bowerstock, P. Brown, and O. Grabar. Cambridge: Belknap Press, 1999.

Geertz, Clifford. *The Interpretation of Cultures.* New York: Basic Books, 1973.

———. *Works and Lives: The Anthropologist as Author.* Cambridge: Polity Press, 1988.

Gerhard, Peter. *The Northern Frontier of New Spain.* Princeton, NJ: Princeton University Press, 1982.

Gibson, Charles. *The Aztecs under Spanish Rule.* Stanford, CA: Stanford University Press, 1964.

Gilchrist, Roberta. *Contemplation and Action: The Other Monasticism.* London: Leicester University Press, 1995.

Gilliam, J. F. "The Plague under Marcus Aurelius." *American Journal of Philology* 82 (1961): 225–251.

Glover, T. R., and Rendall, Gerald H., trans. *Tertullian [Apologeticus and De Spectaculis] Minucius Felix [Octavius].* Cambridge, MA: The Loeb Classical Library, Harvard University Press, 1931.

Goehring, James E. "Withdrawing from the Desert: Pachomius and the Development of Village Monasticism in Upper Egypt." *Harvard Theological Review* 89 (1996): 267–285.

Golan, David. "Hadrian's Decision to Supplant 'Jerusalem' by 'Aelia Capitolina'." *Historia* 35 (1986): 226–239.

Goldhill, Simon. *Foucault's Virginity: Ancient Erotic Fiction and the History of Sexuality.* Cambridge, UK: Cambridge University Press, 1995.

Gomez Canedo, Lino. *Evangelizacion y conquista, experiencia franciscana en Hispanoamerica.* Mexico: Editorial Porrúa, 1977.

Goodich, Michael. *Vita Perfecta: The Ideal of Sainthood in the Thirteenth Century.* Stuttgart: Anton Hiersemann, 1982.

Goody, Jack. *The Development of the Family and Marriage in Europe.* Cambridge, UK: Cambridge University Press, 1983.

Gradie, Charlotte M. *The Tepehuan Revolt of 1616*. Salt Lake City: University of Utah Press, 2000.

Graf, Fritz. *Magic in the Ancient World*. Cambridge, MA: Harvard University Press, 1997.

Grant, Patrick. *The Transformation of Sin: Studies in Donne, Herbert, Vaughan, and Traherne*. Montreal: McGill-Queen's University Press, 1974.

Grant, Robert M. *Greek Apologists of the Second Century*. Philadelphia: Westminster Press, 1988.

Grattan, J. H. G., and Singer, Charles. *Anglo-Saxon Magic and Medicine*. London: Oxford University Press, 1952.

Gregory I, Pope. *The Dialogues of S. Gregorie, 1608/St. Gregory: English Recusant Literature 1558–1640*, Vol. 240. Ed. D. M. Rogers. Ikley: The Scolar Press, 1975 [1608].

Griffen, William B. *Indian Assimilation in the Franciscan Area of Nueva Vizcaya*. Anthropological Papers of the University of Arizona 33. Tucson: University of Arizona Press, 1979.

Grijalva, Juan de. *Cronica de la Orden de N.P.S. Augustin en las provincias de la Nueva España... de 1533 hasta el de 1592*. Mexico: Imprenta Victoria, 1924 [1624].

Gruzinski, Serge. *The Conquest of Mexico*. Trans. Eileen Corrigan. Cambridge, UK: Cambridge University Press, 1993.

Gundry, Robert H. *A Survey of the New Testament*. Grand Rapids, MI: Academie Books, 1970.

Gunn Allen, Paula. *The Sacred Hoop*. Boston: Beacon Press, 1986.

_____, ed. *Spider Woman's Granddaughters*. New York: Fawcett Columbine, 1989.

Gutiérrez, Ramón A. *When Jesus Came, the Corn Mothers Went Away: Marriage, Sexuality, and Power in New Mexico, 1500–1846*. Stanford, CA: Stanford University Press, 1991.

Hackett, C. W. *Historical Documents Relating to New Mexico, Nueva Vizcaya, and Approaches Thereto, to 1773*. Collected by Adolph and Fanny R. Bandelier, 3 vols. Washington, DC: Carnegie Institution of Washington, 1923–1937.

Hackett, L. W. *Malaria in Europe*. London: Oxford University Press, 1937.

Hall, G. "Ministry, Worship and Christian Life." In *Early Christianity Origins and Evolution to AD 600*, pp. 101–112. Ed. Ian Hazlett. Nashville: Abingdon Press, 1991.

Hall, Stuart. "Old and New Identities, Old and New Ethnicities." In *Culture, Globalization and the World-System*, pp. 41–68. Ed. A. King. London: Macmillan, 1991.

Halsall, Guy. "Social Identities and Social Relationships in Early Merovingian Gaul." In *Franks And Alamanni in the Merovingian Period, An Ethnographic Perspective*, pp. 141–165. Ed. Ian Wood. Rochester, NY: Boydell Press, 1998.

Hammond, George P., and Rey, Agapito, eds. and trans. *Obregon's History of 16th Century Exploration in Western America*. Los Angeles: Wetzel Publishing Company, 1928.

———, ed. and trans. *Narratives of the Coronado Expedition 1540–1542*. Albuquerque: University of New Mexico Press, 1940.

Hanson, R. P. C., trans. and ed. *The Life and Writings of the Historical St. Patrick*. New York: Seabury Press, 1983.

Haring, C. H. *The Spanish Empire in America*. San Diego: Harcourt Brace Jovanovich, 1947.

Harnack, Adolf. *Militia Christi, the Christian Religion and the Military in the First Three Centuries*. Trans. D. M. Grace. Philadelphia: Fortress Press, 1981 [1905].

Haselgrove, Colin. "Roman impact on rural settlement and society in southern Picardy." In *From the Sword to the Plough: Three Studies on the Earliest Romanisation of Northern Gaul*, pp. 127–189. Ed. N. Roymans. Amersterdam, Amersterdam University Press, 1966.

Heather, P. J. *Goths and Romans*. Oxford: Clarendon Press, 1991.

Heather, Peter, and Mathews, John. *The Goths in the Fourth Century*. Liverpool, UK: Liverpool University Press, 1991.

Hedrick, Basil C. and Riley, Carroll. *Documents Ancillary to the Vaca Journey*. University Museum Studies 5. Carbondale: Southern Illinois University Museum, 1976.

Heffernan, T. J. *Sacred Biography, Saints and Their Biographies in the Middle Ages*. New York: Oxford University Press, 1988.

Hefner, Robert. "Introduction: World Building and the Rationality of Conversion." In *Conversion to Christianity*, pp. 3–44. Ed. R. Hefner. Berkeley: University of California Press, 1993.

Heimann, P. M. "Voluntarism and Immanence: Conceptions of Nature in Eighteenth-Century Thought." In *Philosophy, Religion, and Science in the 17th and 18th Centuries*, pp. 393–405. Ed. John W. Yolton. Rochester, NY: University of Rochester Press, 1990.

Hemming, John. *Red Gold: The Conquest of the Brazilian Indians*. Cambridge, MA: Harvard University Press, 1978.

Hen, Yitzhak. *Culture and Religion in Merovingian Gaul A.D. 481–751*. New York: Brill, 1995.

Heraughty, Patrick. *Inishmurray, Ancient Monastic Island*. Dublin: O'Brien Press, 1982.

Herbert, Christopher. *Culture and Anomie: Ethnographic Imagination in the Nineteenth Century*. Chicago: University of Chicago Press, 1991.

Hillgarth, J. N. *Christianity and Paganism, 350–750*. Philadelphia: University of Pennsylvania Press, 1986.

Hinson, E. Glenn. *The Evangelization of the Roman Empire*. Macon, GA: Mercer University Press, 1981.

Hoare, F. R., ed. *The Western Fathers: Being the Lives of SS. Martin of Tours, Ambrose, Augustine of Hippo, Honoratus of Arles and Germanus of Auxerre*. New York: Sheed and Ward, 1954.

————, trans. "Constantius of Lyon, The Life of Saint Germanus of Auxerre." In *Soldiers of Christ: Saints and Saints' Lives from Late Antiquity and the Early Middle Ages*, pp. 75–106. Ed. Thomas F. X. Noble and Thomas Head. University Park: Pennsylvania State University Press, 1995.

Hodge, F. W., Hammond, G. P., and A. Rey, eds. *Fray Alonso de Benavides' Revised Memorial of 1634*. Albuquerque: University of New Mexico Press, 1945.

Hodgen, Margaret T. *Early Anthropology in the Sixteenth and Seventeenth Centuries*. Philadelphia: University of Pennsylavania Press, 1964.

Hodgkin, Thomas. *The Letters of Cassiodorus*. London: H. Frowde, 1886.

Hood, A. B. E., ed. and trans. *St. Patrick: His Writings and Muirchu's Life*. London: Phillimore, 1986.

Hopkins, Donald R. *Princes and Peasants: Smallpox in History*. Chicago: University of Chicago Press, 1983.

Howe, John. "The Conversion of the Physical World." In *Varieties of Religious Conversion in the Middle Ages*, pp. 63–78. Ed. James Muldoon. Gainesville: University Press of Florida, 1997.

Howe, Nicholas. "Historicist Approaches." In *Reading Old English Texts*, pp. 79–100. Ed. Katherine O'Brien O'Keefe. Cambridge, UK: Cambridge University Press, 1997.

Hughes, L. *The Christian Church in the Epistles of St. Jerome*. London: Society for Promoting Christian Knowledge, 1923.

Huizinga, Johan. *The Waning of the Middle Ages*. New York: St. Martin's Press, 1967 [1919].

Hulme, Peter. *Colonial Encounters, Europe and the native Caribbean, 1492–1797*. London: Methuen, 1986.

Hummer, Hans J. "Franks and Alamanni: A Discontinuous Ethnogeesis." In *Franks and Alamanni in the Merovingian Period: An Ethnographic Perspective*, pp. 9–21. Ed. Ian Wood. Rochester, NY: Boydell Press, 1998.

Jackson, Ralph. *Doctors and Diseases in the Roman Empire*. London: British Museum Publications, 1988.

Jackson, Robert H. *Indian Population Decline: The Missions of Northwestern New Spain, 1687–1840*. Albuquerque: University of New Mexico Press, 1994.

Jackson, Robert H., and Castillo, Eduardo. *Indians, Franciscans, and Spanish Colonization*. Albuquerque: University of New Mexico Press, 1995.

James, Edward, ed. *Gregory of Tours: Life of the Fathers*. Liverpool, UK: Liverpool University Press, 1991.

James, Montague Rhodes. *The Apocryphal New Testament*. Oxford: Clarendon Press, 1963.

James, Simon. *Exploring the World of the Celts*. London: Thames and Hudson, 1993.

Jameson, F. *The Political Unconscious: Narrative as a Socially Symbolic Act*. Ithaca, NY: Cornell University Press, 1981.

Jiménez, Ramon L. *Caesar against the Celts*. New York: Sarpedon, 1995.

Johnson, Elizabeth. "Marian Devotion in the Western Church." In *Christian Spirituality: High Middle Ages and Reformation*, pp. 392–414. Ed. Jill Raitt. New York: Crossroad, 1987.

Johnston, William. *The Modern Epidemic: A History of Tuberculosis in Japan*. Cambridge, MA: Harvard University Press, 1995.

Jonas, Hans. *The Gnostic Religion: The Message of the Alien God and the Beginnings of Christianity*. 2nd ed. Boston: Beacon Press, 1963.

Jones, Lindsay. *The Hermeneutics of Sacred Architecture, Experience, Interpretation, Comparison. Volume One: Monumental Occasions*. Cambridge, MA: Harvard University Press, 2000.

Jones, Stephen D. *Deconstructing the Celts: A Skeptic's Guide to the Archaeology of the Auvergne*. Oxford: Archaeopress/BAR (British Archaeological Reports), 2001.

Jones, W. H. S. *Malaria: A Neglected Factor in the History of Greece and Rome*. Cambridge, UK: Bowes & Bowes, 1907.

Kamen, Henry. *Inquisition and Society in Spain in the Sixteenth and Seventeenth Centuries*. Bloomington: Indiana University Press, 1985.

Kay, Margarita A. "The Florilegio Medicinal: Source of Southwestern Ethnomedicine." *Ethnohistory* 28 (1977): 251–259.

Kee, Howard Clark. "From the Jesus Movement toward Instiutional Church." In *Conversion to Christianity*, pp. 47–63. Ed. R. Hefner. Berkeley: University of California Press, 1993.

Keenan, Sister Mary Emily, S.C.N., trans. "Life of St. Anthony by St. Athanasius." In *The Fathers of the Church, Volume 15, Early Christian Biographies*, pp. 127–216. Ed. Roy J. Deferrari. New York: Fathers of the Church, 1952.

Kessell, John L. *Kiva, Cross, and Crown*. Albuquerque: University of New Mexico Press, 1987.

———. *Spain in the Southwest*. Norman: University of Oklahoma Press, 2002.

Keyes, Charles F. "Charisma: From Social Life to Sacred Biography." *JAAR Thematic Studies* 48 (1982): 1–45.

Keyes, G. *Christian Faith and the Interpretation of History: A Study of St. Augustine's Philosophy of History*. Lincoln: University of Nebraska Press, 1966.

Kieckhefer, Richard. "Imitators of Christ: Sainthood in the Christian Tradition." In *Sainthood: Its Manifestations in World Religions*, pp. 1–42. Ed. Richard Kieckhefer and George D. Bond. Berkeley: University of California Press, 1988.

———. "Major Currents in Late Medieval Devotion." In *Christian Spirituality: High Middle Ages and Reformation*, pp. 75–108. Ed. Jill Raitt. New York: Crossroad, 1987.

Klingshirn, William E. *Caesarius of Arles: The Making of a Christian Community in Late Antique Gaul*. Cambridge, UK: Cambridge University Press, 1994.

Klor de Alva, J. Jorge. "Spiritual Conflict and Accomodation in New Spain: Toward a Typology of Aztec Responses to Christianity." In *The Inca and*

Aztec State, 1400–1800: Anthropology and History, pp. 345–366. Ed. G. Collier, R. Renaldo, and J. Wirth. New York: Academic Press, 1982.

_____. "The Postcolonization of the (Latin) American Experience: A Reconsideration of 'Colonialism'." In *After Colonialism, Imperial Histories and Postcolonial Displacements*, pp. 241–275. Ed. Gyan Prakash. Princeton, NJ: Princeton University Press, 1995.

Kozak, David L., and Lopez, David I. *Devil Sickness and Devil Songs: Tohono O'Odham Poetics*. Washington, DC: Smithsonian Institution Press, 1999.

Kramer, Heinrich, and Sprenger, James. *The Malleus Maleficarum*. Trans. with introductions and notes by Montague Summers. New York: Dover Publications, 1971 [c. 1489].

La Piana, George. "Foriegn Groups in Rome During the First Centuries of the Empire." *The Harvard Theological Review* XX (1927): 183–403.

Ladd, Edmund J. "Zuni on the Day the Men in Metal Arrived." In *The Coronado Expedition to Tierra Nueva: The 1540–1542 Route Across the Southwest*, pp. 225–233. Eds. Richard and Shirley Flint. Niwot, CO: University Press of Colorado, 1997.

Lamberis, Vasiliki. *Divine Heiress: The Virgin Mary and the Creation of Christian Constantinople*. London: Routledge, 1994.

Lange, Charles, and Riley, Carroll L. *The Southwestern Journals of Adolph F. Bandelier: 1883–1884*. Albuquerque: University of New Mexico Press, 1970.

Latourette, K. S. *A History of the Expansion of Christianity*. 7 Vols. London: Eyre & Spottiswood, 1938–1945.

Laurence, Ray. "Afterword: Travel and Empire." In *Travel and Geography in the Roman Empire*, pp. 167–176. Eds. Colin Adams and Ray Laurence. London: Routledge, 2001.

Lavrin, Asunción. *Sexuality and Marriage in Colonial Latin America*. Lincoln: University of Nebraska Press, 1989.

LeBlanc, Steve. *Prehistoric Warfare In The American Southwest*. Salt Lake City: University of Utah Press, 1999.

Le Goff, Jacques. *The Medieval Imagination*. Trans. Arthur Goldhammer. Chicago: University of Chicago Press, 1985.

_____. *Medieval Civilization: 400–1500*. Trans. Julia Barrow. Oxford: Basil Blackwell, 1988.

Leclerq, Jean, O.S.B. *The Love of Learning and the Desire for God*. New York: Fordham University Press, 1982.

Lewis, Robert, ed. *Lotario Dei Sgni (Pope Innocent III) De Miseria Condicionis Humane*. Athens: University of Georgia Press, 1978.

Liebeschuetz, J. H. W. G. *Barbarians and Bishops: Army, Church, and State in the Reigh of Arcadius and Chrysostom*. Oxford: Clarendon Press, 1990.

Limon, Graciela. *Song of the Hummingbird*. Houston: Arte Publico Press, 1996.

Lincoln, Bruce. *Myth, Cosmos, and Society: Indo-European Themes of Creation and Destruction*. Cambridge, MA: Harvard University Press, 1986.

Littman, R. J., and Littman, M. L. "Galen and the Antonine Plague." *American Journal of Philology* 94 (1973): 243–255.

Lockhart, James. *The Nahuas after the Conquest*. Stanford, CA: Stanford University Press, 1992.

Lucas, Thomas M., S.J. *Landmarking: City, Church & Jesuit Urban Strategy*. Chicago: Loyola Press, 1997.

Luibheid, Colm, trans. *John Cassian: Conferences*. New York: Paulist Press, 1985.

Lupher, David A. *Romans in a New World: Classical Models in Sixteenth-Century Spanish America*. Ann Arbor: University of Michigan Press, 2003.

Lyman, J. Rebecca. *Christology and Cosmology*. Oxford: Clarendon Press, 1993.

Lynch, Joseph H. *Godparents and Kinship in Early Modern Europe*. Princeton, NJ: Princeton University Press, 1988.

———. *The Medieval Church*. New York: Longman, 1992.

———. *Christianizing Kingship: Ritual Sponsorship in Anglo-Saxon England*. Ithaca, NY: Cornell University Press, 1998.

MacCormack, Sabine. *Religion in the Andes: Vision and Imagination in Early Colonial Peru*. Princeton, NJ: Princeton University Press, 1991.

Macherey, Pierre. *A Theory of Literary Production*. London: Routledge, 1978.

Mackenthun, Gesa. *Metaphors of Dispossession*. Norman: University of Oklahoma Press, 1997.

MacMullen, Ramsay. *Christianizing the Roman Empire (A.D. 100–400)*. New Haven, CT: Yale University Press, 1984.

———. "What Difference Did Christianity Make?" *Historia* 35 (1986): 322–343.

———. *Christianity and Paganism in the Fourth to Eighth-Centuries*. New Haven, CT: Yale University Press, 1997.

Magoulias, H. J. "The Lives of the Saints as Source of Data for the History of Byzantine Medicine in the Sixth and Seventh Centuries." In *Byzantinische Zeitscrhrift, Bergrundet Von Karl Krumbacher*, pp. 127–150. Ed. Hans-Georg Beck, F. W. Deichmann, and H. Hunger. Munich: C.H. Beck'sche, 1964.

Maravall, Jóse A. *Culture of the Baroque: Analysis of a Historical Structure*. Minneapolis: University of Minnesota Press, 1986.

Markus, R. A. *From Augustine to Gregory the Great, History and Christianity in Late Antiquity*. London: Variorum Reprints, 1983.

———. *The End of Ancient Christianity*. Cambridge, UK: Cambridge University Press, 1990.

Martin, A. Lynn. *The Jesuit Mind: The Mentality of an Elite in Early Modern France*. Ithaca, NY: Cornell University Press, 1988.

———. *Plague? Jesuit Accounts of Epidemic Disease in the 16th Century*. Kirksville, MO: Sixteenth Century Journal Publishers, 1996.

Martin, David. *Tongues of Fire: The Explosion of Protestantism in Latin America*. Oxford: Basil Blackwell, 1990.

Martin, Henri-Jean. *Print, Power, and People in 17th-Century France*. Trans. David Gerard. Metuchen, NJ: The Scarecrow Press, 1993.

Martin, Janet, ed. *Peter the Venerable: Selected Letters*. Toronto: Pontifical Institute of Medieval Studies, 1974.

Martin, Malachi. *The Jesuits*. New York: Touchstone Books, 1987.

Marx, Karl. *The Eighteenth Brumaire of Louis Bonaparte*. New York: International Publishers, 1963 [1852].

Marx, Karl, and Engels, Frederick. *The German Ideology*. Moscow: Progress Publishers, 1964 [1845–1846].

Mathisen, Ralph. *Roman Aristocrats in Barbarian Gaul*. Austin: University of Texas Press, 1993.

McCluskey, Stephen C. *Astronomies and Cultures in Early Medieval Europe*. Cambridge, UK: Cambridge University Press, 1998.

McCormick, Michael. *Origins of the European Economy: Communications and Commerce, A.D. 300–900*. Cambridge, UK: Cambridge University Press, 2001.

McCutcheon, Russell T. *Manufacturing Religion: The Disourse on Sui Generis Religion and the Politics of Nostalgia*. Oxford, UK: Oxford University Press, 1997.

McElroy, Ann, and Townsend, Patricia A. *Medical Anthropology in Ecological Perspective*. North Scituate, MA: Duxbury Press, 1979.

McGrath, Alister. *Reformation Thought: An Introduction*. Oxford: Basil Blackwell, 1988.

McHugh, Michael P. *The Carmen de Providentia Dei Attributed to Prosper of Aquitaine: A Revised Text with an Introduction, Translation, and Notes*. Washington, DC: Catholic University of America Press, 1964.

McInerny, Ralph. *A First Glance at St. Thomas Aquinas*. Gary, IN: University of Notre Dame Press, 1990.

McKenna, Stephen. *Paganism and Pagan Survivals in Spain up to the Fall of the Visigothic Kingdom*. Washington, DC: Catholic University of America, 1938.

McLaughlin, Megan. *Consorting with Saints: Prayer for the Dead in Early Medieval France*. Ithaca, NY: Cornell University Press, 1994.

McNamara, Jo Ann. *A New Song: Celibate Women in the First Three Christian Centuries*. New York: The Institute for Research and in History, 1983.

———. "An Unresolved Syllogism, The Search for a Christian Gender System." In *Conflicted Identities and Multiple Masculinities*, pp. 1–24. Ed. Jacqueline Murray. New York: Garland Publishing, 1999.

McNary-Zak, Bernadette. *Letters and Asceticism in Fourth-Century Egypt*. New York: University Press of America, 2000.

McNaspy, Clement J., S.J. *Conquistador Without a Sword*. Chicago: Loyola University Press, 1984.

McNeill, William H. *Plagues and Peoples*. New York: Doubleday, 1976.

McNulty, Patricia, trans. and ed. *St. Peter Damian: Selected Writings on the Spiritual Life*. London: Faber and Faber, 1959.

Meeks, Wayne A. *The First Urban Christians: The Social World of the Apostle Paul*. New Haven, CT: Yale University Press, 1983.

Mendieta, Fray Geronimo de. *Vidas Franciscanas*, ed. Juan B. Iguiniz. Mexico: Universidad Nacional Autónoma, 1945.

———. *Historia Eclesiastica Indiana*. 2 vol. Ed. with an introduction by Francisco Solano y Perez-lila. Madrid: Ediciones Atlas, 1973 [1585].

Merrill, William L. "Conversion and Colonialism in Northern Mexico: The Tarahumara Response to the Jesuit Mission Program, 1601–1767." In *Conversion to Christianity*, pp. 129–163. Ed. R. Hefner. Berkeley: University of California Press, 1993.

Métraux, Alfred. "Jesuit Missions in South America, Part 2." In *Handbook of South American Indians, Volume 5: Comparative Ethnology of South American Indians*, pp. 645–653. Ed. J. Steward. Washington, DC: The Smithsonian Institution Press, 1949.

Mignolo, Walter D. "Cartas, crónicas y relaciones del descubrimiento y la conquista." In *Historia de la literatura hispanoamericana, época colonial, Volume I*, pp. 57–116. Ed. Luis I. Madrigal. Madrid: Cátedra, 1982.

———. *Local Histories/Global Designs: Coloniality, Border Thinking, and Subaltern Knowledges*. Princeton, NJ: Princeton University Press, 2000.

———. "Introduction and Commentary." In *Natural and Moral History of the Indies* [1590] by José de Acosta, pp. xvii–xxviii, 451–518. Ed. Jane E. Mangan, trans. Frances López-Morillas. Durham, NC: Duke University Press, 2002.

Miles, Margaret. *Plotinus on Body and Beauty*. Oxford: Basil Blackwell, 1999.

Millett, M. *The Romanization of Britian*. Cambridge, UK: Cambridge University Press, 1990.

Mills, Kenneth. *Idolatry and Its Enemies: Colonial Andean Religion and Extirpation, 1640–1750*. Princeton, NJ: Princeton Univeristy Press, 1997.

Mills, Kenneth, and Taylor, William B. *Colonial Spanish America: A Documentary History*. Wilmington, DE: Scholarly Resources, 1998.

Minns, Denis, O.P. *Irenaeus*. Washington DC: Georgetown University Press, 1994.

Moore, James T. *Indian and Jesuit*. Chicago: Loyola University Press, 1982.

Morner, Magnus. *The Political and Economic Activities of the Jesuits in the La Plata Region: The Hapsburg Era*. Stockholm: Library and Institute of Ibero-American Studies, 1953.

Morrell, Juliene, Ven. Mother, O.P., trans., with the Dominican Nuns of Corpus Cristi Monastery. *A Treatise on The Spiritual Life by Saint Vincent Ferrer, O.P.* London: Black Friars, 1957.

Morris, Joan. *The Lady Was a Bishop*. New York: Macmillan, 1973.

Morrison, Kenneth M. "Sharing the Flower: A Non-Supernaturalistic Theory of Grace." *Religion* 22 (1992): 207–219.

Mota Padilla, Matias de la. *Historia de la Conquista del Reino de la Nueva Galicia*. Guadalajara: Tallers Gráficos de Gallardo y Alvares del Castillo, 1924 [1742].

Motolinía, Fray Toribio de Benavente. *Historia de los Indios de la Nueva España*. Ed. and ann. Edmundo O'Gorman. Mexico: Editorial Porrúa, 1969 [1541].

———. *Memoriales e Historia de los indios de la Nueva España*. Intro. Fidel de Lejarza. Madrid: Ediciones Atlas, 1970[c. 1535].

Motulsky, Arno G. "Metabolic Polymorphisms and the Role of Infectious Diseases in Human Evolution." In *Human Populations Genetic Variation, and Evolution*, pp. 222–252. Ed. Laura N. Morris. San Francisco: Chandler Publishing Company, 1971.

Mueller, Sister Mary Magdeleine, O.S.F., ed. and trans. *Saint Casesarius of Arles; Sermons*, Vol. I (1–80). New York: Fathers of the Church, 1956.

Muhlberger, Steven. *The Fifth-Century Chroniclers, Prosper: Hydatius, and the Gallic Chonicler of 452*. Leeds: Francis Cairns, 1990.

Muldoon, James. "Introduction: The Conversion of Europe." In *Varieties of Religion Conversion in the Middle Ages*, pp. 1–10. Ed. James Muldoon. Gainesville: University of Florida Press, 1997.

Munro, Dana Carleton, ed. *Life of St. Columban by the Monk Jonas*. Felinfach: Llanerch Publishers, 1993 [1895].

Musurillo, Herbert, ed. and trans. *The Acts of the Christian Martyrs*. Oxford: Clarendon Press, 1972.

Nabhan, Gary. *Gathering the Desert*. Tucson: University of Arizona Press, 1985.

Nader, Helen. *Liberty in Absolutist Spain: The Hapsburg Sale of Towns, 1516–1700*. Baltimore, MD: Johns Hopkins University Press, 1990.

Navarro Garcia, Luis. *Sonora y Sinaloa en el Siglo XVII*. Sevilla: Escuela de Estudios Hispano-Americanos, 1967.

Naylor, Thomas B., and Polzer, Charles W., S.J. *The Presidio and Militia on the Northern Frontier of New Spain, 1500–1700*. Tucson: University of Arizona Press, 1986.

Necker, Luis. *Indios Guaranies y Chamanes Franciscanos, Las Primeras Reducciones del Paraguay (1580–1800)*. Biblioteca Paraguaya de Antropología, Vol. 7. Asuncion: Centro de Estudios Antropológicos, Universidad Católica, 1990.

Neel, James V., et al. "Notes on the Effects of Measles and Measles Vaccine in a Virgin Soil Population of South American Indians." *American Journal of Epidemiology* 91 (1970): 418–429.

Nentvig, Juan, S.J. *Rudo Ensayo*. Trans. and ann. Alberto F. Pradeau and Roberto R. Rasmussen. Tucson: University of Arizona Press, 1980 [1764].

The New Jerusalem Bible. Garden City, NY: Doubleday, 1985.

Nichols, Stephen G., Jr. *Romanesque Signs: Early Medieval Narrative and Iconography*. New Haven, CT: Yale University Press, 1983.

Nieremberg, Juan E., S.J. (with Andrade Cassini). *Varones Illustres de la Compañia de Jesus*. 3 vols. Bilbao, 1889 [1666].

Noffke, Suzanne, O.P., trans. *The Letters of Catherine of Siena*. Binghamton, NY: Center of Medieval and Renaissance Studies, 1988.

O'Gorman, Edmundo, ed. *Apologética Historia Sumaria, by Fray Bartolomé de Las Casas*. 2 vols. Mexico: Universidad Nacional Autónoma de México Instituto de Investigaciones Históricas, 1967 [c. 1558].

O'Malley, John W. *The First Jesuits*. Cambridge, MA: Harvard University Press, 1993.

———. *Religious Culture in the Sixteenth Century*. Brookfield, VT: Variorum, 1993.

O'Meara, M. "Planting the Lord's Garden in New France: Gabriel Sagard's *Le Grand Voyage* and *Histoire du Canada*." *Rocky Mountain Review* 46 (1992): 11–25.

Olin, John C. *Erasmus, Utopia, and the Jesuits*. New York: Fordham University Press, 1994.

Oliver, James H., and Palmer, Robert E.A. "Minutes of an Act of the Roman Senate." *Hesperia* 24 (1955): 320–349.

Orsi, Robert. *Thank You, St. Jude: Women's Devotion to the Patron Saint of Hopeless Causes*. New Haven, CT: Yale University Press, 1996.

Ortiz, Alfonso. *The Tewa World*. Chicago: University of Chicago Press, 1969.

———, ed. *Handbook of North American Indians (Volume 10): Southwest*. Washington, DC: Smithsonian Institution Press, 1983.

Ortner, Sherry B. "Resistance and the Problem of Ethnographic Refusal." *Comparative Studies In Society and History* 37 (1995): 173–193.

Pagden, Anthony. *The Fall of Natural Man*. Cambridge, UK: Cambridge University Press, 1982.

Pagels, Elaine. "What Became of God the Mother? Conflicting Images of God in Early Christianity." In *Gnosticism in the Early Church*, pp. 295–307. Ed. with intro. David M. Scholer. New York: Garland Publishing Company, 1993.

Pailes, Richard A., and Reff, D. T. "Colonial Exchange Systems and the Decline of Paquime." In *The Archaeology of West and Northwest Mesoamerica*, pp. 353–363. Ed. Michael S. Foster and Phil C. Weigand. Boulder, CO: Westview Press, 1985.

Painter, Muriel. *With Good Heart: Yaqui Beliefs and Ceremonies in Pascua Village*. Tucson: University of Arizona Press, 1986.

Palacios, Silvio, and Zoffoli, Ena. *Gloria y Tragedia de las Misiones Guaraníes*. Bilbao: Mensajero, 1991.

Parrinder, Geoffrey. *West African Religion*. London: Epworth Press, 1949.

Paxton, Frederick. *Christianizing Death: The Creation of a Ritual Process in Early Medieval Europe*. Ithaca, NY: Cornell University Press, 1990.

Payer, Pierre J. *Sex and the Penitentials, The Development of a Sexual Code 550–1150*. Toronto, Can.: University of Toronto Press, 1984.

Pennington, Campbell W. *The Pima Bajo, Volume II: Vocabulario en la Lengua Nevome*. Salt Lake City: University of Utah Press, 1979.

———. *The Pima Bajo, Volume I: The Material Culture*. Salt Lake City: University of Utah Press, 1980.

Pérez de Ribas, Andrés. *History of the Triumphs of Our Holy Faith Amongst the Most Barbarous and Fierce People of the New World*. Trans. Daniel T. Reff,

Maureen Ahern, and Richard Danford. Tucson: University of Arizona Press, 1999 [1645].

──────. *Corónica y Historia Religiosa de la Provincia de la Compañia de Jesus de Mexico.* 2 Vols. Mexico: Sagrado Corazon, 1896 [c. 1653].

Perkins, Judith. *The Suffering Self: Pain and Narrative Representation in the Early Christian Era.* London: Routledge, 1995.

Peter, Jean-Pierre. "Disease and the Sick at the End of the Eighteenth Century." In *Biology of Man in History*, pp. 81–94. Ed. E. Forster and O. Ranum, trans. E. Forster and P. Ranum. Baltimore, MD: Johns Hopkins University Press, 1975.

Peters, Edward. *The Magician the Witch and the Law.* Philadelphia: University of Pennsylvania Press, 1978.

Petersen, Joan M. *The Dialogues Of Gregory The Great in Their Late Antique Cultural Background.* Toronto: Pontifical Institute of Medieval Studies, 1984.

Petroff, Elizabeth A. "Women in the Early Church, St. Perpetua and St. Macrina." In *Medieval Women's Visionary Literature*, pp. 60–69. Ed. E. A. Petroff. Oxford University Press, 1986.

Pfefferkorn, Ignaz. *Sonora: A Description of the Province.* Trans. Theodore E. Treutlein. Albuquerque: University of New Mexico Press, 1949.

Phelan, J. L. *The Millennial Kingdom of the Franciscans in the New World.* 2nd ed. Berkeley: University of California Press, 1970 [1956].

Pickles, Christopher. *Texts and Monuments: A Study of Ten Anglo-Saxon Churches of the Pre-Viking Period.* Oxford, UK: Archaeopress, 1999.

Pizarro, Joaquín Martínez. *A Rhetoric of the Scene: Dramatic Narrative in the Early Middle Ages.* Toronto, Can.: University of Toronto Press, 1989.

Polzer, Charles W., S.J. *Rules and Precepts of the Jesuit Missions of Northwestern New Spain, 1600–1767.* Tucson: University of Arizona Press, 1976.

Poole, Stafford, C. M. *Pedro Moya de Contreras: Catholic Reform and Royal Power in New Spain, 1571–1591.* Berkeley: University of California Press, 1987.

──────. *Our Lady of Guadalupe: The Origins and Sources of a Mexican National Symbol, 1531–1797.* Tucson: University of Arizona Press, 1995.

Pounds, N. J. *An Historical Geography of Europe.* Cambridge, UK: Cambridge University Press, 1990.

Powell, Philip Wayne. *Soldiers, Indians and Silver: The Northward Advance of New España, 1550–1600.* Berkeley: University of California Press, 1952.

Prakash, Gyan. "Writing Post-Orientalist Histories of the Third World: Indian Historiography Is Good To Think." In *Colonialism and Culture*, pp. 353–388. Ed. N. B. Dirks. Ann Arbor: University of Michigan Press, 1992.

Price, Betsey B. *Medieval Thought: An Introduction.* Oxford: Basil Blackwell, 1992.

Price, Lorna. *The Plan of St Gall.* Berkeley: University of California Press, 1982.

Price, Richard M. "The Holy Man and Christianization from the Apocryphal Apostles to St Stephen of Perm." In *The Cult of the Saints in Late Antiquity and the Middle Ages*, pp. 215–240. Ed. James Howard-Johnston and Paul Antony Hayward. Oxford, UK: Oxford University Press, 1999.

Quinn, Frederick. "How Traditional Dahomian Society Interpreted Smallpox." *ABBIA, Revue Culturelle Camerounaise* 20 (1967): 151–166.

Quinn, Patricia A. *Better than the Sons of Kings*. New York: Peter Lang, 1989.

Rabasa, José. "Crónicas religiosas del Siglo XVI." In *Historia de la Literatura Mexicana*, pp. 321–350. Ed. Beatriz Garza Cuarón and Georges Baudot. Mexico City: Siglo XXI, 1996.

Rabinow, Paul, ed. *The Foucault Reader*. New York: Random House, 1984.

Radding, Cynthia. *Wandering Peoples: Colonialism, Ethnic Spaces, and Ecological Frontiers in Northwestern Mexico, 1700–1850*. Durham, NC: Duke University Press, 1997.

Rama, Angel. *The Lettered City*. Durham, NC: Duke University Press, 1996.

Ramsey, Boniface, O.P., trans. *The Sermons of St. Maximus of Turin*. New York: Newman Press, 1989.

——. *John Cassian: The Conferences*. New York: Paulist Press, 1997.

Rees, B. R. *Pelagius: Life and Letters*. Woodbridge, UK: Boydell Press, 1998.

Reff, Daniel T. "The Location of Corazones and Senora: Archaeological Evidence from the Rio Sonora Valley, Mexico." In *The Protohistoric Period in the American Southwest, AD 1450–1700*, pp. 94–112. Ed. David R. Wilcox and W. Bruce Masse. Arizona: Arizona State University Anthropological Research Papers 24. Tempe, 1981.

——. *Disease, Depopulation, and Culture Change in Northwestern New España, 1518–1764*. Salt Lake City: University of Utah Press, 1991.

——. "Contextualizing Missionary Discourse: The Benavides' Memorials of 1630 and 1634." *Journal of Anthropological Research* 50 (1994): 51–68.

——. "The 'Predicament of Culture' and Spanish Missionary Accounts of the Tepehuan and Pueblo Revolts." *Ethnohistory* 42 (1995): 63–90.

——. "Text and Context: Cures, Miracles, and Fear in the Relación of Alvar Núñez Cabeza de Vaca." *Journal of the Southwest* 38 (1996): 115–138.

——. "The Jesuit Mission Frontier in Comparative Perspective: The Reductions of the Rio de la Plata and the Missions of Northwestern New Spain, 1588–1700." In *Contested Ground*, pp. 16–31. Ed. Donna Guy and Thomas Sheridan. Tucson: University of Arizona Press, 1998.

Reta, J. Oroz. "The Role of Divine Attraction in Conversion According to St. Augustine." In *From Augustine to Eriugena: Essays on Neoplatonism and Christianity in Honor of John O'Meara*, pp. 155–168. Ed. F. X. Martin and J. Richmond. Washington, DC: Catholic University of America Press, 1991.

Reyman, Jonathan E., ed. *The Gran Chicchimeca: Essays on the Archaeology and Ethnohistory of Northern Mesoamerica*. Sydney: Avebury, 1995.

Ricard, Robert. *The Spiritual Conquest of Mexico*. Berkeley: University of California Press, 1966 [1933].

Riché, Pierre. *Daily Life in the World of Charlemagne*. Trans. Jo Ann McNamara. Philadelphia: University of Pennsylvania Press, 1978 [1973].

Ricoeur, Paul. *Hermeneutics and the Human Sciences: Essays on Language, Action, and Interpretation.* New York: Cambridge University Press, 1981.

———. *Time and Narrative, Volume I.* Trans. Kathleen McLaughlin and David Pellauer. Chicago: University of Chicago Press, 1984.

Ridley, Ronald T. *Zosimus: New History.* Sydney: Austalian Association for Byzantine Studies, 1982.

Riley, Carroll L. *The Frontier People.* Albuquerque: University of New Mexico Press, 1987.

Robertson, Duncan. *The Medieval Saints' Lives: Spiritual Renewal and Old French Literature.* Lexington, KY: French Forum Publishers, 1995.

Rolfe, John C., trans. *Ammianus Marcellinus.* 3 vols. Cambridge, MA: Harvard University Press, 1935.

Rousselle, Aline. "From Sanctuary to Miracle-Worker: Healing in Fourth-Century Gaul." In *Biology of Man in History*, pp. 95–127. Ed. E. Forster and O. Ranum and trans. E. Forster and P. Ranum. Baltimore, MD: Johns Hopkins University Press, 1975.

———. *Croire et Guérir. La Foi en Gaule Dans l'Antiquité Tardive*, pp. 109–32, Paris: Fayard, 1990.

Rousseau, Phillip *Ascetics: Authority and the Church.* Oxford, UK: Oxford University Press, 1978.

———. *Pachomius: The Making of a Community in Fourth-Century Egypt.* Berkeley: University of California Press, 1985.

———. "Ascetics as Mediators and as Teachers." In *The Cult of the Saints in Late Antiquity and the Middle Ages*, pp. 45–62. Ed. James Howard-Johnston and Paul Antony Hayward. Oxford, UK: Oxford University Press, 1999.

Rowe, William, and Schilling, Vivian. *Memory and Modernity: Popular Culture in Latin America.* London: Verso, 1991.

Roymans, Nico. "The sword or the plough. Regional dynamics in the romanization of Belgic Gaul and the Rhineland area." In *From the Sword to the Plough: Three Studies on the Earliest Romanisation of Northern Gaul*, pp. 9–126. Ed. N. Roymans. Amersterdam: Amersterdam University Press, 1996.

Rubia García, Antonio. *La santidad controvertida: Hagiografía y conciencia criolla alrededor de los venerable no canonizados de Nueva España.* Mexcio City: UNAM, 1999.

Ruiz de Montoya, Antonio. *Conquista Espiritual hecha por los religiosos de la Compañia de Jesus en las provincias del Paraqguay, ParanA, Uruguay y Tape.* Bilbao: Corazon de Jesus, 1892 [1639].

———. *The Spiritual Conquest.* Trans. Clement J. McNaspy, S.J. St. Louis: Institute of Jesuit Sources, 1993 [1639].

Russell, J. B. *The Devil: Perceptions of Evil from Antiquity to Primitive Christianity.* Ithaca, NY: Cornell University Press, 1977.

———. *Lucifer: The Devil in the Middle Ages.* Ithaca, NY: Cornell University Press, 1984.

———. *Mephistopheles.* Ithaca, NY: Cornell University Press, 1986.

Russell, J.C. "Late Ancient and Medieval Population." *Transactions of the American Philosophical Society*, New Series Vol. 48, Part 3. Philadelphia: American Philosophical Society, 1958.

Russell, James C. *The Germanization of Early Medieval Christianity*. Oxford, UK: Oxford University Press, 1994.

Sahagún, Fray Bernardino de. *Historia General de las cosas de Nueva Espana*, 2nd ed. Mexico: Editorial Porrúa, 1969.

———. *Primeros Memoriales*. Paleography of Nahuatl Text and English. Trans. Thelma Sullivan, completed by H. B. Nicholson et al. Norman: University of Oklahoma Press, 1997[c. 1560].

Sahlins, Marshall. *Islands of History*. Chicago: University of Chicago Press, 1985.

Sale, Kirkpatrick. *Conquest of Paradise*. New York: Penguin Books, 1991.

Sallares, Robert. *The Ecology of the Ancient Greek World*. London: Duckworth, 1991.

Salomon, Frank. *Nightmare Victory, The Meaning of Conversion among Peruvian Indians (Huarachorí, 1608)*. Discovering the Americas 1992 Lecture Series, Working Papers No. 7. Department of Spanish and Portuguese, University of Maryland. College Park: University of Maryland, 1990.

Salomon, Frank, and Urioste, George L., trans. and eds. *The Huarochiri Manuscript: A Testament of Ancient and Colonial Andean Religion*. Austin: University of Texas Press, 1991.

Salway, Benet. "Travel, Itineria and Tabellaria." In *Travel and Geography in the Roman Empire*, pp. 22–66. Eds. Colin Adams and Ray Laurence. London: Routledge, 2001.

Sauer, Carl O., *The Distribution of Aboriginal Tribes and Languages in Northwest Mexico*. Ibero-Americana 5. Berkeley: University of California Press, 1934.

———. *Aboriginal Population of Northwest Mexico*. Ibero-Americana 10. Berkeley: University of California Press, 1935.

Sauer, Carl O., and Brand, Donald E. "Prehistoric Settlements of Sonora with Special Reference to Cerros de Trincheras." *University of California Publications in Geography* 5 (1931): 67–148.

———. *Aztatlan: Prehistoric Mexican Frontier on the Pacific Coast*. Ibero-Americana 1. Berkeley: University of California Press, 1932.

Schaefer, Stacy, and Furst, Peter T. *People of the Peyote*. Albuquerque: University of New Mexico Press, 1996.

Schaferdick, Knut. "Christian Mission and Expansion." In *Early Christianity Origins and Evolution to AD 600*, pp. 65–78. Ed. Ian Hazlett. Nashville: Abingdon Press, 1991.

Schmitt, J. C. "The Rationale of Gestures in the West: Third to Thirteenth Centuries." In *A Cultural History of Gesture*, pp. 59–70. Ed. J. N. Bremmer and H. Roodenburg. Oxford, UK: Oxford University Press, 1991.

Schneider, Jane. "Spirits and the Spirit of Capitalism." In *Religious Orthodoxy and Popular Faith in European Society*, pp. 24–53. Ed. E. Badone. Princeton, NJ: Princeton University Press, 1990.

Schneider, Jane, and Lindenbaum, Shirley, eds. "Frontiers of Christian Evangelism." *American Ethnologist* (Special Issue) (1987): 14.

Scott, James C. *Weapons of the Weak: Everyday Forms of Peasant Resistance*. New Haven, CT: Yale University Press, 1985.

Seed, Patricia. "More Colonial and Postcolonial Discourse." *Latin American Research Review* 28 (1993): 146–152.

———. *Ceremonies of Possession in Europe's Conquest of the New World, 1492–1640*. Cambridge, UK: Cambridge University Press, 1995.

Service, Elman R. *Primitive Social Organization*. New York: Random House, 1962.

Sharp, Joanne P., Routledge, P., Philo, C., and Paddison, R. "Entanglements of Power: Geographies of Domination/Resistance." In *Entanglements of Power: Geographies of Domination/Resistance*, pp. 1–42. Eds. J. P. Sharp, P. Routledge, C. Philo, and R. Paddison. London: Routledge, 2000.

Shaul, David L. "The State of the Arte: Ecclesiastical Literature on the Northern Frontier of New Spain." *The Kiva* 55 (1990): 167–175.

Shaw, Brent. "War and Violence." In *Late Antiquity: A Guide to the Postclassical World*, pp. 130–170. Ed. G. W. Bowerstock, P. Brown, and O. Grabar. Cambridge: Belknap Press, 1999.

Sheridan, Thomas. "The Limits of Power: The Political Ecology of the Spanish Empire in the Greater Southwest." *Antiquity* 66 (1992): 153–171.

———. "The Yoemem (Yaquis): An Enduring People." In *Paths of Life: American Indians of the Southwest and Northern Mexico*, pp. 35–40. Eds. Thomas Sheridan and Nancy J. Parezo. Tucson: University of Arizona Press, 1996.

———. *Empire of Sand: The Seri Indians and the Struggle for Spanish Sonora, 1645–1803*. Tucson: University of Arizona Press, 1999.

Sheridan, Thomas E., and Naylor, T., eds. *Raramuri, A Tarahumara Colonial Chronicle 1607–1791*. Flagstaff, AZ: Northland Press, 1979.

Shiels, W. E., S.J. *Gonzalo de Tapia (1561–1594): Founder of the First Permanent Jesuit Mission in North America*. New York: United States Catholic Historical Society, 1934.

———. "The Critical Period in Mission History." *Mid-America* (New Series) 10 (1939): 97–109.

Slack, Paul. "Responses to Plague in Early Modern Europe: The Implications of Public Health." In *In Time of Plague*, pp. 111–131. Ed. Arien Mack. NY: New York University Press, 1991.

Smart, Ninian. *The Religious Experience of Mankind*. 3rd ed. [1969] NY: Scribner.

Smith, Jonathan Z. *Map Is Not Territory*. Leiden: E.J. Brill, 1978.

———. *Drudgery Divine: On the Comparison of Early Christianities and the Religions of Late Antiquity*. London: School of Oriental and African Studies, University of London, 1990.

Soustelle, Jacques. *Daily Life of the Aztecs*. Stanford, CA: Stanford University Press, 1961.

Spicer, Edward H. *Cycles of Conquest: The Impact of Spain, Mexico, and the United States on the Indians of the Southwest, 1533–1960*. Tucson: University of Arizona Press, 1962.

———. *The Yaquis: A Cultural History*. Tucson: University of Arizona Press, 1980.

Spiegel, Gabrielle. "History, Historicism and the Social Logic of the Text in the Middle Ages." In *The Postmodern History Reader*, pp. 180–203. Ed. Keith Jenkins. London: Routledge, 1997.

Stancliffe, Clare. "From Town to Country: The Christianization of the Touraine, 370–600." In *The Church in Town and Countryside*, pp. 43–59. Ed. Derek Baker. Oxford: Basil Blackwell, 1997.

———. *St. Martin and His Hagiographer*. Oxford: Clarendon Press, 1983.

Stanford, Peter. *The Devil: A Biography*. New York: Henry Holt and Company, 1996.

Stark, Rodney. *The Rise of Christianity: A Sociologist Reconsiders History*. Princeton, NJ: Princeton University Press, 1996.

Steneck, Nicholas H. *Science and Creation in the Middle Ages*. Notre Dame, IN: Notre Dame University Press, 1976.

Stern, Steve J. *Perus' Indian Peoples and the Challenge of Spanish Conquest*. Madison: University of Wisconsin Press, 1982.

———. "New Approaches to the Study of Peasant Rebellion and Consciousness: Implications of Andean Experience." In *Resistance, Rebellion, and Consciousness in the Andean Peasant World, 18th to 20th Centuries*, pp. 3–28. Ed. S. Stern. Madison: University of Wisconsin Press, 1987.

Stodder, Ann L., Martin, D. L., Goodman, A. H., and Reff, D. T. "Cultural Longevity and Biological Stress in the American Southwest." In *The Backbone of History*, pp. 481–505. Eds. R. H. Steckel and J. Rose. Cambridge, UK: Cambridge University Press, 2002.

Strenski, Ivan. "Religion, Power, and Final Foucault." *Journal of the American Academy of Religion* (1998): 345–367.

Sullivan, Daniel David. *The Life of the North Africans as Revealed in the Works of Saint Cyprian*. Washington, DC: Catholic University of America, 1933.

Sullivan, Lawrence E. *Icanchu's Drum: An Orientation to Meaning in South American Religions*. New York: Macmillan, 1988.

———. *Native Religions and Cultures of North America*. New York: Continuum, 2000.

Sullivan, Richard E. "Early Medieval Missionary Activity: A Comparative Study of Eastern and Western Methods." *Church History* 23 (1954): 17–35.

———. *Christian Missionary Activity in the Early Middle Ages*. Brookfield, VT: Variorum, 1994.

———. "What Was Carolingian Monasticism?" In *After Rome's Fall: Narrators and Sources of Early Medieval History – Essays Presented to Walter Goffart*, pp. 251–289. Ed. A. Callander Murray. Toronto, CAN: University of Toronto Press, 1998.

Sweet, David. "The Ibero-American Frontier Mission in Native American History." In *The New Latin American History*, pp. 1–48. Eds. Erick Langer and Robert H. Jackson. Lincoln: University of Nebraska Press, 1995.

Taft, Robert. "Liturgy and Eucharist I. East." In *Christian Spirituality: High Middle Ages and Reformation*, pp. 415–26. Ed. Jill Raitt. New York: Crossroad, 1987.

Talbot, C. H., and Hammond, E. A. *The Medical Practicioners in Medieval England: A Biographical Register*. London: Wellcome Historical Medical Library, 1965.

Tapahonso, Luci. *Blue Horses Rush In*. Tucson: University of Arizona Press, 1998.

Taylor, Thomas, trans. *The Arguments of the Emperor Julian against the Christians*. Chicago: Ares Publishing, 1980.

Taylor, William B. "The Virgina of Guadalupe in New Spain: An Inquiry into the Social History of Marian Devotion." *American Ethnologist* 14 (1987): 9–33.

———. *Magistrates of the Sacred: Priests and Parishioners in Eighteenth-Century Mexico*. Stanford, CA: Stanford University Press, 1996.

Tello, Fray Antonio. *Libro Segundo de la Cronica Miscelanea en que se trata de la conquista Espiritual y Temporal de la Santa Provincia de Xalisco*. Guadalajara: La Republica Literaria, 1891 [1650].

Thompson, E. A. *The Early Germans*. Oxford: Clarendon Press, 1965.

———. *The Visigoths in the Time of Ulfila*. Oxford: Clarendon Press, 1966.

———. "Britain, A.D. 406–410." *Britanna* 8 (1977): 303–318.

———. *Romans and Barbarians: The Decline of the Western Empire*. Madison: University of Wisconsin Press, 1982.

———. *Saint Germanus of Auxerre and the End of Roman Britian*. Woodbridge, UK: Boydell Press, 1984.

———. *The Huns*. Oxford: Basil Blackwell, 1996.

Tiessen, Terrance L. *Irenaeus on the Salvation of the Unevangelized*. Metuchen, NJ: The Scarecrow Press, 1993.

Tinker, George. *Missionary Conquest*. Minneapolis: Fortress Press, 1993.

Todd, Malcolm. "*Famosa Pestis* and Britain in the Fifth Century." *Britania* 8 (1977): 319–325.

Torquemada, Fray Juan de. *Monarquia Indiana*. 3 vols. Mexico: Editorial Porrúa, 1969 [1615].

Toynbee, Arnold. *An Historian's Approach to Religion*. 2nd ed. Oxford, UK: Oxford University Press, 1979.

Treutlein, Theodore E. "The Economic Regime of the Jesuit Missions in the Eighteenth Century." *Pacific Historical Review* 8 (1939): 284–300.

———, trans. and ed. *Missionary in Sonora: The Travel Reports of Joseph Och, S.J., 1755–1767*. San Francisco: California Historical Society, 1965.

Trevor-Roper, H. R. *The European Witch-Craze of the 16th and 17th Centuries*. Harmondsworth, UK: Penguin Books, 1967.

Trexler, Richard C. "From the Mouths of Babes: Christianization by Children in 16th Century New Spain." In *Religious Organization and Religious Experience*, pp. 115–135. Ed. J. Davies. New York: Academic Press, 1982.

Tylenda, Joseph N., S.J. *Jesuit Saints and Martyrs*. Chicago: Loyola University Press, 1984.

Tyson, Joseph B. *A Study of Early Christianity*. New York: Macmillan, 1973.

Valantasis, Richard. "Porphyry on the Life of Plotinus and the Order of His Books." In *Religions of Late Antiquity in Practice*, pp. 50–61. Ed. R. Valantasis. Princeton, NJ: Princeton University Press, 2000.

Van Dam, Raymond. *Leadership and Community in Late Antique Gaul*. Berkeley: University of California Press, 1985.

————, trans. *Gregory of Tours: Glory of the Martyrs*. Liverpool, UK: Liverpool University Press, 1988.

————. *Saints and Their Miracles in Late Antique Gaul*. Princeton, NJ: Princeton University Press, 1993.

Van Engen, John, trans. *Devotio Moderna: Basic Writings*. New York: Paulist Press, 1988.

Verano, John, and Ubelaker, Douglas, eds. *Disease and Demography in the Americas*. Washington, DC: Smithsonian Institution Press, 1992.

Vetancurt, Fray Agustin de. *Teatro Mexicano, Descripción Breve De Los Sucesos Ejemplares, Históricos Y Religiosos Del Nuevo Mundo De Las Indias*. Mexico: Edirotial Porrúa, 1970 [1697–1698].

Wacher, John. *The Towns of Roman Britain*. London: B.T. Batsford, 1975.

Waldron, Harry Neff. "Expressions of Religious Conversion Among Laymen Remaining Within Secular Society in Gaul, 400–800 A.D." Ph.D. Dissertation, Ohio State University, Columbus, 1977.

Wallace-Hadrill, J. M. *Early Medieval History*. Oxford: Basil Blackwell, 1975.

Walsh, P. G., trans. *Letters of St. Paulinus of Nola*, Vol. I: Letters 1–22. Westminster, MD: Newman Press, 1966.

Ward-Perkins, Bryan. *From Classical Antiquity to the Middle Ages: Urban Public Building in Northern and Central Italy AD 300–850*. Oxford: Clarendon Press, 1984.

Webb, J. F., trans. *The Lives of the Saints*. Baltimore, MD: Penguin Books, 1965.

Weber, David J. "John Francis Bannon and the Historiography of the Spanish Borderlands." *Journal of the Southwest* 29 (1987): 331–336.

————. *The Spanish Frontier in North America*. New Haven, CT: Yale University Press, 1992.

Weber, Max. *The Sociology of Religion*. Trans. Ephraim Fischoff. Boston: Beacon Press, 1963.

————. *Economy and Society*. 2 vols. Berkeley: University of California Press, 1968 [1956].

Weigand, Phil. "Minería y Intercambio de Minerales en Zacatecas Prehispánica." In *Zacatecas III: Anuario de Historia*, pp. 138–195. Ed. C. Esparanza Sanchez. Zacatecas, Mexico: Universidad Autónoma de Zacatecas, 1981.

————. "Evidence for Complex Societies During the Western Mesoamerican Classic Period." In *The Archaeology of West and Northwest Mexico*, pp. 47–92. Ed. Michael Foster and P. C. Weigand. Boulder, CO: Westview Press, 1985.

Weigand, Phil C., and Harbottle Garman. "The Role of Turquoises in the Ancient Mesoamerican Trade Structure." In *The American Southwest and Mesoamerica, Systems of Prehistoric Exchange*, pp. 159–177. Eds. Jonathan E. Ericson and Timothy Baugh. New York: Plenum Press, 1993.

Weinstein, Donald, and Bell, R. M. *Saints and Society: The Two Worlds of Western Christendom, 1000–1700*. Chicago: University of Chicago Press, 1982.

Wells, Peter S. *The Barbarians Speak: How the Conquered Peoples Shaped Roman Europe*. Princeton, NJ: Princeton Univesity Press, 1999.

Whitby, Michael, and Whitby, Mary, trans. *Chronicon Paschale 284–628 AD*. Liverpool, UK: Liverpool University Press, 1989.

White, Hayden. "Figuring the Nature of the Times Deceased: Literary Theory and Historical Writing." In *The Future of Literary Theory*, pp. 19–43. Ed. R. Cohen. London: Routledge, 1989.

Whittaker, C. R. *Frontiers of the Roman Empire: A Social and Economic Study*. Baltimore, MD: Johns Hopkins University Press, 1994.

Wilken, Robert L. "Pagan Criticism of Christianity: Greek Religion and Christian Faith." In *Early Christian Literature and the Classical Intellectual Tradition*, pp. 117–134. Ed. W. R. Schodel and R. L. Wilken. Paris: Editions Beauchesne, 1979.

————. *The Christians as the Romans Saw Them*. New Haven, CT: Yale University Press, 1984.

Williams, Michael A. "The Life of Antony and the Domestication of Charismatic Wisdom." *Journal of the American Academy of Religion Thematic Studies* 48 (1982): 23–45.

Williamson, G. A., trans. *Eusebius: The History of the Church from Christ to Constantine*. Harmondsworth, Middlesex, UK: Dorset Press, 1965.

Wilson, Chris. "Understanding the Nature and Importance of Low-growth Demographic Regimes." In *Asian Population History*, pp. 24–44. Ed. Ts'ui-jung Liu et al. Oxford, UK: Oxford University Press, 2001.

Winstead, Karen. *Virgin Martyrs: Legends of Sainthood in Late Medieval England*. Ithaca, NY: Cornell University Press, 1997.

Winterbottom, Michael, trans. *Gildas: The Ruin of Britain and Other Works*. London: Phillimore, 1978 [540 C.E.].

Wood, Ian. "The Missionary Life." In *The Cult of the Saints in Late Antiquity and the Middle Ages*, pp. 167–183. Ed. James Howard-Johnston and Paul Antony Hayward. Oxford, UK: Oxford University Press, 1999.

————. *The Missionary Life: Saints and the Evangelisation of Europe, 400–1050*. London: Longman, 2001.

Woolf, Alex. "Romancing the Celts, A Segmentary Approach to Acculturation." In *Cultural Identity In The Roman Empire*, pp. 111–124. Eds. Ray Laurence and Joanne Berry. London: Routledge, 1998.

Woosley, Anne I., and Ravesloot, John C., eds. *Culture and Contact, Charles C. Di Peso's Gran Chichimeca*. Dragoon, AZ: Amerind Foundation, 1993.

Wright, A. D. *The Counter-Reformation, Catholic Europe and the Non-Christian World.* London: Weidenfeld and Nicolson, 1982.

_____. *Catholicism and Spanish Society Under the Reign of Philip II, 1555–1598, and Philip III, 1598–1621.* Lewiston, Australia: Edwin Mellen Press, 1991.

Wright, D. "The Latin Fathers." In *Early Christianity Origins and Evolution to AD 600*, pp. 148–163. Ed. Ian Hazlett. Ashville, NC: Abingdon Press, 1991.

Wright, Wilmer C., trans. *The Works of the Emperor Julian.* Vol. 2. London: William Heinemann, 1913.

Wuellner, Wilhelm. "Greek Rhetoric and Pauline Argumentation." In *Early Christian Literature and the Classical Intellectual Tradition*, pp. 177–188. Eds. W. R. Schodel and R. L. Wilken. Paris: Editions Beauchesne, 1979.

Zambrano, P. Francisco, S.J. *Diccionario bio-bibliográfico de la Compañia de Jesus en Mexico.* 16 vols. Mexico: Editorial JUS, 1961–1977.

Zamora, Margarita. *Reading Columbus.* Berkeley: University of California Press, 1993.

Zimmer, Carl. *Evolution: The Triumph of an Idea.* New York: HarperCollins, 2001.

Zinn, Grover A., trans. *Richard of St. Victor.* New York: Paulist Press, 1979.

Zinsser, Hans. *Rats, Lice, and History.* Boston: Little, Brown and Company, 1934.

Zubillaga, Félix, S.J., ed. *Monumenta antique Florida (1566–1572).* Monumenta Missionum Societatis Jesu, Vol. 3. Rome: Institum Historicum Societatis Jesu, 1946.

_____, ed. *Monumenta Mexicana, Vol. I* (1570–1580). Rome: Institum Historicum Societatis Iesu, 1956.

_____, ed. *Monumenta Mexicana, Vol. II* (1581–1585). Rome: Institum Historicum Societatis Iesu, 1959.

_____, ed. *Monumenta Mexicana, Vol. III* (1585–1590). Rome: Institum Historicum Societatis Iesu, 1968.

_____, ed. *Monumenta Mexicana, Vol. IV* (1590–1592). Rome: Institum Historicum Societatis Iesu, 1971.

_____, ed. *Monumenta Mexicana, Vol. V* (1592–1596). Rome: Institum. Historicum Societatis Iesu, 1973.

Index